The Complete Guide to Motorcycle Mechanics

Learning Resource Centre
New College Stamford
Drift Road
Stamford
L ncs

...29

WITHDRAWN

D0321974

New College Stamford LRC
Drift Road Stamford Lincs.
PE9 1XA
Tel: 01780 484339

The Complete Guide to Motorcycle Mechanics

Second Edition

MOTORCYCLE MECHANICS INSTITUTE
A Division of Clinton Technical Institute
Phoenix, Arizona
Orlando, Florida

PRENTICE HALL CAREER & TECHNOLOGY, Upper Saddle River, New Jersey 07458

Library of Congress Cataloging-in-Publication Data
The Complete guide to motorcycle mechanics / Motorcycle Mechanics
Institute.—2nd ed.
    p.   cm.
    Includes index.
    ISBN 0-13-225889-7
    1. Motorcycles—Maintenance and repair.   I. Motorcycle Mechanics
Institute (U.S.)
    TL444.C65   1994
629.28´775—dc20
                                                        93-14849
                                                        CIP

Acquisitions Editor: Ed Francis
Editorial/production supervision: Tally Morgan, WordCrafters Editorial Services, Inc.
Cover design: Marianne Frasco
Buyer: Ilene Sanford
Editorial assistant: Gloria Schaffer

© 1994, 1984 by Motorcycle Mechanics Institute
Phoenix, AZ 85027

All rights reserved. No part of this book may be reproduced, in any form or by any means,
without permission in writing from the publisher.

Printed & bound by Antony Rowe Ltd, Eastbourne
Transferred to digital print on demand 2002

ISBN 0-13-225889-7

Prentice-Hall International (UK) Limited,London
Prentice-Hall of Australia Pty. Limited, Sydney
Prentice-Hall Canada Inc., Toronto
Prentice-Hall Hispanoamericana, S.A., Mexico
Prentice-Hall of India Private Limited, New Delhi
Prentice-Hall of Japan, Inc., Tokyo
Pearson Education Asia Pte. Ltd., Singapore
Editora Prentice-Hall do Brasil, Ltda., Rio de Janeiro

Contents

Preface

Traditionally, motorcycles have been viewed as an inexpensive and easily maintained method of transportation. The result is a generation of self-trained mechanics. But recent technology has increased the complexity of motorcycle systems and created the need for formally trained motorcycle technicians.

Instructors at the Motorcycle Mechanics Institute in Phoenix, Arizona, and Orlando, Florida, have been training entry-level technicians for over 15 years. Although knowledgeable in the latest service techniques and endorsed by the manufacturers who provide service manuals, publications, and training aids, we recognized the need for a suitable instructional textbook. *The Complete Guide to Motorcycle Mechanics,* first published in 1984, was designed to fill that need.

The Complete Guide to Motorcycle Mechanics is based on our philosophy that to cope with an increasingly advanced technology, it is important to have a theoretical comprehension as well as a practical grasp of the various systems. Therefore, the explanation of each system includes the theory and principles of operation, the practical applications of this theory, the technical aspects of the system, and representative service procedures. The text is designed as a guide for students in either secondary or postsecondary courses and should prove of interest to all motorcycle enthusiasts.

The content of the book includes career opportunities; the metric system; internal combustion engine theory; two- and four-stroke engine design and operation; transmission, clutch, primary, and final drive systems; lubrication; cooling; fuel delivery and carburetion; fuel injection and turbocharging; basic electrical theory; ignition and charging systems; starter motors; lighting and accessory systems; wheels and tires; frames; brake and suspension systems; two- and four-stroke engine tune-up and service; shop safety and tools; riding safety; and much more.

Every effort has been made to present the most current and accurate information to prepare a student for a successful career as a motorcycle technician. Please direct any questions or comments concerning the text to *Director of Publications, Motorcycle Mechanics Institute, a Division of Clinton Technical Institute, 2844 West Deer Valley Road, Phoenix, Arizona 85027.*

Acknowledgments

Special thanks and recognition are due to the Motorcycle Mechanics Institute instructors and staff who contributed their time and knowledge in the preparation of the first and second editions of this text. Contributors to the first edition include: John White, for chapter 1; David Pfaff, for Chapter 2; Dan Mariani, for Chapters 3 and 8; Gary Andresakis and Craig Etzel, for Chapters 4 and 5; Larry Barrington, for Chapters 6, 18, and 19; Charlie Lawlor, for Chapter 7; Craig Etzel and Dan Mariana, for Chapter 9; Eric Anderson, for Chapters 10 through 13; Bernie Thompson, for Chapters 14 and 15; Rich Brown, for Chapter 16; Larry Alcorn and Dave Bush, for Chapter 17; and Craig Etzel, for Chapter 20. Special thanks go to Ray Bailey of Yamaha Motor Corporation, U.S.A. for his review of the first edition manuscript and for his many valuable suggestions.

Contributors to the second edition include: John White, for Chapter 1; Dave Koshollek, for Chapter 4; Larry Barrington, for Chapters 5, 8, and 13 through 18; Mario J. Kowalski, for Chapters 6 through 8 and Chapters 13 and 15; Eric Anderson, for Chapters 9 through 12; and Bob Drapp for Chapter 16. Special thanks go to Tony Mills, Tire Specialist/Industry Consultant, of Tony Mills International, Inc., for the extensive information he provided for Chapters 13 and 15, and to Dennis Adam Pinti, Quality Control Manager, Yuasa Exide Battery Corporation, for the detailed information he provided for Chapter 9.

Figures that do not have credit lines were prepared by members of the Motorcycle Mechanics Institute. Particular thanks go to Craig Etzel and Dave Bush for the photographs and drawings they contributed. Thanks also to the instructors who reviewed the first edition: Arnie Beaman, Larry Barrington, Craig Etzel, and David Pfaff; and to those who reviewed the second edition: Larry Barrington, Rick Lewis, Eric Anderson, Dave Bush, Dave Koshollek, Steve Ehle, Mario Kowalski, Bob Mahaffey, and Bernie Thompson. Special thanks to Gary Green for his valuable assistance.

Sincere appreciation and thanks go to the following manufacturers and organizations and the people who represent them for the information and illustrations they supplied: American Honda Motor Company; Harley-Davidson Motor Company, Inc.; Kawasaki Motors Corporation, U.S.A.; American Suzuki Motor Corporation; Yamaha Motor Corporation, U.S.A.; Champion Spark Plug Company; Exxon Company, U.S.A.; Heli-Coil

Products, Division of Mite Corporation; HP Books; Jennings & Lovell, Inc.; Mr. Gordon Jennings; *Motorcyclist Magazine*, Peterson Publications; Motorcycle Safety Foundation; Robert Bentley, Inc.; S-K Hand Tool Division/Dresser Industries; S & S Products; Sun Electric Corporation; S & W Engineered Products; L.S. Starrett Company; Bowman Distribution; Barnes Group, Inc.; Haynes Publishing Group; BMW of North America; Brush Research Manufacturing Company, Inc.; and Yuasa Exide Battery Corporation.

Finally, sincere thanks and recognition are due to Carol Borrowdale for undertaking the difficult task of organizing and supervising the first and second editions; for utilizing her skills and talents in rewriting, revising, and editing the manuscripts, locating and securing the illustrations, and for attending to the many details that producing such a text requires.

Motorcycle Mechanics Institute

A Note to the Reader

The Complete Guide to Motorcycle Mechanics provides technical information for the entry-level motorcycle technician and a foundation for using the motorcycle manufacturers' service manuals. Many general and basic service procedures are provided throughout this text, as well as safety precautions that should be observed when performing service procedures. Exact service procedures pertaining to specific models and related safety precautions can be found in the motorcycle manufacturers' service manuals.

Motorcycle safety begins with proper operation of the vehicle, and detailed information about this can be found in the manufacturer's service manual. When you service a motorcycle, use common sense and follow the basic safety considerations presented in this book as well as the specific safety precautions provided in the motorcycle manufacturer's service manual. If you have a safety question or concern when servicing a motorcycle, using special tools or equipment, or when using chemicals, contact the manufacturer of the vehicle, equipment, or chemical to obtain a detailed explanation of the correct procedures and safety precautions. Services that demand special tools and require extensive skill and knowledge may best be performed by an experienced professional motorcycle technician.

chapter 1

Working in the Motorcycle Industry

The growing motorcycle industry offers a variety of job opportunities, and each of these jobs requires specific training. This chapter explores briefly the growth of the motorcycle industry, the jobs that are available, the skills that are necessary to obtain these jobs, and where to get the training that is required.

INDUSTRY GROWTH Recent technological breakthroughs and advances have created new industries and revolutionized others. The impact of new technology on the motorcycle industry has been dramatic. The "backyard" mechanic will find it increasingly difficult to cope with modern electronic ignition and fuel systems, complicated drive trains, and turbocharged engines. Today's sophisticated machinery requires the skills of a professionally trained and qualified motorcycle technician (Fig. 1-1).

Recent polling of motorcycle dealers indicates that many are having difficulty finding professionally trained technicians. Poorly trained service department staff can erode profits. As the motorcycle industry continues to grow, the demand increases for professionally trained, competent entry-level technicians.

JOB OPPORTUNITIES There are several job levels in a motorcycle service facility which provide a solid career and the possibility of advancement for those entering the field of motorcycle mechanics. These jobs are:

> Technician—entry-level apprentice, line
> Service writer
> Parts manager
> Service manager

This section describes the necessary skills and responsibilities of each position and the path to advancement.

Figure 1-1   Student working on a motorcycle.

Technician

The service technician is essential for a profitable service facility because the reputation of the facility is based on the quality of the technician's work. Like automobile mechanics, beginning motorcycle technicians usually start at the apprentice level. However, figures show that there is one auto mechanic for approximately 230 cars but only one motorcycle technician for every 750 motorcycles; therefore, an apprentice advances rapidly to a line technician if the proper skills are demonstrated (Fig. 1-2). The requirements for this position include a good work record, the ability to work well with others, enthusiasm, initiative, a professional appearance, and of course, a good mechanical education.

Usually, an apprentice technician works with an experienced line technician in the early phase of his or her career. This allows continued "hands-on" learning. Once the apprentice and line technician requirements are met, there are several avenues for promotion, depending on the technician's interests.

Service Writer

Typically, this is the first stepping-stone from mechanic to manager. The service writer diagnoses the problem described by the customer, puts the problem into mechanically understandable terms, assigns the work to a technician with the proper skills, and informs the customer of the progress of the work. The service writer is also responsible for maintaining the proper paperwork for regular and warranty work. The service writer and service manager work together to administer warranty and policy adjustments in the best interest of the customer and the dealership. Because of the importance of good customer relations, the service writer must be courteous, efficient, and fair in addition to being mechanically knowledgeable.

Parts Manager

The parts manager position is often overlooked when discussing potential job opportunities, but it is one of the most important positions in a service facility. The parts manager controls many thousands of dollars worth of parts inventory. The inventory dollar investment must bal-

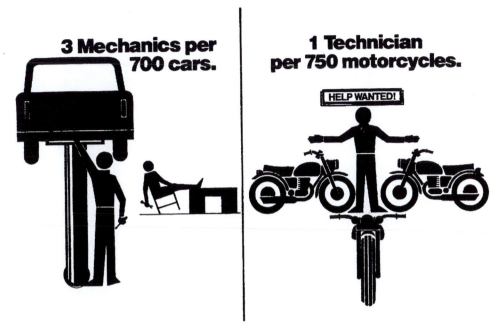

Figure 1-2 There is one auto mechanic for 230 cars, and one motorcycle technician for 750 motorcycles.

ance with customer service. This means that if there is a set inventory dollar figure that must be maintained, it is the parts manager's responsibility to see that the bulk of the inventory consists of the 20 percent of the parts that are used 80 percent of the time. The balance of the inventory is stocked based on usage. Nothing cripples a service facility more than having to wait for a common part that is on order. A sound mechanical and administrative background as well as knowledge of parts and part usage are the requirements for this management position.

Service Manager

The service manager is responsible for all aspects of shop operation from customer relations to administrative paperwork. The service manager supervises the technicians and helps them with problem jobs. This position includes promoting the dealership to customers, administering shop policies, and maintaining the quality of the service facility. This top management position is difficult and demanding because the service manager must skillfully balance customer demands and dealership goals. In addition to possessing a strong mechanical background and a work record that indicates dependability, the service manager must be pleasant, yet businesslike, to promote good customer relations and to gain the respect of the other employees (Fig. 1-3).

WHERE TO TRAIN The new technology has almost eliminated learning by trial and error in the backyard or by looking over someone's shoulder in a service shop. Increased sales and the lack of qualified technicians have created the necessity for educational programs that will produce well-trained entry-level motorcycle technicians in a reasonable amount of time. Educational programs in the field of motorcycle mechanics can now be found in many high schools, colleges, and vocational schools.

High Schools: Many high schools have developed or are in the process of developing a program of education in motorcycle mechanics. Motorcycle manufacturers are becoming aware of the need for increased training, and many assist in the creation of high school training programs.

Figure 1-3   Service manager working with a customer.

Colleges: Many colleges, especially community colleges, offer classes or a two-year degree in motorcycle mechanics.

Vocational Schools: Vocational schools such as the Motorcycle Mechanics Institute have been teaching courses in motorcycle mechanics for many years. In addition to many years spent exclusively training motorcycle technicians, some vocational schools also offer financial aid and job placement.

Since the first step to a satisfying career is a proper education, take the time to explore your educational options thoroughly and find the best school to meet your training needs.

chapter 2

Measurement Systems

There is a number of measurement systems in existence, but the two prevalent systems are the English and metric. Measurement systems are used throughout our daily lives. When we measure in pounds, gallons, inches, and feet, we are using the English system of measurement. Motorcycle technicians must also be able to use the metric measuring system because nearly all motorcycles sold in the United States are manufactured using metric measurements. A motorcycle technician must make precise measurements with accuracy. Precision measurement tools such as the vernier caliper, dial indicator, and micrometer are used to measure the length, location, and thickness of a part.

This chapter presents a brief history of the English and metric systems and explains the metric system. You will learn how to use the metric system, how to convert English measurements to metric, and how to use measurement tools.

A BRIEF HISTORY The basis of any measurement system is arbitrary. In other words, each measurement system was originally based on someone's whim or assumption. For example, the English system, which was brought to England by the Romans, designated 1 inch as the width of a soldier's thumb and 1 foot as the length of his foot. Since Roman soldiers came in different sizes, these measurements were not precise. But because these soldiers controlled the populace, the system was effective.

The metric system was based on an assumption of the earth's size. In 1670, Gabriel Mouton defined a meter as a certain part of the size of the earth based on his estimate of the earth's size. Since he could not precisely determine the earth's size, the basis for the meter was as arbitrary as Roman thumbs. But because the people of the time were impressed with what appeared to be an exact and scientific basis, they accepted the system.

A measurement system is useful not because it is scientific but because it is accepted. The conquered people of England were forced to accept and adopt the Romans' measurement system. Later people, because they felt that Mouton's system was scientific and sound, adopted his system. But neither the Romans' whim nor Mouton's assumption made either system functional. It is when a measurement system is accepted and used that a practical, working measurement system is established.

Obviously, because almost all motorcycles sold in the United States are manufactured using the metric system, the metric system is an essential tool for motorcycle technicians. In 1901, the U.S. Congress adopted the metric system, and since 1968 all metric motorcycles have had International Standard Order (ISO) bolts. That means that for a given size bolt there is only one standard thread size. Although you may not yet be familiar or comfortable using it, the metric system is an established and accepted measurement system.

THE METRIC SYSTEM

The metric system has many advantages that become obvious when it is compared to the English system. When English standard measurements were determined, no relationship was developed between measurements of length, weight, or volume. A foot consists of 12 inches, and 3 feet make up a yard. The ratios are different: 12:1 in one case and 3:1 in the other. Two different units of measurement are both called an ounce. Sixteen fluid ounces make a pint and 16 weight ounces make a pound, but a fluid ounce is not the same amount as a weight ounce. The English system becomes especially complicated when applied to the field of motorcycle mechanics. The system uses two different methods for measuring nuts and bolts, which requires that the technician use two different tool kits: standard and Whitworth. As you will see, the metric system solves or avoids most of the problems of the English system.

Metric units are related to the size of the earth and the properties of water:

meter = part of the size of the earth

gram = the weight of 1 cubic centimeter of water

0° Celsius = the freezing point of water

100° Celsius = the boiling point of water

The metric system divides every measuring unit into tens and many of the units are related to each other. The basic unit names are meter, liter, and gram. Each of these names acts as a suffix in the name for the part of the basic unit. The prefixes that denote the part of the unit remain the same no matter which suffix is used:

Prefix	Basic units	Unit of measurement	
kilo-	meter, liter, gram	1000	
hecto-	meter, liter, gram	100	
deca-	meter, liter, gram	10	
	meter, liter, gram	1	
deci-	meter, liter, gram	0.1	1/10
centi-	meter, liter, gram	0.01	1/100
milli-	meter, liter, gram	0.001	1/1000

There are seven basic units in the metric system, but motorcycle technicians use only five. They are:

meter = unit for measuring length

liter = unit for measuring volume

gram = unit for measuring weight

kilogram per square centimeter (kg/cm^2) = unit for measuring pressure

degree Celsius = unit for measuring temperature

To help you visualize these units:

meter = about a yard

liter = about a quart

gram = fairly small; a penny weighs 3 grams

kilogram = a little more than 2 pounds

$2.0 \, kg/cm^2$ = normal street tire pressure

22°C = normal room temperature

A complete list of the metric units used to measure length, volume, weight, pressure, and torque is provided in the Appendix. The following table shows the units most often used by motorcycle technicians and an example of what they are used to measure:

Quantity	Used to measure
Length	
kilometer	Length of a road
meter	Stopping distance of a motorcycle
centimeter	Length of a shaft
millimeter	Diameter of a piston
Volume	
liter	Size of a gas tank
cubic centimeter	Size of an engine (also called a milliliter)
Weight	
kilogram	Weight of a motorcycle
gram	Weight of a piston
Pressure	
kilogram per square centimeter (kg/cm^2)	Tire or fluid pressure
kilopascals (kPa)	Tire or fluid pressure
Torque	
kilogram-meter (kg-m)	Tightness of a fastener
Newton-meter (Nm)	Tightness of a fastener

CONVERSIONS   Once you understand the metric system, you must then be able to make conversions. Conversions are rules for converting or changing a measurement from one system to another. Conversions are necessary because motorcycle technicians often work with English measurement tools, but service manuals usually give specifications in metric measurements.

Conversions are normally written as mathematic forms called formulas. A formula is a "fill-in-the-blank" type of statement. Here is a conversion that is not written as a formula:

There are 2.54 centimeters in every inch. If a measurement in inches is multiplied by 2.54, the result is the same measurement in centimeters.

Here is the same conversion written as a formula:

inches × 2.54 = centimeters

Using a formula with a calculator is easy. Just enter the numbers and symbols into the calculator in the same order that they are presented in the formula and read the answer.

Fractions

The English system uses fractions to indicate parts of the whole, and the metric system uses decimals. To convert a fraction into a decimal, the top number (numerator) of the fraction must be divided by the bottom number (denominator). Here is how a formula for converting a fraction is written using the fraction 1/2:

$$1 \div 2 = 0.5$$

Other examples:

$$(3/4) \qquad 3 \div 4 = 0.75$$
$$(7/16) \qquad 7 \div 16 = 0.4375$$

Rounding Off Decimals

The decimal numbering system uses a base of 10. Digits to the left of the decimal point indicate multiples of a positive power of 10, or whole numbers, as follows:

$$1. = \text{one}$$
$$10. = \text{ten}$$
$$100. = \text{one hundred}$$
$$1000. = \text{one thousand}$$
$$10,000. = \text{ten thousand}$$

Digits to the right of the decimal point indicate parts or fractions of a whole number as follows:

$$0.1 = \text{one tenth}$$
$$0.01 = \text{one one hundredth}$$
$$0.001 = \text{one thousandth}$$
$$0.0001 = \text{one ten thousandth}$$

Sometimes a decimal number will have many decimal places. The decimal places are the numbers to the right of the decimal point. You will probably want to round off the number to one, two, or three decimal places depending on the accuracy of the measurement required. (In most English-to-metric conversions you will round off to two places or to hundredths. In most metric-to-English conversions you will round off to three places or to thousandths.) Here is the rounding-off procedure:

You have a decimal number with three decimal places. You want to round off to two decimal places. If the third decimal place number is 5 or more, drop the third decimal place number and add one to the second decimal place number.

EXAMPLES:

1.376 rounds off to 1.38
1.375 rounds off to 1.38

If the third place number is less than 5, the second decimal place number stays the same and the third place number is dropped.

EXAMPLE:

1.374 rounds off to 1.37

No matter what decimal to which you want to round, it is only the number after that decimal place that determines whether or not you add one.

EXAMPLES:

3.74936 rounded off to three decimal places = 3.749
3.74936 rounded off to two decimal places = 3.75
3.74936 rounded off to one decimal place = 3.7

Conversions within the Metric System

Occasionally, motorcycle technicians need to convert one metric unit measurement to another metric unit measurement. To make this type of conversion, use the following list and procedure:

$$\text{meter}$$
$$\text{kilo—hecto—deca—liter—deci—centi—milli}$$
$$\text{gram}$$

To convert from one unit to another, count the number of places moved in the list and note the direction. Move the decimal point the same number of places in the same direction. For example, to convert 137.63 millimeters to centimeters, the decimal point would be moved one place to the left:

$$137.63 \text{ millimeters} = 13.763 \text{ centimeters}$$

Other examples:

$$17 \text{ grams} = 170 \text{ decigrams}$$

$$4 \text{ kilograms} = 40 \text{ hectograms}$$

$$5 \text{ centimeters} = 0.05 \text{ meter}$$

The length and width of a gas tank is measured in centimeters, but the volume of the tank is measured in liters. Use the following formulas to convert cubic centimeters (cc) to liters and liters to cubic centimeters:

$$cc \times 0.001 = \text{liters}$$

$$\text{liters} \times 1000 = cc$$

Conversion Table

Two complete tables of conversions and formulas are located in the Appendix. This is a partial table of the conversions that motorcycle technicians use most often:

Length (shafts and springs)

mm × 0.03937 = inches
cm × 0.3937 = inches
inches × 2.54 = cm
inches × 25.4 = mm

Weight (motorcycles and pistons)

pounds × 0.4536 = kg
kg × 2.205 = pounds
grams × 0.03527 = ounces
ounces × 28.35 = grams

Volume (engines and gas tanks)

cubic inches × 16.388 = cc
cc × 0.06102 = cubic inches
cubic inches × 0.01639 = liters
liters × 61.02 = cubic inches
liters × 1.057 = quarts
quarts × 0.9463 = liters
liters × 0.2642 = gallons
gallons × 3.785 = liters

Pressure (tire pressure)

pounds per square inch (psi) × 0.0703 = kg/cm^2
kg/cm^2 × 14.224 = psi
psi × 6.89 = kPa

Torque wrench reading

ft-lb × 0.1383 = kg-m
kg-m × 7.233 = ft-lb
kg-m × 100 = kg-cm
ft-16 × 1.3556 = Nm
kg-m × 9.807 = Nm

Easy Rules to Remember

1 cm = approximately 1/2 inch

1 liter = approximately 1 quart

4 liters = approximately 1 gallon

1 kilometer = approximately 1/2 mile

1 kilogram = approximately 2 pounds

Easy rules for small measurements include:

1 millimeter = about 40 thousandths of an inch

0.10 millimeter = about 4 thousandths of an inch

To convert millimeters to thousandths of an inch, just multiply by 0.03937.

Using Conversion Tables

Here are some examples that require the use of conversion tables. We suggest that you make these conversions and see if you get the same answers.

1. You are doing a tune-up on a new model. You look in the service manual for the valve clearances and it reads:

0.007 inch	What is that in mm?	(*answer:* 0.18)
0.002 inch		(*answer:* 0.05)
0.003 inch		(*answer:* 0.08)
0.004 inch		(*answer:* 0.10)

2. A service manual usually lists valve clearances in millimeters because most motorcycles are metric. But many technicians have feeler gauges that measure only in thousandths. Make these conversions:

0.05 mm = _____	(*answer:* 2 thousandths)
0.10 mm = _____	(*answer:* 4 thousandths)
0.15 mm = _____	(*answer:* 6 thousandths)

   Notice that all you have to do is multiply by 0.03937.

3. You need to set the points during a tune-up. The service manual reads, "0.35 to 0.40 millimeter." What is that in thousandths of an inch? (*answer:* 14 to 16)

   Perhaps the clearance for the points is listed in thousandths of an inch. What are the following in millimeters?

16 thousandths (0.016 inch)	(*answer:* 0.41 mm)
20 thousandths (0.020 inch)	(*answer:* 0.51 mm)

4. Motorcycle technicians often need to measure shafts and springs. An accurate measurement is especially important because the length will indicate if a spring is weakening. Here are some lengths. Convert them.

Shaft: 13.73 cm	(*answer:* 5.406 in)
Spring: 4.93 cm	(*answer:* 1.941 in)
Fork spring: 68.7 cm	(*answer:* 27.047 in)

5. If a container measures 7 cm × 4 cm × 5 cm:

How many cc's does it hold?	(*answer:* 140)
How many liters?	(*answer:* 0.14)
How many quarts?	(*answer:* 0.15)

USING MEASUREMENT TOOLS

Because parts can only be machined within certain tolerances, acceptable ranges that permit parts to fit and function as intended have been established. The difference between the maximum and minimum measurements in an approved range is the *tolerance*. When two parts mate or are interchanged in an assembly, part tolerance is vitally important. Service manuals provide part specifications and tolerances.

Measurement tools are used to measure the inner and outer dimensions of parts. These measurements must then be compared to the specifications and tolerances provided in the service manual to determine if a part can be used.

Motorcycle technicians use several types of measuring tools. This section explains how to use rulers, vernier calipers, feeler gauges, micrometers, and dial indicators. These instruments are manufactured to make either English or metric measurements, and they include scales or dials by which the measurements are read. Telescoping gauges and small hole gauges are also used to take measurements, but these tools do not provide a scale or dial for readings. This section also explains how to make comparison measurements using these instruments.

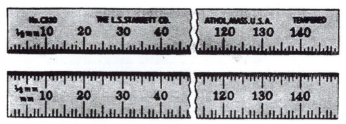

Figure 2-1   Metric rulers (The L.S. Starrett Company).

Rulers

You are already familiar with English rulers, yardsticks, and tape measures. These are usually marked off in inches and are accurate to approximately 1/32 of an inch.

Metric rulers are marked off in centimeters, and each centimeter has 10 millimeters marked off within it. Metric rulers are accurate to approximately 5 mm (Fig. 2-1).

Rulers are placed next to the object being measured, and the size of the object is determined by comparing it to the scale of the ruler. Vernier calipers, micrometers, and dial indicators fit in the object being measured, and the size is indicated on the scale by a pointer.

Vernier Caliper

Vernier calipers are commonly used by technicians. They are accurate to approximately 0.02 mm or 0.001 inch.

A caliper is made of two pieces (Fig. 2-2). The main piece is a long beam which has a scale on it. At one end of the beam are a pair of nibs or points and jaws. The nibs and jaws are attached to a collar that slides back and forth on the beam.

When using the vernier caliper to measure a spring, open the jaws and place the spring between them. Gently slide the jaws closed. The nibs or points are used to measure the inside dimensions. The depth gauge is used to measure the height and length. The measurement will be indicated on the beam's main scale.

The purpose of the vernier scale is to determine the size indicated on the beam's main scale with more accuracy. At first glance, the vernier scale appears to be a short section of the scale on the beam, but actually each division is smaller than those on the beam. Only one line of the vernier scale will correspond with another line on the beam. To determine the measurement of an object, find the line of the vernier scale that corresponds with a line on the main scale (Figs. 2-3, 2-4, and 2-5).

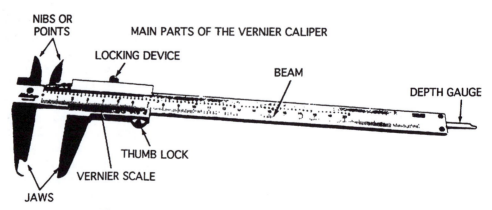

Figure 2-2   (Yamaha Motor Corporation, U.S.A.).

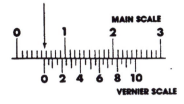

Figure 2-3 Main scale reading of 5.00 (Yamaha Motor Corporation, U.S.A.).

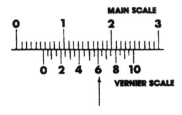

Figure 2-4 Vernier scale reading of 0.60 (Yamaha Motor Corporation, U.S.A.).

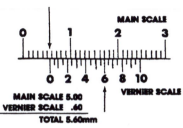

Figure 2-5 Total reading of 5.60 mm (Yamaha Motor Corporation, U.S.A.).

Feeler Gauge

A feeler gauge is a flat strip of metal that is placed between two parts to measure the space between them. Feeler gauges are manufactured in various thicknesses and each size is very accurate. The size is indicated on the gauge leaf.

Feeler gauges are manufactured to make either English or metric measurements. An English feeler gauge gives measurements in thousandths of an inch (Fig. 2-6). A metric gauge gives measurements in one hundredths of a millimeter. Also available are feeler gauge sets with both English and metric measurements stamped on the individual blades.

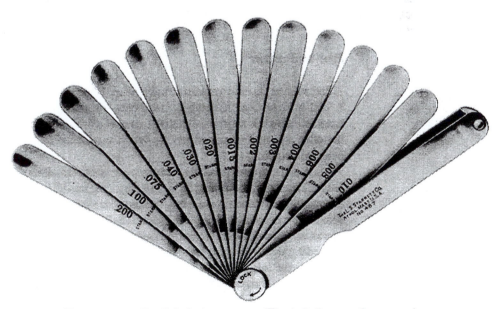

Figure 2-6 English feeler gauges (The L.S. Starrett Company).

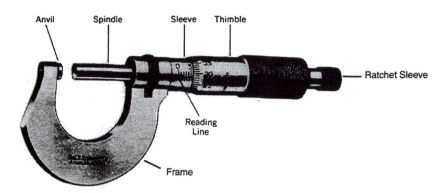

Figure 2-7   Metric micrometer (The L.S. Starrett Company).

Micrometer

A micrometer is the most precise measuring tool used by motorcycle technicians. A good-quality micrometer can measure down to 0.001 mm or 0.0001 inch depending on whether it is a metric or English scale micrometer.

A micrometer appears to be sturdy, but it is fragile and should be handled carefully (Fig. 2-7). Place the object to be measured between the anvil and spindle, and turn the knob to tighten the anvil and spindle around the object. Be careful not to overtighten a micrometer. Many micrometers have a small knob or ratchet sleeve on the end of the large knob that prevents overtightening. Use this ratchet sleeve to close the micrometer.

The main scale of an English micrometer is divided into tenths of an inch, and each of those is divided into four parts. The scale on the rotating knob reads from 0 to 25. As the knob is turned, it rotates once for each quarter of each tenth of an inch, which permits measurements to one thousandths of an inch.

The main scale of a metric micrometer is divided into millimeters, and each millimeter is divided in half. The rotating scale has 50 spaces, which permits measurements to 1/100 mm. With the addition of a vernier scale on the sleeve, the metric micrometer can measure down to 0.001 mm and the English micrometer can measure down to 0.0001 inch.

There are several types of micrometers, but all micrometer scales are read in essentially the same way. Because it is used for very small measurements, it is important for the micrometer to be carefully lined up and for it to be neither too loose nor too tight around the object to be measured.

Dial Indicator

A dial indicator is used to measure movement. It has an accuracy of approximately 1/100 mm. A dial indicator can be held in place with a bracket or used with a magnetic mount. A magnetic mount is a magnet attached to one end of an arm. The dial indicator is clamped into the other end of the arm, which can be adjusted to hold the indicator against the surface being measured.

A dial indicator is usually used to measure the small movements of metal parts such as shafts. When the measuring rod is pushed up, the needle in the dial makes one revolution for each millimeter of rod movement. The small scale counts off the number of times the needle completes a revolution (Figs. 2-8, 2-9, and 2-10). A dial indicator can also be mounted so that it presses against a shaft. When the shaft is slowly turned, the needle should remain still. If the needle moves, the shaft is not straight. A dial indicator is essential to measure piston movement in order to set ignition timing.

All measurement tools are sold with an instruction booklet that explains the care and handling of the tool and how to read its scale. Be sure to read the instructions before using the tool.

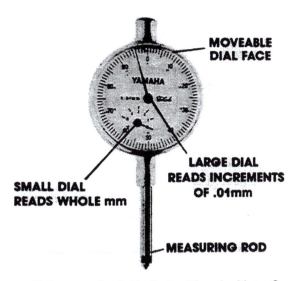

Figure 2-8   Main parts of a dial indicator (Yamaha Motor Corporation, U.S.A.).

Figure 2-9   Large scale reading of 0.81 (Yamaha Motor Corporation, U.S.A.).

Figure 2-10   Small scale reading of 3.00 (Yamaha Motor Corporation, U.S.A.).

Telescoping Gauge

A telescoping gauge is used with a micrometer to measure the diameter of bores such as cylinders. Telescoping gauges are available in sets that range from 5/16 to 6 inches (8 to 150 mm). Be sure to select the appropriate gauge for the bore to be measured. Insert the gauge into the bore, and release the handle lock screw. Rock the gauge sideways to ensure that you are measuring the full diameter. This is especially important when measuring large-diameter bores.

Once the gauge is inserted properly, lightly tighten the locking screw. Roll the gauge up or down through the bore. This motion will push the gauge plungers in to conform to the bore's diameter. Now tighten the locking screw, and again roll the gauge through the bore while feeling for a light drag.

Remove the gauge and place it between the micrometer's spindle and anvil. As you close the micrometer, try to feel the same amount of resistance on the gauge between the spindle and anvil as you felt while rolling the gauge through the bore. If the spindle and anvil put excessive pressure on the gauge, the plungers will depress and the measurement will be incorrect.

Repeat this procedure at least twice to verify the accuracy of the reading.

Small Hole Gauge

A small hole gauge is used to measure inside dimensions. These gauges are available in sets that range from 1/8 to 1/2 inch (3 to 13 mm) and 1/16 to 1/2 inch (1.5 to 13 mm). There are several small hole gauge designs, but basically the gauge consists of two parallel halves that expand or contract as the adjusting screw at the top is turned. Contract the gauge before placing it in the slot to be measured. Then turn the adjusting screw to expand the gauge, and move it back and forth in the slot, making sure that the edges of the gauge conform to the size of the slot. Lock the gauge and remove it from the slot. Use a micrometer to measure the small hole gauge.

chapter 3

Internal Combustion Engine Theory

There are motorcycles available to suit the taste of every rider, but whether the motorcycle is a full-dress touring model or a state-of-the-art motocross rocket, each is propelled by an internal combustion engine. This chapter explains the internal combustion engine process by first examining the physical laws involved in the process. The actual combustion process will be described, including the factors that influence combustion and engine performance. The abnormalities that may occur in the combustion process will be presented, followed by some practical knowledge about the engine and its ability to perform work.

PHYSICAL LAWS INVOLVED IN COMBUSTION Thermodynamics and gas laws provide an understanding of what makes combustion possible.

Thermodynamics

Thermodynamics, the science of heat and energy, has established laws to predict the effects of heat and the transfer of energy. The following laws are at work in the combustion process:

> Energy cannot be created or destroyed.
>
> Energy can be changed from one form to another.
>
> No conversion of energy is 100 percent efficient.

Gas Laws

Laws have been formulated to predict the behavior of expanding gases. There are some complications to consider, but the following laws provide a basic explanation of how an engine works:

> If air is compressed, its temperature increases.
>
> Air that is heated seeks to expand.
>
> The more air is compressed and heated, the greater its pressure.

Physical Laws at Work

Combustion changes chemical energy to heat energy. An engine works by compressing the air/fuel mixture into a small space and by taking advantage of its expansion as it is heated. Before it is compressed, the air/fuel mixture is gaseous and contained in a cylinder. The air/fuel mixture is then compressed by a piston and ignited by a spark plug, which causes the mixture to burn. This burning, called *rapid oxidation*, is actually a chemical reaction that happens very quickly. During rapid oxidation, the fuel and oxygen in the air combine to form new molecules, primarily carbon dioxide (CO_2) and water (H_2O). While the fuel and oxygen are

17

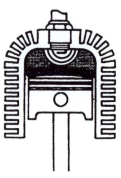

Figure 3-1 Combustion lag.

Figure 3-2 Active combustion.

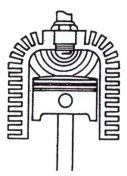

Figure 3-3 Postcombustion activity.

converting to become new molecules, they lose some of their internal energy. That energy is released as heat, which causes a tremendous increase in pressure in the cylinder, which forces the piston down. Some of the heat is absorbed by the surrounding cylinder.

THE INTERNAL COMBUSTION PROCESS

There are three phases in the internal combustion process: combustion lag, active combustion, and postcombustion activity.

Combustion Lag

The piston compresses a gaseous mixture of the proper air/fuel ratio. The spark plug ignites a small portion of the mixture at the firing tip. A ball of fire spreads outward and begins to consume the remaining air/fuel mixture. The burning inside the cylinder is a chain reaction of burning fuel that spreads to the far reaches of the combustion chamber. But this ball of fire that initiates combustion does not immediately spread outward. Before the chain reaction spreads, a short period of slow burning takes place. This slow burning is known as *combustion lag* (Fig. 3-1).

Active Combustion

This second phase begins once the initial lag is overcome and as the chain reaction begins to accelerate outward at greater speeds. Rapid temperature and pressure buildup occurs as the charge is consumed. The chain reaction of burning molecules accelerates, and the chemical conversion causes heat to be released rapidly. This heat makes the molecules vibrate faster and faster, similar to water becoming steam when boiled. In accordance with the gas laws, the tremendous increase in temperature causes the pressure in the cylinder to increase proportionately. This ignition spark is timed so that the charge is almost completely burned while the piston is near top dead center (Fig. 3-2).

Postcombustion Activity

After most of the charge has been consumed and while the piston is changing direction at top dead center, burning contributes very little toward producing power. As the piston descends and the volume inside the cylinder increases, which allows the pressure to drop, power is absorbed by the piston. The cylinder now eliminates spent gases to prepare for the next cycle of fresh air/fuel mixture. All engines begin to release exhaust gases out of the cylinder well before the piston reaches bottom dead center (Fig. 3-3).

FACTORS INFLUENCING COMBUSTION AND ENGINE PERFORMANCE

There are several factors that influence the combustion process and engine performance. They are compression ratio, volumetric efficiency, bore and stroke, air/fuel ratio, and residual gases.

Compression Ratio

The *compression ratio* is the difference in the volume of air when the piston is at bottom dead center compared to the volume of air trapped when the piston is at top dead center (Fig. 3-4).

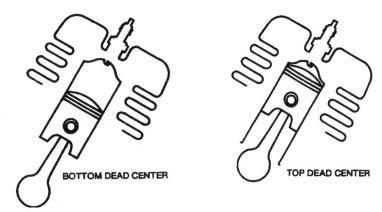

Figure 3-4 Compression ratio = difference in volume of air when the piston is at BDC when compared to piston at TDC.

The following formula, which is known as the *full stroke ratio*, provides an understanding of the effects of compression ratio on engine performance:

$$CR = \frac{CV + CCV}{CCV}$$

CR = compression ratio

CV = cylinder volume

CCV = combustion chamber volume

The compression ratio of an engine is a dominant factor in engine performance. In many cases, increasing the compression ratio will result in a power increase (Figs. 3-5 and 3-6).

Volumetric Efficiency

Volumetric efficiency and compression pressure are related. *Volumetric efficiency* is a measure of how much air is actually inhaled by the engine compared to how much it could hold according to the size of the cylinder. An engine that can inhale a full charge of air/fuel mixture has a high volumetric efficiency. An engine with a high compression ratio may not be powerful if it has a low volumetric efficiency. This is because a cylinder that is not completely packed with a charge of air will not create much heat during compression.

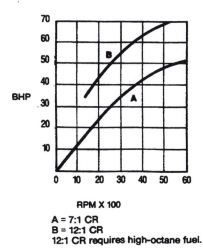

RPM X 100

A = 7:1 CR
B = 12:1 CR
12:1 CR requires high-octane fuel.

Figure 3-5 Graph showing the relationship between compression ratio and horsepower at a given rpm. (From *The Design and Tuning of Competition Engines*, by Phillip H. Smith, 6th edition revised by David N. Wenner, 1977, Robert Bentley, Inc., Cambridge, Mass.)

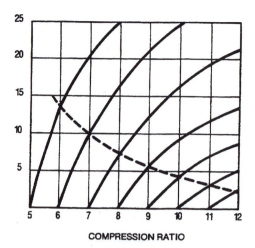

COMPRESSION RATIO

Figure 3-6   Raising the compression ratio from 6:1 to 7:1 increases power 10%. Raising the compression ratio from 9:1 to 10:1 increases power only 4%. The progressive decrease in power is a result of raising the compression ratio. (From *The Design and Tuning of Competition Engines*, by Phillip H. Smith, 6th edition revised by David N. Wenner, 1977, Robert Bentley, Inc., Cambridge, Mass.)

Bore and Stroke

The combustion process and engine performance are also influenced by the size or displacement of the engine. The engine displacement is determined by the diameter of the cylinder and the distance the piston moves when traveling from bottom dead center to top dead center.

The diameter of the engine cylinder is called the *bore*. How far the piston travels from bottom dead center to top dead center is called the *stroke*. The engine displacement can be found by using this formula:

bore × bore × stroke × 0.7854 × number of cylinders = displacement

Air/Fuel Ratio

Only certain ratios of air and gasoline mixtures burn satisfactorily. The theoretical, chemically correct air/gasoline ratio for complete fuel combustion is known as the *stoichiometric ratio*. The stoichiometric ratio is approximately 14.7 parts air to 1 part gasoline measured by weight. Maximum power is obtained by decreasing the amount of air in this ratio by approximately 10 percent. Minimum fuel consumption is achieved by increasing the amount of air in the mixture by approximately 10 percent.

Air density is the thickness of air. Humidity, temperature, and elevation all affect air density. High humidity increases air density. When the air density increases, the oxygen in the air also increases, and this can result in a leaner air/fuel ratio. High temperature and/or increased elevation decrease air density. When the air density decreases, the oxygen in the air decreases, and this can result in a richer air/fuel ratio.

Since an engine operates at many different speeds, loads, and temperatures, the stoichiometric ratio must change to meet the different operating conditions (Fig. 3-7). This job of changing ratios is handled by the carburetor or by a fuel injection system.

Residual Exhaust Gases

During compression the fresh charge is always diluted to some extent by exhaust gases that are left from the previous cycle. These gases slow the speed of burning. Four-stroke valve tim-

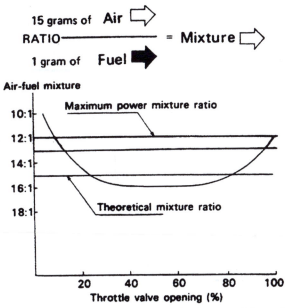

Figure 3-7 Air/fuel ratio (Motorcycle Carburetor Manual, Haynes Publishing Group).

ing, two-stroke port timing, ignition timing, and carburetion specifications are determined by the manufacturer to compensate for the presence of these residual gases.

ABNORMAL COMBUSTION

Up to this point what has been described is an internal combustion engine operating under ideal conditions. Combustion has been described as an even, smooth burning of the air/fuel mixture (Fig. 3-8). In practical applications normal combustion is the goal, but it is not always achieved. There are two common types of abnormal combustion: preignition and detonation.

Preignition

During normal combustion the mixture is ignited by a spark plug. The ignition system ensures that the spark fires at precisely the right time. But sometimes the mixture ignites before the spark plug fires. This is known as *preignition*.

Preignition is caused by an object in the combustion chamber that becomes hot enough to ignite the mixture before the spark (Fig. 3-9). A carbon deposit from fuel or oil, an overheated spark plug, or the edge of a gasket that protrudes into the combustion chamber can ignite the mixture before normal sparking takes place. Usually, preignition occurs in an engine that has high mileage or has been improperly serviced. Incorrect ignition timing or an improper air/fuel mixture will also lower the efficiency of an engine, drive up temperatures, and cause preignition.

Power is lost during preignition because the piston must overcome the pressure buildup before reaching top dead center. During preignition the heat from combustion is present in the chamber for a period of time that is longer than normal. This can overheat the engine parts. Some of the effects of preignition are excessive heat buildup and abnormal pressure rise. This excessive heat and pressure could lead to piston seizure, loss of power, or a melted piston, spark plug, or both. Maintaining a good state-of-tune is the easiest way to keep preignition under control.

Detonation

Also called *autoignition, detonation* is a violent explosion of the last part of the gases to burn that is caused by an excessive rise in pressure and temperature. Normally, the flame front sweeps

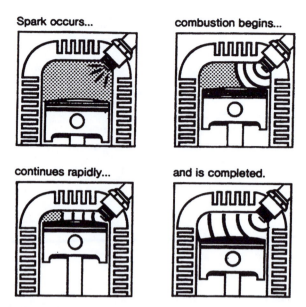

Figure 3-8   Normal combustion (Champion Spark Plug Company).

through the combustion chamber and consumes the entire charge, including the gas mixture in the far reaches of the chamber. But if the speed of this burning is too slow, the end gases can reach detonation temperature before they are consumed by the main charge. These end gases can ignite spontaneously if they become hot enough. If they reach detonation temperature before being burned, they will explode. This explosion sends out a tremendous pressure wave that bounces off the cylinder walls with a sound like a hammer hitting metal. This is the source of pinging and rattling sounds (Fig. 3-10).

The rapid rise in pressure caused by detonation causes a terrific load to be placed on the piston. Bearings are pounded, spark plugs can disintegrate, and the top of the piston can actually be blown to pieces. In many situations detonation is not severe enough to destroy an engine immediately. Mild cases will not break pistons, bearings, or connecting rods. But the extra pounding drastically shortens the service life of these components.

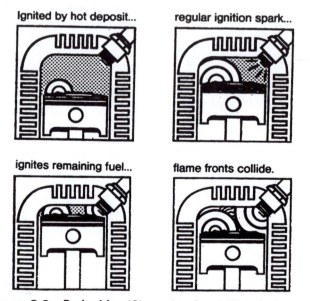

Figure 3-9   Preignition (Champion Spark Plug Company).

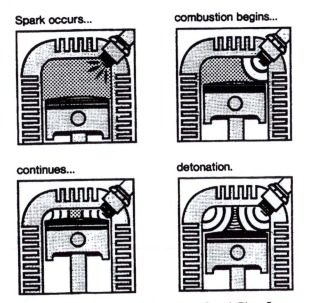

Spark occurs... combustion begins...

continues... detonation.

Figure 3-10 Detonation (Champion Spark Plug Company).

To prevent detonation, the engine conditions must be correct, and end gases must be consumed before they explode. To keep temperatures at an acceptable level, the air/fuel mixture must burn in a controlled manner. The octane rating of gasoline controls the burning, and this is explained in Chapter 9.

ENGINE DESIGN AND COMBUSTION

Most engines perform somewhere between normal combustion and detonation. There are several factors in engine design which can either aggravate or prevent abnormal combustion. These factors are compression ratio, engine load, fuel quality, turbulence, and state-of-tune.

Compression Ratio

The compression ratio creates power. An excessive compression ratio can create detonation, especially when coupled with a dense charge of intake gases. Motorcycle cylinder head design is very efficient and allows a high compression ratio. The effects of excessive compression ratio can be prevented through the use of a good-quality fuel. A high compression ratio requires high-octane fuel, which is not generally available today.

Engine Load

Engine load is what the engine must overcome to perform work. A heavily weighted motorcycle that is pulling up a steep hill makes extreme demands on the engine. Under such severe loads, the rider must use full throttle to extract maximum horsepower. Engine temperature rises rapidly under these heavy loads. The compressed charge reaches higher temperatures, which can lead to detonation. Detonation is also likely when riding in a gear that is too high; this is commonly known as *lugging the engine*. If a rider uses full throttle instead of downshifting for more power, the motorcycle will be in a gear that is too high for the low speed of the engine. The engine speed will rise very slowly and eventually match the load. But until this occurs, the engine receives too much air because the throttle is wide open. This creates a lean air/fuel mixture which burns slowly and causes the end gases to overheat. Detonation soon follows.

Fuel Quality

Early gasolines burned with an uncontrollable reaction rate. The pressure rise in the cylinder was steep, which caused the end gases to detonate. In 1921, Thomas Midgeley discovered tetraethyllead. When used in fuel, which is known today as *leaded gas*, this additive raises the octane rating of gas by slowing the reaction rate. For years, leaded gas allowed higher compression ratios to be used without creating detonation. Today, because of environmental standards, most lead is removed from gas. Other additives are used but not with the same effectiveness as that of tetraethyllead.

Turbulence

Knowing that fuel quality was receding, engine designers searched for ways to improve combustion efficiency and suppress detonation. They discovered that an air/fuel mixture that is in rapid motion tends to burn more efficiently. Inducing turbulence in the combustion chamber allows the fire to rush to the far corners of the chamber and consume the entire charge more quickly.

Two early researchers, Harry Ricardo and Harry Weslake, were the first to identify that a swirling mixture is more efficient. Weslake found that in a four-stroke engine, offsetting the intake valve induces a circular swirl of incoming gases. Ricardo found that compacting the combustion chamber over the center of the piston reduces detonation. The outer edges of the chamber are very close to the piston when it approaches top dead center. This area, known as the *squish band*, actually forces the charge toward the center and induces turbulence. This is called the *squish effect*. A squish-type cylinder head also reduces the distance the flame front must travel and allows it to reach the end gases sooner. Most two-stroke engines use the squish-type cylinder head (Fig. 3-11).

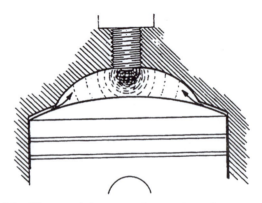

Figure 3-11 The squish area above the piston squeezes the charge toward the center of the chamber, promoting turbulence. (From *The Two-Stroke Tuner's Handbook*, by Gordon Jennings, 1973, HPBooks, Tucson, Ariz.)

Modern-day innovations to induce turbulence include a twin-swirl combustion chamber and an induction control system. The twin-swirl design uses four valves per cylinder and induces two separate swirling motions by dividing the chamber into two segments. The induction control system includes separate subports that interconnect at the intake manifolds. These subports shoot a stream of air into each incoming charge and cause it to move rapidly through the chamber (Figs. 3-12 and 3-13).

State-of-Tune

Detonation can be prevented by maintaining a good state-of-tune. An engine that is out of tune can suffer from advanced timing, which occurs when the spark plug fires too soon. The ef-

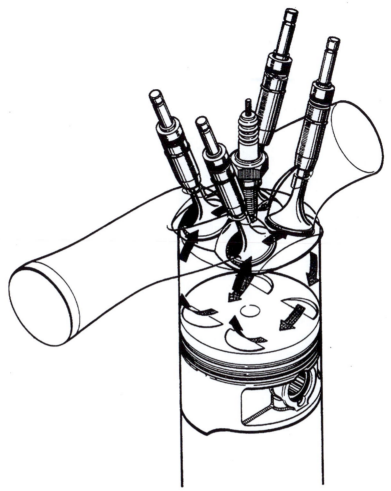

Figure 3-12 Twin-swirl combustion chamber (TSCC) (American Suzuki Motor Corporation).

fects of this advanced timing are similar to preignition; combustion temperatures are present for a longer time than normal and the end gases overheat. A good state-of-tune is also important for multicylinder engines that use a carburetor with each cylinder. Each cylinder must receive the same amount of air/fuel mixture. A couple of cylinders that are out of adjustment can cause the other cylinders to work harder. This imbalance in the engine raises temperatures and once again makes conditions ripe for detonation to occur.

FACTORS DETERMINING EFFICIENT COMBUSTION

To determine the efficiency of the combustion process, several factors must be considered and measured. These factors are heat efficiency, cylinder pressures, force at the crankshaft, and mechanical power.

Heat Efficiency

The heat of combustion raises the temperature of gases inside the cylinder and causes them to expand. Higher percentages of heat converted to work mean more efficiency. The measurement of heat and its conversion to work is known as *thermal efficiency*. A good four-stroke engine may be 35 percent efficient. The rest of the heat is either released with the exhaust or absorbed by the cylinder and dissipated to the outside air.

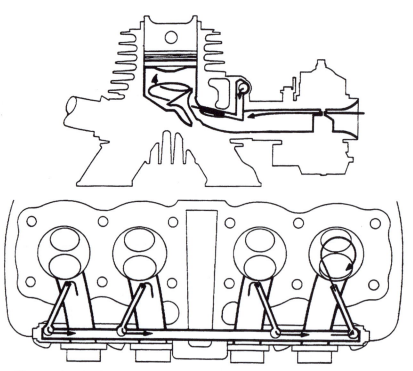

Figure 3-13 Induction control system (Yamaha Motor Corporation, U.S.A.).

Cylinder Pressure

The efficiency of combustion is directly related to how much pressure is built up in the cylinder. The more pressure is created, the more efficient the combustion process. The pressure on top of the piston(s) is the *indicated mean effective pressure* (IMEP). A more useful figure is the *brake mean effective pressure* (BMEP), which is measured in pounds per square inch. BMEP is the calculated pressure at the crankshaft that takes into account the frictional losses caused by the rings, pistons, and bearings in the engine. The engine's ability to intake a full charge and the compression ratio are major factors in developing cylinder pressure.

Force at the Crankshaft

Torque is the twisting force at the end of a rotating shaft. Engine displacement and BMEP determine how much torque is produced at the end of the crankshaft. Torque is not the same as horsepower. Torque (measured in kilograms or pounds) applied to a lever (measured in feet or meters) performs the same amount of work regardless of how long it takes. The formula for determining torque is:

$$\text{torque (in ft-lb)} = \frac{\text{BMEP} \times \text{displacement}}{2473}$$

Increases in BMEP or displacement cause torque to change.

Mechanical Power

Horsepower (hp), a measure of mechanical power, is determined by work and its relationship to time. The more work done in a specific amount of time equals more horsepower.

1 hp = 33,000 ft-lb of work done in 1 minute, or 550 ft-lb per second

Horsepower is a direct result of torque and engine speed (revolutions per minute, or rpm). Given an amount of torque, an engine will increase horsepower with increased rpm. Horsepower will increase until lower cylinder pressures cause torque to decrease. At higher speeds there is less time available for air/fuel intake. With reduced time available for intake, less cylinder filling results in less BMEP and torque.

Horsepower that is measured at the crankshaft takes into account the frictional losses in the engine. Regardless of the amount of power produced by efficient combustion, poor mechanical engine design will reduce horsepower because of the amount of friction that must be overcome. The lower the frictional losses, the higher the mechanical efficiency of the engine.

A clear understanding of the combustion process is necessary to evaluate an engine's combustion efficiency. This is basic to motorcycle mechanics. A good technician will be able to understand how an engine's thermal and mechanical efficiency—cylinder pressures, torque, and horsepower—affect engine performance.

chapter 4

The Four-Stroke Engine

This chapter explains four-stroke engine components, operation, and designs. A brief overview of four-stroke engine components is first presented, followed by an explanation of four-stroke engine operation. Various four-stroke engine designs and configurations are described. Detailed information about four-stroke engine components is provided, including general service and maintenance guidelines. Information about four-stroke engine carburetion, lubrication, and cooling systems is presented in subsequent chapters.

FOUR-STROKE ENGINE COMPONENTS

Four-stroke engine design includes many of the following components:

Cylinder head
  Valves, springs, valve guides, and seals
  Rocker arms and adjusters
  Cam chains and tensioners
  Tappets and lifters
  Shims and buckets
  Pushrods
Cylinder
  Piston
  Piston rings
Crankshaft
  Connecting rod
  Engine balancers
Crankcase
  Bearings and bushings
  Seals and gaskets

The following description of the main internal components of a single-cylinder four-stroke engine (Fig. 4-1) will provide a basic understanding of how the components interact.

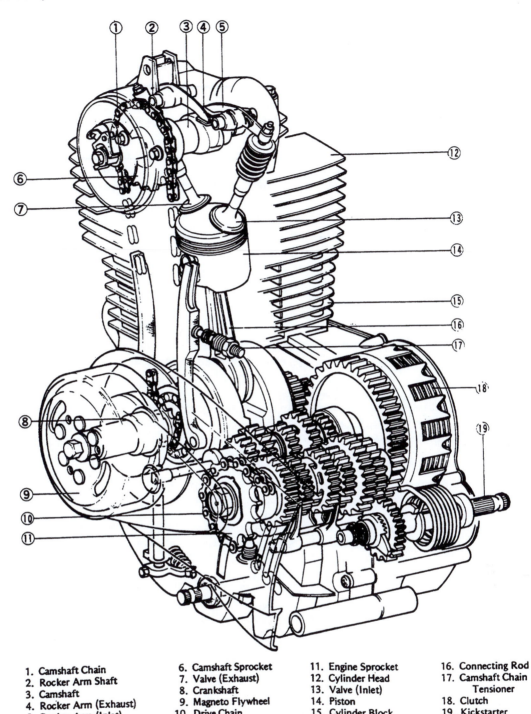

1. Camshaft Chain	6. Camshaft Sprocket	11. Engine Sprocket	16. Connecting Rod
2. Rocker Arm Shaft	7. Valve (Exhaust)	12. Cylinder Head	17. Camshaft Chain
3. Camshaft	8. Crankshaft	13. Valve (Inlet)	Tensioner
4. Rocker Arm (Exhaust)	9. Magneto Flywheel	14. Piston	18. Clutch
5. Rocker Arm (Inlet)	10. Drive Chain	15. Cylinder Block	19. Kickstarter

Figure 4-1 Single-cylinder four-stroke engine (Kawasaki Motors Corporation, U.S.A.).

The crankshaft, which is supported in the crankcase, is composed of a left flywheel and shaft, a right flywheel and shaft, and a crankpin to which the connecting rod is attached. The crankshaft changes the up-and-down motion of the piston into circular motion. The weight of the crankshaft creates an inertia effect that causes rotational momentum, which is the tendency to keep turning after combustion takes place. The crankshaft is also weighted so as to provide a counterbalance to the natural imbalance caused by the piston and rod motion.

The connecting rod connects the crankpin and the crankshaft assembly to the piston pin in the piston. A piston pin is also known as a wrist pin. The piston and piston rings create a sealed chamber that contains the air/fuel mixture and power produced in the cylinder.

The cylinder head seals the end of the cylinder to create the combustion chamber. The intake and exhaust valves control the flow of gases in and out of the combustion chamber. The intake and exhaust valves are directly or indirectly controlled by the camshaft and the rocker arms or shim devices.

FOUR-STROKE ENGINE OPERATION

A single-cylinder four-stroke engine completes four operations and four piston strokes in two crankshaft revolutions to complete one four-stroke cycle. The completion of a cycle produces one power stroke. The four operations that are required for the engine to produce power are:

1. Intake stroke
2. Compression stroke
3. Timed ignition/power stroke
4. Exhaust stroke

Intake Stroke

Intake occurs when the air/fuel mixture enters the cylinder. The intake stroke begins when the intake valve is just beginning to open, and the piston is close to the cylinder head. As the piston moves away from the cylinder head, the volume above the piston expands. This increased volume creates a negative pressure area, or vacuum, in the cylinder. Because the intake valve is open, a path is completed through the intake manifold and carburetor. In an effort to balance the pressure difference between the atmospheric pressure of the outside air and the negative pressure in the cylinder, the outside air moves through the carburetor toward the cylinder (Fig. 4-2). The intake valve closes and seals the combustion chamber when the piston is near the crankshaft.

Compression Stroke

As both the intake and exhaust valves close, the piston begins moving toward the cylinder head. As it moves, the piston compresses the air/fuel mixture which entered during the intake stroke. Compressing the air/fuel mixture into a smaller space creates a high-energy mixture of air and fuel molecules (Fig. 4-3).

Figure 4-2   Intake stroke (American Suzuki Motor Corporation).

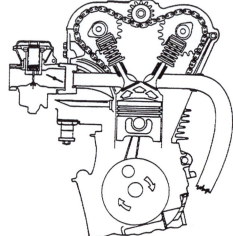

Figure 4-3   Compression stroke (American Suzuki Motor Corporation).

Timed Ignition/Power Stroke

As explained in Chapter 3, because of combustion lag, ignition takes place at some point before the piston reaches top dead center. Four-stroke engines have various timing specifications, but the goal in each engine is to create peak power just after the piston passes top dead center. The heated gases created by combustion expand rapidly and force the piston away from the cylinder head (Fig. 4-4). Because the piston is attached to the crankshaft by the connecting rod and shafts, the linear movement of the piston produces the rotary movement of the crankshaft.

Exhaust Stroke

Most of the power created during the power stroke occurs in the first half of piston travel. The remaining expanding gases start pushing the exhaust gases out of the cylinder through the exhaust valve during the end of the power stroke. Before the piston reaches bottom dead center of the power stroke, the exhaust valve begins to open. This is the beginning of the exhaust stroke. As the exhaust stroke continues, crankshaft inertia keeps the crankshaft turning, which forces the piston back toward the cylinder head.

As the cylinder volume decreases, the exhaust gases are pushed out of the cylinder through the exhaust valve (Fig. 4-5). As the exhaust gases leave the cylinder, a negative pressure, or vacuum, is created. Before the exhaust valve is completely closed, the intake valve starts to open and the fresh air/fuel mixture enters. This fresh mixture pushes the remaining spent exhaust gases out of the closing exhaust valve. This point in the cycle, when both valves are open, is referred to as *valve overlap*. More information about valve overlap, which is determined by camshaft design, is presented later in this chapter.

The intake, compression, power, and exhaust strokes repeat and continue during four-stroke engine operation.

FOUR-STROKE ENGINE DESIGNS A modern motorcycle engine is very different from the first model that was created over 100 years ago when an internal combustion engine was installed in a bicycle frame (Figs. 4-6 and 4-7). The crude design, inefficient fuel burning, and minimal power output of the first engines have little in common with today's engines. However, single-cylinder, V-twin, opposed-twin, radial, and in-line four-cylinder engines were designed before 1920, and today's motorcycles are refined versions of these early designs. Developments in technology have affected motorcycle castings and designs, fuels, components, carburetion, and ignition systems. As

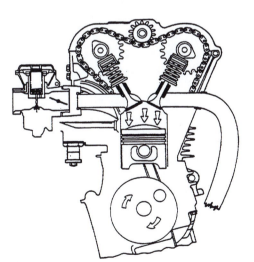

Figure 4-4 Timed ignition/power stroke (American Suzuki Motor Corporation).

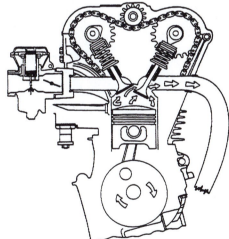

Figure 4-5 Exhaust stroke (American Suzuki Motor Corporation).

Figure 4-6   1930 Four-cylinder Indian (Kent Myers).

combustion became better understood, methods were found to make it more efficient. Improvements in metallurgy, machining, and production have provided the quality and precision that are found in modern motorcycles.

Every year new four-stroke motorcycle engines are developed with new features and improvements. Today's motorcycles are designed to be faster, lighter, more efficient, and longer lasting. Continuing developments in manufacturing and materials allow engines to be lighter, create less friction, resist more heat, and provide more horsepower. High-quality steel alloys, aluminum alloys, magnesium, plastics, and ceramics are now being used on motorcycles. Water cooling, which was initially used in most automotive engine designs but few motorcycles, is now commonplace in four-stroke motorcycle engine design.

Four-Stroke Engine Configurations

The number of cylinders determines the number of power strokes produced relative to crankshaft rotation. The engine layout and configuration are factors in cooling and vehicle handling. Compression ratio, cam design, and engine displacement are factors that determine the amount of horsepower and torque that can be produced.

Single-Cylinder Engines: These are the least complicated of the four-stroke engines. The single-cylinder engine uses the fewest number of parts and produces less horsepower than a multicylinder engine of equal displacement. The basic design may include an overhead cam, or it may use pushrods and rocker arms. The engine cylinder is usually positioned vertically. Most single-cylinder engines are used in small, lightweight motorcycles, but a few engines are rated at 600 cc displacement or larger. Many single-cylinder, large-displacement engines use counterbalancer systems to smooth out the power pulses created by the single-cylinder design.

V-Twin Engines: V-twin engines were developed in the early 1900s and are still very popular (Figs. 4-8 and 4-9). The V-twin design allows for the greatest amount of engine displacement in the smallest overall area. Harley-Davidson engines have always been a 45° V-twin design with both rods sharing the same crankpin. One rod is forked to accept the other rod inside of it.

European manufacturers build V-twin engines with a 90° V and use offset rods. These engines have less vibration, but the engine is a little wider than the 45° design.

Japanese manufacturers produce several models of V-twins; the degrees between cylinders vary between models.

Vertical Twin Engines: Today's vertical twin engines are more efficient than their early British counterparts because of improved manufacturing processes and better ignition systems. The engines are smaller and narrower than a four-cylinder engine and use either a 180° or 360° crankshaft layout. The crankshaft layout can be determined by observing the position of the pistons when the cylinder head is removed. If both pistons move together, it is a 360° layout. If one piston is up while the other is down, it is a 180° layout (Fig. 4-10).

To achieve smooth engine operation, many manufacturers use a gear- or chain-driven counterbalancer to offset the forces creating vibration. Used in many engine designs, a counterbalancer requires additional parts but very little maintenance (Fig. 4-11).

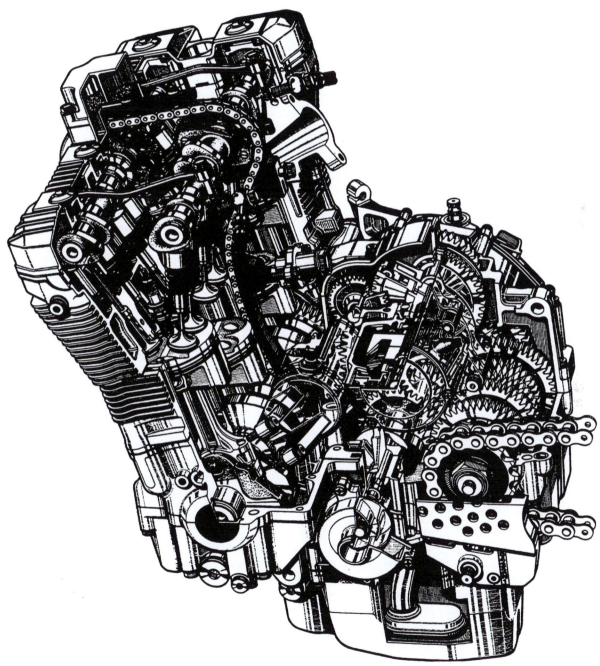

Figure 4-7   A modern motorcycle engine (American Suzuki Motor Corporation).

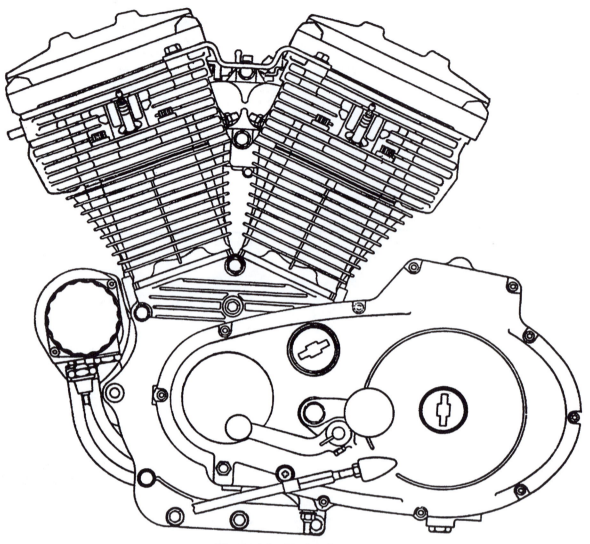

Figure 4-8   Harley-Davidson V-twin engine.

Horizontally Opposed Twin-Cylinder Engines: The horizontally opposed twin engine, often called a flat twin, usually mounts the crankshaft in line with the motorcycle's wheelbase (Fig. 4-12). The crankshaft layout is a 180° degree design. Because the cylinders oppose each other and there are two crankpins, the pistons move in and out at the same time. This design allows the engine to be mounted lower in the frame, which improves weight distribution. The BMW Boxer Twin is a popular model of this design.

Horizontally Opposed Multicylinder Engines: The horizontally opposed four- and six-cylinder engines are similar to the flat twin design with additional cylinders on each side. Because the cylinders lie side by side, the engine is liquid-cooled to ensure rear cylinder cooling. The opposed multicylinder engine is mounted lower in the frame than an in-line engine to improve weight distribution. The Goldwing produced by the American Honda Motor Company is a popular model of this design.

In-Line Multicylinder Engines: The in-line multicylinder engine is found in three-, four-, and six-cylinder designs (Figs. 4-13 and 4-14). The cylinders may be vertical, horizontal, or positioned at some angle in between. The cylinders may be transversely positioned from left to right or longitudinally positioned with the chassis from front to rear. An in-line multicylinder engine is usually designed so that the power strokes are spaced to occur at an equal

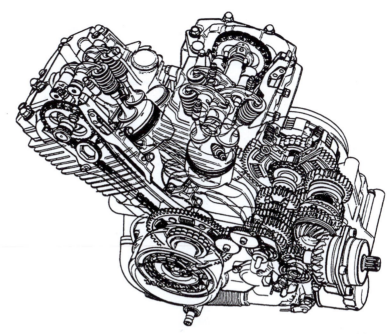

Figure 4-9   Japanese V-twin engine (American Honda Motor Company).

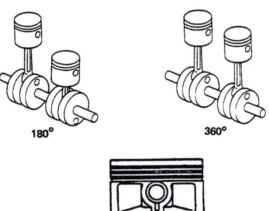

180°   **360°**

Figure 4-10   Crankshaft layouts (American Suzuki Motor Corporation).

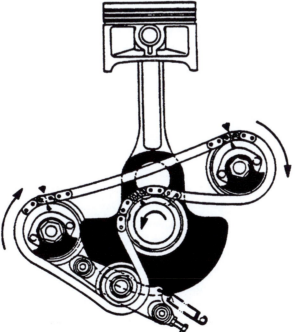

Figure 4-11   Chain-driven counter-rotating balancer (American Suzuki Motor Corporation).

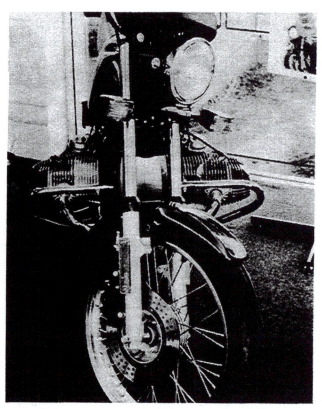

Figure 4-12 Opposed twin-cylinder engine.

number of degrees apart. For example, in an in-line four-cylinder engine, all four power strokes occur in two full turns of the crankshaft or 720° of rotation. The crankshaft, camshaft, and ignition system are designed so that there are 180° between each power stroke. This design creates a smooth-running engine.

V-Four Engines: The V-four engine is similar to two V-twin engines placed side by side (Fig. 4-15). This design is more compact than the in-line four-cylinder engine and produces minimal vibration. The crankshaft is forged, and a pair of connecting rods is mounted to a common crankpin.

FOUR-STROKE ENGINE COMPONENTS

This section explains differences in the design and function of four-stroke engine components and assemblies.

Cylinder Heads

At one time, many cylinder heads were made of cast iron, but most four-stroke engine cylinder heads are now made of aluminum alloy. Aluminum is preferred because it is lightweight and transfers heat better than most metals. Aluminum cylinder heads use valve seats made of several metals to create an alloy that is compatible with today's unleaded fuels. The valve seats have an interference fit in the cylinder head. An interference fit is created when the outside diameter of the valve seat is larger than the hole bored in the cylinder head. Because the expansion rate of most alloy seats is similar to aluminum, the seat stays tight in the head even when the engine reaches operating temperature.

Cylinder head cooling is accomplished using air, oil, or water. Cylinder heads that are air cooled have large fins, and the heads are positioned in the chassis for maximum airflow. Liquid-cooled models are equipped with a body of fluid in a cooling jacket. Liquid cooling

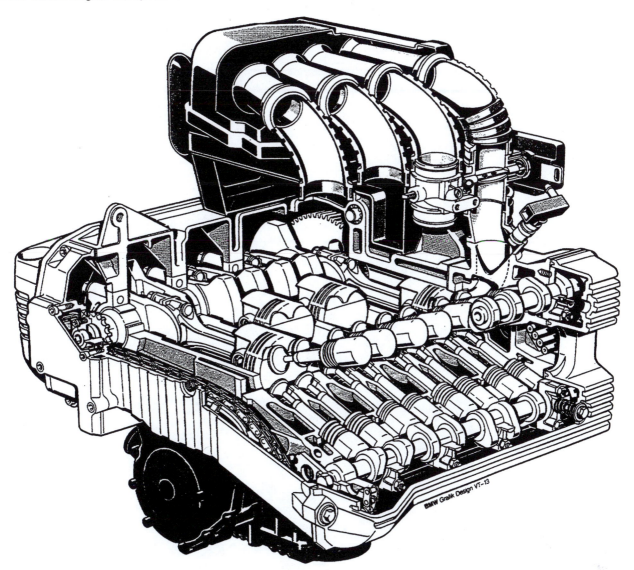

Figure 4-13   Horizontal in-line multicylinder engine (BMW of North America, Inc.).

controls heat more consistently, and the cooling jacket helps reduce mechanical noise (Fig. 4-16).

Four-stroke engine cylinder head designs vary in an effort to meet the following goals:

To create sufficient turbulence within the combustion chamber

To create a squish area

To eliminate restrictions when the air/fuel flows through valve ports

The shape of the combustion chamber within the cylinder head and the position of the valves within the combustion chamber create turbulence. Turbulence is essential to keep the air/fuel mixture well atomized, which is required for complete combustion. The squish area also helps promote turbulence and forces the combustible mixture toward the spark plug to reduce flame travel. The valves and ports are also arranged to reduce air/fuel flow restrictions. The amount of bend in a port, the size of the port, and the diameter of the valve all affect the amount of air/fuel flow.

Some popular four-stroke cylinder head designs include the following:

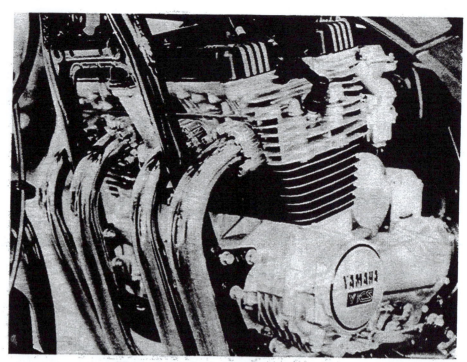

Figure 4-14   In-line four-cylinder engine.

Figure 4-15   Liquid-cooled V-4 engine.

Hemispherical Cylinder Head: This design has many variations. The old-fashioned design offered fairly good port flow, but it did not produce sufficient turbulence for today's fuels (Fig. 4-17). The old design also created a longer distance for flame travel which increased the possibility of detonation.

Side Squish Combustion Chamber: This is a two-valve hemispherical design utilizing a large squish area opposite the spark plug. This creates good turbulence and forces the air/fuel mixture toward the spark plug. This design uses a flat-top piston to reduce gas and flame travel interference (Fig. 4-18).

Shallow Hemispherical Chambers: This design normally utilizes a flat-top or low-dome piston. Two intake valves and two exhaust valves are arranged to reduce the height of the combustion chamber. A squish area is built in around the outside edges of the combustion chamber. This promotes turbulence and forces the air/fuel mixture toward the center where the spark plug is located (Fig. 4-19).

Semispherical Combustion Chamber: This design utilizes two exhaust valves and three intake valves. The third intake valve promotes greater flow by increasing the overall valve area. The spark plug is centrally located, and there is a squish area around the outer edge of the combustion chamber. The cylinder head is contoured to further improve air/fuel direction and turbulence (Fig. 4-20).

Overhead Cam Cylinder Heads: Many cylinder heads today support one or more camshafts. Ball bearings or plain bearings can be used, or the cam can be supported between the cylinder head and the valve cover.

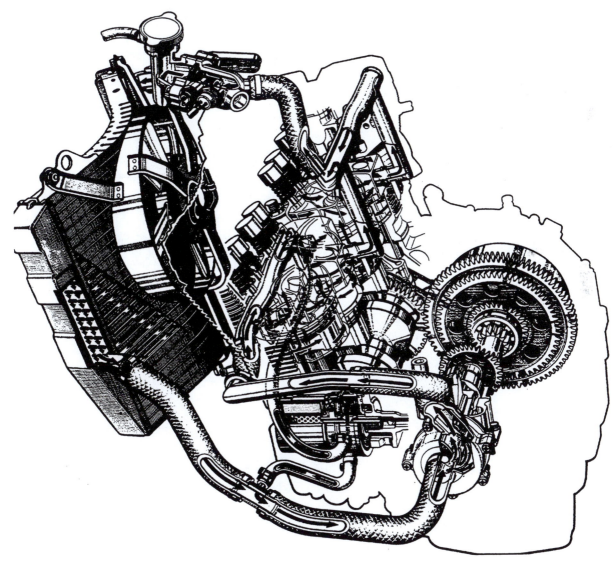

Figure 4-16   Liquid-cooled four-stroke engine (American Suzuki Motor Corporation).

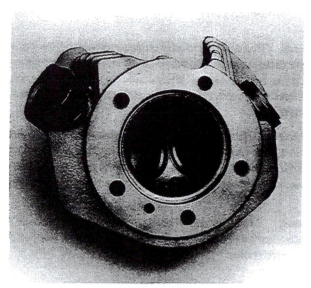

Figure 4-17   Hemispherical cylinder head.

Figure 4-18   Side squish combustion chamber.

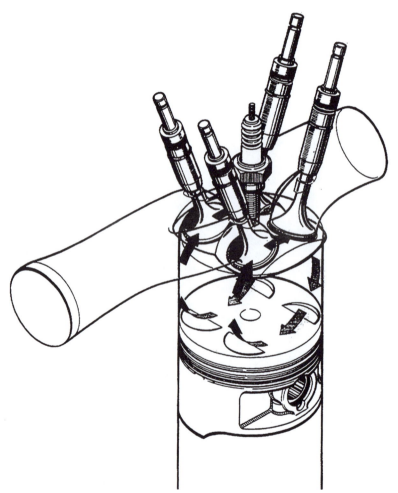

Figure 4-19   Twin-swirl combustion chamber (TSCC) (American Suzuki Motor Corporation).

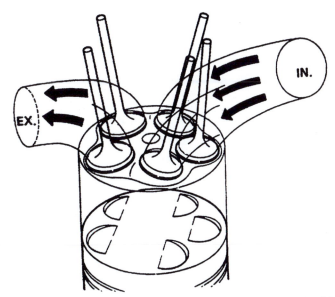

Figure 4-20 Semispherical combustion chamber (Yamaha Motor Corporation, U.S.A.).

General Cylinder Head Service

This section provides guidelines for inspecting, cleaning, rebuilding, and assembling four-stroke engine cylinder heads.

Inspection Areas

Check all gasket and sealing surfaces to be sure that they are flat and smooth. Make sure threaded holes and fasteners are in good condition. Check for damage such as broken cylinder head fins and cracks around the valve guides and spark plug threads. Look for oily ports; this indicates excessive oil consumption. Check for wear or damage at the camshaft bearing support areas.

Cleaning

Because some cylinder heads are painted, clean the head with a degreaser that will not harm the paint and will wash off with water.

Rebuilding

Damaged threaded devices in a cylinder head can be repaired or replaced. Damaged gasket surfaces can be machined. Valve seats can be cut or ground to the manufacturer's specifications. Most valve seats are designed with three angles, usually 60°, 45°, and 30°, so that the valve contact area meets a specified width. The angles may vary slightly between manufacturers, so consult the appropriate service manual before machining.

In some instances and with the proper equipment, worn valve seats can be replaced, structural cracks can be repaired, worn camshaft bearing surfaces can be remachined, and broken fins can be rebuilt.

Cylinder Head Assembly

Always use a torque wrench and follow the manufacturer's recommendations for the amount of fastener torque and correct assembly sequence. Incorrect assembly will result in leakage and component damage.

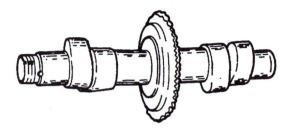

Figure 4-21   Twin-cylinder single-overhead cam (Yamaha Motor Corporation, U.S.A.).

Valve Train

A four-stroke engine valve train includes many of the following components:

> Camshafts, gears, sprockets, and chains
> Tappets and pushrods
> Hydraulic valve lash adjusters
> Rocker arms
> Shims and buckets
> Valves, springs, seals, and guides

Camshaft

The component used to initiate and control the valve action is called a cam (Fig. 4-21). A shaft with at least one lobe is called a camshaft, and it is usually made of cast or billet steel. The lobes are machined to provide the proper timing for opening and closing the valves. The

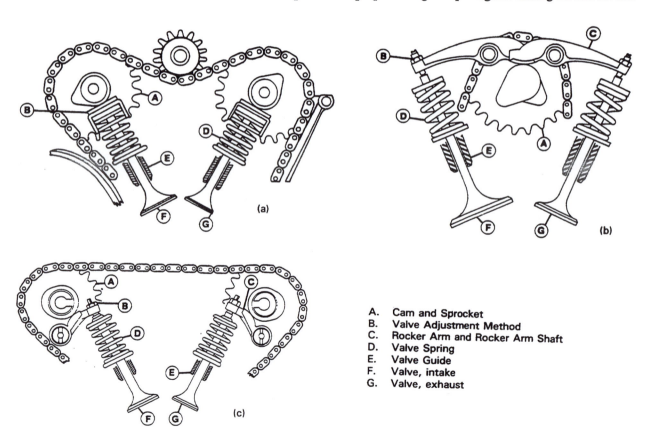

A.   Cam and Sprocket
B.   Valve Adjustment Method
C.   Rocker Arm and Rocker Arm Shaft
D.   Valve Spring
E.   Valve Guide
F.   Valve, intake
G.   Valve, exhaust

Figure 4-22   Three overhead cam-valve designs: (a) double overhead cam shim bucket; (b) single overhead cam rocker arm; and (c) Double overhead cam rocker arm. (American Suzuki Motor Corporation).

camshaft lobes control the valve movement. How far the valve opens is controlled by the height of the cam lobe, or by the height of the cam lobe and the leverage of the rocker arm. The valve lifter or tappet rests on the camshaft lobe and is lifted by the cam lobe to activate the rocker arm assembly to open the valves.

Camshafts that are located over the combustion chamber are known as overhead cams. Engines with double overhead cams use one cam for intake valves and the other for exhaust valves (Fig. 4-22). Cams located in the crankcase use pushrods to activate the rocker arms and valves (Fig. 4-23).

The purpose of the camshaft is to control the opening and closing of the intake and exhaust valves in relation to crankshaft rotation. With the exception of a few engines that use belts, gears, or rotating shafts with bevel gears, most motorcycle engines use a cam chain. The cam chain runs between the crankshaft and the camshaft and turns the cam at one-half crankshaft rotation. Chain slack is controlled by a chain tensioner (Fig. 4-24). The cam chain tensioner is either automatically or manually adjusted to provide the proper amount of tension. The camshaft timing sequence is set by aligning special timing marks on the crankshaft, cam gear, or sprockets. Consult the appropriate service manual for instructions on camshaft timing.

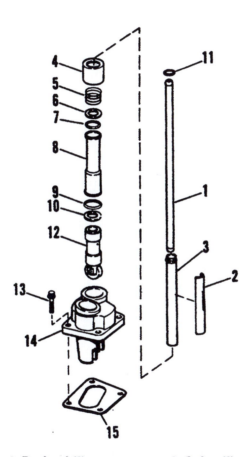

1. Pushrod (2)	**9. O-ring (2)**
2. Spring cap retainer (2)	**10. Spacer (2)**
3. Upper push rod cover (2)	**11. O-ring (2)**
4. Spring Cap (2)	**12. Tappet (2)**
5. Spring (2)	**13. Bolt (4)**
6. Spacer (2)	**14. Tappet guide**
7. O-ring (2)	**15. Gasket**
8. Lower push rod cover (2)	

Figure 4-23   Rocker arm pushrod and cover (Harley-Davidson Motor Company, Inc.).

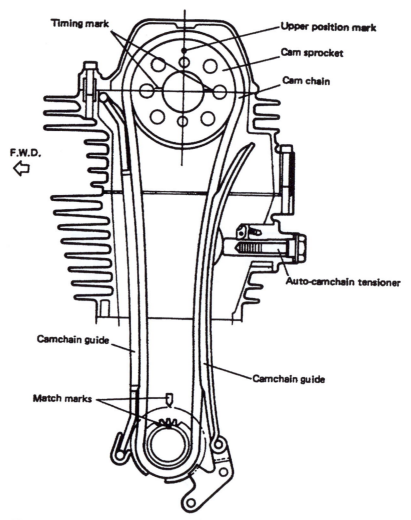

Figure 4-24 Cam chain and tensioner (Yamaha Motor Corporation, U.S.A.).

Valve lift is determined by the camshaft design, or by the camshaft design and rocker arm leverage or ratio. The amount of valve lift can be computed by multiplying the amount of cam lift by the rocker arm ratio. For example, a Harley-Davidson Evolution Big Twin engine which has a rocker arm ratio of approximately 1.63 and a cam lift of 0.290 inches produces a valve lift of 0.4727 inches:

$$\text{cam lift} \times \text{rocker arm ratio} = \text{valve lift}$$
$$0.290 \text{ inch} \times 1.63 = 0.4727 \text{ inch}$$

Duration is the amount of time a valve is open in relation to crankshaft rotation. This is measured at an equal amount of lift when the valve is just beginning to open or close. The point of measurement varies between manufacturers.

The intake valve typically starts to open just before the piston reaches top dead center (Fig. 4-25), and the exhaust valve is still open. Exhaust gases leaving from the previous power cycle help pull the fresh intake mixture into the cylinder. The intake valve remains open while the piston travels from top dead center to bottom dead center and stays open just after the piston reaches bottom dead center. This allows the momentum of the moving fresh air/fuel mixture to fill the cylinder for better volumetric efficiency.

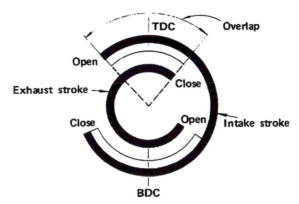

Figure 4-25   Valve timing (Yamaha Motor Corporation, U.S.A.).

Both intake and exhaust valves are closed as the piston moves through the compression stroke and part of the power stroke. About two-thirds through the power stroke, the exhaust valve opens to relieve the cylinder of the spent gases. The exhaust valve remains open while the piston travels from bottom dead center to top dead center and closes just after the piston reaches top dead center. The exiting exhaust gases help draw in the fresh air/fuel mixture.

Valve overlap occurs between the exhaust and intake strokes when both valves are open. The cam design, amount of cam lift, and timing duration primarily determine the characteristics of a four-stroke engine. Conservative timing specifications in which the intake and exhaust valves are barely open at top dead center tend to create peak power and torque at lower rpm ratings. To create peak power and torque at higher rpm ranges, the valve overlap is increased to 30° or more. This timing specification is commonly seen in high-performance four-stroke engines. The intake and exhaust valves open sooner and stay open longer. This helps pack more fresh air/fuel mixture into the cylinder for a stronger power stroke. However, there is a drawback to this design. When valve overlap becomes excessive, engine efficiency in the lower rpm ranges suffers. The engine must rotate fast enough so that there is no loss of compression or air/fuel mixture through the valves, which are open for a longer period of time. When the engine rotates fast enough to trap the mixture inside, there is a noticeable power increase. Many refer to this as "being on the cam" or achieving peak power.

Tappets and Pushrods

Tappets are used in pushrod-style engines. Tappet design can be as simple as a hardened steel cylinder or block. Current Harley-Davidson engines use roller tappets and hollow pushrods which connect the tappet to the rocker arms. Some tappets or pushrods are adjustable to compensate for valve train wear. This is called *adjusting valve lash*. Valve lash is the total amount of clearance in all valve train components for one valve (Fig. 4-26).

Automatic Hydraulic Valve Lash Adjusters

Automatic hydraulic valve lash adjusters are used on some models and are usually located either in the tappet body or rocker arm area (Figs. 4-27 and 4-28). They are designed to create zero valve lash at all operating temperatures. When the engine warms up, all components expand from the temperature increase, and the valve lash changes. Automatic hydraulic valve lash adjusters require no maintenance.

Most automatic hydraulic valve lash adjusters operate on the same principle. The adjuster has an internal plunger and check valve, which is fed oil while the engine is running. The check valve controls the flow of oil into the adjuster. Oil enters, completely fills the adjuster body, and takes up all valve lash. As the valve is lifted and valve spring pressure is applied to the plunger, the check valve closes. Because oil does not compress, the valve receives full lift from the cam. The hydraulic unit is designed so that it cannot override the valve spring pressure. This ensures that the valve fully closes to seal the combustion chamber and transfer heat from the valve to the cylinder head where it can be dissipated.

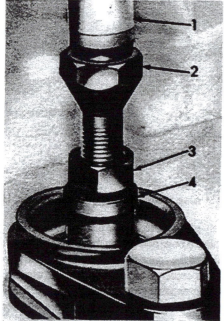

1. Push rod
2. Tappet adjusting screw
3. Tappet adjusting screw locknut
4. Tappet body

Figure 4-26 Adjusting tappets
(Harley-Davidson Motor Company,
Inc.).

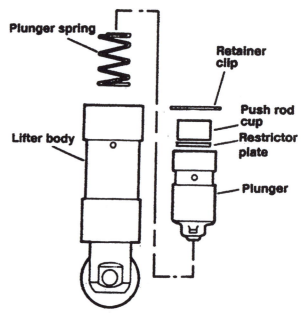

Figure 4-27 Tappet assembly (Harley-Davidson
Motor Company, Inc.).

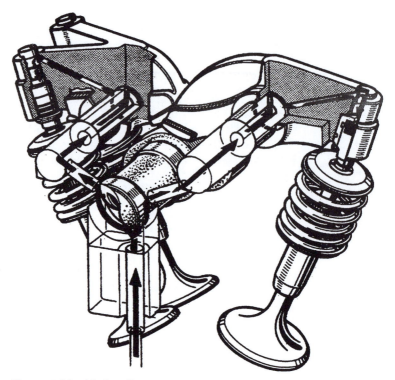

Figure 4-28 Hydraulic valve lash adjuster in the rocker arm area
(American Suzuki Motor Corporation).

Figure 4-29   Rocker arms (American Suzuki Motor Corporation).

Rocker Arms

Rocker arms are made of cast steel, forged steel, or aluminum and are located above the cylinder head. They may be activated by pushrods, or they may be in direct contact with the cam lobe. On some models, the rocker arms have a screw and nut to adjust valve lash. On other models, the rocker arms are not adjustable, and the valve lash is controlled by removable shims of various thicknesses (Fig. 4-29).

Some motorcycles use an eccentric shaft to adjust valve lash or to adjust the position of the rocker arm in relation to the valve. The bearing surface of the rocker arm shaft is machined so that it is off center. When a lock nut is loosened, the shaft can be rotated. Rotating the shaft causes the rocker arm to move closer to or farther from the valve, and this changes the valve lash adjustment.

Shims and Buckets

Many current engine designs use disk-shaped shims of various thicknesses to adjust valve lash. The shims can be located on top of the shim bucket, between the bucket and valve tip, or on top of the valve spring retainer (Fig. 4-30). Special tools are used to replace shims. The cam must be removed to replace the shims on some models.

Valves

Four-stroke engines use poppet valves for intake and exhaust. Poppet valves are typically made of a steel or stainless steel alloy that contains chromium and nickel. Poppet valves may be one piece or may be constructed of two pieces that are welded together (Fig. 4-31).

Both intake and exhaust valves operate in extreme temperatures, but the exhaust valve is the hottest component in the engine and often exceeds temperatures of 1500°F. Valves must withstand drastic temperature variations, severe impact, the effects of friction, and wear well. To meet these demands, many exhaust valve heads are composed of austenitic steel, and the stems welded to the head are made of steel alloy. Austenitic steel becomes harder and more brittle as the engine operating temperature rises. This helps the head to withstand impact and temperature variations, and reduces stem wear as it moves in

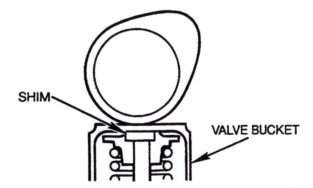

Figure 4-30   Shim under bucket (American Honda Motor Company).

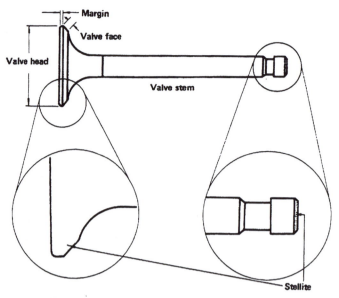

Figure 4-31   Four-stroke valve (Yamaha Motor Corporation, U.S.A.).

the valve guide. Stellite in various thicknesses may be welded to the valve stem tip and face to aid in impact and abrasion resistance. Valves with a thin coating of stellite cannot be resurfaced. Consult the appropriate service manual for the proper valve machining procedure.

Valve Springs

A valve spring is used to close the valve after it is opened by the cam action. The closed valve seals the combustion chamber. The valve spring must be strong enough to control the valve train and follow the cam profile. If the spring pressure is insufficient, the valve "floats." Valve floating occurs when the valve does not fully close, or the valve train improperly follows the cam profile.

Most four-stroke valve springs are made of coil-wound steel alloy wires. A spring set usually consists of one inner and one outer spring. A valve spring collar is positioned between the springs and the cylinder head. The valve spring collar, also known as the spring seat, keeps the springs from wearing into the soft aluminum head and locates the inner and outer springs. A valve spring retainer is located on the other end of the springs and held in position by valve retainers or cotters (Fig. 4-32).

The desmodromic system uses a special clothespin-type spring to assist closing the valves at idle speeds. Each valve is equipped with two rocker arms. One rocker arm opens the valve; the other closes it. Each rocker arm is activated by two cam lobes. One cam lobe contacts the rocker arm to open the valve; the other cam lobe closes it. Shims in various thicknesses are used to adjust the valves. This system reduces spring tension and has the ability to accurately follow radical cam lobes (Fig. 4-33).

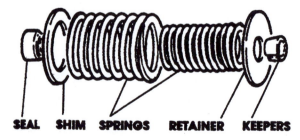

SEAL   SHIM   SPRINGS   RETAINER   KEEPERS

Figure 4-32   A valve spring set (Yamaha Motor Corporation, U.S.A.).

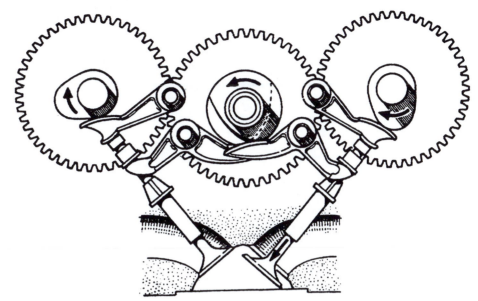

Figure 4-33   Desmodromic valve operation (Motorcycle Basics Manual, Haynes Publishing Group).

Valve Guides and Seals

The purpose of the valve guide is to ensure precise valve movement so that a good seal is maintained between the valve and valve seat. Current production motorcycle engines also use valve guide seals to prevent excess oil from leaking through the valve stem and guide. Too much oil entering the combustion chamber causes excessive carbon deposits and hydrocarbon emissions as well as rapid oil consumption.

Because the cylinder head is made of relatively soft metals, a valve guide is pressed into the cylinder head and then sized to provide the proper clearance between the valve stem and valve guide. Valve guides are made of cast iron, steel, or silicone bronze.

General Valve Train Service

This section provides guidelines for inspecting, servicing, and assembling the valve train components.

Inspection and Service

Consult the appropriate service manual when inspecting and measuring camshafts, gears, sprockets, chains, and tensioners for wear or damage. High-wear areas include the cam lobes and journals, cam chains, and tensioner blades. Most of these components cannot be rebuilt and must be replaced.

Inspect and measure tappets and rollers for wear and damage. Most cannot be rebuilt, but some early Harley-Davidson roller tappets can be rebuilt with a tappet roller kit. Inspect pushrods for wear at the ends or excessive bend. Hydraulic valve lash adjusters cannot be rebuilt and must be replaced if damaged or worn. Replace rocker arms if the contact surfaces are pitted or grooved; rocker arms should not be rebuilt. Shims are slow to wear but should be replaced if necessary.

Inspect the valves and measure the wear at the stem, stem tip, keeper groove, and margin. Valves that are bent, warped, or accidentally dropped must be replaced. To determine if a valve is bent, insert the valve into the valve guide so that it contacts the valve seat. Rotate the valve while holding it against the seat and look through the port. If light shines through the valve and seat surface and appears to rotate with the valve, the valve is bent and should be replaced.

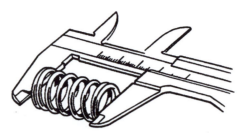

Figure 4-34   Measuring valve spring free length (American Honda Motor Company).

Some manufacturers allow valve refacing. Consult the service manual for the minimum margin width specification. This width specification must be maintained or the valve margin will become too thin and intense heat will cause it to warp or burn.

Measure valve guides for excessive wear. Worn-out valve guides can be replaced and resized with a reamer or hone to create the correct stem to guide clearance. Guides are available in oversizes to provide the correct interference fit when installed into the cylinder head. Guide oversize is determined by the guide's outside diameter. Most standard and oversized guides have the same inside diameter.

Measure the valve springs to ensure they meet the manufacturer's specified free length and tension and that they are within the maximum bend specification (Fig. 4-34). Valve seals cannot be reused and should be replaced with the appropriate installation tool.

Valve Train Assembly

Camshaft lobes and journals should be prelubed with a molybdenum-based commercial lubricant, which is available at most high-performance shops. Valves, seals, valve guide bores, tappets, rocker arms, pushrod ends, shims, and buckets should be prelubed with the appropriate motor oil.

Pistons

Pistons fit snugly in a round cylinder and transfer combustion power directly to the connecting rod and indirectly to the crankshaft. Pistons are made of lightweight aluminum alloy and can be cast or forged. Cast pistons are manufactured by pouring molten metal into a mold. Forged pistons are manufactured by using high pressure to ram metal into a die. Because forging produces a more condensed mass, forged pistons are typically heavier and stronger than cast pistons. Most modern pistons contain large amounts of silicon to increase wear resistance and to help control expansion when the piston is heated.

Piston designs are varied, but all strive to create a shape that expands at operating temperature to closely fit the cylinder and minimize piston slap. Piston slap reduces piston ring sealing and increases noise. The pistons commonly used in Japanese models are tapered from top to bottom. The pistons used in Harley-Davidson and some European models are barrel faced. The diameter of most four-stroke pistons is oval. The piston crown can be flat, domed, or specially shaped to create optimum compression. Most piston crowns have valve reliefs machined or cast in to provide adequate clearance for the valves as they open (Fig. 4-35). Slipper pistons have flat sides which make them lighter and reduce friction (Fig. 4-36).

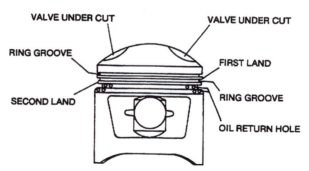

Figure 4-35   Four-stroke piston (Yamaha Motor Corporation, U.S.A.).

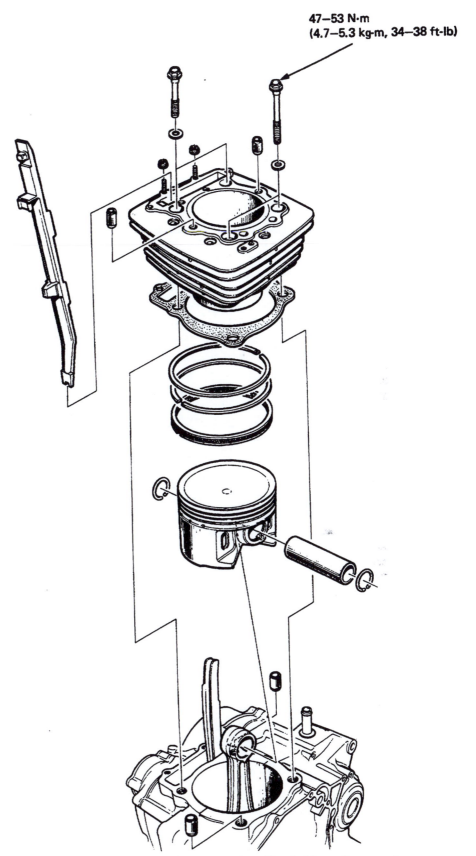

47—53 N·m
(4.7—5.3 kg-m, 34—38 ft-lb)

Figure 4-36 Slipper piston (American Honda Motor Company).

Piston coatings, which are becoming more popular, help reduce friction and heat and extend the life of the piston. Special coatings, usually containing some form of molybdenum, are applied to the piston skirt to reduce friction. Ceramic coatings are applied to the piston crown to insulate the piston from the heat of combustion.

Piston wrist pin bores are centered or offset. Offset wrist pin bores are designed to reduce noise caused by piston rocking at the point of combustion or top dead center of the power stroke. Piston wrist pins are made of steel and positioned with a floating fit in the connecting rod, piston, or both. Usually, special retainers or Teflon buttons secure the pin in the piston. Special tools are normally required for correct piston pin removal and installation.

Piston ring lands are the area that supports the piston rings. The lands normally have a smaller diameter than the bottom of the piston to reduce cylinder contact and noise when the piston rocks.

Piston ring grooves are designed so that the piston rings have minimum side clearance. This provides support and improves ring sealing. The piston rings are pushed out against the cylinder by their ring tension and by the pressure of expanding gases from combustion to seal the cylinder. When the piston changes direction at the top and bottom of the stroke, the rings move in their groove from one land surface to the other. Oil holes or slots in the bottom groove provide a path that allows excess cylinder wall oil to return to the crankcase.

Piston rings perform two important functions. Piston rings seal the cylinder to trap the power of combustion and prevent the oil used to lubricate the piston skirt from entering the combustion chamber. Excessive oil in the combustion chamber reduces the power of combustion, promotes detonation, and creates carbon deposits. Excessive carbon deposits restrict the smooth flow of gases, create hot spots which promote preignition and detonation, and accelerate the wear of all internal engine components.

Four-stroke engines use three types of piston rings: compression, scraper, and oil control rings (Fig. 4-37). The upper rings, or compression rings, seal the combustion chamber. The middle ring acts as a scraper to remove any oil that leaked past the bottom ring. The bottom ring, or oil control ring, prevents oil from entering the combustion chamber.

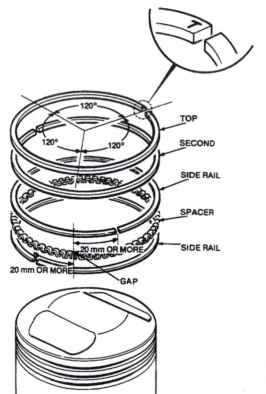

Figure 4-37 Four-stroke piston rings, staggered ring gaps, and positions (American Honda Motor Company).

Manufacturers select the material for ring construction based on the cylinder wall material and finish. Cast iron and plated rings are normally used with cast iron and steel cylinders. Soft cast iron rings are normally used with plated cylinders. Compression and scraper rings are usually made of cast iron or steel and may be chrome plated or coated with a molybdenum material. Because the surface finishes vary depending on the cylinder material and manufacturer's demands, the piston rings are carefully tested and selected to achieve the best results. When replacing pistons and rings, it is best to use the manufacturer's original parts.

Because weight is a major consideration in ring design, most manufacturers use thin rings. A thick ring weighs more and has more inertia to overcome than a lighter ring. Compression ring faces may be plain, barrel faced, or tapered. Usually, the scaper ring is a reverse-twist taper-faced ring that twists in the ring groove to scrape excess oil from the cylinder wall. A commonly used oil control ring set is the steel side sealing oil control type. This type is usually made as a three-piece set. Two narrow chrome-plated steel rings or rails are pushed against the cylinder wall by a ring expander or spacer. The oil is then pushed downward or exits through the holes or slots in the ring groove.

General Piston Service

This section provides guidelines for inspecting and servicing pistons and piston components. Some assembly tips are also included.

A piston should not be reused if the ring grooves or wrist pin retainer grooves have been damaged, or the piston has been dropped, fractured, or dented. Piston rings are normally replaced whenever the top end is serviced unless the engine has very low mileage and wear.

Cleaning

Clean the piston with carbon-desolving degreaser that is water soluble. Bead-blast only the dome; do not bead-blast the ring lands or the piston rings will not properly seal. All carbon must be carefully removed from the ring grooves without marring the piston.

Measuring

The size of most pistons can be determined by measuring at the bottom of the piston skirt, 90° from the wrist pin (Fig. 4-38). However, the barrel-faced pistons used in American and some European models cannot be accurately measured. The manufacturers provide a chart to determine excessive clearance and oversize dimensions. Piston-to-cylinder clearance is calculated by accurately measuring the cylinder and subtracting the piston's largest diameter.

Installation Tips

Before installing the piston, apply 20 weight motor oil to the piston skirt with a paper towel. Be careful not to overlubricate the piston prior to installation as this will cause the cylinder to glaze and prevent proper ring sealing.

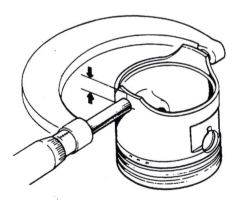

Figure 4-38 Measuring piston diameter at the skirt (American Honda Motor Company).

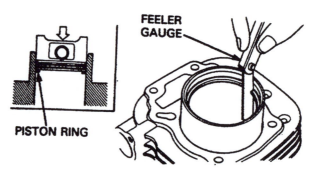

Figure 4-39   Measuring ring end gap (American Honda Motor Company).

Consult the appropriate service manual, and locate the directional markings to determine the correct direction for piston installation. These directional markings are normally found on the piston crown. Install piston pin retainers with the appropriate special tool. Set the end gap so that it is aligned with the connecting rod and positioned away from any piston notches. Some retainers require specific installation instructions regarding inside and outside surfaces. Always follow the instructions in the appropriate service manual.

Before installing rings on a piston, install the ring squarely in the cylinder, and measure the end gap with a feeler gauge (Fig. 4-39). Compare the measurement to the service manual specification. If the rings are made of cast iron and the surfaces are not plated, the ends of the rings may be filed to provide the correct minimum clearance.

Identify the compression, scraper, and oil control rings. To determine correct ring direction, locate the letters or numbers on the top two rings. These letters or numbers always face the piston crown when the rings are correctly installed.

Consult the service manual to determine the proper ring end gap placement (Fig. 4-40). Normally, you should alternate the ring end gaps. For example, position the end gap of the top ring to the left and the end gap of the middle ring to the right. Do not align any two ring end gaps with each other. Position ring end gaps in the piston pin end areas, not on the thrust surface. Ring installation is easier when a piston ring installation tool is used.

After installing the rings, verify that the correct side clearance exists by inserting a feeler gauge between the ring and the ring land. Check all the way around (Fig. 4-41).

Cylinders

Four-stroke cylinders come in many designs and materials. The most common cylinders are made of aluminum, and the cylinder liner is made of cast iron or steel that is cast or pressed in. A cast-in liner is preferred because it provides better heat transfer and is less likely to become loose in the cylinder casting.

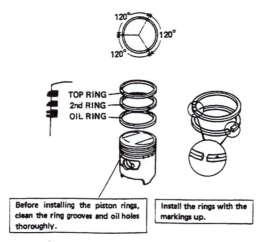

Figure 4-40   Positioning ring end gap (American Honda Motor Company).

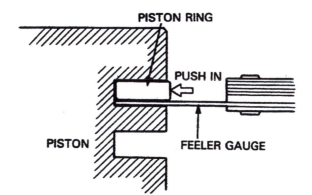

Figure 4-41 Verifying ring side clearance (American Honda Motor Company).

Cylinders may be air cooled with large fins, liquid cooled by oil spray, or water cooled by a glycol-based coolant. The coolant flows through a cooling jacket that surrounds the cylinder. Air-cooled engines generally run at lower compression ratios to reduce heat. They may also have greater piston-to-cylinder clearance because the heat and expansion cannot be accurately controlled. Liquid-cooled engines are more effectively cooled, so these engines can run at higher compression ratios.

In some four-stroke engines, the cylinder is built into the crankcase to reduce the number of required parts and to reduce coolant leakage. In this design, the crankcase and cylinder are composed of aluminum, and the cylinder liner or sleeve is pressed or cast in.

Cylinder coatings are becoming more commonly used to reduce cost, weight, and friction. A popular coating contains nickel and silicon carbide known as Nikasil. The aluminum cylinder is first plated with nickel, and then silicon carbide is applied. The coating process creates an excellent bond to the cylinder, transfers heat well, and provides a surface that resists corrosion, friction, and piston seizure.

Cylinder finishes and their corresponding piston ring materials are designed to create a good piston ring seal while providing sufficient oil for lubrication. Cast iron and steel cylinders are normally honed with abrasive stones to create a 45° to 60° crosshatch (Fig. 4-42). The crosshatch grooves hold small amounts of oil for ring lubrication.

General Cylinder Service

This section provides guidelines for removing, inspecting and measuring, and installing cylinders.

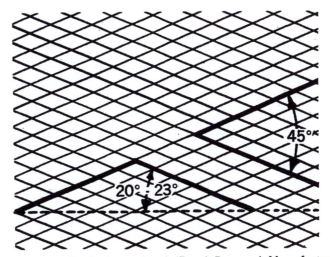

Figure 4-42 Typical crosshatch (Brush Research Manufacturing Company, Inc.).

Cylinder Removal

Before removing a cylinder from the piston, always place a rag under the cylinder to protect the lower end of the engine from contamination by broken rings or wrist pin clips that may be trapped between the piston and cylinder.

Inspecting and Measuring

Inspect the cylinder gasket surfaces for flatness and scarring. If the surfaces exceed the manufacturer's specifications, the cylinder may leak fluids or distort when assembled, causing improper piston-to-cylinder clearances (Fig. 4-43).

Measure the cylinder in at least six locations to determine whether the cylinder exceeds the manufacturer's wear or distortion specification. To determine the piston-to-cylinder clearance, measure the diameter of the piston and subtract this measurement from the smallest and largest measurements of the cylinder's diameter. Some manufacturers state that the cylinder should be mounted in cylinder torque plates before measuring or resizing. Because torque plates stress and shape the cylinder like running conditions, they provide the most accurate method of measuring and resizing (Fig. 4-44).

Excessively worn, distorted, or damaged cylinders that are not plated can usually be resized by boring and honing. Oversized pistons are available for most models to fit oversized cylinders to new vehicle specifications. Piston oversizes are usually stamped on the piston crown in English or metric measurements.

Plated cylinders, like those with Nikasil coatings, cannot be machined and should never be honed or refinished. Excessively worn or damaged plated cylinders should be replaced. Some manufacturers supply oversized pistons that can be installed in a moderately worn plated cylinder to restore the piston-to-cylinder clearance to specification.

Cylinder Installation

Before installing a cylinder, wash it in warm soapy water and use a cylinder brush to remove dirt and honing abrasive. When the cylinder is clean, rinse and dry it. Then clean and

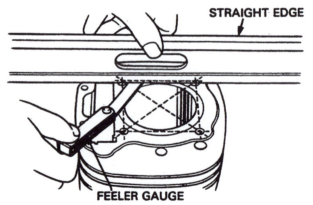

Figure 4-43   Checking gasket surface (American Honda Motor Company).

Figure 4-44   Torque plates (Harley-Davidson Motor Company, Inc.).

prelube the cylinder bore with paper towels and 20 weight motor oil. You will know the cylinder is clean when you can wipe the bore with a clean paper towel and it is not soiled.

When installing the cylinder onto the piston, use piston ring compressors to press the rings into the piston grooves. This prevents the rings from bending or breaking while installing the cylinder (Fig. 4-45).

Crankshaft Assemblies

The crankshaft changes the up-and-down motion of the piston into rotating motion which turns the gears or sprockets to produce vehicle movement. The piston is connected to the crankshaft by the wrist pin and connecting rod (Fig. 4-46). The distance from the crankpin center to the crankshaft center is called the *throw*. Twice the length of the throw is known as the *stroke*.

Crankshaft Designs

There are two basic crankshaft designs: a one-piece unit and a multipiece unit. One-piece crankshafts are forged or cast and then machined or ground to close tolerances. One-piece crankshafts use two-piece connecting rods that require plain bearings and a high-pressure lubrication system. Oil holes drilled into the crankshaft supply lubrication to the bearings and pistons (Fig. 4-47). Forged one-piece crankshafts are very strong and usually cannot be serviced. Bearings can be replaced to restore the proper fit and exact clearance. A fit that is too tight causes excess friction and heat; a fit that is too loose causes oil pressure loss and engine noise.

Multipiece crankshafts are pressed or bolted together and use a one-piece connecting rod. Low oil pressure is required, and splash lubrication may be used on the connecting rod and crankshaft bearings. Most multipiece crankshafts may be disassembled to renew the bearings, rods, and pins. A hydraulic press and special tools are required for this operation.

Connecting Rods

A connecting rod connects the piston to the crankshaft. The small end or top of the connecting rod may have a wrist pin bearing or bushing that supports the wrist pin in the piston. The big end or bottom of the connecting rod contains either plain or roller bearings. This end of the rod connects the rod to the crankshaft's crankpin. The center part of the connecting rod is called the *beam*, and it is usually in the shape of an I-beam. The connecting rod has oil holes or slots to provide lubrication. The rod may be made of cast or forged steel or heat-treated aluminum.

Connecting rods may be one- or two-piece. The one-piece rod is used with multipiece pressed or bolted crankshafts and uses a roller or caged bearing. This type of rod

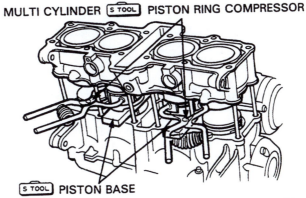

MULTI CYLINDER [S TOOL] PISTON RING COMPRESSOR

[S TOOL] PISTON BASE

Figure 4-45 Using ring compressors to install cylinders (American Honda Motor Company).

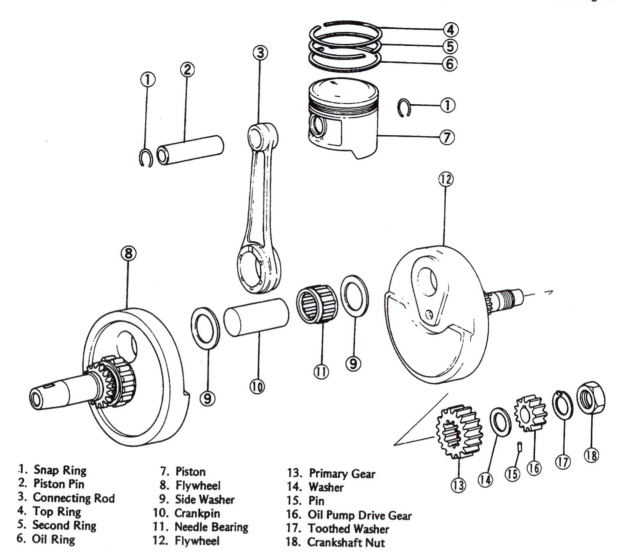

.1. Snap Ring	7. Piston	13. Primary Gear
2. Piston Pin	8. Flywheel	14. Washer
3. Connecting Rod	9. Side Washer	15. Pin
4. Top Ring	10. Crankpin	16. Oil Pump Drive Gear
5. Second Ring	11. Needle Bearing	17. Toothed Washer
6. Oil Ring	12. Flywheel	18. Crankshaft Nut

Figure 4-46   Single crankshaft and piston (Kawasaki Motors Corporation, U.S.A.).

bearing requires very little lubrication. The two-piece connecting rod is used only in four-stroke engines that have a one-piece crankshaft. The two-piece connecting rod requires a high-pressure oil system to lubricate the plain bearing on the big end (Fig. 4-48). A rod cap with marks for alignment is bolted to the rod.

Connecting rods are designed to withstand the high stresses of engine operation such as the piston's direction reversal at the top and bottom of each stroke and the rapid acceleration from the power stroke (Fig. 4-49).

Crankshaft Balancing

An imbalance is created by the power pulses of the power stroke and the weight and momentum of the piston and rod assembly as it reverses direction at the top and bottom of each stroke. This imbalance must be counterbalanced to provide smooth engine operation, preserve the engine bearings, and eliminate excessive vibration. Excessive vibration contributes to vehicle damage and rider discomfort.

Engine manufacturers have found several solutions to counteract imbalance. All crankshafts are counterweighted and balanced to offset the natural imbalance. In multi-

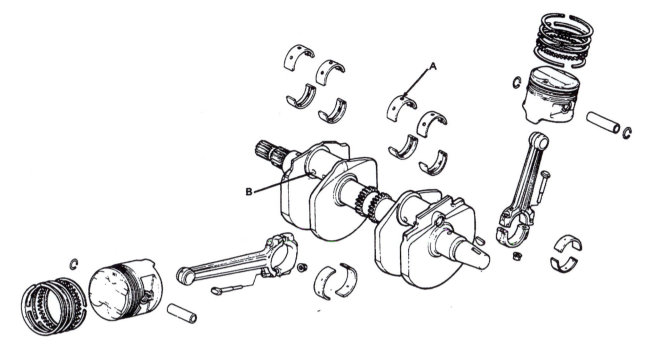

A. Plain Bearing Oil Holes
B. Journal Oil Holes

Figure 4-47 Forged crankshaft with plain bearings showing oil holes (American Honda Motor Company).

cylinder engines, each cylinder is positioned and its firing sequence is arranged so as to off-set the natural imbalance created by another cylinder. Some motorcycles use isolation devices, which are usually made of some rubber derivative, to absorb engine vibration and to prevent it from being transmitted to the chassis. Counterbalance weights, timed with engine rotation, may be mounted to shafts driven by gears or chains and rotated inside the crankcase. Most chain-driven counterbalancer systems include adjustment devices, which can be manually tightened to achieve the correct chain tension (Fig. 4-50). This service is normally performed at major maintenance intervals. Counterbalancers are found on many single-cylinder four-stroke engines as well as on some engines with two or more cylinders.

General Crankshaft Assembly Service

Crankshaft service of any kind is considered major mechanical repair and should be performed only by an experienced technician. Crankshaft balancing is performed in only a few specialty

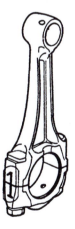

Figure 4-48 Two-piece connecting rod (American Honda Motor Company).

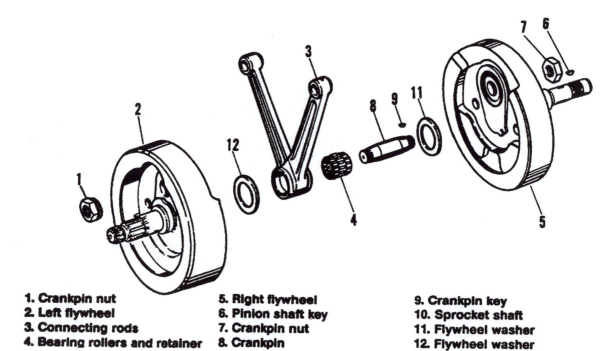

1. Crankpin nut
2. Left flywheel
3. Connecting rods
4. Bearing rollers and retainer

5. Right flywheel
6. Pinion shaft key
7. Crankpin nut
8. Crankpin

9. Crankpin key
10. Sprocket shaft
11. Flywheel washer
12. Flywheel washer

Figure 4-49   Harley-Davidson connecting rod assembly (Harley-Davidson Motor Company, Inc.).

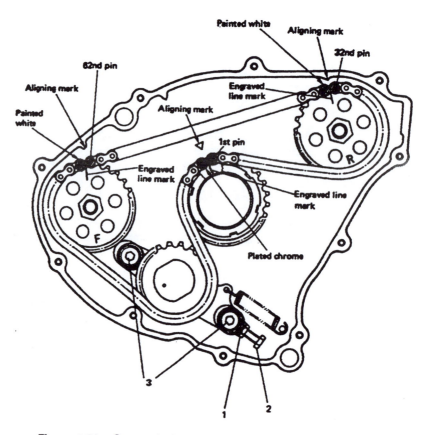

Figure 4-50   Counterbalance weights and adjuster (American Suzuki Motor Corporation). Locknut (1); stopper bolt (2); setting bolts (3).

shops because it requires a great deal of technical knowledge, and the equipment required to perform this service is expensive. This section provides general guidelines for rebuilding crankshafts and servicing connecting rods and counterbalancers.

Crankshaft Service

Usually, severely worn and damaged crankshaft parts are replaced and not rebuilt. Multipiece crankshafts must be retrued to a close tolerance after being reassembled. One-piece crankshafts that use plain bearings must be carefully measured to determine the correct bearing size. The new bearings should be selected according to the manufacturer's bearing selection chart provided in the service manual.

Before installing any crankshaft assembly, the oil passages must be checked to ensure oil can freely flow through them. This is accomplished by forcing engine oil through the oil passages with an oil squirt can.

Connecting Rod Service

Worn or damaged connecting rod bearings, races, and bushings can usually be replaced. The connecting rods used in Harley-Davidson engines can be resized to accept oversized bearings and crankpins.

Two methods are used to identify fractures in a connecting rod. A dye check indicates surface fractures. Magnafluxing exposes internal as well as surface fractures. Magnafluxing is the preferred method, but it requires special equipment that creates a magnetic field at the fracture points. Iron powder is applied, and the powder stands up straight in the fractured areas.

Counterbalancer Service

Counterbalancers with mechanical adjusters can be adjusted to achieve the correct tension. After the adjustment is made, the counterbalancer normally maintains the appropriate tension for a long time. A worn counterbalancer chain with excessive slack can be replaced. Replacing the chain sometimes requires extensive disassembly of the engine crankcase.

Crankcases

Four-stroke engine crankcases support the crankshaft and transmission shafts, seal the crankshaft and transmission areas, and route lubricants and coolants. The crankcase may include the cylinders. Crankcases are usually made of a lightweight aluminum alloy. Locating pins or dowels in the crankcases align the case halves or covers and locate the bearing position. Mounting pads are built into the crankcase to secure it to the chassis.

There are three basic crankcase designs: the one-piece case which has a retainer cover fastened to one side, the vertically split case which is fastened together, and the horizontally split case which is also fastened together (Figs. 4-51 and 4-52).

The mating surfaces of the crankcase halves may be sealed by either a gasket or a flexible oil-resistant sealer. A crankcase should never be assembled without a gasket if one is specified. Omitting a required gasket would alter or eliminate necessary clearances and cause extensive damage.

General Crankcase Service

Crankcase repair requires great technical skill, knowledge, and special tools. Crankcase fractures should be repaired only by a qualified welder who is experienced in motorcycle repair. This section provides general guidelines for crankcase disassembly and bearing and sealer service.

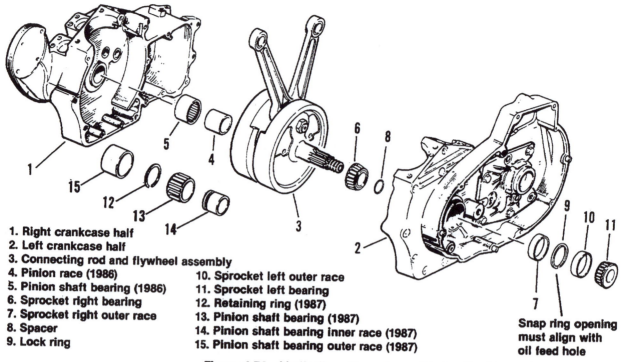

1. Right crankcase half
2. Left crankcase half
3. Connecting rod and flywheel assembly
4. Pinion race (1986)
5. Pinion shaft bearing (1986)
6. Sprocket right bearing
7. Sprocket right outer race
8. Spacer
9. Lock ring

10. Sprocket left outer race
11. Sprocket left bearing
12. Retaining ring (1987)
13. Pinion shaft bearing (1987)
14. Pinion shaft bearing inner race (1987)
15. Pinion shaft bearing outer race (1987)

Snap ring opening
must align with
oil feed hole

Figure 4-51   Vertically split crankcase (Harley-Davidson Motor
Company, Inc.).

Crankcase Disassembly

After all fasteners are removed, the case halves must be gently separated. Special tools may be required to separate the case halves. Never strike a crankshaft or transmission shaft to separate the crankcases.

Special tools are required to reassemble some crankcase halves when components such as bearings have an interference fit on the shaft. During final assembly of the crankcase, the fasteners must be tightened in the proper sequence to the manufacturer's torque specifications (Fig. 4-53).

Bearing Service

Some crankcases are equipped with bearings that can be replaced or rebuilt. Bearings that can be rebuilt must be resized or fitted to the meet the manufacturer's recommendations. These procedures require a great deal of skill and special tools.

Sealer Service

Manufacturers normally specify in service manuals the exact sealer to be used to seal the crankcase halves. Failure to use the specified sealer could result in leaks or severe engine damage.

Bearings and Bushings

The purpose of a bearing is to reduce friction and to allow movement while carrying a load. Bearings are required to handle loads that range from slow engine cranking to maximum engine rpm. Bearings carry radial, axial, and thrust or side loads.

Bearings are the most precisely manufactured of all motorcycle components. They are rated by the amount of clearance between the balls and the races or metal rings on which they rotate. A bearing must always be replaced with one of the same rating. Correct bearing installation is critical.

There are many different bearing types and sizes that are designed for specific uses.

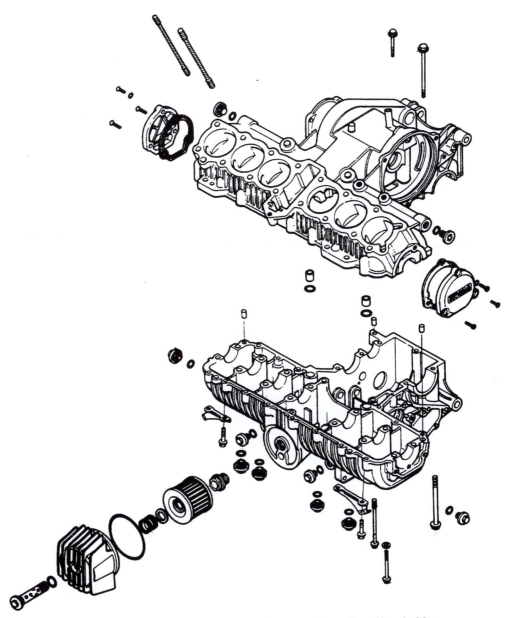

Figure 4-52 Horizontally split crankcase (American Honda Motor Company).

Ball and Roller Bearings: These familiar bearings consist of a multipiece assembled unit that is usually made of a carbon, chromium, nickel, and steel alloy. Bearing components include the inner race, rollers or balls, an outer race, and usually a retaining cage. The inner race connects the rotating shaft to the bearing. The outer race is stationary in the case. The balls or rollers rotate between the races. The retaining cage guides and supports the balls or rollers and keeps them an equal distance apart (Fig. 4-54).

The difference between a ball and a roller bearing is that the ball is spherical and the roller bearing is a cylinder that is normally two to three times as wide as its diameter. Roller bearings generally carry more load than ball bearings because they have a larger load bearing area.

Needle Bearings: A needle bearing is a type of roller bearing. The needle bearing is several times longer than its diameter (Fig. 4-55). It can be found on some connecting rods, transmission

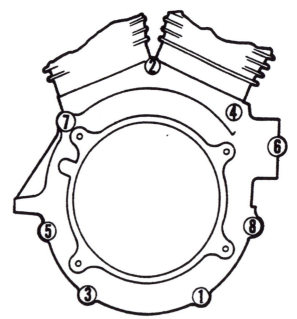

Figure 4-53 Harley-Davidson crankcase torque sequence (Harley-Davidson Motor Company, Inc.).

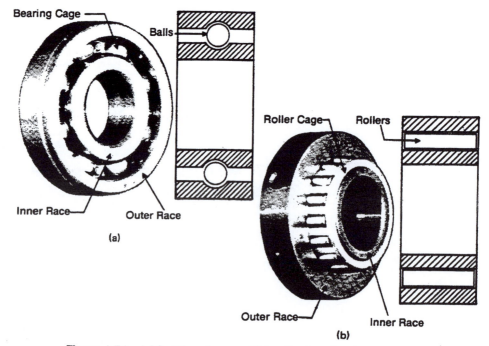

Figure 4-54 (a) Ball bearing; and (b) roller bearing (American Suzuki Motor Corporation).

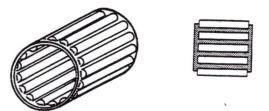

Figure 4-55 Needle bearing (American Suzuki Motor Corporation).

shafts, swing arms, and camshafts. The end of the bearing may be flat or have a point that guides it into the bearing cage. The bearing may be fully open, caged and open, or caged with one end closed.

Needle bearings must be kept exceptionally clean as dirt will prevent bearing rotation and cause the bearing to fail quickly. Needle bearings must be prelubed before installation. Needle bearings that have an interference fit require special installation. They must be pressed in by applying pressure only to the numbered side.

Plain Bearings: The construction of the plain or babbit bearing is quite different from the roller, ball, and needle bearings, but the functions are the same. The plain bearing may be either one- or two-piece. The two-piece bearing is also called a *split sleeve*. A plain bearing is constructed of softer metal material (Fig. 4-56). Alloys of aluminum, zinc, antimony, and lead, called babbit, are used for the bearing surface and mated to a steel back. There is a very close clearance between the soft bearing material and the crankshaft journal. The bearing and journal are cushioned by pressurized oil. Rotating the shaft in the oil causes the shaft to float inside the bearing; this is called the *wedge effect*. Special passageways are designed in the crankshafts, rods, and camshafts to provide a supply of oil to the bearing surfaces. Often the plain bearing will have an oil hole that must be aligned with oil passageways.

Tapered Roller and Thrust Bearings: Tapered roller bearings and thrust bearings are designed specifically to handle thrust loads. Tapered roller bearings are used on chassis wheels, steering heads, and Harley-Davidson crankshafts (Fig. 4-57). Thrust bearings may be found on some transmissions and clutches.

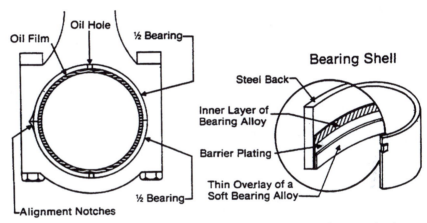

Figure 4-56 Plain bearing (American Suzuki Motor Corporation).

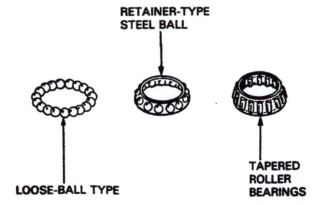

Figure 4-57 Tapered roller bearings (American Honda Motor Company).

It is very important that a tapered roller bearing has the proper fit to prolong the life of the bearing. The fit is usually determined by precision-ground spacers.

General Bearing Service

This section provides information about bearing lubrication and installation guidelines.

Bearing Lubrication

Ball, roller, and needle bearings require some form of lubrication. Bearings that are located in the wheel, steering head, and swing arm are usually packed in a thick grease. Engine bearings receive lubrication from engine oil that is delivered by pumped pressure or by splash. Excess oil on these bearings can restrict movement and cause additional friction and hydroplaning. Hydroplaning occurs when the bearing skids rather than rotates. Lack of sufficient oil to the bearings increases friction and heat and eventually leads to seizure.

The greatest amount of plain bearing wear occurs when the engine starts and stops. When a plain bearing engine is started, the wedge effect is not present, there is no initial oil pressure, and only residual surface lubrication is present. Under these conditions some oxidation may take place on the bearing surface and journal, which in time could cause pitting. It is very important to have a continuous supply of clean oil to ensure efficient plain bearing operation.

Bearing Installation

The installation procedures for ball, roller, and needle bearings vary from engine to engine depending on whether or not the bearing is pressed onto a shaft or into the cases. Many bearings are held in place by special retainers or locating pins. It is important that the bearing is installed straight, and if it is pressed into position, that it be pressed on only in the area of support. If the bearing requires a tight fit on a shaft, you should press against the inner race. If the bearing requires a tight fit in the case, you should press against the outer race.

One-piece plain bearings are pressed into a housing so that the oil holes are aligned with oil passageways. Split sleeve bearings are usually notched to ensure proper positioning and to reduce the chances of spinning. The clearance of the split sleeve bearing can be measured with a plastigauge (Fig. 4-58). The one-piece bearing must be measured with a dial bore gauge. To determine the necessary bearing clearance, subtract the diameter of the shaft from the dial bore gauge measurement, or measure the width with a plastigauge installed between the parts when fully assembled. Then disassemble and measure the width of the compressed plastigauge.

Figure 4-58   Measuring bearing clearance with a plastigauge.

Sealing Devices

A flat or round surface that does not move but contacts a rotating or sliding surface must be sealed to prevent air, oil, or coolant from leaking. Sealing is accomplished using fiber, paper, metal or rubber gaskets, o-rings, or liquid sealers.

Gaskets and O-Rings

Gaskets and o-rings are used to seal cylinder heads, valve covers, cylinders, crankcase covers, and crankcase halves (Fig. 4-59). Although most modern gaskets do not require an additional sealer, you should consult the appropriate service manual for the manufacturer's recommendations.

To successfully replace gaskets, you must ensure that the surfaces to be sealed are flat, smooth, and clean. Follow the manufacturer's specifications for fastener torque and tightening sequence. Be sure to replace old gaskets with new ones. Gaskets are crushed when the mating surfaces are torqued, and they never regain their original shape.

Liquid Sealers

Liquid sealers are specifically designed to seal a wide variety of surfaces such as:

Fiber gaskets to metal

Metal to metal

Metal to rubber

Metal to silicone rubber

Areas exposed to high temperatures

Areas with large gaps between them

Areas exposed to gasoline, oil, or coolant

Surfaces that greatly expand and contract

It is essential to select the appropriate sealer for the surfaces to be sealed. Follow the manufacturer's recommendations. Avoid using a silicone-type sealant that is not designed for use in engines. Some of these silicone sealers break up inside the engine and contaminate the lubrication system. This causes engine seizure.

Rotating Surface Seals

Unless they are enclosed within the cases, the camshaft and crankshaft ends must be sealed. Transmission shafts and other rotating shafts within an engine are also sealed to prevent oil loss and to keep contaminants from entering the engine. Rotating surface seals are usually made of neoprene, and may be supported by an outside metal body. The lip or lips contact the circumference of the shaft. The seal lip may be held with light tension against the shaft by a supporting spring. The seal keeps dirt from entering the engine, prevents oil from leaving the engine, and seals out air. The oil keeps the lip of the seal lubricated so that it does not wear rapidly (Fig. 4-60).

Prior to installation, rotating surface seals must be lubricated. They must be installed straight and to the proper depth to ensure correct contact with the part to be sealed. Universal seal drivers and special tools are used for installation. Whenever possible, seals should be pressed in, not tapped. Using clear tape will prevent the seal lip from being damaged during installation by sharp edges on the shaft. Simply wrap the sharp edges of the shaft with a short length of clear tape to create a smooth edge.

Note the direction in which the old seal was installed, and consult the service manual to determine the correct seal position. The spring side of the seal is usually installed toward the area to be sealed. For example, on most engines, the spring side of the crankshaft seal faces the crankshaft.

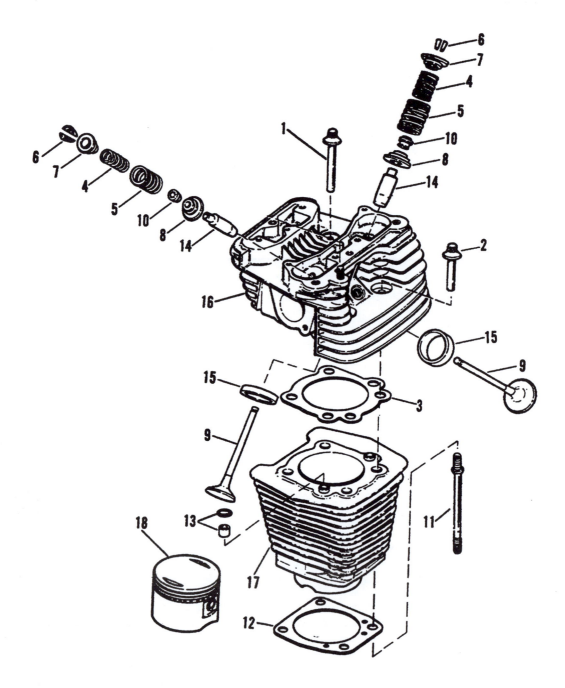

1. Head bolt, long (2)
2. Head bolt, short (2)
3. Cylinder head gasket
4. Inner valve spring (2)
5. Outer valve spring (2)
6. Valve keeper (4)

7. Upper collar (2)
8. Lower collar (2)
9. Valve (1) intake, (1) exhaust
10. Valve stem seal (2)
11. Cylinder stud (4)
12. Cylinder base gasket

13. O-ring and insert (2)
14. Valve guide (2)
15. Valve seat (2)
16. Cylinder head
17. Cylinder
18. Piston

Figure 4-59 Engine gaskets and O-rings (Harley-Davidson Motor Company, Inc.).

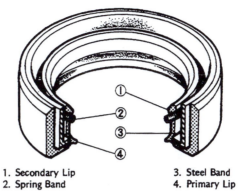

1. Secondary Lip   3. Steel Band
2. Spring Band   4. Primary Lip

Figure 4-60   Seal with spring and lip (Kawasaki Motors Corporation, U.S.A.).

Exhaust Systems

A four-stroke engine exhaust system is designed to meet the following goals:

Direct exhaust gases from the engine's combustion chamber.

Reduce the noise produced by combustion. The amount of acceptable noise is determined by the U.S. Environmental Protection Agency (EPA).

Reduce exhaust emissions. Catalytic converters are used on some models to substantially reduce exhaust emissions through chemical action.

Enhance engine performance.

Complement the motorcycle's styling.

Four-stroke exhaust systems are made of chromed or painted steel, stainless steel, or aluminum. There is one tube for each exhaust port, and the tubes may be single or double walled. Double walls provide better heat insulation, so a double-walled exhaust tube maintains its luster longer. A muffler, collector, or equalizer tube may be attached to each tube or a series of tubes.

The mufflers on production motorcycles are normally constructed entirely of metal and have a series of baffles in different shapes. Baffles reduce the noise created by the engine's power stroke. It is a violation of EPA regulations to alter or remove a motorcycle's stock exhaust system if the motorcycle is to be used on public roads.

Equalizer tubes, which are round or box-shaped, are designed to reduce the positive pressures in the exhaust tubes and maintain a more consistent negative pressure. This helps to remove all exhaust gases from the combustion chamber, especially at lower engine speeds, to reduce exhaust emissions.

The Exhaust Ultimate Power Valve (EXUP) system designed by Yamaha Motor Corporation, U.S.A. is a unique exhaust system design. A microcomputer-controlled exhaust valve located in the exhaust system collector varies the diameter of the exhaust tube according to the engine rpm (Fig. 4-61). At low rpm's, the exhaust valve decreases the diameter of the tube. At high rpm's the diameter is increased. This reduces the positive pressures in the exhaust tubes. The positive pressures inhibit the exhaust gases from exiting the combustion chamber. Reducing the positive pressures also reduces exhaust emissions.

General Exhaust System Service

This section provides guidelines for exhaust system service.

Routine exhaust system inspections should include checking the tightness of the fasteners and the tubes for corrosion, fractures, and exhaust leaks. Corrosion can be reduced by

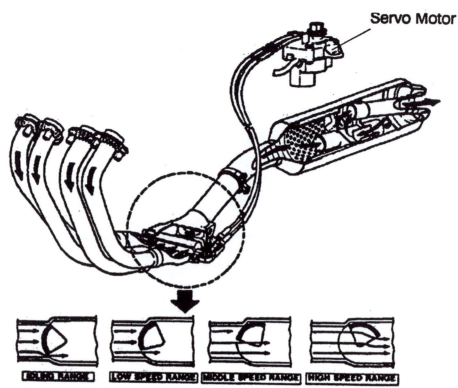

Servo Motor

Figure 4-61 Yamaha EXUP system (Yamaha Motor Corporation, U.S.A.).

regularly operating the vehicle for at least 30 minutes so that moisture from the exhaust system evaporates.

Never run a motorcycle for more than a few minutes without air flowing over the exhaust system. For example, when tuning a motorcycle, be sure the exhaust system is cooled and protected by a strong fan, even if the vehicle is equipped with a liquid cooling system. New exhaust systems can be completely discolored by heat if not sufficiently cooled.

Do not use abrasive liquids to clean the exhaust pipes. Always remove fingerprints, oil, and grease from the pipes before starting the motorcycle. Failure to do so will permanently stain the tubes.

To avoid serious burns, do not touch the exhaust pipes after running a motorcycle.

chapter 5

The Two-Stroke Engine

This chapter describes two-stroke engine components, systems, and engine designs. Two-stroke operation, engine formulas, and some basic service procedures are explained.

TWO-STROKE ENGINE COMPONENTS

A two-stroke engine is a simply constructed engine (Fig. 5-1). The piston, cylinder, and crankcase serve dual roles in developing power. This section explains the purpose and designs of two-stroke engine components. Basic two-stroke engine components include the following:

> Cylinder heads
> Cylinders
> Pistons
> Piston rings
> Wrist pins
> Connecting rods
> Crankshaft
> Cases
> Bearings and bushings
> Seals

Cylinder Heads and Cylinders

Cylinder heads are designed to contain the fuel mixture in a small area which is the combustion chamber. The spark plug is usually mounted in the center of the cylinder head at the top of the combustion chamber. The cylinder head is usually sealed to the cylinder with a gasket. Because a great deal of heat is generated during the combustion process, the cylinder head is also designed to promote heat transfer, which aids in engine cooling. Cylinder heads are either finned for air cooling or surrounded by water jackets for liquid cooling.

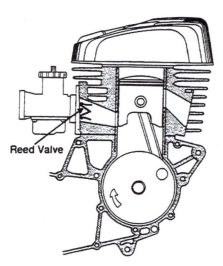

Reed Valve

Figure 5-1 Cutaway view of a two-stroke engine with a reed valve (American Suzuki Motor Corporation).

Most two-stroke engines use a simple cylinder head made of aluminum. Two-stroke heads create either a conical or trench-type combustion chamber to provide a "squish" effect. This design allows the compressed mixture of air, fuel, and oil to be packed tightly around the spark plug (Fig. 5-2).

A basic cylinder consists of a round, tubelike opening called a *bore*. Early cylinders were cast iron and the bore was machined to the correct size. The majority of modern cylinders consist of an aluminum housing with a steel or cast iron liner or sleeve pressed in to form the bore. This makes the cylinder lighter and improves heat transfer. Some other cylinders in use today consist of a bore that is plated or fused to an aluminum casting. This design further reduces weight and friction and improves heat transfer, but it cannot be bored.

The purpose of the cylinder bore is to seal and guide the piston so that it can react to the power of the expanding gases. The piston moves up and down within the cylinder and seals the combustion gases into the upper cylinder area. The piston-to-cylinder fit must be precise.

Cylinders are finned or jacketed for cooling and usually fitted to the engine cases with studs or bolts that are positioned next to the lower cylinder flange. Usually, a gasket seals the cylinder to the cases. When a cylinder is assembled, it must be torqued to the manufacturer's specifications to ensure a good seal.

Two-stroke engine cylinders have a variety of passageways called *ports* cut into the cylinder sleeve that align with ports in the cylinder wall. The ports channel gases into and out of the engine (Fig. 5-3). The ports must have beveled edges to prevent the piston rings from snagging, and they must be accurately aligned in the cylinder to ensure unrestricted movement of gases through the engine (Fig. 5-4).

Intake Port: The intake port is located on the lower half of the cylinder opposite the exhaust port on all but rotary valve and case reed engines. This port allows the air/fuel/oil mixture to travel from the carburetor into the crankcase.

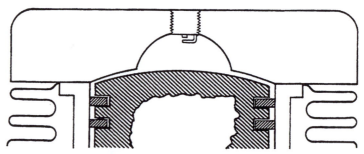

Figure 5-2 Two-stroke cylinder head with piston at top dead center (American Suzuki Motor Corporation).

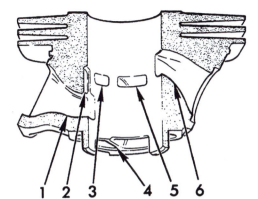

Intake Port [1]
Rear Boost Port [2]
Rear Transfer Port [3]
Transfer Port Divider [4]
Main Transfer Port [5]
Exhaust Port [6]

Figure 5-3   Cylinder Ports (Yamaha Motor Corporation, U.S.A.).

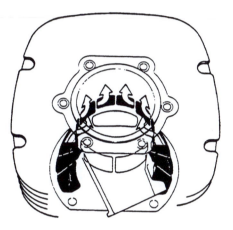

Figure 5-4   Two-stroke engine cylinder ports (American Suzuki Motor Corporation).

Transfer Port: The transfer port inlet is located at the bottom of the cylinder where the cylinder surface matches with the crankcase. The transfer port connects the crankcase compression chamber to the cylinder. The compressed air/fuel/oil mixture in the crankcase is transferred to the cylinder through this port. The transfer port outlet is aligned with the exhaust port and located approximately 90° from the exhaust port.

There are many different transfer port configurations. Some two-stroke engines have only one, but usually there are two to four transfer ports. Most transfer ports are cast into the cylinder barrel.

Exhaust Port: The exhaust port is located on the upper portion of the cylinder opposite the intake port. The spent combustion gases travel through this port to the exhaust system.

Booster Port: On reed valve engines there may be one or more booster ports located at the rear of the cylinder opposite the exhaust port. Booster ports are designed to allow an extra amount of air/fuel/oil mixture to flow from the intake port to the combustion chamber, thus bypassing the crankcase and transfer ports. Some reed valve engines are designed so that when the piston comes down and pressurizes the mixture trapped in the booster ports, the compressed mixture under the piston crown flows out and up through the booster ports.

Pistons

A two-stroke piston performs more functions than a four-stroke piston because the piston also serves as an engine valve. In a two-stroke engine, the piston is used to compress the air/fuel/oil mixture in the combustion chamber, and it is used as a sliding valve to open and close the ports. The crown of a two-stroke piston is domed and controls the exhaust and transfer ports. The skirt of a two-stroke piston is cut away on the nonthrust sides to allow the air/fuel/oil mixture to flow to the transfer ports. The piston skirt can also be used to control intake.

The piston in some two-stroke engines that use reed valves may have a portion of the skirt cut away, or there may be holes in the middle portion of the piston skirt (Figs. 5-5 and 5-6). These holes are located on the intake side of the piston, and they allow the intake port to open to accept an air/fuel/oil charge before the intake skirt of the piston reaches the intake port. This increases the effectiveness of the intake.

In a rotary valve engine, the piston does not have any control of intake, but it does control crankcase pressure (Fig. 5-7). Some pistons also have one or more holes on the middle to upper exhaust side of the piston. These small holes help cool and lubricate a bridge in the exhaust port.

The two-stroke piston must also withstand more heat than a four-stroke piston because it is under power every time it descends, as opposed to a four-stroke piston, which descends under power every other time.

Piston Installation: Piston installation requires determining the proper clearances to allow for the expansion of parts under heat so that they will not contact each other during operation. Two-stroke engine pistons are either cast or forged. Cast pistons usually expand less than forged pistons because of the differences in manufacturing. The piston is measured with a micrometer to determine the proper clearance, and it is measured perpendicular to the wrist pin at the bottom of the skirt. This method of measuring will not be possible on some pistons if the skirt is cut away. Consult the manufacturer's specifications for measuring information.

Piston-to-Cylinder Clearances: The amount of piston-to-cylinder clearance depends on the type of piston that is used. Follow the piston manufacturer's clearance specifications.

Piston-to-Connecting Rod Clearances: The wrist pin should have a light-press fit to the piston. Excessive play will cause the piston or rod to break. The wrist pin end play is also

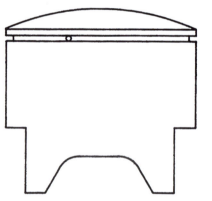

Figure 5-6   A two-stroke engine piston with cutaway below the wrist pin and intake port holes (Yamaha Motor Corporation, U.S.A.).

Figure 5-5   Piston intake skirt cutaway.

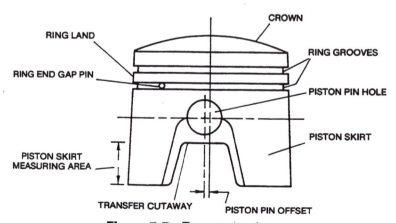

Figure 5-7   Two-stroke piston.

important. A wrist pin must be matched to the piston with the proper fit. Piston pin clips are used to secure the wrist pin in the piston.

Piston Rings

A two-stroke engine uses one or two piston rings to hold the compression pressure in the combustion chamber and to prevent blow-by. Piston rings are usually found in three configurations (Fig. 5-8). The commonly used ring is a standard, rectangular cross section. This type of ring is long-lasting and easily manufactured, but it usually does not seal well in uneven bores. A keystone ring is wedge-shaped to allow burning gases to act on a tapered bearing and to improve the seal. The third type of ring is known as a *dyke* or *L-ring*. The dyke ring is L-shaped and provides an excellent sealing surface. Rings may have surface coatings of chromium or Teflon to improve the service life and to prevent scuffing during break-in.

Weight is a major consideration in ring design. A thick ring weighs more and has more inertia to overcome at the direction change than a lighter ring. A ring is either chrome plated, soft iron, or a combination of both. Select a ring based on the cylinder bore surface; unlike surfaces provide better sealing. Cylinders with alloy chrome, electrofusion plating should use a soft-iron ring. Cylinders with liners that are pressed in can use chrome-plated or iron rings for sealing.

Ring Installation: When rings are installed, they must be checked for the proper fit in the cylinder and the proper groove clearance, and the end gap must be established. Many rings only fit one groove and are not interchangeable with other rings. Rings may have markings to show which side should be up. Two-stroke piston rings are positioned with a locating pin to prevent the ends of the rings from rotating into the port areas.

Wrist Pins

A wrist pin is used to transfer motion from the piston to a single connecting rod. The wrist pin slides through a bearing in the top of the rod to provide a pivot point. This enables the rod to change angles as the crankshaft rotates. The wrist pin is usually held in place by a set of wrist pin clips to prevent the wrist pin from sliding out and causing damage to the cylinder (Fig. 5-9).

Connecting Rods

A connecting rod links the piston to the crankshaft. The small end of the connecting rod contains the wrist pin bearing that connects with the piston. The wrist pin holds the piston to the connecting rod and is held in place by a circlip on each end. The big end of the connecting rod contains caged roller bearings. This end of the rod connects to the crankpin. The center part of the connecting rod is called the *beam,* and it is usually in the shape of an I-beam. Some connecting rods have slots or holes to provide adequate lubrication.

Most two-stroke engines use a one-piece connecting rod. The rod is on a multipiece pressed crankshaft and uses a roller bearing on the big end and a needle bearing on the small end.

Figure 5-8   Ring types (American Suzuki Motor Corporation).

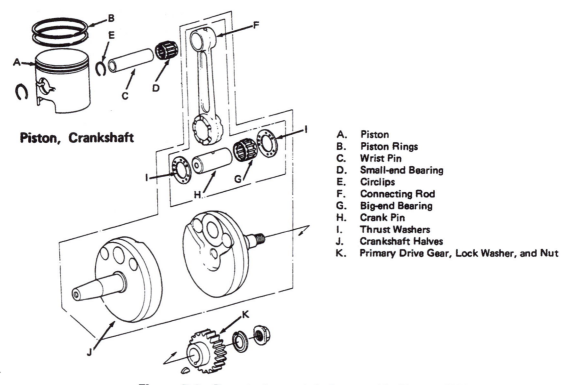

Piston, Crankshaft

A. Piston
B. Piston Rings
C. Wrist Pin
D. Small-end Bearing
E. Circlips
F. Connecting Rod
G. Big-end Bearing
H. Crank Pin
I. Thrust Washers
J. Crankshaft Halves
K. Primary Drive Gear, Lock Washer, and Nut

Figure 5-9 Two-stroke crankshaft assembly (Kawasaki Motors Corporation, U.S.A.).

Connecting rods are designed to withstand the high stresses of engine operation and are composed of forged steel. The connecting rod must also withstand the piston's stop at the top and bottom of each stroke and rapid acceleration from the power stroke under pressure.

Service and Installation: A one-piece connecting rod must be separated from the crankshaft to be serviced. Connecting rods must be checked for wear, lubricated, and installed with the proper clearances.

Crankshafts

The reciprocating motion of the piston is converted to rotating motion by the crankshaft. When the piston is on its upstroke, no power is applied to the crankshaft, but the momentum allows the crankshaft to continue rotating. Once the crankshaft is rotating, its inertia tends to keep it rotating. This rotation enables the piston to continue through its nonpower stroke.

Two-stroke engines use multiple-piece crankshafts. These crankshafts use a one-piece connecting rod, and mist lubrication may be used on either the needle or roller bearings. Some two-stroke crankshafts can be rebuilt. Most of these crankshafts may be pressed apart to renew the bearing(s), rod(s), and crankpin(s). A hydraulic press and some special tools are required for this operation.

Cases

The crankcase is the lower part of the engine where the crankshaft rotates. The engine cases hold the crankshaft and transmission shafts in place and supply the main engine-mounting points. Atmospheric pressure and the partial vacuum created by the piston cause air to flow through the carburetor to pick up a charge of air/fuel/oil and then to flow into the crankcase and later into the cylinder. When the piston has closed off the intake port, the crankcase is sealed. As the piston moves down, the air/fuel/oil mixture trapped below it in the crankcase is pressurized and forced through the transfer ports.

Cases must be strong enough to handle the load and vibrations that the engine design produces. The cases are generally made of a cast aluminum alloy with additional bossing in the areas where extra strength is required. Cases are machined, drilled, and surfaced on assembled areas. Often locating pins are pressed into the cases to help secure the shafts and align the cases.

There are two basic types of cases in use: the two-piece vertically split case and the two-piece horizontally split case. The two-piece vertically split case is commonly used on two-stroke single-cylinder engines. A two-piece horizontally split case is most commonly used for multiple-cylinder two-stroke engines (Fig. 5-10). Usually, cases also have some outer covers that are bolted on to enclose the clutch, ignition, and other components.

Most cases use either a gasket or some form of flexible sealant. Crankcase seals are used to seal the crankcase pressure and vacuum from the primary and ignition side of the engine and from the outside air and oil. Most crank seals are made of neoprene and are designed to

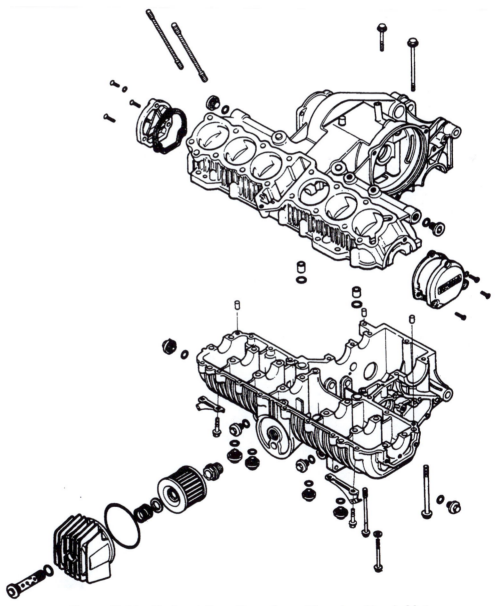

Figure 5-10 Horizontally split crankcase (American Honda Motor Company).

fit tightly on the crankshafts. The ignition side seal may require more frequent replacement because it is not lubricated. A gasket must be used if the case is designed for one. Omitting the gasket eliminates shaft end play and results in binding, clearance problems, or leaks. Consult the service manual for the gasket assembly procedure.

In multiple-cylinder two-stroke engines, each cylinder is enclosed in an individual, sealed compartment. A labyrinth or neoprene seal is used to isolate the cylinder compartments (Fig. 5-11).

Some engine gaskets have been eliminated through better machined mating surfaces and the use of flexible sealants. If the case is manufactured for use with a sealant, do not use a gasket. Be sure to use the sealer that is specified by the manufacturer.

The transmission area of the crankcase is vented to atmospheric pressure to prevent a pressure buildup which could cause gaskets and seals to leak. This vent is controlled on today's street motorcycles to meet Environmental Protection Agency requirements. Further information on venting is presented in Chapter 8.

Case Assembly and Service: Some engines require special tools to pull the cases together. Never use the case securing bolts to pull the case together. After the cases are assembled with the proper gaskets or sealers, the cases must be torqued together. Use a torque wrench and follow the manufacturer's torquing sequence to achieve the best seal and to prevent warping. Actual case maintenance is simple; periodically inspect the case for cracks and leaks. Check the torque of the engine-mounting bolts.

Bearings

The purpose of a bearing is to reduce friction and to allow movement while carrying a load. Generally, bearings are required to handle loads that range from slow engine cranking to maximum engine rpm. Bearings carry radial, axial, and thrust or side loads.

Bearings are the most precisely manufactured of all motorcycle components. They are rated by the amount of clearance between the balls and the races or metal rings on which they rotate. A bearing must always be replaced with one of the same rating, and correct bearing installation is critical.

There are many different bearing types and sizes that are designed for specific uses.

Ball and Roller Bearings: These familiar bearings consist of a multiple-piece assembled unit that is usually made of a carbon, chromium, nickel, and steel alloy. Bearing components include the inner race, rollers or balls, an outer race, and usually a retaining cage. The inner race connects the rotating shaft to the bearing. The outer race is stationary in the case to allow the balls or rollers to be fitted between the races, to supply the basic clearance, and to support the

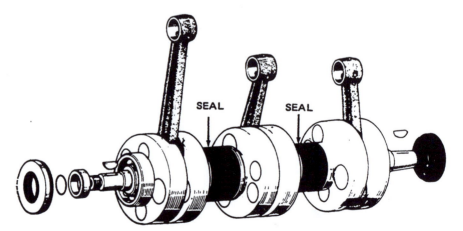

Figure 5-11   Three-cylinder two-stroke crankshaft with two labyrinth seals (Kawasaki Motors Corporation, U.S.A.).

rotating load. The bearing assembly usually includes a retaining cage that guides and supports the balls or rollers and keeps them an equal distance apart.

Needle Bearings: A needle bearing is another type of roller bearing. The needle bearing is several times longer than its diameter (Fig. 5-12). It may be found on some connecting rods, transmission shafts, and swing arms. The needle bearing is compact and distributes a load over a wider area.

Bearing Lubrication: Ball, roller, and needle bearings require some form of lubrication. Two-stroke engine main bearings are lubricated with premixed gas/oil or by injector oil pumps. Two-stroke transmission bearings are lubricated by the splash method.

Excess oil on the bearing restricts movement and causes additional friction and hydroplaning, which is a skidding rather than a rolling motion. Lack of sufficient oil to the bearings increases friction and heat and eventually leads to seizure.

Bearing Installation: The bearing installation procedure varies from engine to engine depending on whether or not the bearing is pressed onto a shaft or into the cases. Many bearings are held in place by retainers or locating pins. It is important that the bearing be in straight, and if it is pressed into position, that it be pressed on only in the area of support.

Types of Engine Sealing

Flat, rotating, and sliding surfaces must be sealed. These surfaces must be clean and flat to facilitate effective sealing. After clean, flat surfaces are joined together, they must be tightened down to the manufacturer's torque specifications.

Flat Surface-to-Surface Seals: A flat surface is sealed with a gasket, O-ring, or semiliquid sealer. Because of the more precise machining on today's motorcycles, there are not as many gaskets in use as there once were. O-rings and liquid sealers have replaced many gaskets. This often makes service easier, reduces cost, and allows a dealer to stock fewer parts. The estimated amount of pressure and heat expansion determines which type of sealing material should be used.

Gaskets are usually used to seal the cylinder head and many side covers. Gaskets are commonly made of a treated fiber material, and some are impregnated with sealant. Head and cylinder base gaskets may be made of a laminated fiber, aluminum, or copper. Most side cover gaskets are subjected to low pressure and are used to seal oil into the cases and to keep air from entering. Because of varying temperatures, gaskets must be able to expand and contract to prevent leaks.

Many of the liquid sealers are more easily removed than gaskets. The majority of today's two-stroke motorcycles use a semiliquid sealer for the case halves.

Rotating Surface Seals: Two-stroke crankshaft ends must be sealed. Transmission shafts and other rotating shafts within a two-stroke engine are sealed to prevent oil from leaving the engine. These seals are usually neoprene and many are supported by an outside metal ring. The lip or lips that contact the circumference of the shaft must be tight. The seal may be held with light tension against the shaft by a supporting spring. The rubber seal must wipe the oil

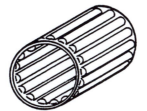

Figure 5-12 Needle bearing (American Suzuki Motor Corporation).

**TWO-STROKE
ENGINE SYSTEMS**

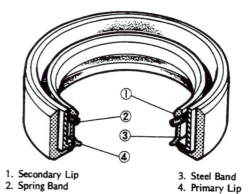

1. Secondary Lip	3. Steel Band
2. Spring Band	4. Primary Lip

Figure 5-13 Seal with spring and lip (Kawasaki Motors Corporation, U.S.A.).

off the shaft, prevent the oil from leaving the engine, and seal out air. The oil keeps the lip of the seal moist enough so that it does not wear rapidly (Fig. 5-13).

Rubber seals must be installed straight and to the proper depth to ensure contact with the part that is sealed. A guide may be used to prevent the lip and spring from rolling out of place during installation.

A two-stroke engine includes intake, exhaust, lubrication, and cooling systems. Intake, lubrication, and cooling system designs vary.

Intake Systems

Most two-stroke engines use one of the following three intake systems.

Piston-Port System: This is the conventional method of controlling the intake port opening. During intake, the piston's movement up the crankcase inlet allows the air/fuel/oil mixture to be inhaled into the crankcase or lower end of the two-stroke engine. This mixture is drawn in by the vacuum that is created underneath the piston as it travels up to the top of the bore. The atmospheric pressure forces a rapidly moving column of air through the carburetor and intake manifold, where it picks up the fuel/oil mixture. This mixture travels through the intake passage and into the crankcase. The opening and closing of the intake port is controlled by the lower edge of the piston skirt. Again, the port opens as the piston travels upward and closes as it travels down (Fig. 5-14).

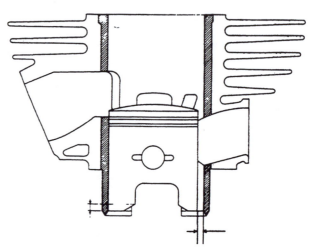

Figure 5-14 Cylinder cutaway showing piston-port design (Kawasaki Motors Corporation, U.S.A.).

Reed Valve System: Reed valve systems use a set of thin flapper valves that are opened by vacuum and closed by pressure. The reeds are forced open by atmospheric pressure as the piston is on its upward stroke and the pressure in the crankcase is below atmospheric pressure. A reed valve engine that has the intake side of the piston cut away pulls the air/fuel/oil mixture as soon as the piston starts its upward stroke. After the piston reaches top dead center and starts down, the pressure difference ceases and the reeds close. The air/fuel/oil mixture is now trapped in the crankcase. The mixture is then compressed by the downward movement of the piston. Reed valves act as a one-way valve and retain the mixture in the chamber to prevent any of the charge from blowing back through the carburetor (Fig. 5-15).

As the piston travels up the cylinder bore, a vacuum is created below it. Some reed valve systems increase the skirt cutaway or use holes in the skirt to allow the mixture to pass through the piston without waiting for the lower edge of the piston to open the port. This allows the crankcase chamber to be filled during most of the piston's upward stroke.

Rotary Valve System: This system controls the intake port with a partially cut away rotating disk that opens and closes the port at the appropriate times. The rotary valve is attached and timed to the engine crankshaft and opens the carburetor-crankcase port when the piston is on its upward stroke. The cutaway area allows the air/fuel/oil charge to enter the vacuum of the crankcase chamber during the entire upward stroke of the piston so that the crankcase temporarily stores the fresh air/fuel/oil mixture. Usually, the carburetors are mounted on the sides of the engine to allow a more direct flow to the rotary valve. The rotary valve closes the intake port on the piston's downward stroke. Generally, this valve system design performs better than the conventional piston porting (Fig. 5-16).

Some models are equipped with a case reed valve assembly that is installed in the cylinder. The reed cage is attached to the base of the cylinder, and the air/fuel/oil mixture passes through the reed cage and into the crankcase (Fig. 5-17).

Some Japanese models use a system that may be incorporated with any of the previously described intake methods but that operates best with reed valves. This system provides a hose and container in which the air/fuel/oil mixture is stored when the port is closed and the car-

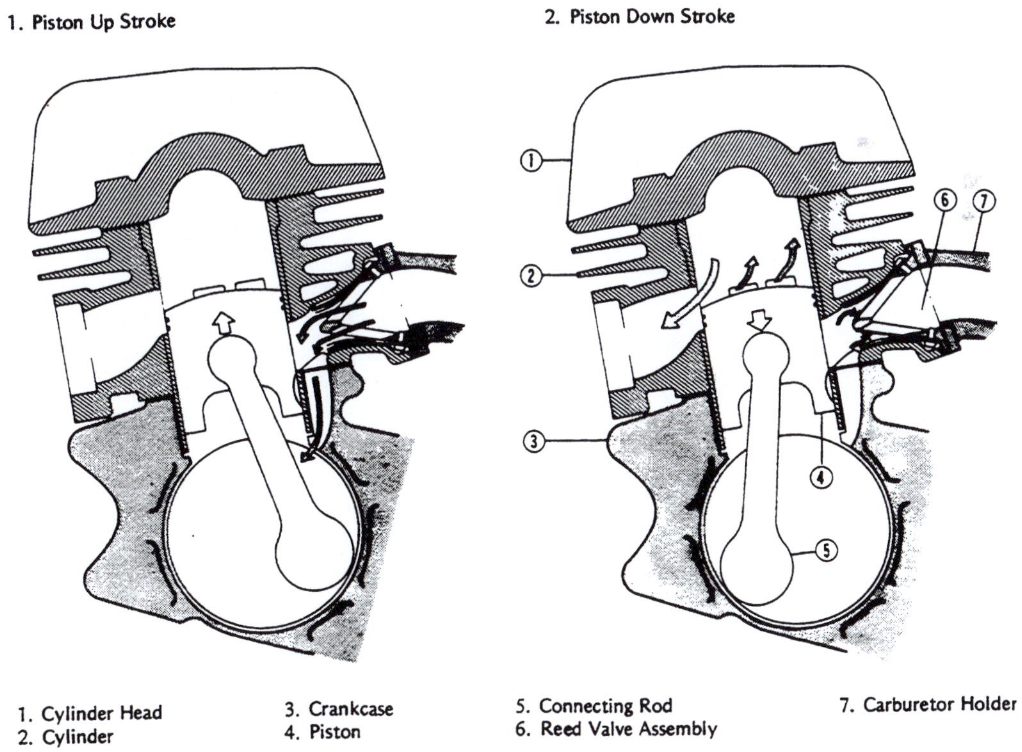

1. Piston Up Stroke   2. Piston Down Stroke

| 1. Cylinder Head | 3. Crankcase | 5. Connecting Rod | 7. Carburetor Holder |
| 2. Cylinder | 4. Piston | 6. Reed Valve Assembly | |

Figure 5-15   Reed valve operation (Kawasaki Motors Corporation, U.S.A.).

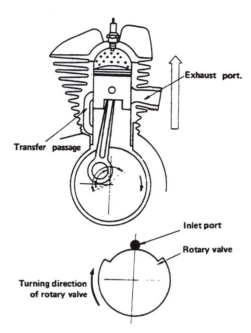
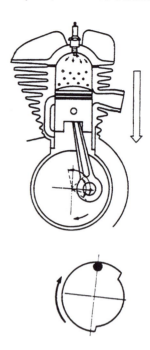

1. **Intake and Compression (in the cylinder)**
   As the piston moves up, the fuel in the cylinder is compressed, and at the same time, the rotary valve clears the inlet port, thus allowing a fresh charge of gas into the crankcase.

2. **Power and Compression (in the crankcase)**
   As the piston approaches TDC, the spark plug produces a spark and ignites the compressed mixture. The resultant combustion pressure forces the piston downward.
   Since the inlet port is already closed, the mixture in the crankcase is compressed by the piston moving downward.

Figure 5-16 Rotary valve operation (Yamaha Motor Corporation, U.S.A.).

buretor is open. This sharply reduces the fluctuations in air speed through the intake tract. This consistent flow of air in turn draws a more consistent flow of fuel into the airstream, so the carburetor can be jetted more precisely.

Exhaust System

The two-stroke engine exhaust system is called an expansion chamber (Fig. 5-18). This type of exhaust system consists of a chamber that operates using the sonic (sound) waves created by the two-stroke engine. The expansion chamber assists the engine by helping to scavenge residual exhaust gases, transferring air/fuel, eliminating charge loss, and adjusting the power band characteristics of the engine.

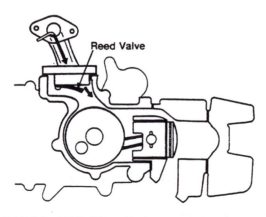

Figure 5-17 Case-reed induction (American Suzuki Motor Corporation).

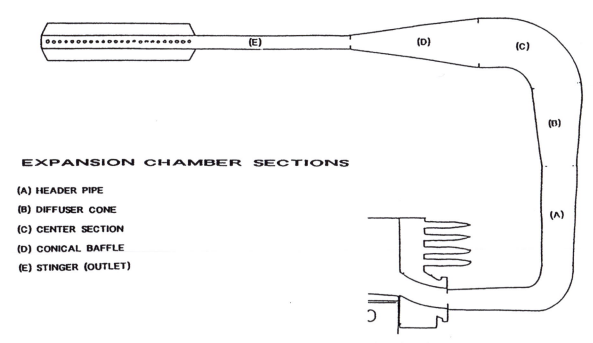

EXPANSION CHAMBER SECTIONS

(A) HEADER PIPE

(B) DIFFUSER CONE

(C) CENTER SECTION

(D) CONICAL BAFFLE

(E) STINGER (OUTLET)

Figure 5-18   Expansion chamber.

An expansion chamber consists of a header pipe, diffuser cone, center section, conical baffle, and stinger pipe. The angle of the header pipe, diffuser cone, and conical baffle helps determine the power band characteristics of the engine. The dimensions of the center section establish the tuned length of the chamber. The stinger pipe restricts the gas flow, which creates back pressures. The back pressures assist the positive waves to force fresh charges of air/fuel back into the secondary area. The amount of power output created by a two-stroke engine depends on the dimensions of the expansion chamber. Operation of the expansion chamber depends on the tuned length of the chamber as well as the expansion and reflection tuning of the chamber.

When the two-stroke engine exhaust port opens, a positive sonic wave is sent down the expansion chamber. The wave expands at the end of the diffuser and continues down the pipe until it reaches the conical baffle, which causes the wave to invert or turn and return up the expansion chamber. The return of the sonic wave creates negative pressure. In a properly tuned expansion chamber, the negative wave reaches the cylinder in time to create a stronger pull during the transfer event so that more air/fuel is taken in and exhaust is pushed out. Because the cylinder is closed, the sonic wave turns again, still creating negative pressure. When the wave reaches the end of the expansion chamber again, pressure equalization created in the chamber causes the wave to turn and create positive pressure. The wave then travels up the exhaust pipe in time to prevent the exit of a new charge of air/fuel that is pushing out the exhaust.

During the manufacture of a two-stroke engine, the expansion chamber is tuned to a specific rpm range (Fig. 5-19). Factors such as the port timing, combustion chamber and crankcase compression ratios, rpm range, and piston displacement are considered to determine the appropriate shape and size of the expansion chamber.

For optimum two-stroke engine performance, the expansion chamber must be compatible with the breathing characteristics of the engine. Poor engine performance will result from a mismatched expansion chamber and port timing.

Lubrication Systems

Two-stroke engines may premix the oil with gasoline or use an oil injection system. The proper oil and mixture ratio or injection system adjustments are essential. The design and operation of two-stroke lubrication systems are described in Chapter 7.

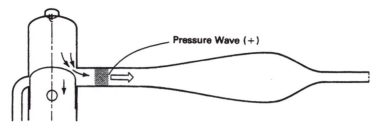

(a) When the exhaust port opens, a pressure wave is generated in the exhaust pipe by the high pressure gas flowing out of the combustion chamber.

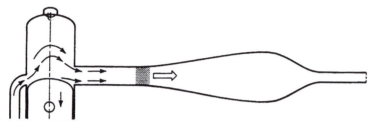

(b) This pressure wave travels through the exhaust pipe at a speed of approximately 1100 ft/s. The high speed of this wave creates a low pressure area behind it which aids in drawing out the exhaust gases.

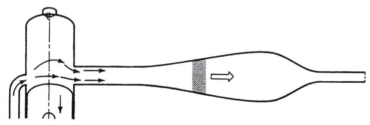

(c) As the pressure wave reaches the widening portion of the expansion chamber, it slows down and loses strength. The exhaust gases following it also slow down but continue to move toward the end of the chamber.

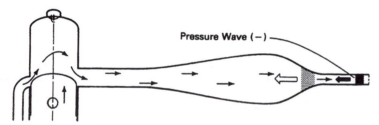

(d) The pressure wave, when traveling through the narrowing part of the expansion chamber, gradually increases in intensity once again. Upon arriving at the narrowest part of the expansion chamber, it is partially reflected back toward the exhaust port of the cylinder. The remainder of the pressure wave continues out the tail pipe (stinger) where the exitting positive pressure wave creates a reverse phase (low pressure wave). The low pressure wave travels back toward the exhaust port.

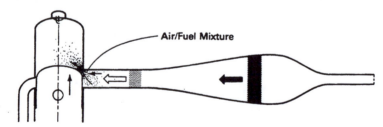

(e) The reflected positive pressure wave, if properly tuned, is directed back to the cylinder exhaust port. It partially prevents from escaping out the exhaust port the fresh air/fuel mixture that is being scavenged out of the combustion chamber. This reflected pressure wave holds the fresh charge in the combustion chamber in an attempt to increase the volumetric efficiency.

The reflected low pressure wave, returning from the end of the tail pipe, arrives at the exhaust port of the cylinder some time behind the arrival of the positive wave. If the low pressure wave is timed to arrive a little before the next opening of the exhaust port, it generates a negative pressure in front of the exhaust port and assists in exhaust scavenging.

Figure 5-19
Expansion chamber operation (Yamaha Motor Corporation, U.S.A.).

Cooling Systems

Heat is generated rapidly in a two-stroke engine. It is essential that this heat be dissipated as quickly as possible to prevent seizure. Two-stroke engines use air or liquid cooling systems.

Air Cooling: An air cooling system uses large, well-spaced fins to dissipate heat. These fins are located on the cylinder, cylinder head, and in the region around the exhaust port where the temperature is the highest.

Liquid Cooling: This system allows more uniform cooling than air cooling, and the heat is carried away more rapidly. With this cooling system, leaner mixtures can be used, working clearances are reduced, and the engine can be designed to produce more power. Liquid cooling allows for less power loss over an extended period of time.

The liquid cooling system consists of a pump, jackets for the cylinder and cylinder head, hoses, and a lightweight aluminum radiator. The crankshaft-driven pump circulates the coolant from the radiator through the cylinder and cylinder head jackets and then back to the radiator. A special radiator cap holds the pressure, so the boiling temperature will be higher. Liquid-cooled, two-stroke engines require a greater liquid flow capacity than four-stroke engines.

Cooling systems are described in more detail in Chapter 7.

TWO-STROKE ENGINE DESIGNS   A single-cylinder two-stroke engine consists of one of each major component: a cylinder, cylinder head, a piston with one or two rings, a wrist pin, connecting rod, and a crankshaft that is contained in a sealed crankcase. A twin-cylinder engine has two of each major component. Two connecting rods are used on a twin crankshaft. A twin crankshaft consists of two single crankshafts that are pressed together to create a twin crankshaft (Fig. 5-20). A four-cylinder two-stroke engine has four of each major component. In multicylinder engines, each cylinder is contained in an individual, sealed compartment within the crankcase.

TWO-STROKE ENGINE OPERATION   In a two-stroke engine, six events take place in two piston strokes (Fig. 5-21). The movement of the piston from bottom dead center to top dead center is called the compression stroke. During the downward movement of the piston, the volume of the engine's crankcase decreases and the trapped air/fuel/oil is pressurized. This is also known as the two-stroke engine's primary compression. The upward stroke is called the compression stroke, and it is also referred to as the combustion compression or secondary compression.

During the compression stroke three events occur:

1. The cylinder is cleaned of lingering burned gases from the previous power stroke.
2. A fresh charge of air/fuel/oil is brought into the cylinder through the transfer ports.
3. The air/fuel/oil mixture is compressed in the combustion chamber in preparation for ignition.

The downward stroke of the piston from top dead center to bottom dead center is called the *power stroke*. The following events occur during this downward movement of the piston:

1. The exhaust port opens and exhaust gases are expelled from the combustion chamber.
2. The volume of the engine crankcase decreases and the air/fuel/oil mixture in the crankcase is compressed and transferred to the cylinder.
3. The power is transferred from the piston to the crankshaft.

1. Crankshaft Assembly
2. Crankshaft 1, left
3. Crankshaft 1, right
4. Crankshaft 2, left
5. Crankshaft 2, right
6. Crank Pin
7. Connecting Rod
8. Connecting Rod Big-end Bearing
9. Washer
10. Labyrinth Seal
11. Bearing
12. Bearing
13. Connecting Rod Small-end Bearing
14. Piston
15. Piston Ring Set
16. Piston Pin
17. Circlip
18. Oil Seal
19. Woodruff Key
20. Circlip
21. Oil Seal
22. Primary Drive Gears
23. Straight Key

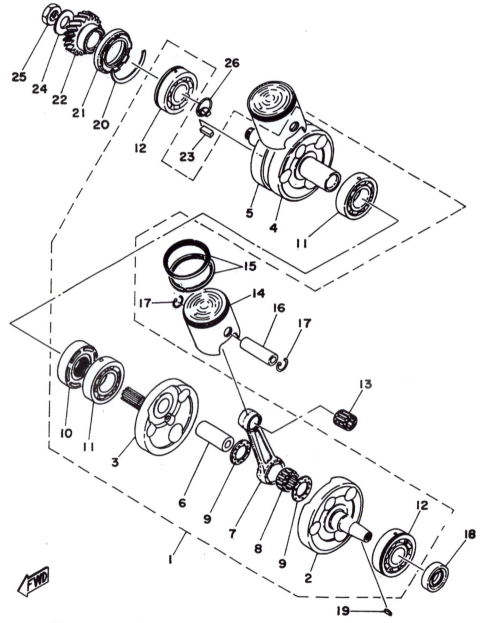

Figure 5-20 Twin-cylinder crankshaft assembly (Yamaha Motor Corporation, U.S.A.).

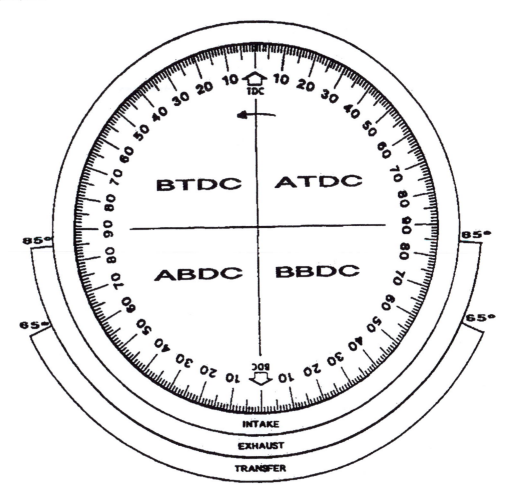

Figure 5-21   Two-stroke timing circle.

Six events are required in order for the two-stroke engine to provide power:

1. Intake
2. Compression
3. Timed ignition
4. Power
5. Exhaust
6. Transfer

This series of events is called the *cycle* and works as follows.

Intake

Intake to the combustion chamber begins with transfer from the crankcase (Fig. 5-22). When the piston is on its downward stroke, the exhaust port opens and then the transfer port opens. It is essential that the exhaust port open first and sufficiently in advance of the transfer port opening to allow time for the pressure in the cylinder to drop below the pressure in

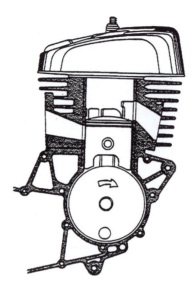

Figure 5-22   Transfer from the crankcase into the combustion chamber (American Suzuki Motor Corporation).

the crankcase. The timing of the transfer port opening is based on the speed at which the engine is required to provide maximum power and the degree to which the mixture is pressurized within the crankcase. When the transfer port is opened, the air/fuel/oil mixture continues to flow into the crankcase even after the piston has passed top dead center.

As the crankshaft turns from bottom dead center, the piston starts on its upward stroke. Intake into the crankcase begins as the piston moves up in the cylinder (Fig. 5-23). When the piston moves up and creates a vacuum, the volume of the crankcase increases, which lowers the pressure within the crankcase to below atmospheric pressure. As soon as the intake port opens, this reduction in pressure causes a mixture of air, fuel, and oil to flow into the crankcase from the carburetor.

Compression

Compression occurs when the air/fuel/oil mixture is compressed by the piston moving upward in the cylinder (Fig. 5-24). The exhaust port is closed and the intake port opens shortly before the piston reaches top dead center, and the air/fuel/oil mixture is compressed.

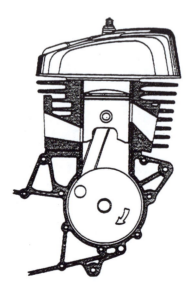

Figure 5-23   Intake into the crankcase (American Suzuki Motor Corporation).

Figure 5-24   Compression (American Suzuki Motor Corporation).

Timed Ignition

While the air/fuel/oil mixture is compressed, the mixture is ignited by a timed electric spark. Ignition occurs as the piston nears the top of its upward stroke. The spark plug ignites the fresh charge and starts it burning. It is very important that the ignition spark occur at precisely the right time. If it occurs too early, the piston must fight to reach the top against a flame front it can barely overcome. If the spark occurs too late, the piston will already be moving down the cylinder and the flame front will follow it weakly rather than driving it strongly. The manufacturer gives the precise piston stroke measurement before top dead center for ignition timing.

Power

The burning air/fuel/oil mixture expands. This forces the piston downward in the cylinder, and the heat energy generated by combustion is converted into mechanical power (Fig. 5-25).

Exhaust

The gaseous products that are formed by the burning air/fuel/oil mixture are expelled from the cylinder so that a new cycle can begin. Once the piston nears the middle of its downward stroke, the cylinder exhaust port begins to open and the burned gases flow out of the open port. Further downward travel of the piston continues to pressurize the crankcase, which forces the fresh charge of air/fuel/oil mixture through the transfer port. The incoming flow of air/fuel/oil mixture from the transfer port helps clean or scavenge any remaining burned gases from the cylinder (Fig. 5-26).

The exhaust port on a two-stroke engine begins to open just as the piston's top edge passes the upper edge of the port when the piston is going down. Under the high pressure of combustion, the gases rush out to the exhaust as the port starts to open. The transfer port design directs the intake charge in a pattern called *loop scavenging*, which helps to push the exhaust gases out (Fig. 5-27). In addition, the column of gas in the exhaust system that is moving out from the previous power stroke, the exhaust stroke, and the resonance of the expansion chamber help to pull the exhaust from the cylinder. If the engine is not properly tuned or the exhaust system is improperly modified, some of the fresh charge is drawn into the exhaust port area, and this fresh mixture is wasted. The results are poor fuel efficiency and a higher output of unburned hydrocarbons.

Figure 5-25 Power (American Suzuki Motor Corporation).

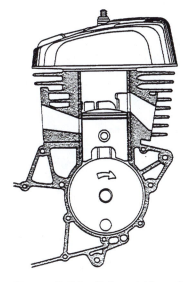

Figure 5-26 Exhaust (American Suzuki Motor Corporation).

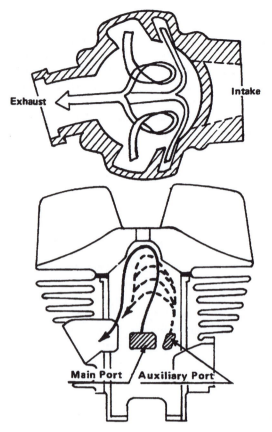

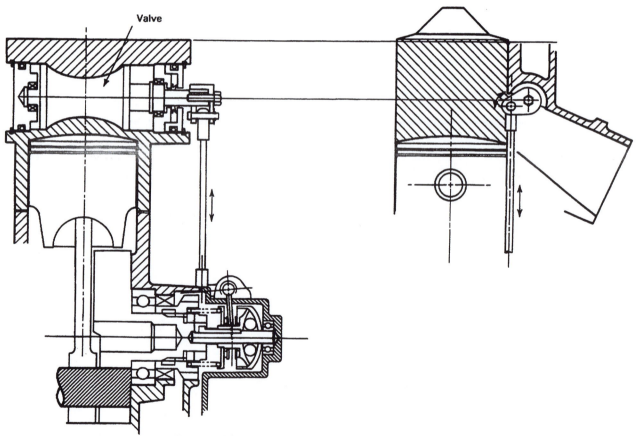

Figure 5-27 Loop scavenging (Kawasaki Motors Corporation, U.S.A.).

Figure 5-28 Cylindrical valve incorporated into exhaust port (Yamaha Motor Corporation, U.S.A.).

Some manufacturers have produced variations on their two-stroke exhaust ports to help control and improve engine power. These exhaust port systems utilize engine rpm's to change exhaust timing. One Yamaha power valve design uses a cylindrical valve that is incorporated into the exhaust port (Fig. 5-28). This valve is cut to match the shape of the port, and it rotates to reduce or increase the exhaust port height, which changes the exhaust timing. In the HPP system designed by Honda, two power valves are positioned near the top of the cylinder and activated by rocker arms located on the engine's water pump shaft (Fig. 5-29). The rocker arm assembly is driven by centrifugal force that increases with the rise of rpm's.

An automatic torque amplification chamber system designed by Honda utilizes exhaust resonance to maintain high power and torque in the lower part of the engine's power band. This system alters the volume of the exhaust system's expansion chamber to produce maximum top-end output. A subchamber which contains a drum-type valve is connected to the exhaust. This valve controls the scavenging characteristics of the expansion chamber. A butterfly valve is activated by a linkage system attached to the crankshaft. At low rpm, when the valve is open, the additional space created by the subchamber enlarges the volume of the exhaust system, thereby increasing the low and midrange power. As the rpm's increase, the centrifugal force activates the linkage to close the butterfly valve and create the necessary exhaust flow for peak power.

Transfer

Transfer is the shortest event that occurs during the cycle. During transfer the piston is moving toward bottom dead center. The difference in pressure above and below the piston pushes a fresh charge of air/fuel through the transfer ports. This fresh charge also helps scavenge residual exhaust gases.

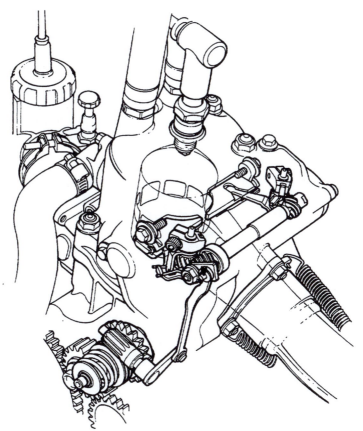

Figure 5-29   Honda power port (HPP) (American Honda Motor Company).

TWO-STROKE When working with two-stroke engines it is sometimes necessary to use the following
ENGINE formulas.
FORMULAS

Compression Ratio

The *compression ratio* is the numerical relationship between the volume in a cylinder at the
beginning of the compression phase and the volume in the combustion chamber at top dead
center (Fig. 5-30). The compression ratio indicates how much the mixture is compressed.
    Manufacturers compute compression ratio by two methods. The first method figures the
ratio with the piston at the base of the cylinder or bottom dead center:

total volume of 110 cc to combustion chamber volume of 10 cc = 110 to 10,
or 11:1 ratio

The second method of determining compression ratio considers only the volume of the
charge above the exhaust port:

total effective volume of 76 cc to combustion chamber volume of 10 cc = 76 to 10,
or 7.6:1 ratio

Displacement

Engine displacement is determined by the diameter of the cylinder and the distance the piston moves in one stroke. Use the formula given on page 20 to find displacement.

Expansion Rate

When working on engines you will often have to refer to the factory specifications for clearances. There are two general expansion rates that help to explain the necessity for these
clearances and why they must be precise. When expanding

iron and steel increase 0.0003 inch per inch per 50°F
aluminum increases 0.0006 inch per inch per 50°F

Because aluminum expands twice as fast as iron, the piston expands much faster than the cylinder. Therefore, it is important to assemble pistons that fit with the proper clearances to
avoid seizure at high temperatures and piston slap at low temperatures.

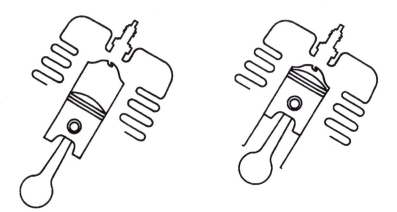

Figure 5-30 Compression ratio = the difference in the volume of
air when the piston is at BDC when compared to piston at TDC.

TWO-STROKE ENGINE SERVICE AND ADJUSTMENTS

Usually, problems with the piston, connecting rod, bearings, crankshaft, and seals can be avoided by following the recommendations in the manufacturer's shop manual. Proper servicing at specified intervals helps to extend the life of the engine and maintain efficient operation. The following are among the most important service procedures:

Adjusting the air/fuel/oil mixture and carburetor

Testing crankcase pressure

Selecting spark plugs

Lubrication

Removing carbon deposits

Maintaining piston clearances

Air/Fuel Mixture and Carburetor Adjustments

There are four major, separate subsystem circuits in a two-stroke carburetor, and each of these circuits has a specific function. These four systems are the float assembly, the idle or slow-speed circuit, the midrange circuit, and the main jet circuit. All of these circuits must be adjusted to the manufacturer's specifications, and the proper jets must be incorporated with the proper system to ensure efficient operation of a two-stroke engine. The design, operation, and servicing procedures for two-stroke engine carburetors are explained in Chapter 8.

Testing Two-Stroke Crankcase Pressure

A vacuum-pressure testing tool is used to check the crankcase pressure and to locate leaks (Fig. 5-31). Crankcase leaks are common in two-stroke engines and usually occur at the crankcase main seals on the left and right sides, at the head and base gaskets, and between the case halves. High idle or excessive exhaust smoke may also indicate a problem at the crankcase seals. Follow the manufacturer's directions for using the vacuum-pressure testing tool.

A pressure testing tool is used to check for pressure leaks at the crankcase seals and base gaskets. Follow the manufacturer's directions for using pressure testers.

Spark Plug Selection

As a general rule, a "hot" spark plug is used for low-speed riding, and a "cold" spark plug is used for high-speed riding. A cold plug has a short heat range and a short insulator nose, and a hot plug has a long heat range and a longer nose. To select the right type of spark plug for the engine, check the color and condition of the spark plug that has been removed from the engine. Consult a spark plug chart for a spark plug with the proper heat range for your applications. The design and selection of spark plugs are described in more detail in Chapter 9.

Two-Stroke Lubrication

Improper lubrication is a major cause of upper-end failure in two-stroke engines. If a two-stroke engine is run without oil or with too little oil, it will seize in a very short time. The proper oil is required in the correct quantity to ensure a smooth film between the moving metal parts to prevent excessive friction and heat. The piston will scuff and gall as a result of insufficient lubrication.

Running the engine with excess oil is not a safeguard against seizure. Fouled plugs, sticking rings, excessive exhaust, a plugged exhaust system, excessive carbon deposits, and poor performance can result from a higher percentage of oil in the mixture than recommended. The servicing of two-stroke lubrication systems is described in Chapter 7.

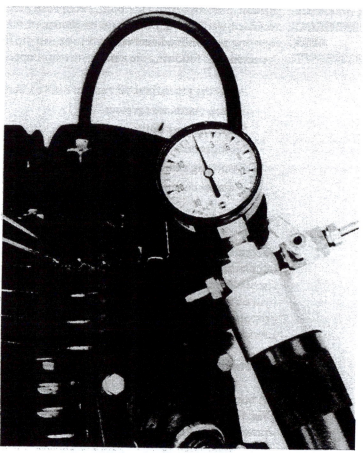

Figure 5-31   Testing crankcase pressure.

Carbon Deposits

A two-stroke engine that has been run for a long period of time develops carbon deposits on the piston crown, cylinder head, and exhaust port. All of this carbon should be removed when servicing the top end. Many mechanics spend hours troubleshooting a two-stroke engine with a restricted exhaust system and are frustrated by continued poor performance until they finally discover that the real problem is a blocked exhaust pipe. The exhaust system, especially the exhaust port, can be clogged with carbon deposits that result from the use of oil in the two-stroke engine. When servicing a two-stroke engine, always clean the carbon from inside the exhaust pipe and muffler baffles and periodically remove carbon deposits from the cylinder head, exhaust port, and piston crown.

Piston Clearances

Pistons must meet precise clearance specifications in a two-stroke engine because of the different expansion rates for aluminum and iron. A typical two-stroke engine requires approximately 0.001 inch of piston-to-wall clearance per inch of cylinder bore. This clearance compensates for the rapid expansion of the piston as opposed to the slower expansion of the cylinder barrel so that there is minimum clearance at normal operating temperatures, and minimum leakage and power loss.

If the piston-to-cylinder clearance is not sufficient, the piston will expand and scuff or score the cylinder wall. Then the rings cannot effectively seal the cylinder wall because of the vertical grooves that are worn in the wall's surface. Compression and combustion gases that escape past the rings through these grooves cause poor performance. If scoring continues and the piston gets too hot, seizure will occur. The piston will develop an interference fit in the cylinder and instantly stop engine rotation. Sometimes a seizure can be predicted when the engine slows down for no apparent reason. One way of safeguarding against seizures is to measure the piston for adequate piston-to-cylinder wall clearances and polish high spots off the piston. Check the manufacturer's specifications for the correct clearances.

Excessive clearances are equally dangerous and can also cause an engine to lock if parts break and lodge in the crankcase and crankshaft area. The piston must travel straight up and down without any wobble or rattle. If the piston rocks in the bore, the skirt may crack and break and damage the lower end of the engine. Inspect pistons for cracks in the skirt area. Even if the skirts do not crack, a rocking piston prevents the necessary ring sealing action so that blow-by is permitted and lower-end vacuum is weak. These conditions cause poor performance and difficult starting. Excessive clearance may be caused by normal wear after high mileage or by poor air filtration.

The complete tune-up and service procedure for two-stroke engines is presented in Chapter 18.

chapter 6

The Drive Train and Starting Systems

The power produced by the engine, to be usable, must be transferred to the rear wheel. Primary drive, transmission, and final drive systems are used together to deliver power to the rear wheel. The primary drive system transfers power from the engine crankshaft into the transmission. When the clutch is engaged, power flows through the clutch into the transmission and is then delivered to the final drive system. The final drive carries the power from the transmission to turn the rear wheel. To turn the engine over, a starting system is located in either the primary drive system or the transmission.

   This chapter first explains the principles on which the operation of a motorcycle drive train is based. The design and operation of each system in the drive train are then explained, followed by the basic service procedures for each system. Finally, the design and operation of motorcycle starting systems and the necessary service procedures are presented.

PRINCIPLES OF OPERATION To understand drive systems, you must first understand types of gears and how they operate, gear ratio, torque and rpm, and power flow.

Types of Gears

A gear transmits power from one shaft to another by meshing with the gear on the other shaft. There are three types of gears commonly used in drive systems: straight-cut or spur gears, helical gears, and beveled gears. The teeth of straight-cut or spur gears are cut straight across the gear's axis. The teeth of helical gears are cut at an angle (Fig. 6-1). Beveled gears are manufactured to make right- or left-angle changes, and they may be straight-cut or helical.

   Gears either rotate freely on a shaft, slide along a shaft, or are fixed to a shaft (Fig. 6-2). Gears that are fixed to a shaft are driving gears. Gears that mesh with a driving gear are driven gears. Some sliding gears have knobs on the side, called *dogs*, that align and interlock with either matching dogs or slots in an adjacent gear. This allows sliding gears to turn freewheeling gears into drive or driven gears.

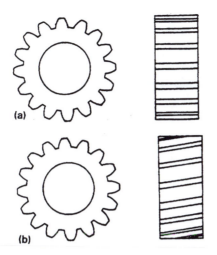

Figure 6-1 (a) Spur gear; (b) helical gear (American Suzuki Motor Corporation).

Gear Ratio

Gear ratio is the numerical relationship that compares the number of times a gear on the input shaft must turn to turn the gear on the output shaft one revolution. For example, an input gear with 20 teeth that meshes with an output gear with 40 teeth produces a 2:1 gear ratio. Gear ratios are used to reduce or increase shaft speed from the power source to the output shaft.

Torque and rpm

Torque is the twisting force of a shaft measured in foot-pounds, kilogram-meters, or newton-meters (Fig. 6-3). The number of revolutions a shaft turns in a minute is the shaft

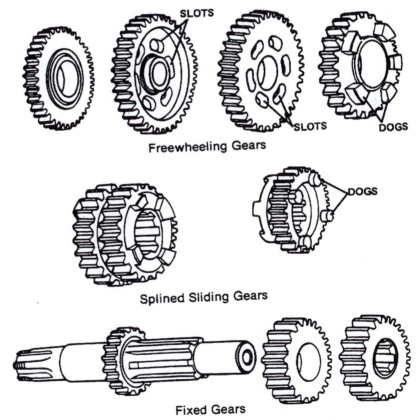

Figure 6-2 (American Suzuki Motor Corporation).

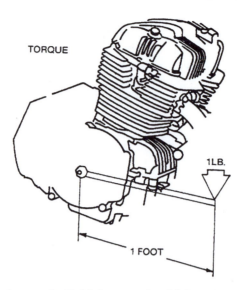

TORQUE

1LB.

1 FOOT

Figure 6-3   (American Honda Motor Company).

rpm. A numerically high gear ratio of 3:1 produces more torque than a low gear ratio of 1:1. Therefore, a low gear ratio requires less input torque to produce the same amount of torque at the output as a high gear ratio. By changing the gear ratios in the drive systems, power is transferred and the speed of the motorcycle is increased and decreased without creating a tremendous change in engine rpm.

Power Flow

Power from the engine is transmitted through the primary drive system into the transmission, and then into the final drive system, which delivers the power to the rear wheel (Fig. 6-4). The devices that convey the power between the engine and the rear wheel differ in each of the following systems.

Primary Drive: The primary drive system includes the clutch. The clutch turns at a slower rpm than the crankshaft because the crankshaft rpm's are too great for the clutch to endure. A gear with a small number of teeth on the end of the crankshaft meshes with a larger gear with many teeth on the clutch. This turns the clutch and provides a reduction of rpm.

Transmission: The transmission provides gear shifting to allow increases in speed without overworking the engine. This is the only point where the rider has the ability to change the gear ratio in the power flow while the motorcycle is in motion.

Final Drive: The final drive system transfers the power to the rear wheel and reduces the rpm at the rear wheel.

PRIMARY DRIVE SYSTEMS   A primary drive system uses gears, chains, or belts to transmit power from the crankshaft to the transmission. The engine and transmission may be a combined unit. Most modern motorcycles use this design because it allows the engine to be more compact.

Early motorcycle designs and some current European and American models place the transmission separate from the engine and use chains or belts to transfer power from the crankshaft to the clutch and then into the transmission. Primary drive components, which are contained in a primary case, include the crankshaft gear or sprocket, the clutch, and its components. Sometimes shifting linkage is included in the primary drive case. Many models also include the kickstarter and the kickstarter gear in this case.

Primary Drive Gear System

Most motorcycles use gears to transfer power from the crankshaft to the transmission (Fig. 6-5). When one gear meshes with another, the power flows out in the reverse direc-

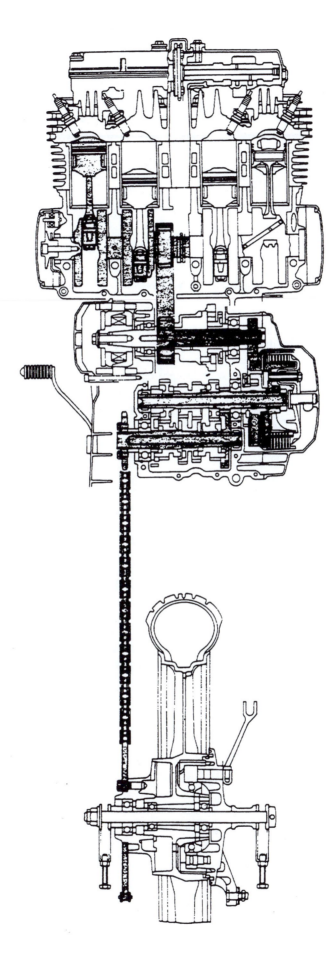

Figure 6-4 Power flow
(Yamaha Motor
Corporation, U.S.A.).

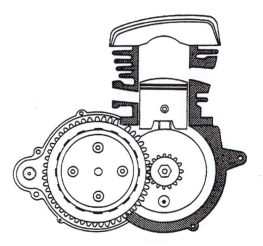

Figure 6-5 Gear-driven primary drive (American Suzuki Motor Corporation).

tion of the input. The power that flows from the crankshaft gear to the clutch gear results in the clutch turning in the opposite direction of crankshaft rotation.

Usually, straight-cut or helical gears are used in a primary gear system. A straight-cut pinion gear, which is the smaller of the two meshing gears, is located on the crankshaft and meshes with a larger straight-cut gear on the clutch. Straight-cut gears do not reduce engine horsepower as much as helical gears, and they are less expensive to manufacture. However, they produce a whining sound. This noise is worse if the gears are too closely engaged. Straight-cut gears may be offset to reduce this noise. Helical gears can be used in place of straight-cut gears to reduce noise. Helical gears operate quietly, but they are more expensive to produce and cause a slight loss of horsepower.

Primary Drive Chain System

In this type of primary drive, chains connect the engine crankshaft to the clutch gear. All primary drive components are the same in this system, but a chain and sprocket are used instead of gears to transfer the power flow. Chains allow the same rotation from shaft to shaft (Fig. 6-6).

There are different types of primary chains used on various motorcycles. Early motorcycles used two or three chains placed side by side. When engine design advanced to produce more horsepower, large, heavy-duty single-unit primary chains were required. Today, triple-row and Hi-Vo-type primary chains are commonly used because they are strong and provide longer service.

Some recent designs use a chain to drive a primary or jack shaft which uses a gear to drive the clutch basket. The primary shaft reduces engine width and can be used to drive an alternator, the ignition system, oil pump, or starter motor.

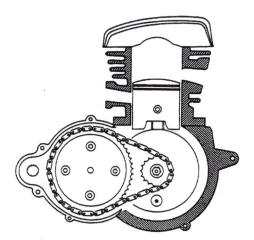

Figure 6-6 Chain-driven primary drive (American Suzuki Motor Corporation).

Figure 6-7 Belt-driven primary drive (Harley-Davidson Motor Company, Inc.).

Primary Drive Belt System

Recently, some motorcycle manufacturers have developed primary drive belts. A belt drive system contains the usual primary drive components but uses a belt in place of a chain (Fig. 6-7). A belt drive system operates quietly and requires less adjustment than a primary chain. Belt drives also have a longer service life and produce a lower horsepower loss.

CLUTCH The clutch is part of the primary drive system. The purpose of the clutch is to engage and disengage the power flow from the crankshaft to the transmission. There are seven clutch variations:

1. Manual, single-plate dry clutch
2. Manual, multiplate dry clutch
3. Manual, multiplate wet clutch
4. Variable ratio clutch
5. Sprag clutch
6. Semiautomatic clutch
7. Torque converter

The first three clutches employ similar parts. The main differences between dry and wet clutches are the type of friction material used and the way the clutch is cooled. Dry clutches are cooled by air and usually use an organic or Kevlar friction material. Older dry clutches used a rayon/asbestos material. Dry clutches should not come in contact with oil as this causes permanent damage to the friction plates. The friction material in a dry clutch does not contaminate the lubrication system as it wears, and this is the primary advantage of a dry clutch.

Wet clutches use a cork/neoprene, paper, or Kevlar friction material and are cooled by the lubrication system. Wet clutches operate more quietly than dry clutches.

Modern motorcycles use either a dry or wet clutch. A wet clutch operates smoother and uses more plates. A dry clutch uses no lubrication and is similar to an automotive clutch. A few American, European, and road-race motorcycles use this type of clutch. A dry clutch can withstand high temperatures and frequent gear shifts without a loss of horsepower caused by heat. A dry clutch must not come in contact with oil. Most modern motorcycles use a wet or oil-bathed clutch that operates in a supply of oil.

Both wet and dry multiplate clutches consist of the following components:

Clutch Outer Basket: The clutch outer basket freewheels off the transmission main shaft. The outer basket is driven by the crankshaft and connected to the drive plates.

Drive Plates: The drive plates are connected to and driven by the clutch outer basket.

Driven Plates: The driven plates are connected to the inner hub and driven by the drive plates.

Inner Hub: The inner hub is splined or connected to the transmission mainshaft and connected to and driven by the driven plates.

Clutch Springs: The clutch springs, which may be coil or diaphragm springs, apply pressure to the pressure plates (Fig. 6-8).

Pressure Plates: There are two types of pressure plates: inner and outer. The pressure plates transfer the clutch spring pressure to the drive and driven plates. Pressure plates are stacked with a friction plate between each metal plate. When the plates are pressed together by the clutch springs, they form one unit and power flows through them.

When a multiplate clutch is engaged, the crankshaft drives the clutch outer basket (Fig. 6-9). The outer basket then turns the drive plates and the clutch springs compress the pressure, friction, and metal plates to drive the inner hub. The inner hub then turns the transmission mainshaft. When the clutch is disengaged, there is no spring pressure. The crankshaft continues to turn the clutch outer basket, and the outer basket turns the drive plates. But because there is no spring pressure, the driven plates are not engaged and the power flow stops.

Variable Ratio Clutch

A variable ratio clutch serves as a clutch and transmission (Fig. 6-10). It consists of a V-belt and a primary and secondary sheave. The primary and secondary sheaves each include a fixed sheave, sheave weights, springs, and a cam sliding sheave. The V-belt is located near the center of the primary sheave and at the outer perimeter of the secondary sheave. As speed increases, the sheave weights are thrown outward by centrifugal force. This causes the primary sliding sheave to move inward and the secondary sliding sheave to move outward. The V-belt is forced toward the outer perimeter of the primary sheave and toward the inner diameter of the secondary sheave.

Sprag Clutch

A sprag clutch engages in only one direction. This type of clutch is found in some primary drives and is used with electric starter motor drives. The sprag clutch is used on electric starters to prevent damage to the starter motor when the engine is engaged. The starter drive disengages from the engine when the speed of the driven portion of the sprag clutch exceeds the speed of the starter.

The sprag clutch is also found in the multiplate wet clutch on some large-displacement motorcycles. It functions to allow part of the clutch to "slip" when the rider downshifts rapidly from a high rpm. This prevents the loss of traction that normally occurs as a result of the engine's compression braking forces.

Some motorcycles and ATVs equipped with a centrifugal clutch use the sprag clutch to provide some engine braking when the centrifugal clutch is disengaged. This helps to provide the rider with better control of the vehicle.

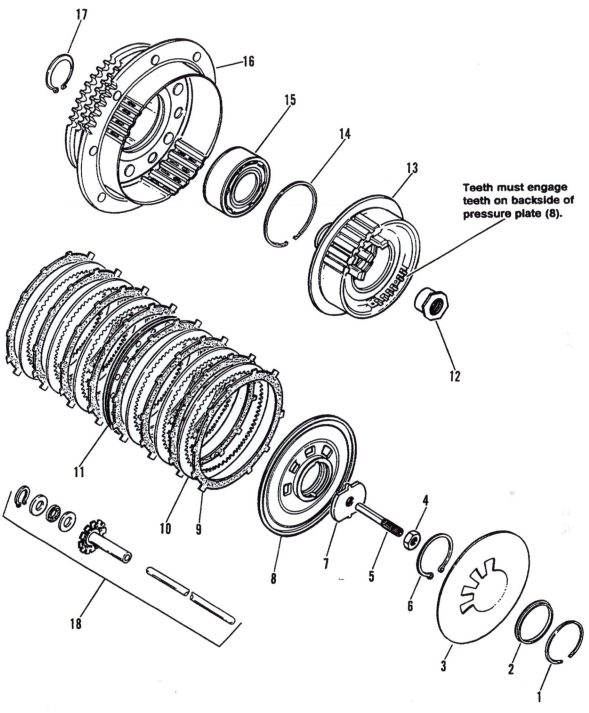

Teeth must engage
teeth on backside of
pressure plate (8).

1. Internal retaining ring
2. Clutch spring seat
3. Diaphragm spring
4. Locknut
5. Adjusting screw
6. Internal retaining ring
7. Release plate
8. Pressure plate
9. Friction plate (8)
10. Steel plate (6)
11. Spring plate
12. Nut (main shaft, left hand threads)
13. Clutch hub
14. Internal retaining ring
15. Double-row ball bearing
16. Clutch shell
17. External retaining ring
18. Push rod components

Figure 6-8 Diaphragm spring clutch (Harley-Davidson Motor
Company, Inc.).

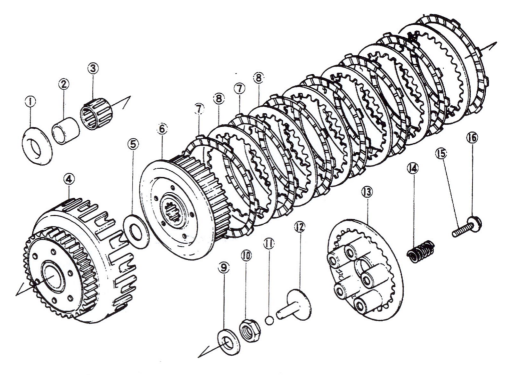

1. Spacer
2. Sleeve
3. Needle Bearing
4. Clutch Housing
5. Thrust Washer
6. Clutch Hub
7. Friction Plate
8. Steel Plate
9. Lockwasher
10. Locknut
11. Steel Ball
12. Spring Plate Pusher
13. Spring Plate
14. Clutch Spring
15. Bolt
16. Washer

Figure 6-9   Clutch (Kawasaki Motors Corporation, U.S.A.).

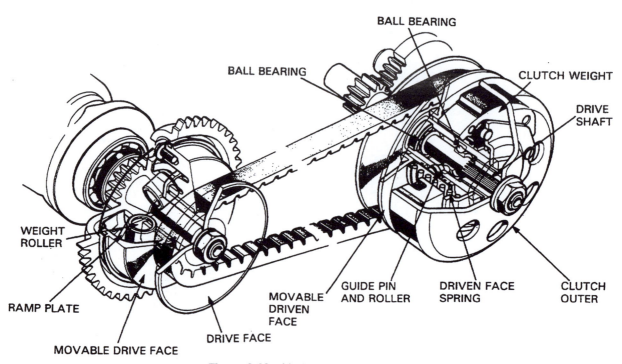

Figure 6-10   Variable ratio clutch (American Honda Motor Company).

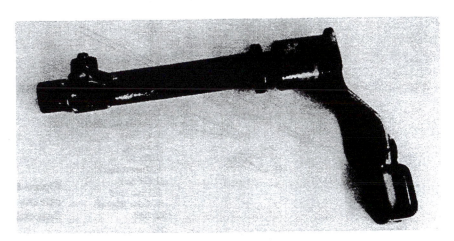

Figure 6-11   Rocker arm release mechanism.

Clutch Release Mechanisms

Manual, single-plate dry clutches, manual, multi-plate wet and dry clutches, variable ratio, and sprag clutches use some type of clutch release mechanism.

The most commonly used clutch release mechanisms are described next.

Rocker Arm Release: The clutch cable is connected to an arm that is connected to the clutch arm. The clutch arm is connected to a pushrod that goes through the transmission to the pressure plate. When the clutch cable is pulled, the pushrod pushes against the pressure plate to release the spring pressure (Fig. 6-11).

Ball-Ramp Release: The clutch cable is connected to a ball-ramp release arm which connects with the pressure plate. As the cable is pulled, the balls roll up a ramp to pull or push the pressure plate away from the clutch plate (Fig. 6-12).

Rack-and-Pinion Release: This release mechanism does not use a pushrod and is common on many two-stroke motorcycles. The clutch cable pulls a lever. The lever is con-

Figure 6-12   Ball-ramp release mechanism.

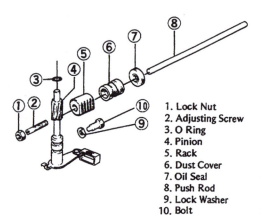

1. Lock Nut
2. Adjusting Screw
3. O Ring
4. Pinion
5. Rack
6. Dust Cover
7. Oil Seal
8. Push Rod
9. Lock Washer
10. Bolt

Figure 6-13 Rack-and-pinion clutch release mechanism (Kawasaki Motors Corporation, U.S.A.).

nected with meshed teeth at the end of a shaft. When the clutch cable is pulled, the teeth on the rotating shaft pull out the pressure plate to release the pressure (Fig. 6-13).

Lever Release: The clutch cable is connected to a lever. When the cable is pulled, a pushrod that is located near the center of the lever pushes against the pressure plate. This release mechanism is simple, but it requires a lot of pressure to activate the release (Fig. 6-14).

Cam Release: The clutch cable is connected to a small arm that is connected to a cam. When the cable is pulled, the cam lobe rotates and pushes a pushrod to release the pressure at the pressure plate (Fig. 6-15).

Screw Release: A threaded screw assembly is connected to a lever. When the lever is pulled, it rotates the screw inward to allow the pushrod to disengage the clutch (Fig. 6-16).

Hydraulic Release: The pushrod is operated by a slave cylinder which is activated by a master cylinder at the clutch lever (Fig. 6-17).

Semiautomatic Clutch

Another type of clutch found on today's smaller motorcycles is the semiautomatic wet clutch. When the rider puts the engine in gear and when the engine rpm increases, the clutch

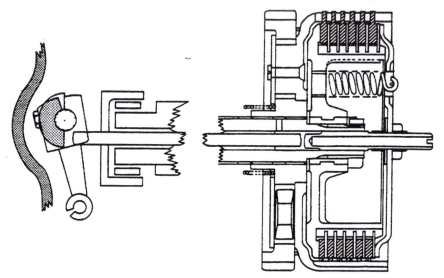

Figure 6-14 Lever release mechanism (American Suzuki Motor Corporation).

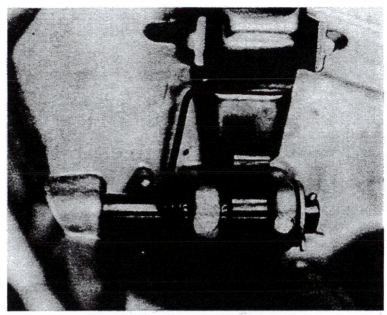

Figure 6-15 Cam release mechanism.

engages through the use of centrifugal weights. Since this clutch relies on centrifugal force to throw the weights out, the rpm must be increased, so the clutch is mounted at the end of the crankshaft. This allows the clutch to spin faster for starting engagement in gear. A gear mounted on the clutch hub meshes with a transmission gear. When the rider shifts gears during acceleration, the clutch can be momentarily disengaged by a linkage (Fig. 6-18).

Torque Converter

Some motorcycles have a completely different power transfer system known as a torque converter. This system uses oil pressure for clutch and transmission engagement. The construction of a torque converter is similar to two propellers. One propeller is driven by the engine to force oil into the other propeller. The oil moving through the propeller turns it to turn the transmission mainshaft (Fig. 6-19). A torque converter must be replaced if a problem develops.

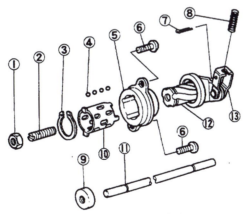

1. Locknut	8. Spring
2. Adjusting Screw	9. Oil Seal
3. Circlip	10. Retainer
4. Steel Ball	11. Push Rod
5. Output Release Gear	12. Inner Release Gear
6. Mounting Screw	13. Release Lever
7. Cotter Pin	

Figure 6-16 Screw release mechanism (Kawasaki Motors Corporation, U.S.A.).

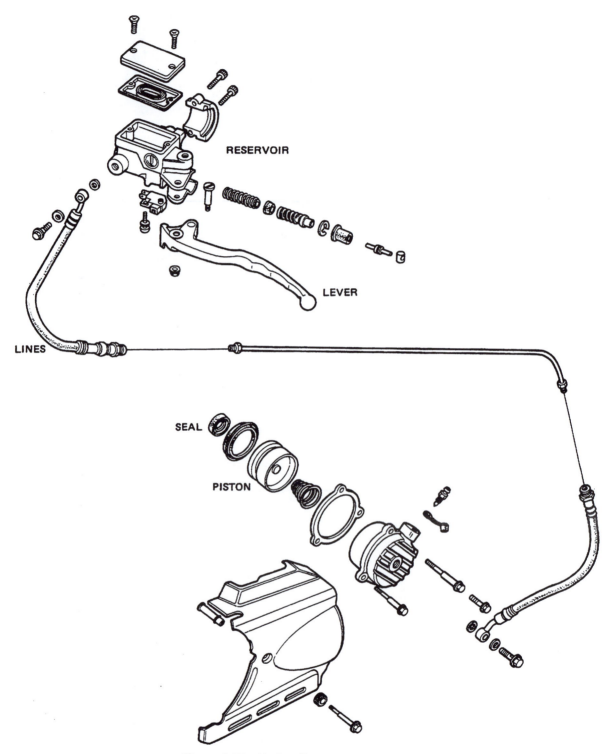

RESERVOIR

LEVER

LINES

SEAL

PISTON

Figure 6-17 Hydraulic clutch release system (American Honda Motor Company).

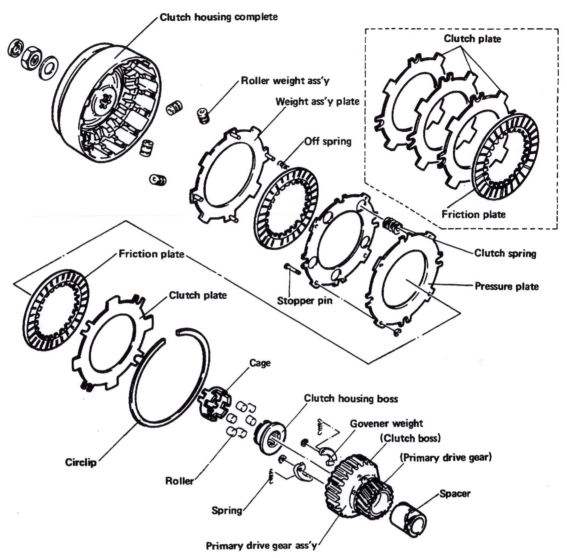

Clutch housing complete

Clutch plate

Roller weight ass'y

Weight ass'y plate

Off spring

Friction plate

Clutch spring

Friction plate

Clutch plate

Stopper pin

Pressure plate

Cage

Clutch housing boss

Govener weight
(Clutch boss)

(Primary drive gear)

Circlip

Roller

Spring

Spacer

Primary drive gear ass'y

Figure 6-18 Semiautomatic clutch (Yamaha Motor Corporation, U.S.A.).

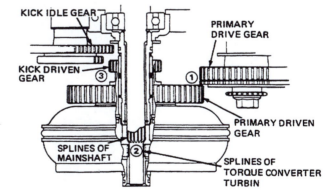

KICK IDLE GEAR

PRIMARY DRIVE GEAR

KICK DRIVEN GEAR

③

①

PRIMARY DRIVEN GEAR

SPLINES OF MAINSHAFT

②

SPLINES OF TORQUE CONVERTER TURBIN

Figure 6-19 Torque converter (American Honda Motor Company).

TRANSMISSION An engine does not produce much power or torque at low engine speed. The transmission uses a series of gears and shafts to increase the torque or turning force. In low gear the transmission gears produce a high gear ratio of about 3:1 instead of 1:1. When the engine has produced enough torque and power, the gear ratio can be changed to allow the final drive to turn faster without higher engine speeds (Fig. 6-20). Gear changing continues until the motorcycle is cruising in top gear. Usually the top gear ratio is approximately 1:1, and the output shaft is moving at approximately the same speed as the clutch. Most motorcycles have five- or six-speed transmissions. Some motorcycles have a top gear ratio of less than 1:1 for an overdrive effect.

The main transmission shaft is connected to the clutch. The smallest gear on the main shaft produces low gear. This gear is fixed and either machined in one piece with the shaft or pressed on. In most cases, both shafts have a combination of fixed, freewheeling, and sliding gears (Fig. 6-21).

Motorcycle transmissions use constant-mesh gears. This means that all gear pairs are always meshing when the transmission is in any gear or in neutral. Motorcycles use one of two types of constant-mesh transmission: indirect or direct drive.

Indirect Drive Transmission

The indirect transmission is used in most Japanese models. The indirect transmission receives power from the primary drive into the input shaft or mainshaft and then directs the power to the countershaft. The countershaft transmits the power to final drive (Fig. 6-22).

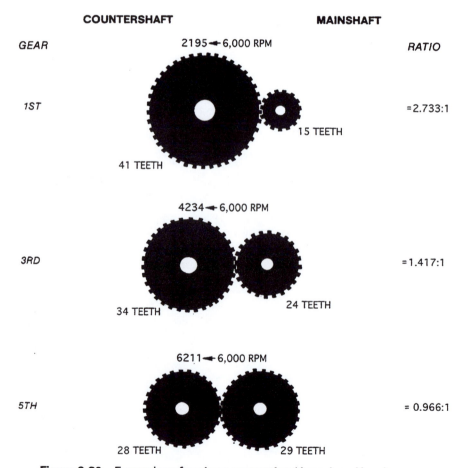

Figure 6-20 Examples of various gear ratios (American Honda Motor Company).

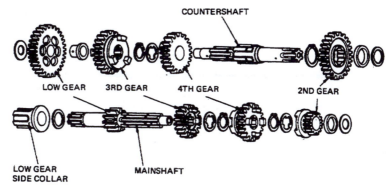

Figure 6-21 Transmission shafts with gears (American Honda Motor Company).

Direct Drive Transmission

Direct drive transmission is used on American and British models and on some Japanese models (Fig. 6-23). To achieve standard engine rotation when a primary chain is used, the transmission must take in the power on one shaft, make a gear ratio change, and then transmit the power to the rear wheel without reversing rotation. That is why a direct drive transmission was designed. In a direct drive transmission, the power enters on the mainshaft and

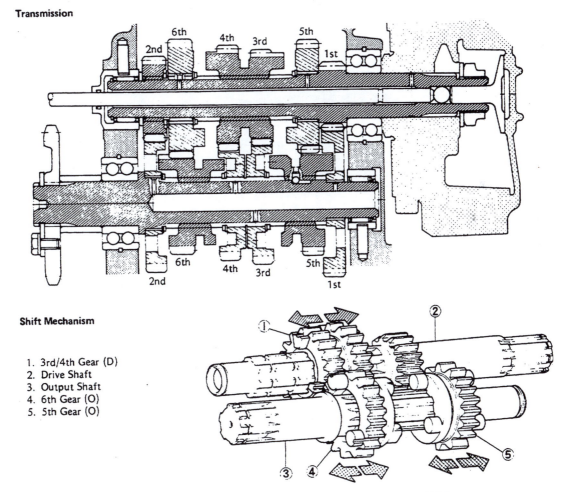

Figure 6-22 Indirect drive transmission (Kawasaki Motors Corporation, U.S.A.).

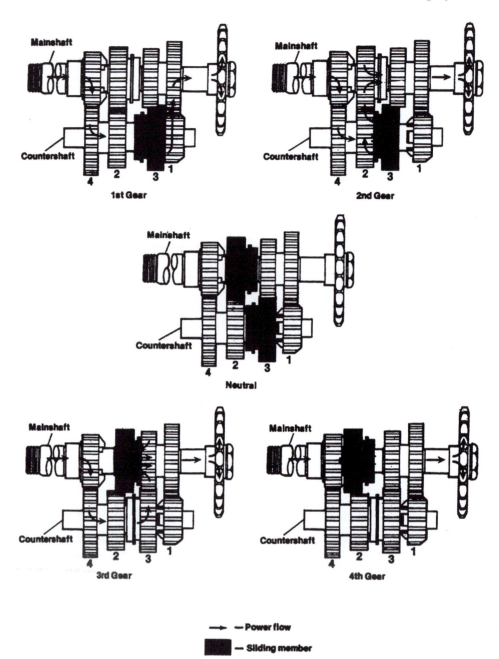

Figure 6-23   Direct drive transmission (Harley-Davidson Motor Company, Inc.).

is transferred to the countershaft, which determines the gear ratio for the lower gears. The power is transferred from the countershaft through the output shaft, which directs the power out over or through the inside of the mainshaft. The sprocket is splined to the output shaft, which is bushed to fit over the mainshaft. In top gear the mainshaft is directly connected to the output shaft and power does not flow through the countershaft.

Dual-Range Transmission

Some small trail bikes and some larger motorcycles that are used for touring incorporate a dual-range transmission (Fig. 6-24). This auxiliary transmission, which is sometimes called a *subtransmission*, is placed into the power flow between the transmission and the final

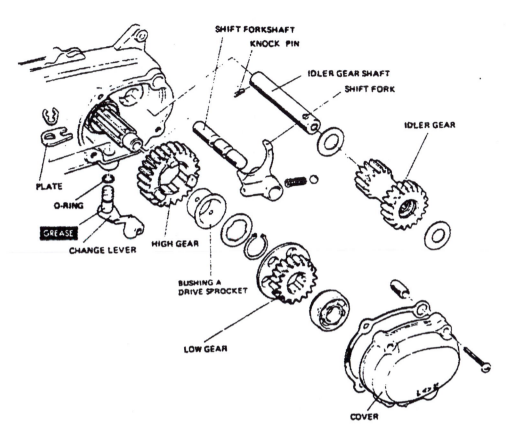

Figure 6-24 Auxiliary transmission (American Honda Motor Company).

drive system. Usually, the dual-range transmission is a two-speed, high and low, manual shift gear box. It consists of four gears, an input shaft, output shaft, and some type of damping device. On a small trail bike, this transmission provides dual-range gear ratios for on-road and off-road use. On a larger, heavier touring motorcycle the dual-range transmission provides quick acceleration in stop-and-go traffic in low range, and a high range for cross-country touring and fuel economy. In theory, a motorcycle that is equipped with a normal five-speed transmission and the dual-range transmission has 10 forward speeds.

Shift Linkage

The transmission includes a shift linkage that moves the shift mechanism. The shift mechanism moves the shift forks, which in turn move a slider gear or shifting clutch. The shift linkage is operated by the rider's hand or foot. There are three basic types of shift mechanisms: claw, floating plate, and ratchet.

Claw Shifter Selector Linkage: The claw shifter linkage consists of a shift shaft that has a foot or hand lever on one end and a fixed arm with a movable shift claw or pawl on the other end (Fig. 6-25). The movable arm has two claws that contact equally spaced steel pins, which are located on the end of the shift mechanism. The movable claw arm includes a spring to provide constant contact with the steel pins.

When pressure is applied to the claw shift linkage, the claw contacts a steel pin and rotates the shift mechanism. After gear selection is made, a return spring located on the shift shaft recenters the claws between the pins to allow for the next up- or downshift. The return spring is located inside the overshift limiter, which is part of the fixed plate on the shift shaft. The edges of the overshift limiter contact the return spring pin and prevent the mechanism from rotating more than one transmission ratio at a time.

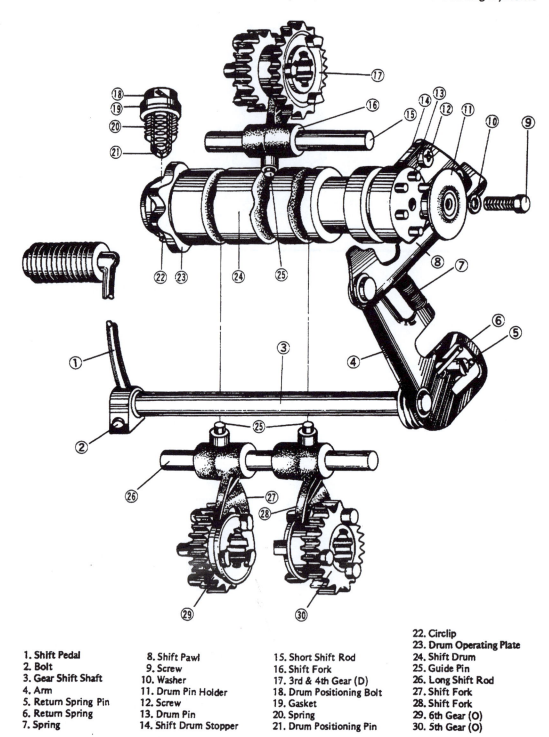

			22. Circlip
			23. Drum Operating Plate
1. Shift Pedal	8. Shift Pawl	15. Short Shift Rod	24. Shift Drum
2. Bolt	9. Screw	16. Shift Fork	25. Guide Pin
3. Gear Shift Shaft	10. Washer	17. 3rd & 4th Gear (D)	26. Long Shift Rod
4. Arm	11. Drum Pin Holder	18. Drum Positioning Bolt	27. Shift Fork
5. Return Spring Pin	12. Screw	19. Gasket	28. Shift Fork
6. Return Spring	13. Drum Pin	20. Spring	29. 6th Gear (O)
7. Spring	14. Shift Drum Stopper	21. Drum Positioning Pin	30. 5th Gear (O)

Figure 6-25   Shift mechanism (Kawasaki Motors Corporation, U.S.A.).

Floating Plate Linkage: This type of linkage also uses a rider-controlled lever to rotate a shift shaft (Fig. 6-26). The shift shaft also has a fixed arm, but a spring-mounted floating plate contacts circular protrusions on the end of the shift mechanism. The floating plate has a square opening, and the upper corners of this opening contact the protrusions. When rotated, a corner of the opening contacts a protrusion to move the shift mechanism. After gear selection is made, the return spring centers the floating plate between the protrusions again

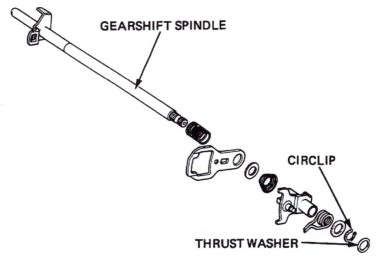

GEARSHIFT SPINDLE

CIRCLIP

THRUST WASHER

Figure 6-26 Floating plate shift linkage (American Honda Motor Company).

to allow for the next up- or downshift. The return spring also prevents excessive movement of the shift shaft so that only one gear ratio change can be made at a time.

Ratchet Linkage: Ratchet linkage also uses a rider-controlled lever to rotate a shift shaft (Fig. 6-27). The shaft has either a sector or planetary gear on the working end. The sector or planetary gear rotates a ratchet that engages the shift mechanism to change the transmission gear ratio. The ratchet linkage also includes an overshift limiter to prevent making more than one transmission ratio at a time.

Shift Mechanisms

The shift mechanism moves the shift forks. There are basically two types of shift mechanisms: a shift drum or cam plate. The shift drum is a cylinder with square-sided grooves. The cam plate is a flat plate that also has square-sided grooves. The grooves in both the shift drum and cam plate are designed to guide shift fork travel. The grooves are accurately machined to prevent achieving two gear ratios at the same time. Both the shift drum and cam plate use a shift detent to help hold the shift fork in position and to locate the next gear ratio position.

Shift Detents

There are many shift detent design variations. Four basic shift detents are: arm and roller, roller and shift mechanism, spring and ball, and spring and plunger. The arm and roller design uses a movable arm that has a roller wheel attached to it. The roller wheel contacts the steel pins on the shift mechanism. A spring ensures constant contact between the roller and the shift mechanism. Some motorcycles use two roller detents: one for neutral, and the other for the other gear ratios. The spring and ball and spring and plunger detents are variations of the arm and roller design. The shift mechanism has a star-shaped stopper cam on which the spring-loaded ball or plunger rides. The neutral position for this type of detent is normally located between the first and second gear ratio.

FINAL DRIVE SYSTEM The final drive system directs the power flow from the transmission to the rear wheel to propel the motorcycle. Different motorcycles use different final drive ratios. The final drive ratio is determined by how many times the transmission shaft must turn to produce one revolution of the rear wheel.

There are three types of final drive systems in use: chain drive, belt drive, and shaft drive.

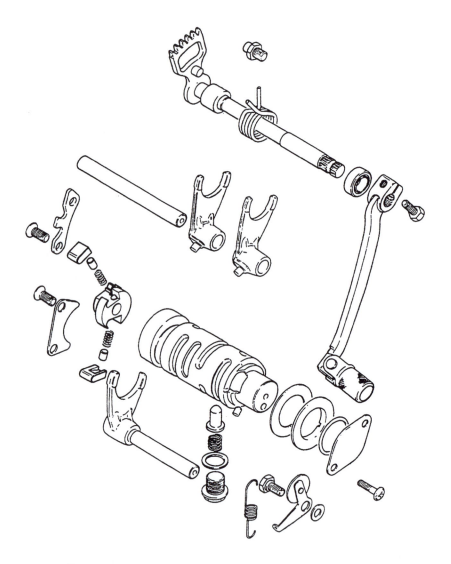

Figure 6-27   Ratchet shift linkage (American Suzuki Motor Corporation).

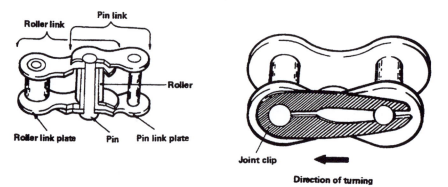

Figure 6-28   Drive chain link and master link (Yamaha Motor Corporation, U.S.A.).

Figure 6-29   O-ring chain
(American Suzuki Motor
Corporation).

Drive chains are composed of inside and outside links. Each inside link consists of two plates, two bushings, and two rollers. The outside link is connected to the inside link and consists of two plates and two pins that are riveted to the plates. Rear drive chains are either endless or connected by a master link (Fig. 6-28). An endless chain is designed to overcome the weak point that a master link may produce. Most manufacturers include an O-ring between the bushings and plates and pins so that each link has four O-rings. The O-rings retain grease on the inside of the roller and protect the roller from contaminants (Fig. 6-29).

Chain Drive System

The chain drive system consists of a sprocket on the transmission shaft and a sprocket attached to the rear wheel. The chain connects each sprocket. When the transmission is engaged and rotating in its normal direction, the sprocket pulls the top of the chain to rotate the rear sprocket (Fig. 6-30).

Figure 6-30   Final drive chain.

When a chain is used, the final drive ratio may be changed to increase speed or torque. Using different-sized sprockets alters the final drive ratio, but the chain and sprockets must be compatible.

Belt Drive System

Belts are currently used on selected Japanese and American models (Fig. 6-31). The belt, which is a Gilmer type, has notches molded into it instead of links to mesh with the sprockets. The belt requires no lubrication, reduces sprocket wear, and operates cleanly and quietly. Usually, the final drive ratio of a belt drive system cannot be changed because the necessary parts are not available.

Shaft Drive System

The shaft drive system consists of a drive or propeller shaft, a universal joint, slip joint, pinion shaft and gear, and a ring gear (Fig. 6-32). The shaft drive system is activated by the rotary motion of the transmission output shaft. The drive shaft is connected to the universal joint, which is used with the slip joint at the other end and located inside the swing arm. The slip joint moves with the rear suspension and provides flexibility. The slip joint rotates the pinion shaft and the pinion gear at the end of the shaft. The pinion gear meshes with a ring gear that is attached to the rear wheel. Both gears are beveled and sealed in an aluminum housing to allow the system to run in oil. This unit is known as the *final drive gear case* (Fig. 6-33).

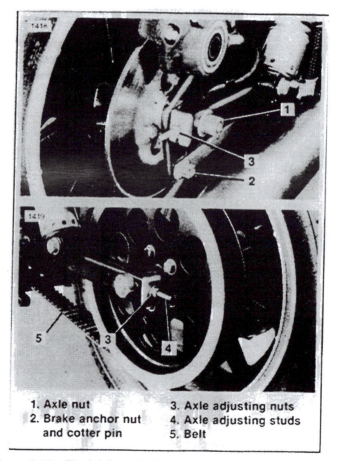

1. Axle nut	3. Axle adjusting nuts
2. Brake anchor nut and cotter pin	4. Axle adjusting studs
	5. Belt

Figure 6-31   Final drive belt (Harley-Davidson Motor Company, Inc.).

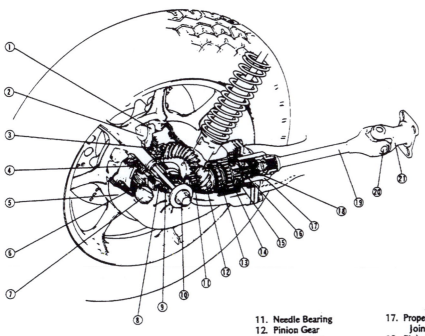

1. Rear Wheel Coupling
2. Rubber Damper
3. Oil Seal
4. Ball Bearing
5. Final Gear Case
6. Ring Gear
7. Final Gear Case Oil Filler
8. Needle Bearing
9. Oil Seal
10. Axle Shaft
11. Needle Bearing
12. Pinion Gear
13. Tapered Roller Bearing
14. Tapered Roller Bearing
15. Oil Seal
16. Grease Seal
17. Propeller Shaft Joint
18. Pinion Shaft Joint
19. Propeller Shaft
20. Universal Joint
21. Universal Joint Coupling

Figure 6-32 Shaft drive system (Kawasaki Motors Corporation, U.S.A.).

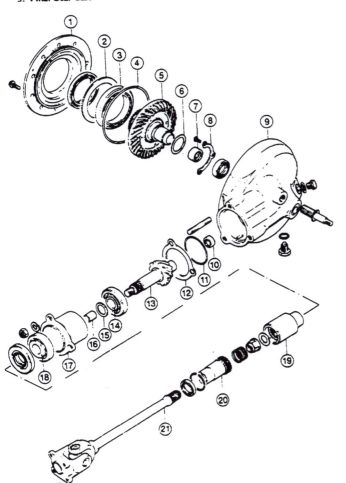

1. Final Gear Bearing Case
2. Shim
3. Ball Bearing
4. O-ring
5. Final Driven Gear
6. Shim
7. Needle Roller Bearing
8. Bearing Holder
9. Final Gear Case
10. Needle Roller Bearing
11. O-ring
12. Shim
13. Final Drive Gear
14. Inner Roller Bearing
15. Shim
16. Spacer
17. Drive Gear
18. Outer Roller Bearing
19. Drive Gear Coupling
20. Propeller Shaft Coupling
21. Propeller Shaft

Figure 6-33 Exploded view of shaft drive (American Suzuki Motor Corporation).

SERVICING Each drive system requires specific servicing procedures. Consult the service manual for
DRIVE SYSTEMS the model you are working on. What follows are the basic servicing procedures for each
system and some tips.

Primary Drive Gear System

Inspect the gear teeth for wear. Some manufacturers list specifications for gear *backlash*.
Backlash is the distance between two meshed teeth, and it is usually measured in thousandths of an inch. Too little clearance reduces the lubrication, wears the teeth, and causes
excessive whining noise. Too much clearance causes the gears to beat against each other,
which produces a howling noise.

Primary Drive Chain System

A primary chain requires lubrication. The engine lubrication system may also lubricate the
primary chain, or there will be a separate reservoir for primary chain lubrication. Determine
if the lubrication system is separate from the engine oil system before tuning or servicing.
The engine oil becomes contaminated by particles thrown off the clutch, chain, or gears and
must be changed periodically.

A primary chain wears with use, so some type of tensioner or guide is placed on chain
systems to control excess slack. The tensioner may be adjusted automatically or manually
(Fig. 6-34). Adjust a manual tensioner to the manufacturer's specifications.

Inspect chains and sprockets for wear. Check for broken rollers and cracked side
plates.

Primary Drive Belt System

Inspect belts for fraying and sprockets for wear. Oil must not contact the belt because the
additives in oil cause the belt to deteriorate.

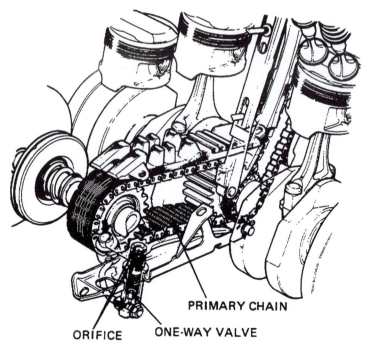

PRIMARY CHAIN

ORIFICE   ONE-WAY VALVE

Figure 6-34   Primary chain tensioner (American Honda Motor
Company).

The shifting linkage that may be found in some primary drive cases may require adjustments. Consult the service manual for the adjustment procedure.

Clutch Service

Usually, the clutch requires adjustments only at the pressure plate or clutch release mechanism and at the hand lever clutch cable. Before making any adjustment, loosen the clutch cable to increase the slack. Any clutch adjustment will alter the cable adjustment. Follow the manufacturer's specifications when adjusting the clutch release mechanism, and adjust the cable at the hand lever for free play. Routine clutch adjustment is necessary because the clutch cable stretches with use.

If the clutch requires maintenance beyond an adjustment, the primary cover must be removed. The components that are likely to wear are the springs, friction plates, clutch hub, clutch basket, release mechanism, and pushrod. Consult the service manual for specifications and procedures. The springs should be measured and must be equal lengths. Measure the thickness of the friction plates with a micrometer or vernier caliper; they must meet the manufacturer's specifications (Fig. 6-35). Determine if the clutch plates have worn grooves in the clutch hub or if the friction plates have worn grooves in the clutch basket. The pushrod must be straight. Inspect for cracks and abnormal wear of the clutch plates, clutch hub, and clutch basket surfaces.

Wet Clutch Service

Wet clutch friction plates should be soaked in the recommended lubricant for 30 minutes prior to installation. Never use shop rags to wipe off or clean wet clutch plates.

All wet clutch steel plates should be installed so that the smooth sides of the splines are facing the direction of disengagement.

Dry Clutch Service

Inspect dry clutch friction and steel plates for wear and to ensure that they meet the minimum thickness specifications. Dry clutch plates that have been contaminated with oil must be replaced. Glazed or cracked plates should also be replaced.

Semiautomatic Clutch Service

Inspect the clutch plates for thickness. Check for excessive wear of the centrifugal roller weights. Measure and inspect the springs, and inspect the clutch hub and basket for abnormal wear (Fig. 6-36). No adjustments can be made. Inspect for broken or bent shifting linkage.

Torque Converter Service

With the exception of an oil change, the torque converter cannot be serviced. Consult the service manual for the oil-changing procedure.

Figure 6-35 Measuring friction plate thickness (American Honda Motor Company).

Figure 6-36 Measuring clutch spring free length (American Honda Motor Company).

Transmission Service

Most transmissions require nothing more than an oil change and occasional linkage adjustment. If the transmission requires servicing beyond a normal adjustment, the engine crankcases of unit transmissions must be taken apart, and sometimes the engine must be disassembled.

Most crankcases consist of two halves. Crankcases may be opened horizontally or vertically. Horizontally split crankcases are common on large street motorcycles, and it is not necessary to dismantle the engine for service. Vertically split crankcases are common on most two-stroke engines and small street motorcycles, and the engine must be dismantled. In either case, do not attempt to open the crankcase without first consulting the service manual.

The transmission must be inspected or rebuilt when the transmission does not stay in gear, does not go into gear, or when it is difficult to shift gears. Inspect the shift forks, gears, shafts, and shift drum.

Shift forks must be straight. If they are bent, they will cause transmission problems. The ends of the shift forks are often covered with hard chrome or other hard materials, and any wear or scoring usually indicates that they are bent. Shift forks cannot be straightened and must be replaced. If a shift fork is replaced, inspect the sliding gear for scoring and replace it if it is scored.

Inspect gears for chips, cracks, or uneven wear, and inspect the dogs for wear (Fig. 6-37). Gear teeth and the ends of dogs should have sharp corners. Inspect gears with slots for dogs and their connecting gears. Inspect freewheeling and sliding gears for scoring in the area where the gear slides or spins on the shaft. If a gear must be replaced, also replace the gear with which it meshes. If a gear is replaced because of a worn dog, the connecting gear should also be replaced.

Inspect shafts for straightness, cracks, and clogged oil holes. All gears must be removed to make this inspection. To remove the gears, remove the circlips and thrust washers that hold the gear in place. Never reuse a circlip. Some circlips must be installed in a certain direction.

Inspect the shift drum. Inspect the cam grooves for wear caused by the pin.

Transmission Reassembly

Assemble the shafts with the gears, thrust washers, and circlips in the proper order. No gear should spin against a circlip. Make sure that the circlip is completely in its groove. Inspect the drive gears on a spline shaft for oil holes. The holes in the gear and shaft must align (Fig. 6-38).

Figure 6-37   Damaged gears.

Figure 6-38 Transmission shaft with oil hole.

Lubricate the transmission and make sure that the transmission shifts through all gears before assembling the case. You may need to rotate the shafts to shift through all gears. Follow the manufacturer's procedure for case assembly.

Dual-Range Transmission Service

Remove the case on the final drive side of the motorcycle. It is not necessary to disassemble the engine. Inspect the four gears and two shafts. Some systems include a spring to reduce rear wheel shock load into the transmission. Consult the service manual for specifications and service procedure.

Final Drive Chain System

Check for minute cracks on the chain's side plates caused by battery acid. If these cracks appear, check for proper routing of the battery vent tube. Final drive chains must be lubricated at frequent intervals. Lubricate the inside rollers and right and left link plates. If the drive chain includes O-rings, lubricate it with a lubricant that is specifically designed for O-ring-type chains.

It is normal for a chain to wear with use. Most motorcycles incorporate a chain adjuster with the rear wheel components (Fig. 6-39). A chain that is too loose for an extended time can jump over the sprockets and break the teeth. Consult the service manual for adjustment procedures and specifications.

Inspect the sprockets for wear. Usually, sprocket teeth wear on the side opposite the direction of rotation. Replace any worn or broken sprockets. Sprockets wear more quickly on motorcycles with high torque output. Check the tightness of the rear sprocket bolts on off-road motorcycles frequently.

Final Drive Belt System

Belts wear slowly unless a sprocket is misaligned. Belts must run to the center of the sprockets or the belt will fray. Check to be sure the belt pulleys are aligned, and follow the service manual procedure and specifications for proper belt tension and adjustment.

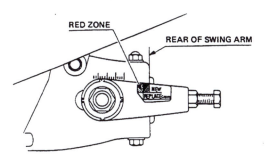

Figure 6-39 Chain adjuster (American Honda Motor Company).

Final Drive Shaft System

The most common problem with this system occurs at the universal joint and drive shaft. The shaft should be solid and without free play. This shaft incorporates bearings, which should also be inspected. Snap rings must be removed to service the universal joint, and they should not be reused. Many universal joints cannot be repaired and must be replaced.

The rear wheel must be removed to service the final drive gear case (Fig. 6-40). This gear case assembly includes two tapered bearings at the pinion gear shaft. Check for the proper end play at the manufacturer's specified intervals. Check the ring and pinion gears for chipped or broken teeth. The backlash must be exact, and the pinion shaft must be straight. This assembly is oil-bathed; consult the service manual for the oil-changing procedure. You may want to inspect the wheel bearings and seals at this time.

STARTING SYSTEMS

The starting system is activated by a kickstarter lever or an electric starting button. There are two types of kickstarting systems: the primary drive starting system and the direct drive starting system.

Primary Drive Starting System

This starting system, which is located in the primary drive, allows the motorcycle to be started in any gear when the clutch is disengaged. This system consists of a kickstarter lever, a drive shaft, drive gear, idler gear, driven gear, and a kick pawl assembly. The kickstarter lever is connected to the drive shaft and drive gear. Pushing the lever down turns the engine over. The lever returns to its normal position, and this movement must disengage the drive gear so that the engine does not rotate in the wrong direction. To ensure safe starting, the drive gear may be manufactured with a ratchet assembly that engages in only one

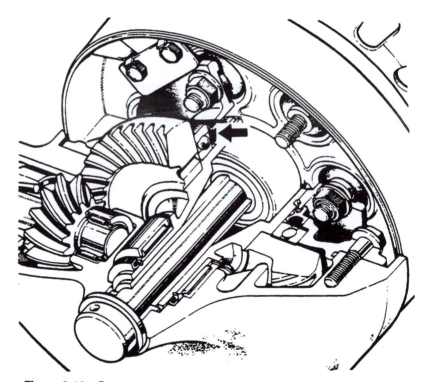

Figure 6-40 Rear gear case on a shaft drive (American Suzuki Motor Corporation).

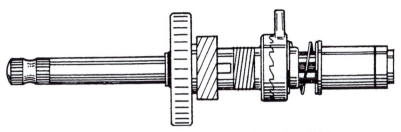

Figure 6-41 Ratchet assembly (American Suzuki Motor Corporation).

direction and freewheels in the other direction (Fig. 6-41). Or the drive gear may be manufactured with spring-loaded pawls that push against the gear and prevent it from rotating in the opposite direction (Fig. 6-42).

The drive gear is meshed with the kickstarter idler gear. The idler gear allows a rotation change of the primary driven gear. The kickstart driven gear on the clutch basket turns the crankshaft to start the engine without turning the transmission when the clutch is disengaged. This starting system is found on most off-road motorcycles (Fig. 6-43).

Direct Drive Starting System

This system is less expensive and is found on most kickstarting street motorcycles. The direct drive starting system is located in the transmission and can only be activated when the transmission is in neutral. When the kickstarter lever is pressed down, the kickstarter gear, which is usually the ratchet type, meshes with the low gear on the mainshaft. This system runs to the transmission and the clutch hub. The clutch must be engaged to allow the starting system power to flow from the clutch plates to the clutch basket to turn the engine over (Fig. 6-44).

Electric Starting System

This system is the most popular and works as well as the automotive system, so many of today's larger motorcycles do not use kickstarters. An electric starting system acts as a quick test of the electrical system. If there is not enough current to activate the starter motor, there may not be enough current to activate the coils and run the other electrical components. The electric starting system operates like the primary drive starting system but uses a small electric motor. The motor uses a gear or chain to turn either the countershaft, mainshaft, or crankshaft (Fig. 6-45). This motor will be described in Chapter 11.

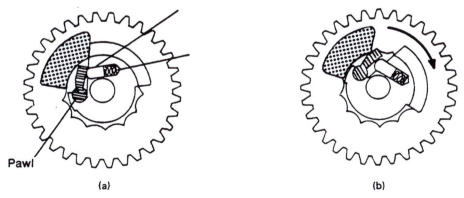

Pawl

(a)   (b)

Figure 6-42 Pawl: (a) disengaged; (b) engaged (American Suzuki Motor Corporation).

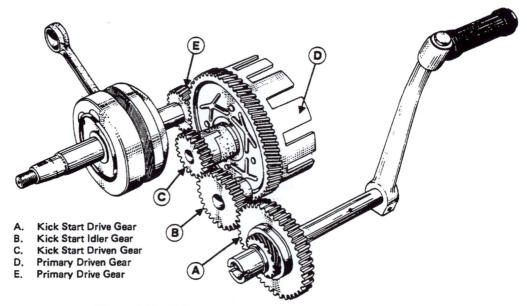

A. Kick Start Drive Gear
B. Kick Start Idler Gear
C. Kick Start Driven Gear
D. Primary Driven Gear
E. Primary Drive Gear

Figure 6-43 Primary kickstarter system (American Suzuki Motor Corporation).

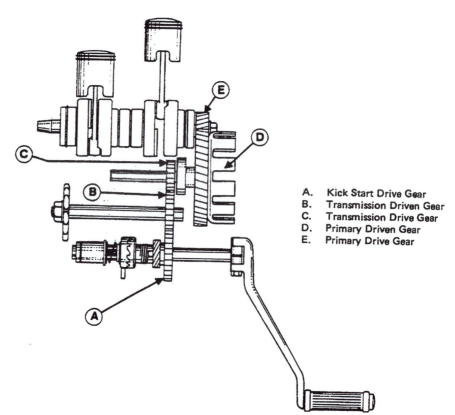

A. Kick Start Drive Gear
B. Transmission Driven Gear
C. Transmission Drive Gear
D. Primary Driven Gear
E. Primary Drive Gear

Figure 6-44 Direct drive starting system (American Suzuki Motor Corporation).

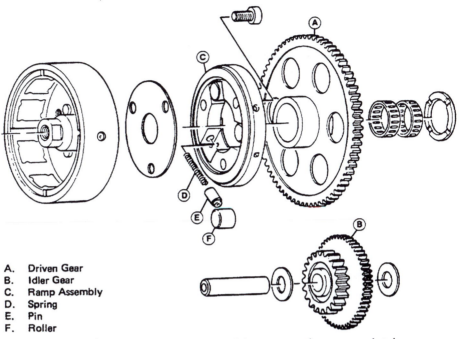

A. Driven Gear
B. Idler Gear
C. Ramp Assembly
D. Spring
E. Pin
F. Roller

Figure 6-45   Electric starter drive gear and one-way clutch
(American Suzuki Motor Corporation).

SERVICING STARTING SYSTEMS

Each starting system must be inspected for wear or damage in specific areas. Consult the service manual for servicing and replacement procedures.

Primary Drive Starting System

Inspect the bolt that is located where the kickstarter lever is splined to the shaft. This bolt tightens the lever to the shaft, and it may come loose and allow stripping of the splines. Inspect the shaft for straightness. Engine backfire, the motorcycle falling from the kickstand, or modifying the engine for high compression may cause this shaft to bend.

Inspect the drive gear, driven gear, and idler gear for broken or cracked teeth. An out-of-tune engine can cause the teeth to break. Check the position of the circlip that secures the idler gear.

Check the return-stop assembly that prevents the shaft from making a complete rotation and returns the shaft to its proper location. Inspect the ratchet engagement jaws for wear. Check the pawls for dirt and wear, and check the spring for weakness. Overheating the engine oil once can weaken this spring.

Direct Drive Starting System

Inspect the bolt at the kickstarter lever and shaft. If the lever occasionally slips or presses down too far, check for broken teeth on the kickstarter drive gear. This gear is usually the thinnest gear on the transmission. The kickstarter shaft is longer than the primary drive starting system shaft and bends more easily. If the starter does not engage, a weak engagement spring at the drive gear could be at fault. On some models, the return spring is located in the primary drive system.

Electric Starting System

Gears or chains are used to activate either the countershaft, crankshaft, or the mainshaft to start the engine. Inspect a chain for excessive stretch and sprocket wear. If the starter motor operates but the motorcycle does not start, the chain may be broken.

A special ratchet or clutch type of gear is located on the end of the starter motor or shaft to prevent the starter from being driven while the engine is running. Inspect the gear teeth for wear and the shaft for straightness.

Some motorcycles use a special drive gear shaft for direction change. If this shaft is bent, it causes binding from the starter motor.

If the motor does not activate the starting system, check the battery voltage at the cable terminal. If voltage is present, consult the service manual for starter replacement or rebuild procedure.

chapter 7

Lubrication and Cooling Systems

Power output is continuously increasing because of the advances in motorcycle engine technology, and this has created an additional strain on vital engine components. To keep pace with engine developments, lubrication and cooling systems have been studied and improved. Research has produced a new breed of synthetic lubricants to compete with highly modified mineral-based oils. Sophisticated liquid-cooled engines have been introduced to prevent high-temperature destruction and reduce overall engine noise.

The first section of this chapter explains the composition of oil, the purpose of lubrication, and the design, operation, and servicing of motorcycle lubrication systems. The second section describes the principles of heat transfer and the design, operation, and servicing of cooling systems.

THE COMPOSITION OF OIL

The composition of oil begins with a stock that is either mineral-, synthetic-, or vegetable-based. The quality of these three oils depends on the base stock as well as the additives used.

Mineral-Based Oils

Mineral-based oils begin as crude oil, which comes from the ground. The crude oil is heated in a process called fractional distillation. This process separates the lubricating oil from the other hydrocarbons in crude oil. Thin and thick stocks are blended into the lubricating oil until the desired viscosity or thickness is achieved. Mineral-based oil performs poorly without additives. Sulfur and phosphorus compounds are added to improve the oil's extreme pressure (EP) properties. Antioxidants, detergent dispersants, viscosity improvers, and other chemicals are added to improve the effectiveness of the oil. The base stocks added to mineral-based oils do not wear out; however, the additives do.

Synthetic-Based Oils

Synthetic-based oils were developed during World War II when petroleum lubricants were not widely available. Synthetic oils are manufactured and consist of many additives that are blended to increase the oil's effectiveness. Synthetic oils operate efficiently over a wider range of temperatures than petroleum-based oils.

Vegetable-Based Oils

Vegetable- or castor-based oils have excellent lubrication properties, but modern synthetics are effective longer and do not produce sludge and varnish. Castor-based oils build up sludge and varnish, which causes piston rings to stick. Because they also break down quickly, castor-based oils are normally used only for racing applications.

THE PURPOSE OF LUBRICATION

The purpose of lubrication is to clean, cool, seal, and lubricate. As oil flows through the engine, it cools the parts by absorbing heat. The circulating, heated oil then falls to the sump or crankcase to be cooled. Some engines also have an oil cooler to further reduce oil temperature and extend the life of the oil. Oil detergents and dispersant additives hold dirt, varnish, carbon, and other contaminants in suspension until they are removed as the oil travels through the oil filter. Contaminants that cannot be removed by the oil filter are suspended and removed when the oil is drained. Oil helps seal the combustion chamber as well as metal-to-metal parts and neoprene seals on sliding or rotating shafts. Lubricating oils have a cushioning effect between moving parts as the oil must be squeezed out before the metals can make contact. Oil also prevents corrosion inside the engine.

Friction occurs any time two moving surfaces contact each other. A lubricant provides a film between moving parts to eliminate contact and reduce friction. Hydrodynamic lubrication occurs when there is no metal-to-metal contact and a film of oil is constantly maintained between moving parts. During hydrodynamic lubrication, friction is primarily caused by the resistance of the oil. Under extreme pressures, or in the absence of a suitable supply of oil, boundary conditions and metal-to-metal contact occurs. The degree of friction depends on the extreme pressure properties of the oil in use.

A motorcycle contains a number of moving parts, and each has special lubrication requirements (Fig. 7-1). The type of oil used is determined by the amount of expected load, the type of load, the type of components, and servicing considerations.

Loads

Loads are identified by the type of motion found at the bearing surfaces. Load motion is either rolling or sliding motion or a combination of the two as found in meshing gears.

Rolling Motion: Ball, roller, and needle bearings operate with a rolling motion. These bearings are also known as antifriction bearings. Theoretically, they can operate without oil, but they function best with a light film of thin oil delivered by splash or mist. Excessive oil causes antifriction bearings to drag, which results in excessive friction and heat buildup. Excessive oil pressure can also cause the bearings to hydroplane which occurs when a bearing skids and stops rolling. Hydroplaning damages bearings by creating flat areas.

Sliding Motion: Plain bearings, bushings, camshaft lobes against rocker arms, and pistons against cylinder walls operate with a sliding motion. A film of oil must be constantly maintained between these moving parts. A rotating shaft must squeeze a wedge of oil out in front of it to ensure adequate lubrication for shaft rotation.

Type of Components

The type of lubrication used also depends on the type of components. Engine bearings are contained in a sealed crankcase. Usually, a supply of oil is poured inside the crankcase or a remote tank and fed to the engine bearings under pressure, or by splash or mist.

Grease, which is oil in a gel form, is the best lubrication for wheel bearings, steering head bearings, and swing arm bearings (Fig. 7-2). A throttle or clutch cable is best lubricated with a dry film or solid lubricant.

Servicing Considerations

Oil coats engine parts and helps to prevent rust and corrosion. Oil also absorbs shock and reduces wear. A layer of oil, especially between gear teeth, absorbs the shock of impact by

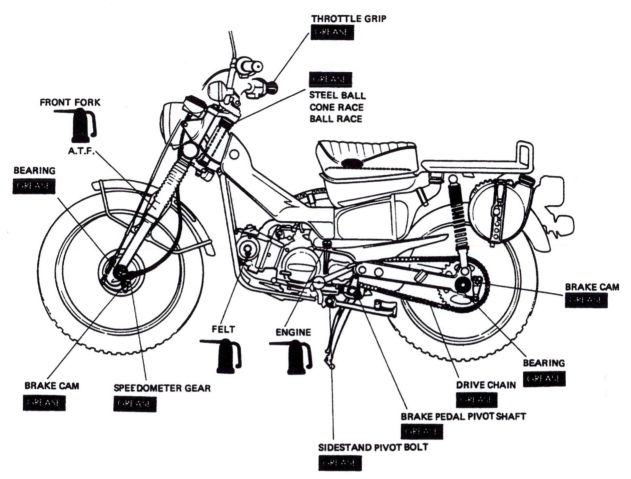

Figure 7-1 Typical lubrication points (American Honda Motor Company).

providing a hydraulic cushion. In addition, a constantly replenished supply of oil prevents engine overheating by carrying away the heat that is produced at load areas.

PROPERTIES OF OIL Any engine oil can provide moderate engine protection for a short period of time. A high-quality oil is one that has a long service life and gives total performance. Total performance includes:

Reducing Friction

The oil's thickness or viscosity is a major factor in reducing friction. A thinner oil creates less drag. Extreme pressure additives, such as zinc or phosphorus, help protect metal surfaces from direct metal-to-metal contact. This contact can occur when the lubricant is squeezed out from between moving surfaces such as cam lobes and gear teeth.

Minimizing Wear

Because oil drains from components while the vehicle is not operated, most wear occurs during the first few seconds after the engine is started. To minimize wear, oil should cling to moving parts after the engine is turned off. In addition, oil must flow efficiently at low temperatures and coat the top-end parts as soon as possible after the engine is started. The extreme pressure ingredients in oil help reduce part wear. When activated by the heat produced under boundary conditions, these ingredients coat engine hot spots and resist being scraped off.

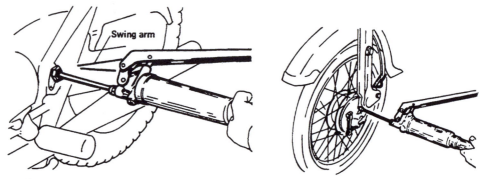

a) Swing arm pivot shaft and brake pedal.   b) Bottom-link fork.

Figure 7-2   Any part for which a grease nipple is provided needs to be greased periodically (Yamaha Motor Corporation, U.S.A.).

Maintaining Viscosity

Lubricants that resist the natural tendency to thicken when cold and thin when heated have a high viscosity index (VI). Engines that operate in varying climates need oil viscosities to match the temperatures. To maintain viscosity, chemical polymers are added to multigrade oils. Chemical polymers are sensitive to temperature and change their molecular shape under high temperatures so the oil flows easily and coats effectively in a wide range of temperatures.

Oxidative Stability

When air and oil come into contact with each other, the oxygen in the air combines with the oil. This is known as *oxidation*. Hot oil reacting with oxygen causes the oil to deteriorate. The oil can thicken as it becomes oxidized and acids can form. Proper attention to refining techniques and adding antioxidants to the oil help slow the rate of oxidation and increase the oil's service life.

Detergent Properties

Detergent dispersants keep dirt particles suspended until the oil goes through the filter or until the oil is changed. Without these dispersants, sludge and varnish will form.

Compatibility with Metals

Sulfur additives react with iron metals to form a low-friction layer. Some gear oils can damage plain bearings if the oil is used in the crankcase because the sulfur reacts to the soft alloys in the bearings.

Pour Point Depressants

Pour point depressants allow the oil to flow easily at lower temperatures. These additives lower the temperature at which the oil would stop flowing.

Foam Inhibitors

Rapidly moving engine parts can create air bubbles in the oil. This places air in the system where only oil is needed or required and can cause damage to the oil pump and bearings. Very small amounts of silicone are commonly used to eliminate foaming.

Other Functions

A good-quality oil should also prevent or carry away deposits, neutralize acids, and protect against rust.

**OIL TESTING AND
CLASSIFICATION**
A number of organizations, including the Society of Automotive Engineers (SAE), the American Petroleum Institute (API), the American Society for Testing and Materials (ASTM), and the National Marine Manufacturers Association (NMMA), are responsible for testing and designating oil ratings.

Oil Classification

Oil sold in this country is classified by its intended use. Oils for different purposes are categorized and labeled according to their viscosity and quality. The American Petroleum Institute (API) has set standards for oil performance and developed a code which is stamped on the container to indicate the oil's purpose and quality. The prefix "S" (spark) indicates that the oil is to be used in a gasoline engine; "C" (compression) designates use in a diesel engine. "S" or "C" is followed by another letter that indicates the oil rating. The further the letter is through the alphabet, the more additives the oil contains and the higher its quality.

Viscosity Ratings

Viscosity is the thickness of oil at a predetermined temperature. The Society of Automotive Engineers (SAE) has established crankcase oil grades based on centistoke viscosity units measured at 100°C (212°F) and centipoise viscosity units measured at a prescribed temperature below 0°C (32°F) (Fig. 7-3). To determine the viscosity of oil, a specific amount is placed in a container that has a metering orifice at the bottom. The oil is brought to the test temperature and then allowed to flow through the metering orifice. Thin oils have a low viscosity and flow more quickly than thick oils, which have a higher viscosity. The higher the SAE viscosity number, the thicker the oil. Low-viscosity oils flow quickly when cold. High-viscosity oils cling better to engine parts when the engine is shut off and resist

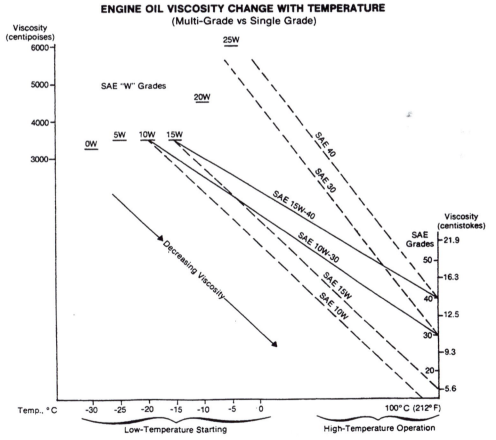

Figure 7-3   (Exxon Company, U.S.A.).

the tendency to thin. Multiviscosity oils perform both functions; they flow easily when cold and provide the protection of a heavier-weight oil as the engine warms to prevent metal-to-metal contact.

Oils tested for winter use are tested at 0°F (−18°C). SAE "W" (winter) grades include: SAE 5W, SAE 10W, SAE 15W, and SAE 20W. Summer grade oils are tested at 212°F (100°C). Summer SAE grades include: SAE 20, SAE 30, SAE 40, and SAE 50. Multiviscosity SAE grades include: SAE 5W-30, SAE 10W-30, SAE 10W-40, SAE 20W-40, and SAE 20W-50.

Engine oils can now be found with energy-conserving ratings which designate that the oils have less fluid friction while still meeting the viscosity requirements. Oils labeled "EC" offer at least a 1 percent reduction in fuel consumption, while oils labeled "EC II" reduce energy consumption by 1.5 percent.

FOUR-STROKE ENGINE LUBRICATION SYSTEMS

The earliest four-stroke motorcycles used a *total loss* lubrication system. Oil stored in a tank circulated to the bearings through an oil line. The oil dripped from the line onto the bearings and some splashed onto the piston and cylinder walls. The oil would then drain from the motorcycle to the ground. Modern motorcycle engines continuously circulate oil through the engine to ensure a constant supply of clean, cool oil.

A four-stroke engine lubrication system consists of a sump (crankcase) or tank to store the oil, an oil pump to pressurize the oil, an oil pressure relief valve, and oil lines and passageways to move the oil where required. Most four-stroke motorcycles also include an oil filter to remove contaminants from the oil and an oil pressure sensor or oil level sensor to warn of lubrication system failure. An oil cooler may be used on some motorcycles to reduce oil temperature and extend the life of the oil.

Sump Systems

The sump is the lower portion of the crankcase where the oil falls and collects after lubricating the major engine components. There are two types of sump systems: wet and dry. In a wet sump system, the oil is stored in the crankcase. Cooling fins may be placed along the sides and bottom of the crankcase to aid in cooling the oil (Fig. 7-4). Hot-running four-stroke engines may use a dry sump system which pulls the oil out of the crankcase and stores it in a separate tank (Fig. 7-5). This provides a lower center of gravity and better cooling of the oil. A pressure pump feeds the oil to the engine, and a scavenge pump pulls the oil from the crankcase and pumps it to the remote oil tank. An anti-leak back valve prevents the oil in the remote tank from leaking back to the sump and filling it with oil, which is known as *wet sumping*. When wet sumping occurs, the excessive oil in the crankcase is thrown up on the cylinder walls by the rotating crankshaft when the engine is started. This can cause excessive smoking and fouling of the spark plugs. The downward movement of the piston(s) can also force oil out of the crankcase breather or vent.

Oil Pumps

There are three main types of oil pumps in use today: trochoid, gear type, and plunger. The designer's choice of oil pump depends on whether the crankshaft bearings are roller or plain, the desired system pressures, and the type of sump in use.

Trochoid Pump: This type of pump is most commonly used today. A trochoid pump consists of a pair of rotors. The inner rotor is shaft driven. The lobes on the rotors squeeze oil out through passages in the pump body. A dry sump engine has two sets of rotors. One rotor is the main pump, and the other scavenges the crankcase and returns oil to the tank. Trochoid pumps are popular because they deliver the high volume of oil and pressure, up to 70 pounds per square inch, which are required by today's multicylinder engines with plain bearing crankshafts. Most trochoid pumps have a spring-loaded valve that bleeds off oil after the oil reaches a predetermined pressure.

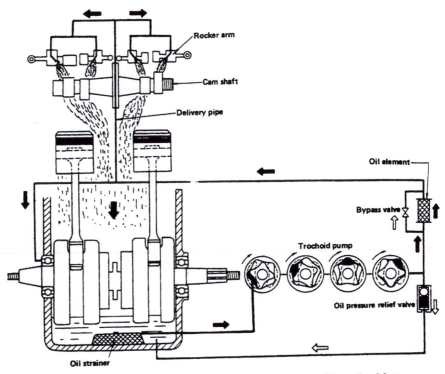

Figure 7-4 Wet sump system with trochoid pump (Yamaha Motor Corporation, U.S.A.).

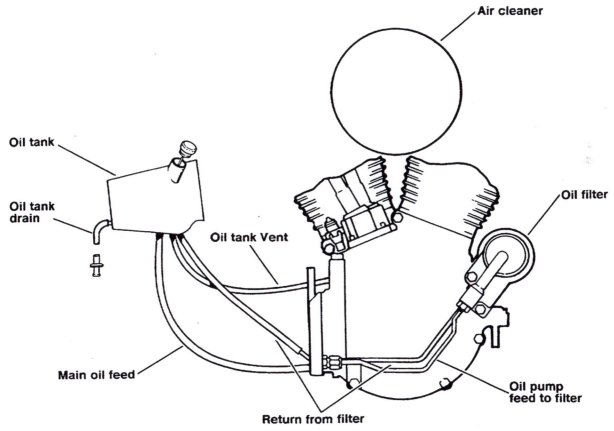

Figure 7-5 Four-stroke dry sump lubrication system (Harley-Davidson Motor Company, Inc.).

Gear and Plunger Pumps: These pumps are found on American and British motorcycles as well as some others. These motorcycles often have transmissions that use a separate supply of oil, which decreases the demand on the pump that lubricates the engine.

Modern motorcycles have efficient oil pumps. Designers take advantage of this and use the pump to feed as many areas as possible with pressurized oil. Some motorcycles use two pumps to ensure that the transmission is well lubricated. Early-model motorcycles rely on splash lubrication of the transmission, and the proper oil level must be maintained.

Most lubrication systems include an oil pressure relief valve to prevent damage that may be caused by excessive oil system pressure.

Oil Passages

Oil passages deliver the oil from the pump to the crankshaft, camshaft, and valves. Most lower ends have holes drilled in the cases to supply oil to the crankshafts and transmission shafts. Crankcases use baffles and deflection plates to ensure that an ample supply of oil is provided during acceleration and cornering. Some models use an external oil line to deliver oil to the top end. Most multicylinder engines simply pump oil up one or more cylinder studs. These studs are sealed with O-rings, which must be replaced any time the engine is overhauled.

Oil Filters

The oil filter removes the dirt and contamination that are suspended in oil by the detergent and dispersant additives. The most simple type of oil filter consists of a wire mesh screen. Because it primarily removes only larger contaminants, this type of filter is often used in conjunction with a paper, fiber, or centrifugal oil filter. Paper filters are available in "spin-on" and insertable styles. Insertable paper filters must be carefully installed to ensure proper operation. Some Harley-Davidson motorcycles use a fiber oil filter that is located in the oil tank. A centrifugal oil filter is a rotating container driven by the crankshaft. As the oil passes through the filter, the heavier contaminants stick to the sides, forming a thick paste that must be periodically scraped away.

Some motorcycles include an oil bypass valve. When the oil flow through the filter is restricted, the valve allows the oil to bypass the filter and provide essential lubrication to critical engine components.

SERVICING FOUR-STROKE LUBRICATION SYSTEMS   Even under ideal operating conditions, oil eventually loses its effectiveness. Oil in an engine crankcase is exposed to high temperatures, water, gas and acid vapors, and dirt. During engine operation, gases blow by the piston rings and enter the oil. All engines use some method for releasing these gases into the atmosphere, but if the crankcase ventilation is poor, these blow-by gases contaminate and dilute the oil. One way to reduce this contamination is to warm the engine thoroughly every time you prepare to ride; the hot engine will drive off the vapors and protect the oil. Short trips promote acid contamination, which reduces the effectiveness of the oil.

Changing the Oil and Filter

Every manufacturer provides a list of service procedures to be followed at specific intervals. Changing the oil and filter are part of these procedures. Before changing the oil and filter, be sure that the necessary tools and replacement parts are at hand:

> Oil drain pan
> Six-point socket and breaker bar
> Funnel
> New oil and a filter

Consult the service manual and use the following procedure:

1. Always drain the oil when it is warm. The detergent and dispersant additives that suspend dirt in the oil work best when the oil is warm, and warm oil flows freely and helps sludge to drain. Before continuing, let the engine components cool to avoid getting burned.

2. Use a six-point socket with a breaker bar. Filter and drain plug bolts are soft, and a six-point socket is the best tool for loosening them.

3. If you are servicing a dry sump system, drain both the tank and the engine.

4. The installation procedure varies depending on the type of oil filter. Consult the appropriate service manual for the correct procedure.

5. Replace any damaged sealing washers with new ones. While the motorcycle is upright on a level surface, check the oil level. Run the engine and check for leaks.

Oil Recommendations

Follow the manufacturer's recommendations for oil brand and viscosity. Generally, a multiviscosity oil is recommended. Use an oil that contains antioxidants, detergents, and dispersants to slow the formation of varnish and sludge deposits.

If you decide to use a synthetic oil, do not mix the old oil with the new as they may not be compatible. Drain all of the oil and change the filter before using a synthetic oil. Some synthetic oils are so slick that they will not allow the piston rings of a new motorcycle to seat. Wait until the motorcycle is broken in before using a synthetic oil. In those motorcycles that share the engine oil with the primary drive, synthetic oil may impregnate the friction plates and cause the clutch to slip.

Racing oil is designed exclusively for racing motorcycles. This oil has good extreme pressure properties, but it lacks the necessary detergents for everyday use.

Engine oils manufactured exclusively for motorcycles have additive packages that are specifically formulated for the extreme conditions under which today's motorcycles operate. These additives allow easier shifting, reduce transmission noise, and extend the life of the oil.

Servicing an Oil Pump

Cleanliness is essential while servicing an oil pump. Dirt particles can score a pump's rotors or plungers and cause reduced pressure output.

You will need a straightedge and feeler gauges. Check the service manual for the clearance specifications and inspect the pump for pockmarks or pitting, sheared woodruff keys, and warping of the pump body. Depending on the type of pump, look for scoring on the rotors, loose-fitting plungers, or chipped gear teeth (Fig. 7-6).

Lubricate the pump while reassembling it. Tighten down the body evenly to prevent warping. Make sure that all mating surfaces are clean to prevent pressure loss.

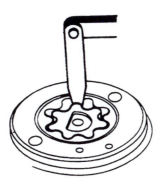

Figure 7-6 Checking oil pump rotor tip clearance (American Honda Motor Company).

Pressure Checking

Some engines have plugs for the installation of oil pressure switches. If plugs are not available, check the oil flow at a cylinder head nut over the stud that acts as an oil passage or at the top fitting of an external line. Check for oil leaks while the engine is running.

TWO-STROKE ENGINE LUBRICATION SYSTEMS
All two-stroke engines separate the transmission from the crankcase and piston. The transmission is filled with standard four-stroke oil or gear oil and is lubricated by splash. The crankcase and piston are lubricated by one of two methods. Either the oil is premixed with the gas, or a pump is used to inject oil into the intake manifold or crankcase to mix with the air/fuel. Oil injection requires an oil tank, pump, and injection lines. The amount of oil that is injected is determined by the throttle opening and rpm. A junction box connects the throttle cable and pump cable so that they open simultaneously (Fig. 7-7).

Two-Stroke Engine Oils

Two-stroke engine oils have extra demands to meet. In addition to performing the four previously listed functions, two-stroke engine oil must prevent preignition, stay suspended in gas, burn cleanly, and must not foul the spark plugs.

The premix and pump systems may use oils with different additives. Premix additives help the oil stay suspended in the gasoline. Pump system oil additives help the oil flow smoothly even in the coldest climates. Take care when selecting two-stroke engine oils. While some two-stroke oils are formulated to be used in both premix and oil injection lubricating systems, others are exclusively designed for one system or the other. Do not mix brands or different types of oils as they may not be compatible and could cause engine damage.

Because the oil is mixed with the gas, two-stroke engine lubrication is complicated. The swirling oil has a tendency to separate and lie at the bottom of the crankcase. After the oil is mixed with the gas, it is shot into the combustion chamber to be burned. Burning oil does not increase power, but if the oil does not burn cleanly, it will quickly lead to a decrease in power. Dirty burning results in carbon deposits which clog the exhaust pipes and ports. A thick layer of carbon on the piston crown and in the combustion chamber raises the compression ratio and leads to overheating. This layer of carbon acts as an insulator and prevents the combustion heat from escaping.

Two-stroke oil used in injection systems must be fairly thin in order to pass through small metering holes in the pump. Four-stroke engine oil should not be used in a two-stroke engine because it is the wrong viscosity, does not burn cleanly, and does not mix well with the gas.

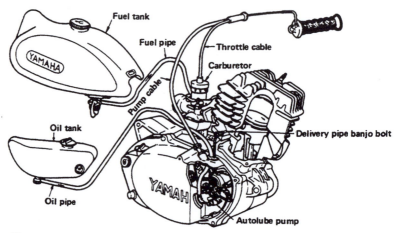

Figure 7-7   Two-stroke lubrication injection system (Yamaha Motor Corporation, U.S.A.).

SERVICING TWO-STROKE ENGINE LUBRICATION SYSTEMS

The premix system requires no service, but a pump system does.

Premix Tips

Premixing oil in the gas tank is one simple method of lubricating a two-stroke engine. Follow the manufacturer's recommendations for the oil-to-gas ratio (Fig. 7-8) and use the following formula to determine how much oil to add to the gas: 128 (the number of ounces in a gallon), divided by the recommended gas-to-oil ratio, multiplied by the number of gallons of gasoline, equals the number of ounces of oil to add. For example, this formula provides the following result when determining the amount of oil to be added to 2 gallons of gas when the manufacturer recommends a 20:1 gas-to-oil ratio:

$$128 \div 20 \times 2 = 12.8 \text{ ounces of oil to add}$$

Because all of the fuel and oil must go through the carburetor jets to reach the engine, changing ratios affects jetting. Adding more oil to the gas increases the mixture's viscosity and makes it more difficult for it to get through the jets. This creates a lean air/fuel mixture because the engine receives less gas from the volume of premix.

Servicing Pump Systems

Regardless of the brand, all pump systems require similar service. The tank must be filled. The pump requires cable adjustment, stroke adjustment, and bleeding.

Cable Adjustment: Injector pump output is calibrated to coincide with the throttle openings. The pump is operated by the throttle cable. To ensure proper synchronization, the pump is aligned by matching two marks. One mark is stationary and the other is on the cable arm. These marks usually align at the full throttle position or at idle. Check the manufacturer's specifications for the model you are servicing.

Stroke Adjustment: Some pumps have an adjustment to regulate the volume of oil injected at idle. The volume is changed by altering the length of the pump stroke. Different-sized shims can be installed to change the stroke.

Bleeding: If the oil tank has run dry or the lines are disconnected or replaced, air must be purged from the lines before the engine is started. Follow the service manual bleeding procedure. The metering orifices of two-stroke pumps may become clogged. Most pumps cannot be repaired and must be replaced. Consult the service manual.

Gas-to-Oil Ratio

		16:1	20:1	24:1	28:1	32:1	36:1	40:1	44:1	48:1
Gallons of Gasoline	1	8.0	6.4	5.3	4.6	4.0	3.5	3.2	2.9	2.7
	2	16.0	12.8	10.7	9.1	8.0	7.1	6.4	5.8	5.3
	3	24.0	19.2	16.0	13.7	12.0	10.7	9.6	8.7	8.0
	4	32.0	25.6	21.3	18.2	16.0	14.2	12.8	11.6	10.7
	5	40.0	32.0	26.7	22.9	20.0	17.8	16.0	14.5	13.3

Figure 7-8 The figures in this premix ratio chart indicate the amount of oil (oz.) required to achieve the desired ratio at the indicated volume of gasoline (Yamaha Motor Corporation, U.S.A.).

TROUBLE-SHOOTING LUBRICATION SYSTEMS   Use the following checklist to troubleshoot two- and four-stroke lubrication systems:

Oil Level Too Low: Normal oil consumption; external oil leaks; worn piston rings.

Oil Contamination: Oil or filter not changed often enough; faulty head gasket.

Low Oil Pressure: Faulty warning light switch; pressure relief valve stuck open; plugged oil pickup screen; oil pump worn.

High Oil Pressure: Pressure relief valve stuck closed; plugged oil filter or metering orifice; incorrect oil being used.

No Oil Pressure: Oil level too low; faulty oil pump; oil pump drive chain broken.

High Engine Temperature: Engine oil level too low; engine oil poor quality or incorrect oil.

COOLING SYSTEMS   Some of the energy produced by combustion is wasted heat. The purpose of a cooling system is to transfer this heat from the engine to the atmosphere as quickly as possible. There are three types of motorcycle cooling systems: internal, liquid, and air cooling. The following sections explain the fundamentals of heat transfer, how each cooling system operates, and how to service each system.

PRINCIPLES OF HEAT TRANSFER   Engine heat dissipates in two steps. First heat travels through the engine, and then it disperses into the air. Heat can be transferred through conduction or convection.

Conduction

Conduction occurs when heat diffuses from a high-temperature region through either solid material or stagnant fluid to a low-temperature region. Thermal conductivity depends on the material's thickness and its resistance to heat flow. Efficient conduction occurs when the engine metal conducts heat well, and there is a short distance between the hot combustion chamber and the cool air. The fewer layers of different material the heat must cross, the more efficient conduction becomes.

Convection

The transfer of heat by convection requires movement. Air or liquid moving over a hot surface picks up the heat and transfers it to the air.

Convection cooling is either natural or forced. Free-flowing air that strikes a hot vertical object rises as it is heated. A motorcycle that is idling at a stoplight is cooled by natural convection, but this cooling is not efficient. As the motorcycle begins to move and gain speed, the volume of air crossing over the engine increases tremendously. This blowing air is forced convection.

COOLING SYSTEM DESIGNS   All motorcycle engines are internally cooled. A motorcycle also has either a liquid or air cooling system.

Internal Cooling

All motorcycle designs provide internal cooling. Oil, oil coolers, rich fuel mixtures, and valve overlap participate in engine cooling.

Oil: Oil acts as a coolant by flowing over hot engine parts and drawing away heat. A thin oil cools efficiently because it pumps easily and has less hydraulic drag. Oil overheats under many conditions such as hot weather and heavy loads. Most oils begin to break down when the engine temperature exceeds 275°F. Sump temperatures may not reach this critical level, but hot spots at big-end bearings and under piston crowns can reach temperatures that exceed the sump temperature by 20 to 30 degrees. Finned sumps, remote oil tanks, and oil coolers are used to cool the oil.

Some manufacturers use the engine oil as the main method of dissipating unwanted heat from the engine. Oil jets squirt oil at the underside of the piston, and the oil absorbs the heat before falling to the crankcase to be cooled. Oil can pool on the cylinder head, which also absorbs heat. The engines of motorcycles that employ oil cooling have a large oil capacity and big oil coolers to eliminate the excess heat.

Oil Coolers: Oil coolers are the most efficient method for cooling engine oil. An oil cooler can reduce oil temperatures by as much as 30 degrees (Fig. 7-9).

Rich Fuel Mixtures: Rich fuel mixtures also cool the engine. Gasoline vapors that flow inside the engine cool critical parts.

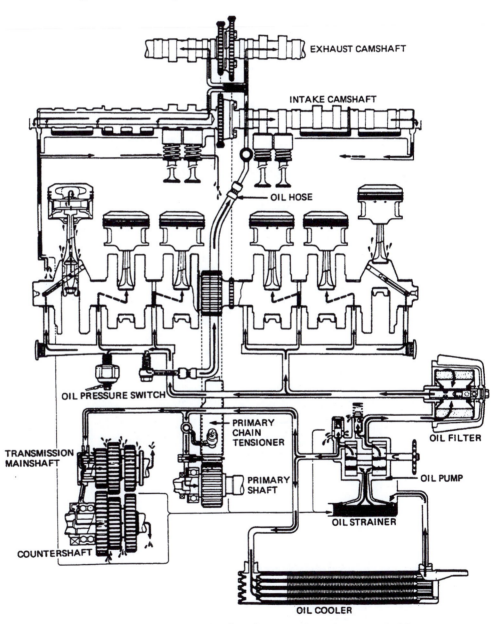

Figure 7-9   Engine lubrication diagram (American Honda Motor Company).

Valve Overlap: When four-stroke engine intake valves open, part of the fresh charge goes directly out the exhaust. This cools the exhaust valve. The combustion chamber, piston crown, and exhaust valve are also cooled when the atomized fuel changes to a vapor. Valve overlap occurs less often today because of EPA emission regulations.

Liquid Cooling

This is the most effective cooling system. Heat is dissipated through a water jacket that surrounds the cylinder and head. The water jacket also reduces engine noise. Liquid cooling eliminates engine hot spots and localized seizures. This system allows motorcycle engines to be tuned for higher power output. An air-cooled engine could overheat and lose power, but a liquid-cooled two-stroke engine can maintain peak power during hard use.

Liquid cooling has some disadvantages. The system is expensive, and the components add weight and complexity to the motorcycle. In some cases the cooling system components make engine servicing more difficult.

A typical liquid cooling system consists of a radiator and reservoir tank, a pump, water jackets, hoses, thermostat, fan, fan switch, temperature gauge and switch, radiator cap, and coolant. The coolant is normally a 50–50 mixture of distilled water and ethylene glycol. Distilled water is used because it does not contain minerals that could cause corrosion problems. Ethylene glycol does not improve heat transfer but rather lowers the freezing point and raises the boiling point of the distilled water. Coolant also contains lubricants, antifoaming additives, and corrosion inhibitors.

The coolant circulates through the jackets that surround the cylinders and heads. The coolant circulates only in the engine until it reaches approximately 180°F (82°C). At this point the thermostat begins to open to allow the coolant to travel to the radiator. Opening the thermostat at this temperature allows rapid engine warm-up and ensures a more constant engine operating temperature.

After the coolant reaches the radiator, heat is dispersed from the radiator into the air through forced convection. Heavy loads combined with high temperature or prolonged idling raise the coolant temperature excessively. For this reason, most systems include an electric fan that is operated by a temperature-controlled switch to assist cooling under these conditions (Fig. 7-10). The reservoir tank retains coolant that has expanded from the heat. After it cools and contracts, the coolant will be pulled back into the radiator.

The radiator cap is designed to pressurize the cooling system to a predetermined point, usually 12 to 14 psi. Pressurizing the cooling system raises the boiling point of the coolant. Every pound per square inch of pressure increases the boiling point of the coolant by approximately 3°F.

Motocross Liquid Cooling: Motocross motorcycles use a simplified system of liquid cooling. There is no thermostat and a high volume of coolant is constantly pumped through the complete system. The main difficulty with motocross cooling systems involves positioning the radiator and hoses so that they are not damaged during rugged riding. Some motocross models use the frame tubes as hoses (Fig. 7-11).

Air Cooling

Air cooling systems use fins of all shapes, sizes, and colors to rid engines of unwanted heat. An air cooling system is satisfactory in most applications. Production costs for motorcycles with air cooling are lower than for motorcycles with liquid cooling systems. But finned engines rely on forced convection to cool properly, and that requires motion. Prolonged idling can lead to serious overheating and possible seizure.

Cylinders and heads are finned to provide a maximum surface area for cooling (Fig. 7-12). The type and thickness of the metal used for the fins determine the cooling efficiency. Cast iron and aluminum alloys are commonly used. The choice of one over the

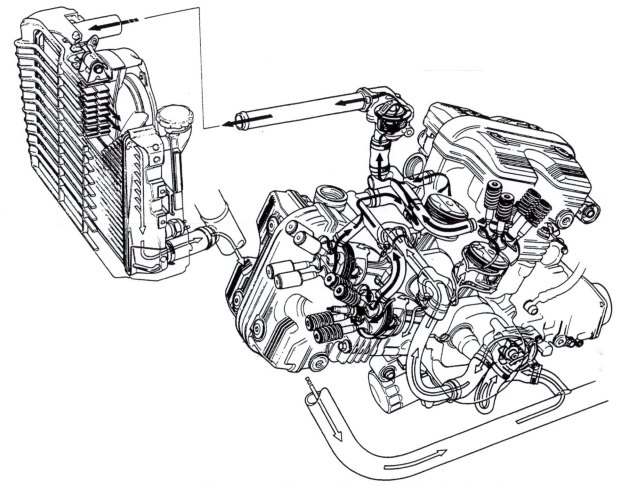

Figure 7-10 Liquid cooling system (American Honda Motor Company).

other depends on the metal's conductivity and on how much the metal distorts under heat. Years ago cast iron was used because of its low distortion. Aluminum alloys dissipated heat more efficiently but distorted badly. Today, cylinders and heads are made of a new aluminum alloy. The metal is thicker near the combustion chamber and exhaust to help stabilize temperatures and reduce uneven expansion.

SERVICING COOLING SYSTEMS   Consult the service manual and use the following procedures.

Servicing Liquid Cooling Systems

Servicing a liquid cooling system consists primarily of topping off the tank, draining and replacing coolant, and flushing the system.

Topping Off the Tank: The plastic reservoir tank is marked to indicate whether the tank is full or low. Add distilled water or the 50–50 coolant mixture. It is not necessary to open the radiator cap.

Draining and Replacing Coolant: Replace coolant at the manufacturer's specified intervals. Never open a radiator cap if the engine is hot. Coolant under pressure can burn you seriously. Drain coolant while the engine is cold. After draining the coolant, inspect the hoses carefully and replace any damaged or rotted hose. Add the coolant mixture and start the engine. With the radiator cap off, continue adding coolant until the level stabilizes at

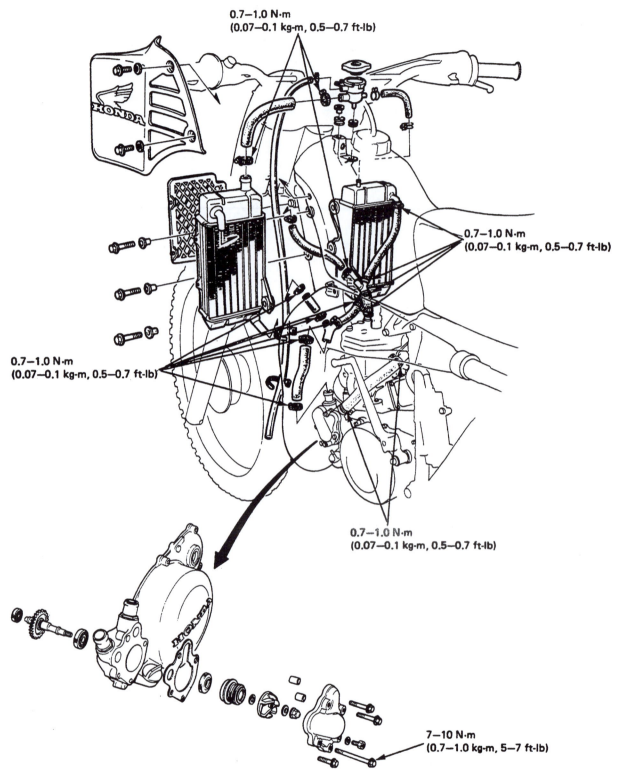

0.7—1.0 N·m
(0.07—0.1 kg-m, 0.5—0.7 ft-lb)

0.7—1.0 N·m
(0.07—0.1 kg-m, 0.5—0.7 ft-lb)

0.7—1.0 N·m
(0.07—0.1 kg-m, 0.5—0.7 ft-lb)

0.7—1.0 N·m
(0.07—0.1 kg-m, 0.5—0.7 ft-lb)

7—10 N·m
(0.7—1.0 kg-m, 5—7 ft-lb)

Figure 7-11 Two-stroke liquid cooling system (American Honda Motor Company).

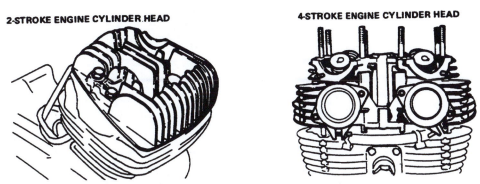

2-STROKE ENGINE CYLINDER HEAD

4-STROKE ENGINE CYLINDER HEAD

Figure 7-12   Air cooling fins (Yamaha Motor Corporation, U.S.A.).

the top of the radiator. The engine must warm up so the thermostat can open. Top off the reservoir tank and replace the radiator cap.

Flushing the System: Flush the system if you find any evidence of lime, scale, or rust in the cooling system. Drain the coolant and replace the drain plug. Add flushing compound, fill the system with water, and replace the radiator cap. Run the engine for 10 minutes at operating temperature and then drain the system. Repeat this procedure twice using plain water. Follow the procedure for replacing coolant.

Troubleshooting Liquid Cooling Systems

Many times an inspection reveals the cause of a problem. Engine temperature that is too low may be caused by a defective temperature gauge or by a thermostat that is stuck open. If the engine temperature is too high, the problem may be caused by:

> Defective temperature gauge
> Blocked coolant passages
> Poor engine tuning, advanced ignition timing
> Thermostat stuck closed
> Low coolant
> Radiator cap not holding pressure
> Defective fan thermostatic switch or motor
> Defective water pump
> Incorrect water-to-coolant ratio

Insufficient coolant may be the result of:

> Leak in the radiator, hose, or water jacket
> Radiator cap not holding pressure
> Coolant leaking to the oil
> Defective head gasket that allows coolant into the cylinders
> Leak or a kink in the hose that runs from the reservoir tank to the radiator

Most test procedures require pressure checking equipment and electrical testers. However, troubleshooting a cooling system without expensive equipment can be accomplished with the following procedure:

1.   Check the coolant protection quality with an antifreeze tester. A 50–50 mixture of water and coolant should be efficient to −34°F (Fig. 7-13).

Figure 7-13   Checking coolant condition with an antifreeze tester.

2. Run the engine and inspect the hoses, radiator, and water jackets for leaks. A leaking radiator cap oozes coolant.

3. If the engine is overheating, the thermostat could be stuck closed. When the engine is cold, remove the radiator cap and fill the radiator if necessary. Run the engine with the cap off. If the thermostat opens, the coolant will bubble. If no bubbling occurs and the pump is working, the thermostat is probably stuck closed.

4. Most systems have a small bleed hole directly below the water pump. If coolant leaks from this hole, the mechanical seal is defective.

Servicing Air Cooling Systems

Use the following procedures to ensure efficient air cooling:

1. Keep the engine clean. Dirt and mud coating the fins act as insulators to keep heat in.

2. Do not block the airflow to the engine.

3. Keep the engine tuned. Lean carburetion or incorrect ignition timing causes the engine to produce excessive heat.

4. Do not overload the motorcycle. The engine works harder and produces more heat when pulling a fairing, saddlebags, and a passenger.

chapter 8

Fuel Systems
and Carburetion

The purpose of a motorcycle fuel system is to store the fuel, mix it with air, and atomize and deliver the combustible mixture to the engine cylinders. The carburetor is the fuel system component that mixes the fuel and air and supplies the proper amounts of the mixture to the engine.

The first section of this chapter explains the design, operation, and servicing of fuel delivery systems. Information regarding fuel and emissions and the Environmental Protection Agency regulations concerning motorcycle emissions follow. The second section describes basic carburetor components and operation. Carburetor systems vary, and the different designs are presented. Finally, the design and operation of electronic fuel injection systems that do not use a carburetor and turbocharging systems that may or may not use a carburetor are discussed.

FUEL SYSTEM COMPONENTS

A fuel delivery system consists of (Fig. 8-1):

> Fuel tank
> Fuel gauge (optional)
> Fuel pump (optional)
> Petcock
> Fuel filter (optional)
> Fuel lines
> Air filter
> Carburetor
> Intake manifold

Fuel Tank

A fuel tank is made of steel, aluminum, fiberglass, or plastic. It is usually mounted on the frame in front of the seat and above the carburetor. The fuel tank is vented to atmospheric

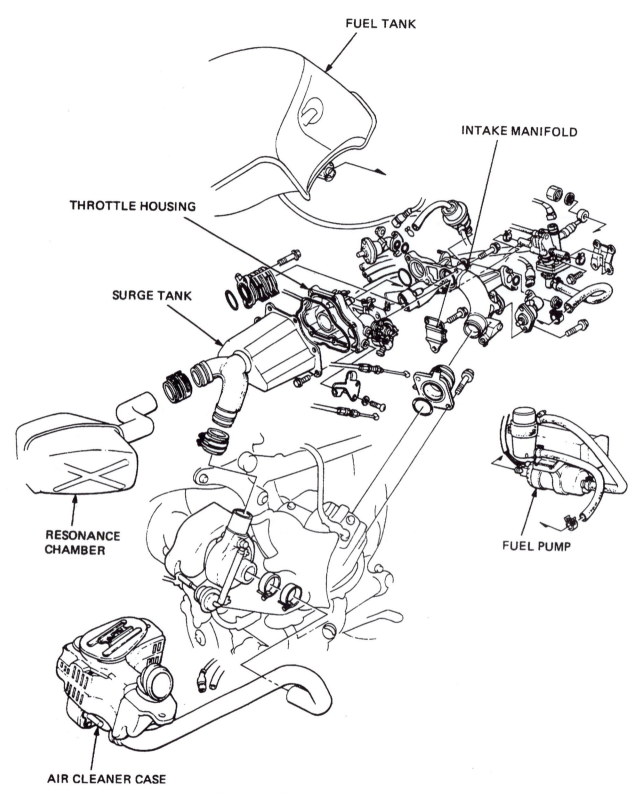

FUEL TANK

INTAKE MANIFOLD

THROTTLE HOUSING

SURGE TANK

RESONANCE
CHAMBER

FUEL PUMP

AIR CLEANER CASE

Figure 8-1 Fuel system components (American Honda Motor Company).

pressure, and gravity pulls the fuel from the tank into the carburetor float bowl. Some tanks include a float arm and float that operate a fuel gauge.

Fuel Pump

Engines with fuel injection or turbocharging systems or motorcycles that are designed with the fuel tank positioned lower than the carburetor require a fuel pump. A fuel pump is driven either mechanically or electrically. A mechanically operated pump is driven off an engine shaft, and two check valves ensure that the fuel travels in the proper direction. Motorcycles that use fuel injection or turbocharging systems normally use an electronic fuel pump with a pressure regulator that maintains uniform pressure in the injection lines.

Petcock

The petcock, also known as the fuel valve, is usually connected to the fuel tank and operated manually by a lever (Fig. 8-2). The lever usually has three positions: on, off, and reserve. When the lever is in the on position, the petcock opens and the fuel travels from the tank through the lines to the carburetor. The off position stops the flow of fuel. Normally, a small amount of fuel is retained in a reserve section of the tank. When the lever is in the reserve position, fuel from the reserve section is available after the main supply is depleted. Some petcocks include a sediment bowl to trap foreign particles that escape through the pickup tubes in the fuel tank.

Some petcocks are vacuum operated (Fig. 8-3). When the engine is not running and the lever is in the on or reserve position, a vacuum-operated petcock automatically prevents fuel from flowing. The lever that operates this petcock has an additional position, the prime position, to override the small vacuum diaphragm that prevents the fuel from leaving the petcock. The prime position is occasionally used when starting the engine.

The electronic vacuum petcock functions like the vacuum petcock. However, an electrical solenoid controls the vacuum to the diaphragm in the petcock. When the fuel tank runs low, a control unit sends voltage to the solenoid, and the solenoid shuts off the vacuum to the diaphragm in the petcock. When the reserve switch is manually turned to the reserve position, a voltage signal notifies the control unit to turn off the voltage to the solenoid. The petcock then functions normally.

Fuel Filter

Some fuel systems include one or two filters that prevent contamination in the fuel from entering the carburetor or fuel pump. Usually, a filter is located in the fuel tank over the

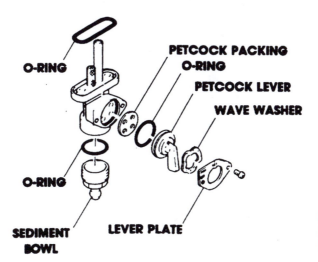

O-RING

PETCOCK PACKING
O-RING

PETCOCK LEVER

WAVE WASHER

O-RING

O-RING

SEDIMENT
BOWL

LEVER PLATE

Figure 8-2 Petcock assembly (Yamaha Motor Corporation, U.S.A.).

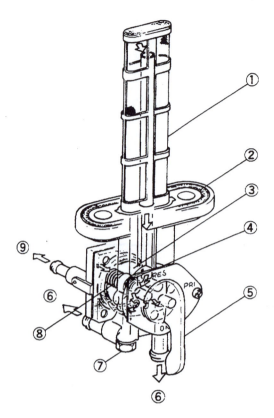

1. Filter	4. O Ring	7. Drain Plug	**Figure 8-3** Vacuum petcock
2. O Ring	5. Tap Lever	8. Spring	(Kawasaki Motors Corporation,
3. Diaphragm	6. Fuel	9. Vacuum	U.S.A.).

pickup tubes that lead to the petcock. An additional filter may be placed in the fuel line between the petcock and carburetor. Fuel filters consist of a nylon mesh or brass screen. Both types of filters require periodic cleaning, and filters in fuel lines may be replaced.

Fuel Lines

A fuel line delivers the fuel from the tank to the carburetor or fuel pump. The fuel lines must be securely attached to the petcock and carburetor to prevent leaks, and the diameter must be large enough so as not to restrict the fuel movement. Fuel lines are usually made of rubber or plastic, and some are reinforced or have an outer cover of nylon. The fuel line should be only as long as necessary and routed to avoid contact with extreme heat or a moving part.

Air Filter

The purpose of an air filter is to clean the air traveling to the carburetor and engine. Filtering the air prevents contamination of the engine components and increases their service life. Usually, an air filter is located inside an air box that is sealed to the carburetor air intake. There are three types of filters used on motorcycles: the paper element, oiled foam, and the oiled gauze filter.

Paper Filter: A paper filter consists of laminated paper fibers that are sealed at the ends or on the sides (Fig. 8-4). The paper filter is molded in a "W" pattern to increase the surface area and to decrease the restriction of air passing through it. Some paper filters include a supportive inner or outer shell of metal screen. Do not use oil on a paper filter. Replace this filter when it becomes excessively dirty; cleaning it with solvent or high air pressure can damage the paper fibers.

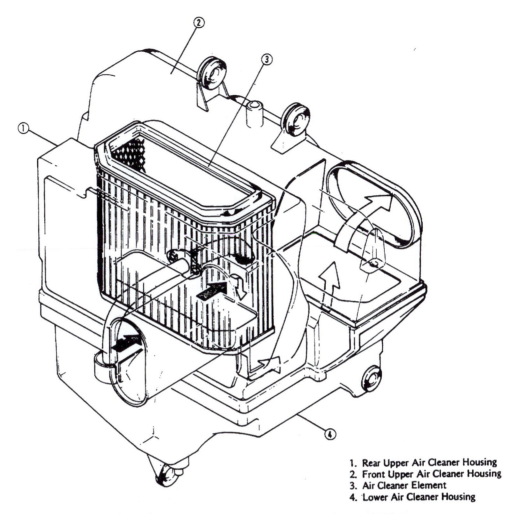

1. Rear Upper Air Cleaner Housing
2. Front Upper Air Cleaner Housing
3. Air Cleaner Element
4. Lower Air Cleaner Housing

Figure 8-4   Air box and paper air filter (Kawasaki Motors Corporation, U.S.A.).

Oiled Foam Filter: Oiled foam filters use oil and cellular foam to trap dirt and contamination (Fig. 8-5). The filter slows the incoming air, and as the air travels through the pores, the particles of contamination are stuck in the oil and left behind.

Gauze Filter: A gauze filter uses features of both the paper and foam filters. A gauze filter also requires oiling, consists of a laminated cloth material, and is formed in a "W" shape. Gauze and oiled foam filters can be washed and reused.

Carburetor

The purpose of the carburetor is to break down the fuel into very small parts so that it may begin to mix with the air. The carburetor varies the amount of fuel and air that are beginning to mix to allow variations of engine rpm. There are several carburetor designs, and these will be explained later in the chapter.

Intake Manifold

Once the air and fuel have begun to mix, the mixture continues on through the carburetor. The intake manifold delivers the mixture from the carburetor to the cylinders, and it allows the air and fuel to continue to mix during this delivery. The intake manifold is clamped,

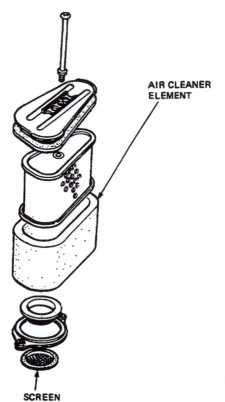

AIR CLEANER
ELEMENT

SCREEN

Figure 8-5 Foam air filter assembly
(American Honda Motor Company).

bolted, and sealed to the carburetor body and cylinder head port to prevent air from leaking into the cylinder. The size and shape of intake manifolds varies depending on the particular engine design, and they may be made of neoprene or aluminum.

SERVICING
FUEL SYSTEMS
Servicing fuel delivery systems is a simple procedure that involves inspecting and cleaning or replacing components. Fuel lines should be replaced when they become brittle with age. Fuel filters should be cleaned or replaced every 4000 to 6000 miles. Usually, the petcock can be removed after the gas tank has been drained; check the sealing O-ring on the petcock for wear. Flush the gas tank and clean the screen over the pickup tubes. Check the O-ring or cork gasket at the gas cap for wear.

FUEL
Today's fuels are made of hydrogen and carbon atoms known as hydrocarbons. Gasoline is removed from crude oil by a process called *fractional distillation*. During fractional distillation, the crude oil is heated to various separation points. Each hydrocarbon boils or vaporizes within a certain temperature range. Crude oil is heated in stages until all the various hydrocarbon classes have been individually vaporized and collected. Additives are then blended with the gasoline to give it distinct properties.

Octane and Octane Numbers

The octane number (ON) or octane rating assigned to fuel is a measure of the fuel's antiknock properties. The antiknock properties provide resistance to detonation. The octane number indicates whether the fuel will "knock" in a given engine under specific operating conditions. The higher the octane number, the higher the fuel's resistance to knock. However, you cannot produce more engine power by using a higher octane fuel than that recommended by the motorcycle manufacturer.

Several methods have been developed for rating octane. Two of the most commonly used methods are the research method and the motor method. The research method assigns a research octane number (RON). The motor method assigns a motor octane number (MON). The octane number displayed on gasoline pumps at fuel stations is the average of the RON and MON numbers.

Use a gasoline with an octane rating that meets the motorcycle manufacturer's minimum requirements.

Fuel Additives

Tetraethyllead was used for many years to prevent detonation and provide some surface lubrication to the valves. However, tetraethyllead has been almost completely replaced by additives that provide less pollution. Today isooctane and heptane are the main additives used in gasoline to resist detonation. While less polluting, these compounds are also considerably more expensive.

Modern gasolines contain a number of chemical additives that are designed to improve fuel quality. These additives are used to:

> Raise the octane number of the fuel
> Control surface ignition
> Reduce spark plug fouling
> Resist gum formation
> Prevent rust
> Reduce carburetor icing
> Remove carburetor or injector deposits
> Minimize deposits in the intake system
> Prevent valve sticking
> Reduce vaporization in hot climates
> Increase vaporization in cold climates

Oxygenated Fuels

An oxygenate is a liquid fuel component such as alcohol or an ether that contains oxygen. Adding oxygen to fuel helps reduce carbon monoxide emissions in some vehicles. The most popular additives, and the maximum amounts in which they can be used, are as follows:

> Methyl tertiary butyl ether (MTBE)—up to 15 percent
> Ethanol alcohol (gasohol)—up to 10 percent
> Methanol alcohol (gasolhol)—up to 5 percent

Additives and octane boosters can be purchased and added to the fuel to improve engine performance and extend engine life. However, they must be mixed in the correct ratio to be effective and prevent damage. Check the manufacturer's recommendations before using additives. Store and handle additives carefully. Many additives contain lead or other substances that are poisonous, irritate the skin, and may damage paint.

MOTORCYCLE EMISSIONS   Motorcycle emissions are a byproduct of the engine's combustion process. During the combustion process, the hydrocarbons in the fuel combine with oxygen in the air and are then released into the atmosphere through the engine exhaust. It is essential to control these emissions. Carbon monoxide is toxic, and under certain conditions hydrocarbons form a photochemical smog.

Environmental Protection Agency Regulations

The U.S. Environmental Protection Agency (EPA) and the California Air Resources Board require that motorcycle manufacturers comply with exhaust emission standards. Motorcycles built after January 1, 1983 must also comply with applicable noise emission standards for one year or a specific amount of miles after the time of sale. Fines have been established to discourage technicians and dealers from altering emission control devices to increase engine performance. Anyone in the business of selling, repairing, or leasing motorcycles is subject to a fine if an emission-related component is removed or rendered inoperable. Federal law prohibits the removal or alteration of any component which conducts exhaust gases. Replacing parts of the intake and exhaust system, as well as any moving part of the vehicle, with parts other than those specified by the manufacturer is also prohibited by federal law.

The manufacturer must design and produce a motorcycle that burns fuel efficiently, and the motorcycle must be serviced periodically to maintain a high level of efficiency. A technician must be able to recognize what causes emissions and how to lower emissions through engine adjustments.

Emission Control Systems

To meet EPA regulations, current motorcycles are produced with systems that help control emissions. A crankcase emission control system routes crankcase emissions through the motorcycle's air cleaner and then into the combustion chamber. The condensed crankcase vapors accumulate in an air/oil separator and drain tube. The separator and drain tube should be periodically emptied and cleaned.

An exhaust emission control system includes a secondary air supply system that introduces filtered air into the exhaust port. Fresh air is drawn into the exhaust port whenever there is a negative pressure pulse in the exhaust system. This charge of fresh air helps promote burning of the unburned exhaust gases and helps to convert a substantial amount of hydrocarbons and carbon monoxide into harmless carbon dioxide and water.

An evaporative emission control system, which is currently required only in California, routes fuel vapors from the fuel tank and carburetor into a charcoal canister. The fuel vapors are stored in the canister and absorbed by the charcoal when the engine is not running. When the engine is started and running, a purge control diaphragm valve opens to allow the fuel vapors in the canister to be drawn into the engine through the carburetor. When the purge control valve opens, an air vent control valve also opens to allow fresh air to be drawn into the carburetor.

The catalytic converter system is designed so that when negative pressure occurs in the exhaust pipes, fresh air is allowed to flow through the air cleaner and reed valve system and then into the exhaust pipes. The two-stage catalytic converter uses this fresh air to convert the hydrocarbons and carbon monoxide in the exhaust gas into water and carbon dioxide. Motorcycles equipped with a catalytic converter must use unleaded gas; other types of fuel will damage the system.

Emission Sources

Many factors determine the amount of emissions that a motorcycle produces. When it is new, the motorcycle engine design specifications limit emissions. But with use and wear the engine requires servicing to return it to peak performance. An increase in emissions can be caused by wear or malfunctions in the engine, ignition system, and carburetor.

Engine: Wear creates a gradual loss of sealing between piston rings and cylinder walls. This leads to a loss in engine compression, which creates inefficient combustion and excessive hydrocarbons and carbon monoxide in the exhaust. Poor sealing also allows the

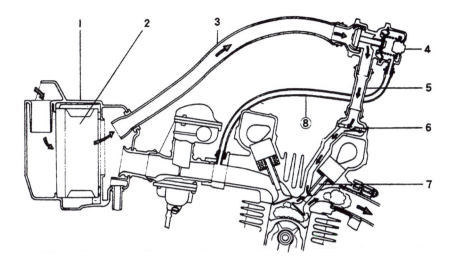

1. Air Cleaner Housing
2. Air Cleaner Element
3. Air Hose
4. Vacuum Switch Valve
5. Air Hose
6. Air Suction Valve
7. Exhaust Valve
8. Vacuum Hose

Figure 8-6 Crankcase ventilation system (Kawasaki Motors Corporation, U.S.A.).

combustion gases to blow by the rings and enter the crankcase. Once in the crankcase, these burned/unburned gases combine with oil vapors and then escape to the atmosphere through the crankcase vent. Until EPA regulations came into effect, most motorcycles simply ran a hose from a crankcase vent to the underside of the motorcycle. The vapors blew onto the ground and unburned hydrocarbons were released into the atmosphere. Today's street motorcycles are required to recirculate and burn crankcase vapors (Fig. 8-6). The hose from the crankcase is either routed directly to the air filter or to a breather/separator where water vapor and other contaminants are separated from the fumes. The contaminants are routed to a sludge trap, which should be emptied during normal servicing.

Ignition System: Unburned hydrocarbons are usually caused by an ignition system malfunction. A weak spark or no-spark condition prevents combustion from taking place or results in poor combustion, which allows unburned fuel vapors to pass through the engine. Unburned hydrocarbons are caused by worn ignition points, early or retarded ignition timing, worn or fouled spark plugs, or a charging system malfunction.

Carburetor: The most common cause of carbon monoxide is rich carburetion. Richer fuel mixtures produce proportionate increases in carbon monoxide (Fig. 8-7). The size of carburetor jets is determined at the factory to meet engine demands and emission standards, and normally, jets do not need adjustment. The slow-speed screws are sealed to prevent tampering, but a slow-speed adjustment may be necessary during carburetor synchronization. After carburetor synchronization, use an exhaust gas analyzer (EGA) to confirm that the emissions have not increased.

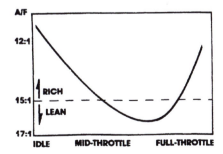

Figure 8-7 Typical air/fuel ratios (Yamaha Motor Corporation, U.S.A.).

Controlling Motorcycle Emissions

Maintaining a good state-of-tune ensures low emissions. Follow the manufacturer's specifications and pay particular attention to ignition timing, valve adjustment, and carburetor synchronization.

Exhaust Gas Analyzer: An exhaust gas analyzer is a valuable servicing tool that produces an accurate analysis of an engine's emissions and indicates the exact amount of hydrocarbons and carbon monoxide in the exhaust. With these data a technician can determine if an engine problem exists, diagnose the problem, and locate its source.

The EGA is either attached or inserted into the exhaust pipe. When in the operational mode it draws the exhaust through a chamber filled with reflected infrared waves and measures emissions at idle and simulated cruise speed. The exhaust is compared with a sample of fresh air, analyzed, and the amounts of carbon monoxide and hydrocarbons are displayed on two meters (Fig. 8-8). Carbon monoxide is measured by the percentage in the total volume of gas; hydrocarbons are measured in parts per million (ppm).

The contents of the exhaust indicate the engine's efficiency. The correct ratio of air and fuel should combine to burn completely. Because carbon monoxide is partially burned fuel, a high carbon monoxide reading indicates that there is too much fuel in the mixture or the air is restricted. High float levels, worn carburetor parts, an improperly adjusted carburetor, or a leaking choke can cause an excessively rich mixture. A dirty air cleaner, restricted carburetor air jet, or blocked air inlet can restrict the amount of air entering the engine.

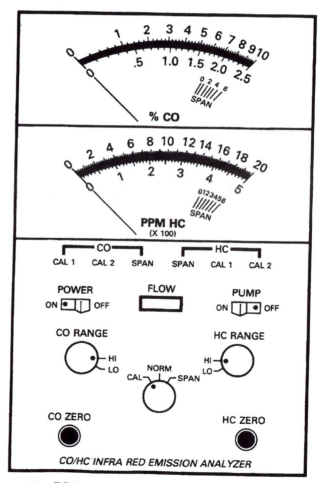

Figure 8-8   EGA meters (Yamaha Motor Corporation, U.S.A.).

Hydrocarbons are raw fuel that has passed through the engine without burning. A high hydrocarbon reading indicates inefficient combustion and wasted fuel caused by an ignition, carburetion, or engine malfunction. However, there are always some hydrocarbons in the exhaust because combustion is never completely efficient.

Study the operations manual carefully before using an EGA. The machine must be checked and calibrated before every use. The motorcycle must also be properly prepared before testing. The idle speed, oil, and engine temperature must be carefully monitored to give accurate readings. An EGA cannot be used on two-stroke motorcycles because the oil in the exhaust coats the mirrors in the EGA and ruins the calibration.

CARBURETION

There are several different types of carburetors, but the fundamental operation is the same for each type. This section first explains the principles of carburetion and the basic carburetor design and operation. Then the design and operation of different types of carburetors and the service procedures for each type are presented.

PRINCIPLES OF CARBURETION

The design and operation of all carburetors are based on the following physical laws:

Liquid takes the shape of its container.

A contained liquid produces pressure in proportion to its depth.

Liquid in two chambers that are connected will be at the same level in both chambers unless there is a difference in air pressure on top of the liquid. Then the level will be higher in the low-pressure chamber.

Air under high pressure moves toward air under low pressure if the two areas are connected by an enclosed pathway.

Air that travels through a constriction increases in speed and decreases in pressure along the sides of the constriction. This is known as the *Venturi principle*.

A liquid can be atomized or broken down into smaller parts.

BASIC CARBURETOR COMPONENTS

A carburetor assembly consists of the following components (Fig. 8-9):

Carburetor body	Float arm and pin
Slide or throttle butterfly	Float needle and seat
Return spring	Air bleed circuit(s)
Slow jet	Fuel or air screw
Needle jet	Cold-starting device
Jet needle	Synchronization screws
Main jet	Gaskets and O-rings
Float bowl and floats	

Carburetor Body: The carburetor body is precisely machined and usually made of aluminum. It supplies the location points for the carburetor components. The diameter of the carburetor's center opening is smaller than either end of the carburetor. This creates a constriction which is called the *venturi* (Fig. 8-10). A carburetor also includes one or more passageways that contain a jet. These passageways allow the fuel from the float bowl to travel to the venturi.

Slide or Throttle Butterfly: A carburetor includes either a slide or throttle butterfly that is mounted inside the carburetor body. The operation of a slide and of a throttle butterfly differs, but both regulate pressure in the venturi. This controls the fuel/air mixture and the amount to reach the engine which controls the engine speed.

The throttle is located on the right handlebar and is connected to the slide or throttle butterfly by a cable. When the rider twists the throttle twist grip counterclockwise, the slide is raised or the throttle butterfly is opened to allow more air through the venturi.

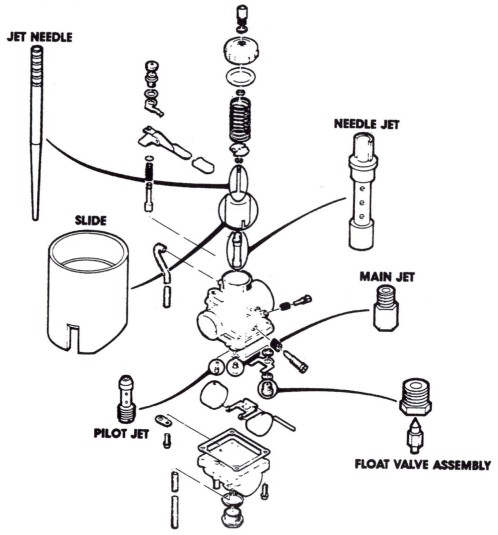

JET NEEDLE

NEEDLE JET

SLIDE

MAIN JET

PILOT JET

FLOAT VALVE ASSEMBLY

Figure 8-9 Exploded slide carburetor (Yamaha Motor Corporation, U.S.A.).

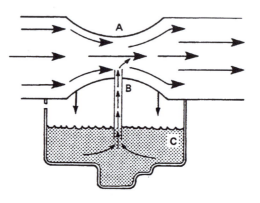

A.   Venturi
B.   Emulsion Tube
C.   Fuel in Float Bowl

Figure 8-10 Venturi (American Suzuki Motor Corporation).

Return Spring: The return spring ensures that the slide or throttle butterfly closes after the rider releases the turning force of the throttle. The return spring is located inside the slide or outside the throttle cable linkage.

Slow Jet: This jet is usually small and made of brass. It is screwed or pressed into the passageway at the lower carburetor body. One end of the jet is submerged in the fuel in the float bowl; the other end has an outlet in or near the venturi. The slow jet provides the proper amount of fuel to the venturi at idle and just above idle. This jet is also called the *pilot or idle jet.*

Needle Jet: This jet is longer and larger than the slow jet, and it is pressed or screwed into the passageway at the lower body directly under the center of the slide. The needle jet operates in conjunction with the jet needle to control the amount of fuel available during the midrange throttle opening.

Jet Needle: This thin, tapered needle connects with the bottom of the slide and moves in and out of the needle jet as the slide is raised or lowered. The jet needle helps control the amount of fuel that is used as the engine increases rpm's during midrange operation.

Main Jet: The main jet is made of brass or plastic and screwed or pressed into place. It is usually located near the bottom of the needle jet. The diameter of the orifice in the main jet is the final factor in determining the amount of fuel that is available from three-quarters to full throttle (Fig. 8-11).

Float Bowl and Floats: The float bowl is connected to the bottom or side of the body below the venturi. The float bowl contains fuel, is vented to atmospheric pressure, and usually includes an overflow tube. One or more hollow floats made of brass or plastic float on the fuel and rise and fall with the fuel level.

Float Arm and Pin: The float arm either has a float attached to it or it is contacted by independent floats. The locating pin holds the float arm in place at the lower body.

Float Needle and Seat: The float needle fits inside the seat and acts as a valve to allow fuel to enter the float bowl. The float needle and seat open and close to maintain a consistent amount of fuel in the float bowl. When the floats raise the float arm, the float arm pushes the needle into the seat, which blocks the fuel from entering the float bowl (Fig. 8-12).

Air Bleed Circuit: The air bleed circuit consists of passageways in the carburetor body that intersect with various jet outlet passageways. The jets meter the fuel, and the air bleed circuit supplies air to initiate this atomization process.

Fuel or Air Screw: A carburetor usually includes either a fuel or air screw to allow adjustments of the air/fuel mixture at slow speeds.

Cold-Starting Device: The carburetor body incorporates some type of cold-starting device to help provide a richer fuel mixture when the cold engine is started. The different cold-starting systems will be explained later in the chapter.

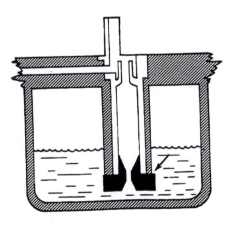

Figure 8-11   Main jet (American Suzuki Motor Corporation).

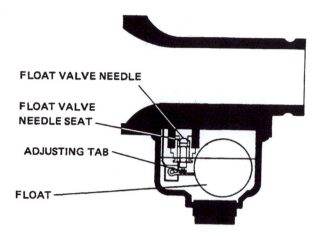

FLOAT VALVE NEEDLE

FLOAT VALVE
NEEDLE SEAT

ADJUSTING TAB

FLOAT

Figure 8-12 Float needle and seat (Yamaha Motor Corporation, U.S.A.).

Synchronization Screws: Synchronization screws are found on most multicylinder, multicarburetor engines. These screws allow adjustment of the slide valves or throttle valves so that they open the same amount to allow an even amount of air to flow into each cylinder. On some models synchronization is accomplished through cable adjusters. After synchronization is achieved, the idle speed may require adjustment.

Gaskets and O-Rings: The carburetor assembly includes several gaskets and O-rings that prevent fuel from leaking out and air from leaking in.

BASIC OPERATION   The negative pressure that occurs on the downstroke of intake sets the air in motion and creates an airstream from the air filter toward the intake valve opening and cylinder. The carburetor is positioned in this airstream between the intake valve and the air filter. As the air passes through the carburetor venturi, the venturi creates an increase in velocity and a drop in pressure.

The pressure difference of 14.7 pounds per square inch (psi) on the fuel in the float bowl and less than 14.7 psi on the fuel in the jet pushes the fuel through the jet and into the venturi (Fig. 8-13). The size of the jet and the amount of pressure difference determine the amount of fuel that travels into the venturi. The jet constricts the fuel to increase the speed of travel and begins to atomize the fuel.

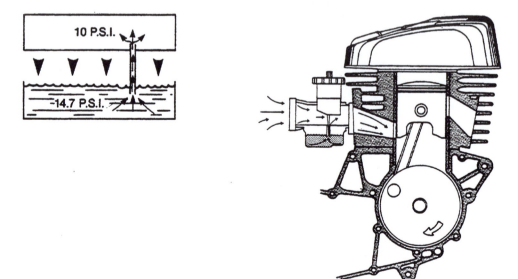

Figure 8-13   Intake operation (American Suzuki Motor Corporation).

CARBURETOR DESIGNS

There are three types of carburetors used on motorcycles today: slide, constant velocity, and fixed venturi. Each of these three types can be used on a four-stroke motorcycle. Most two-stroke motorcycles use a slide carburetor.

Slide Carburetors

The slide carburetor is also called a *variable venturi carburetor*. The rider can control the size of the venturi opening by operating the throttle to raise and lower the slide. This controls the air volume, velocity, and pressure in the venturi (Fig. 8-14).

When the engine is idling, the slow jet and its passages supply fuel to the venturi. The slide is closed, and a very small amount of air rushes beneath the slide and through the venturi. This creates the richer mixture that is required for slow-idle speed. The normal air-to-fuel ratio is approximately 15 or 16 parts air to 1 part fuel measured by weight; at idle the air/fuel ratio is approximately 10:1.

In most slide carburetors, the slow jet operates in conjunction with an air bleed circuit. The air bleed circuit allows air to travel through a passage from the air filter side of the carburetor to a point that is past the slow jet restriction but before the fuel outlet to the venturi. This additional air helps to complete the atomization process and begins dispersing the air with the fuel (Fig. 8-15). The slow jet fuel passage or the air bleed passage may include an adjustment screw to vary the fuel mixture at idle.

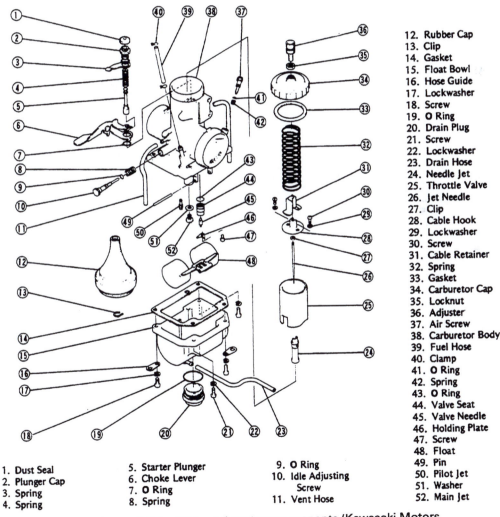

12. Rubber Cap
13. Clip
14. Gasket
15. Float Bowl
16. Hose Guide
17. Lockwasher
18. Screw
19. O Ring
20. Drain Plug
21. Screw
22. Lockwasher
23. Drain Hose
24. Needle Jet
25. Throttle Valve
26. Jet Needle
27. Clip
28. Cable Hook
29. Lockwasher
30. Screw
31. Cable Retainer
32. Spring
33. Gasket
34. Carburetor Cap
35. Locknut
36. Adjuster
37. Air Screw
38. Carburetor Body
39. Fuel Hose
40. Clamp
41. O Ring
42. Spring
43. O Ring
44. Valve Seat
45. Valve Needle
46. Holding Plate
47. Screw
48. Float
49. Pin
50. Pilot Jet
51. Washer
52. Main Jet

1. Dust Seal
2. Plunger Cap
3. Spring
4. Spring
5. Starter Plunger
6. Choke Lever
7. O Ring
8. Spring
9. O Ring
10. Idle Adjusting Screw
11. Vent Hose

Figure 8-14   Slide carburetor components (Kawasaki Motors Corporation, U.S.A.).

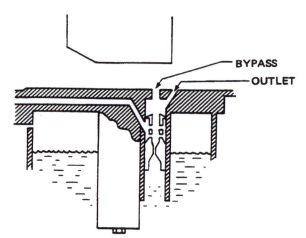

Figure 8-15 Slow-speed circuit with air bleed outlet and bypass (American Suzuki Motor Corporation).

Some types of slide carburetors have more than one passage or bypass port to the venturi from the slow jet. This allows additional fuel to escape the slow jet circuit as the throttle is opened just above idle speed.

Engine rpm increases when the rider moves the throttle twist grip and the slide moves to increase the venturi opening. The slide is cut away on the side that faces the incoming air. The larger the cutaway, the more air is available to the venturi. An increase in fuel must accompany the increase in air to the venturi to maintain the correct mixture. The slide cutaway controls the amount of air available during the transition from the slow jet to the jet needle and needle jet. The cutaway size is usually stamped on the bottom of the slide. The larger the number, the greater the size of the cutaway.

The jet needle and needle jet control the midrange mixture. As the slide moves to allow more air into the venturi, the jet needle moves out of the needle jet to allow more fuel to enter the venturi with the air. The slide cutaway and the needle jet work together to provide a smooth transition from idle as the engine increases rpm's. The slow-speed circuit continues to provide fuel, but this is a small amount of the total fuel supplied to the venturi.

Slide and constant-velocity carburetors use one of two types of needle jets: a primary or bleed type (Fig. 8-16). A primary needle jet usually consists of a hooded projection into the venturi and a single air bleed passage located just below the venturi. The primary needle jet controls the degree of negative pressure at the needle jet outlet and helps to complete the atomization process.

The bleed-type needle jet has no projection into the venturi; instead, the air bleed passage corresponds with the many holes along the needle jet. This perforated tubing efficiently atomizes the fuel before it leaves the needle jet.

The jet needle may have a clip that can be raised or lowered to change the mixture or the time of transition. If the jet needle is positioned lower in the needle jet, the clip position is raised, the transition occurs later, and the mixture is leaner for the same throttle opening. If the jet needle is raised, the clip position is lowered, the transition occurs earlier, and the mixture is richer (Fig. 8-17). Many of today's jet needles cannot be adjusted because of EPA regulations. Jet needles and tapers are available in various sizes.

As the engine continues to increase rpm's, the air velocity increases and the pressure difference between the venturi and the float bowl becomes greater. The increased pressure difference causes more fuel to be pushed through the slow, needle, and main jets. The main jet is either connected to the bottom of the needle jet or it is aligned and sealed with the needle jet. The main jet determines how much fuel leaves the needle jet outlet.

Constant-Velocity Carburetors

The components and operation of a constant-velocity carburetor are similar to a slide carburetor with two main differences. First, the throttle cable connects to a throttle butterfly valve instead of a slide. The throttle butterfly valve is a flat disk or plate at the engine side

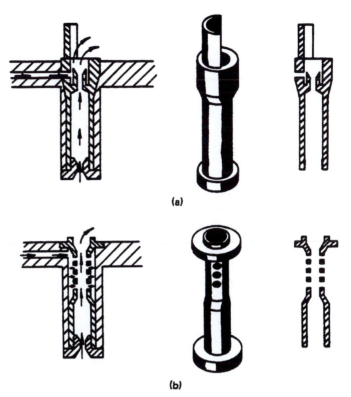

Figure 8-16   Needle jets: (a) primary; (b) bleed (American Suzuki
Motor Corporation).

of the carburetor that controls the amount of engine vacuum available to the venturi
(Fig. 8-18).

Second, the slide in a constant-velocity carburetor operates in conjunction with either
a vacuum-operated piston or a diaphragm, which is why this design is often called a *vacuum carburetor*. A hole in the bottom of the slide allows the negative pressure in the venturi to travel through the slide and up into an enclosed area above the vacuum piston or diaphragm. The lower piston or diaphragm chamber is vented to atmospheric pressure by a
passage from the chamber to the carburetor air inlet. The amount of pressure difference between the upper and lower chambers determines how far the slide rises. As the pressure
drops in the venturi and upper chamber, the atmospheric pressure in the lower chamber
helps to push the slide higher. The correct amount of air and fuel is supplied based on
engine vacuum demand (Fig. 8-19).

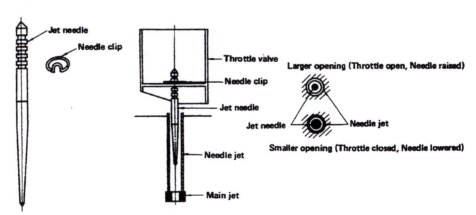

Figure 8-17   Jet needle clip positions (Yamaha Motor Corporation,
U.S.A.).

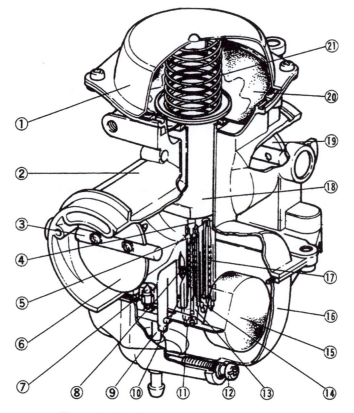

1. Upper Chamber Cov
2. Carburetor Body
3. Choke Shaft
4. Jet Needle
5. Needle Jet
6. Choke Valve
7. Float Valve Needle
8. Pilot Jet
9. Overflow Pipe
10. Plastic Plug
11. Secondary Main Jet
12. Drain Screw
13. Needle Jet Holder
14. Primary Main Jet
15. Float
16. Float Chamber
17. Bleed Pipe
18. Vacuum Piston
19. Throttle Shaft
20. Diaphragm
21. Spring

Figure 8-18 Constant-velocity carburetor components (Kawasaki Motors Corporation, U.S.A.).

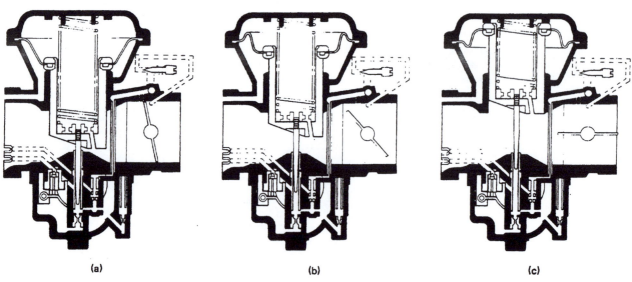

(a) (b) (c)

Figure 8-19 Sequence of constant-velocity carburetor operation: (a) idle; (b) half throttle; (c) full throttle (Yamaha Motor Corporation, U.S.A.).

This system, unlike the slide carburetor, automatically compensates for changes in the mixture that are caused by changes in altitude. Because atmospheric pressure drops as altitude increases, the pressure difference in the upper and lower chambers is reduced, which provides less fuel to the engine.

Many constant-velocity carburetors use the same jet systems as slide carburetors. But the slow-speed circuit has several bypass ports to provide additional fuel to the airstream just as the throttle butterfly is opened. This assists the transition from idle to midrange. A fuel screw allows adjustments of the idle mixture. Some constant-velocity carburetors use a primary main jet that is positioned after the bypass ports to control the mixture until the jet needle and needle jet are reached. The main jet is still connected to the bottom of the needle jet, but it is called the *secondary main jet* in this type of carburetor. The secondary main jet does not control the mixture until the pressure difference raises the slide at least halfway up (Fig. 8-20).

Some constant-velocity carburetors include an air cutoff valve. This additional system helps enrich the mixture under rapid deceleration and reduces lean misfire. The air cutoff valve is located on the carburetor body and consists of a diaphragm that is operated by manifold vacuum. When the throttle valve is suddenly closed, the increase in pressure moves the diaphragm plunger and partially blocks the air to the slow jet circuit. This provides the engine with less air to the slow jet and gives the engine a richer mixture (Fig. 8-21).

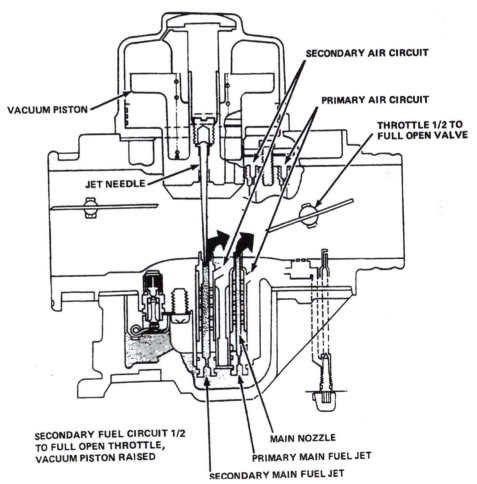

Figure 8-20 Three-jet carburetor (American Honda Motor Company).

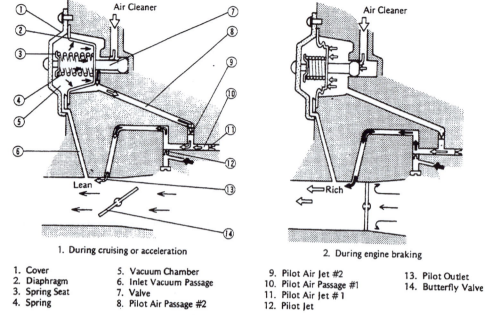

1. During cruising or acceleration   2. During engine braking

1. Cover	5. Vacuum Chamber	9. Pilot Air Jet #2	13. Pilot Outlet
2. Diaphragm	6. Inlet Vacuum Passage	10. Pilot Air Passage #1	14. Butterfly Valve
3. Spring Seat	7. Valve	11. Pilot Air Jet #1	
4. Spring	8. Pilot Air Passage #2	12. Pilot Jet	

Figure 8-21   Air cutoff valve (Kawasaki Motors Corporation, U.S.A.).

Fixed Venturi Carburetors

The fixed venturi carburetor design is simple and the operation is precise. The shape of the venturi is determined by the manufacturer. A slide is not used to vary the size of the opening nor is a moving jet needle used. The float system is similar to those of slide and constant-velocity carburetors (Fig. 8-22).

The jetting sequence is similar to the carburetors previously described, but a fixed venturi carburetor includes more precise bypass ports and air bleed circuits to smooth the transition from one jet to the next. Usually, the slow jet circuit operates in conjunction with an air bleed circuit, and there are three to five bypass ports (Fig. 8-23). A fuel screw is

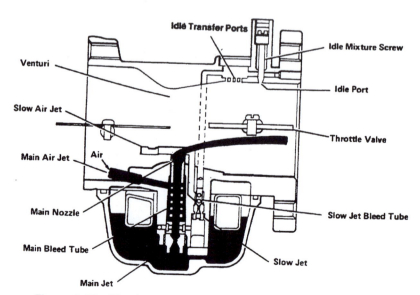

Figure 8-22   Fixed venturi carburetor (Harley-Davidson Motor Company, Inc.).

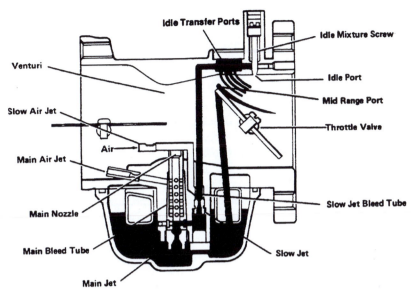

Figure 8-23   Several bypass ports on a slow jet system (Harley-Davidson Motor Company, Inc.).

located near the leading edge of the throttle butterfly. Some fixed venturi carburetors include a midrange port with a jet or fixed passage from the float bowl to a single outlet. This port is uncovered by the throttle butterfly before the butterfly is half opened. The main jet operates with a main bleed tube and an air bleed circuit to deliver fuel when the throttle is approximately half opened.

A fixed venturi carburetor often includes an accelerator pump. The accelerator pump forces a precise amount of fuel at a specific time into the carburetor air intake. Usually, a plunger or diaphragm is connected to a passage, and a nozzle delivers a fine spray of fuel into the carburetor air intake. The accelerator pump is synchronized to the throttle opening. When the throttle returns to a lesser position, the plunger or diaphragm chamber fills again with fuel. One or two ball check valves maintain the proper fuel level and cause the fuel to move in the proper direction. The accelerator pump helps reduce engine hesitation caused by a lean mixture, assists the transition of fuel from the bypass ports to the main jet, and improves performance. An accelerator pump may also be used on slide and constant-velocity carburetors (Fig. 8-24).

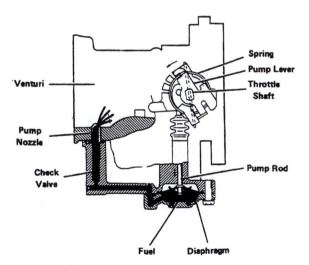

Figure 8-24   Accelerator pump (Harley-Davidson Motor Company, Inc.).

Carburetor Variations

The way in which air flows through a carburetor depends on the engine configuration and manufacturing design. Most carburetors are based on the *sidedraft* design, and air flows horizontally from one side of the carburetor to the other. In a *downdraft* carburetor design, the air flows vertically from top to bottom of the carburetor (Fig. 8-25). In the *semi-down-draft* carburetor design, the airflow is angled. This design is popular on some models because the airflow traveling to the combustion chamber follows a straighter path. There are fewer twists or turns as the air travels through the carburetor, so there is less chance of air/fuel separation. A straighter airflow path can increase the volume of air/fuel entering the combustion chamber and produce more efficient combustion.

Carburetor slides can be round, square, flat, or the radial-flat slide design, which is half round and half flat. The flat and radial-flat carburetors provide a very narrow venturi area. The more narrow the venturi area, the greater the concentration of negative pressure under the slide. This results in smoother transition and better throttle response.

SERVICING CARBURETORS Servicing carburetors requires adjustments, synchronization, and cleaning.

Carburetor Adjustments

Carburetor adjustments include adjusting the throttle cable, the idle adjustment screws, the air or fuel screw, and carburetor synchronization. Carburetor adjustments should only be made when the engine compression is good, the valves are properly adjusted, the ignition system is timed and operating properly, and the air filter is clean.

Throttle Cable Adjustment: Loosen the throttle cable before making any adjustments. Idle adjustments affect the cable length. After all adjustments have been made, consult the service manual and adjust the throttle cable to its proper length (Fig. 8-26).

Air Screw Adjustment: The air screw is a blunt-nosed adjustment screw that is located on the air filter side of the carburetor. The air screw projects into the air bleed circuit. As the air screw is turned in, air in the passage is blocked to create a rich mixture at idle. When it is screwed out, more air is allowed to pass and this creates a leaner mixture at idle. Consult the manufacturer's specifications for the correct adjustment setting (Fig. 8-27).

Fuel Screw Adjustment: The fuel screw is located at the engine side of the carburetor. This screw has a fine point that projects into a slow jet outlet passage. As the fuel screw is

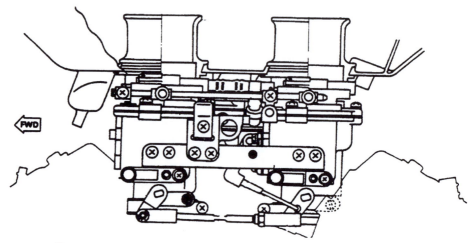

Figure 8-25 Downdraft carburetors (Yamaha Motor Corporation, U.S.A.).

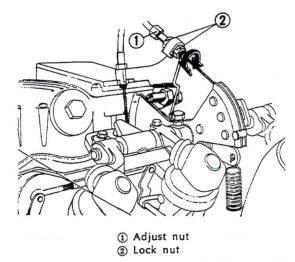

① Adjust nut
② Lock nut

Figure 8-26   Carburetor cable linkage and adjustment (American Honda Motor Company).

turned in, the fuel is blocked to create a leaner mixture at idle. When it is screwed out, more fuel passes, which enriches the mixture. Some carburetors use a limiter cap to cover the fuel screw. Check the manufacturer's specifications for the correct adjustment setting. This adjustment affects the mixture at idle. Some carburetors have both fuel and air screws.

Carburetor Synchronization: Proper synchronization is essential to efficient carburetor operation. A carburetor synchronization adjustment is required to adjust the carburetor throttle valve openings and to synchronize the vacuum in each carburetor intake port. This procedure should be performed during routine engine maintenance or whenever the carburetors are disassembled and reassembled.

Synchronization should be made when the engine is in good mechanical condition and running at operating temperature while the transmission is in neutral. Use fans to prevent the engine from overheating.

Locate the fittings that are positioned either on the cylinder head port or in an area on the cylinder head port, the intake boot, or at the front of the carburetor. Install an adapter or

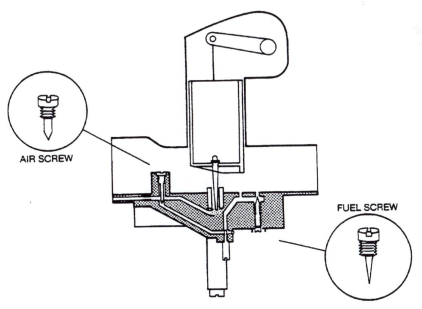

Figure 8-27   Air and fuel screws (American Suzuki Motor Corporation).

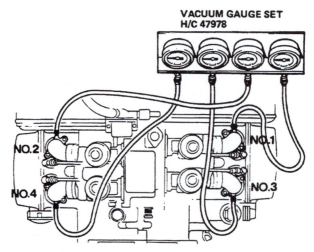

Figure 8-28   Carburetor synchronization using vacuum gauges (American Honda Motor Company).

connect a vacuum gauge or mercury stick to the fitting or adapter (Fig. 8-28). Consult the service manual, and adjust the idle rpm to the specified idle speed.

If the motorcycle is equipped with a base carburetor, consult the service manual to determine the location of the base carburetor and the carburetor synchronization adjusting screws (Fig. 8-29). Turn the synchronization adjusting screws until the difference between the vacuum in the base carburetor intake port and the vacuum in the remaining carburetor intake ports meets the manufacturer's specifications.

If these adjustments do not improve the engine response, clean the carburetor, check the float setting, and inspect the carburetor mounting for air leaks.

Cleaning: A carburetor that is excessively dirty or that has been allowed to sit with fuel in it for a prolonged period should be cleaned in a special cleaner. Completely disassemble the carburetor and set aside all rubber and plastic parts. Place the remaining parts in the cleaner and follow the manufacturer's directions and recommendations. Rinse the parts in warm water and blow them dry with compressed air.

Servicing Two-Stroke Engine Slide Carburetors

Many of the jets on modern carburetors are fixed and cannot be adjusted; however, the jetting of a two-stroke engine slide carburetor must be changed if significant altitude differences are encountered. The internal jetting varies depending on whether the engine is oil-

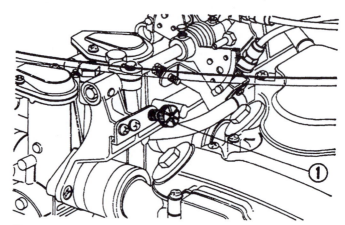

Figure 8-29   Throttle stop screw (American Honda Motor Company).

injected or uses a fuel/oil premix. If the fuel and oil are premixed, the carburetor jets are larger so that the proper amount of fuel can move with the oil through the jet. If the engine has an oil injection system, the oil pump must be synchronized to the throttle cable movement. Consult the service manual for the correct adjustment procedure.

Servicing Constant-Velocity Carburetors

Synchronize the carburetor as described previously. Set the throttle butterflies to open equally. If the carburetor uses a vacuum piston, check the piston for the proper clearance and for contamination. Dirt wears the seal and decreases the slide's responsiveness. If a vacuum diaphragm is used, inspect it under a bright light for holes or cracking. A leak in the diaphragm prevents a pressure difference and produces no slide movement. The engine may idle, but it will not respond to midrange throttle opening.

COLD-STARTING SYSTEMS

All carburetors include a cold-starting system to provide and control the richer mixture that is necessary to start the engine. Cold-starting mixtures are approximately 3 parts air to 1 part fuel. Some European carburetors use a tickler cold-starting circuit, but most modern motorcycles use either a mixture enricher or a plate air restrictor system.

Tickler System

This system uses a pin and spring-loaded rod that projects into the float bowl. When the rider pushes the pin down, the rod further submerges the floats. This causes the float needle to come off the seat and allows more fuel to enter the float bowl. As long as the rider holds the pin down, fuel enters the float bowl. When the fuel begins to run out of the overflow tube, the fuel level is high and closer to the outlet ports for starting. The engine is easily flooded with this system, and overflowing gas is hazardous. Emission standards no longer allow this type of system to be used on street motorcycles.

Mixture Enricher System

When activated, a mixture enricher operates like a minicarburetor. It consists of a passageway into the float chamber, a fuel supply jet, an air bleed circuit, an outlet port past the slide on the engine side of the carburetor, and a plunger valve that opens to allow the air bleed and fuel jet passages to meet (Fig. 8-30). The air combines with the fuel and moves toward the engine. This type of cold-starting system operates when the throttle valve is closed.

Plate Air Restrictor System

This system controls the air that is available during starting. A disk valve or sliding plate blocks the air to the carburetor venturi at any throttle opening. The disk or plate has a hole cut into it to allow some air to pass. Or it has a spring-loaded window that the air pushes open to prevent the mixture from becoming too rich (Fig. 8-31).

ELECTRONIC FUEL INJECTION

Electronic fuel injection has long been used on cars, heavy diesel equipment, and racing engines. An electronic fuel injection system increases performance and fuel economy because it monitors engine conditions and provides the correct air/fuel mixture based on the engine's demand. An electronic fuel injection system includes a computer, a fuel delivery system, and an air delivery system (Fig. 8-32). There are two types of electronic fuel injection systems: indirect injection and direct injection. The indirect injection system is most commonly used. In this design, the injector is located in the intake manifold or throttle body. In the direct injection system, the injectors are located in the combustion chamber. The direct injection system requires very high fuel pressure.

Both systems utilize an onboard computer that monitors air and engine temperature, ignition timing, throttle position, air volume, and fuel pressure. The computer receives in-

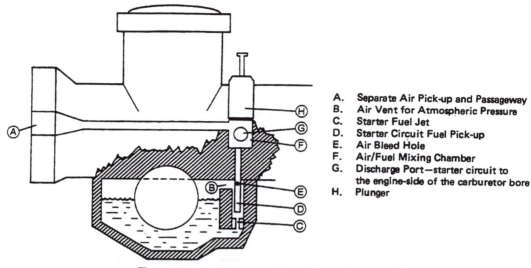

A. Separate Air Pick-up and Passageway
B. Air Vent for Atmospheric Pressure
C. Starter Fuel Jet
D. Starter Circuit Fuel Pick-up
E. Air Bleed Hole
F. Air/Fuel Mixing Chamber
G. Discharge Port—starter circuit to the engine-side of the carburetor bore
H. Plunger

Figure 8-30 Mixture enricher (American Suzuki Motor Corporation).

formation from sensors located at various points in the engine and uses this information to determine the proper air/fuel ratio for the given operating condition.

A fuel injection system eliminates the carburetor, but the fuel delivery system is more complex. The fuel delivery system consists of a fuel tank, fuel filters, fuel pump, fuel injectors, pressure regulator, and feed and return lines (Fig. 8-33). A fuel filter is used in both the fuel tank and the fuel line to remove any contamination that could damage the fuel pump or injectors. The fuel pump is electronically driven and controlled by the computer to supply each injector with an equal amount of fuel. The amount of time the injectors are open is known as the *discharge duration*. The longer the discharge duration, the richer the air/fuel mixture. Constant fuel pressure is delivered to the injectors. The pressure regulator ensures equal pressure on the fuel at each injector based on the amount of pressure at the intake manifold. The pressure regulator controls the return line to the fuel tank. It operates to bleed off excessive pressure created by the fuel pump and returns fuel to the fuel tank.

Most air delivery systems include a conventional air filter, an airflow meter, a surge tank, and a throttle butterfly valve (Fig. 8-34). After passing through the air filter, the incoming air passes through the airflow meter. The airflow meter monitors the air temperature and the rate at which the air moves through the engine. This information is transmitted

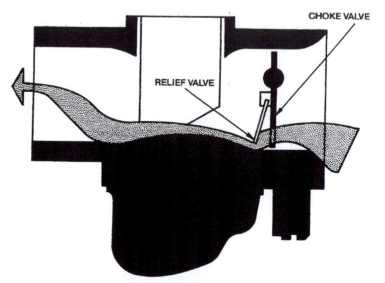

CHOKE VALVE

RELIEF VALVE

Figure 8-31 Plate air restricter with spring-loaded window (American Honda Motor Company).

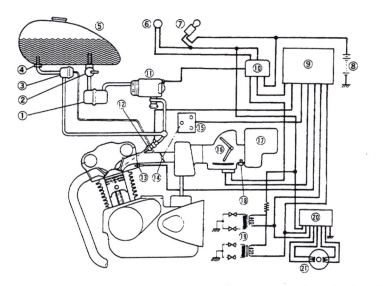

1. Fuel Filter: removes impurities from fuel.
2. Fuel Tap
3. Pressure Regulator: controls pressure in fuel line.
4. Check Valve
5. Fuel Tank
6. Starter Button
7. Ignition Switch
8. Battery
9. Control Unit: receives various signals from sensors, and controls opening time of injectors.
10. Relay: controls power supply to fuel pump and Control Unit.
11. Fuel Pump: draws in fuel from tank and delivers pressurized fuel to fuel line.
12. Injectors: inject atomized fuel against inlet valves upon signal from Control Unit.
13. Engine Temperature Sensor: signals engine temperature to Control Unit.
14. Throttle Valves: control rate of air flow drawn into engine.
15. Throttle Valve Switch: is located on one end of throttle valve shaft, and signals idle and full-load positions of throttle valves to Control Unit.
16. Air Flow Meter: measures rate of air flow drawn into engine, and signals Control Unit; contains air temperature sensor and fuel pump contacts.
17. Air Cleaner
18. Air Temperature Sensor: measures temperature of air flowing through air flow meter, and signals Control Unit.
19. Ignition Coils
20. IC Igniter
21. Pick-up Coils

Figure 8-32 Schematic diagram of fuel injection system (Kawasaki Motors Corporation, U.S.A.).

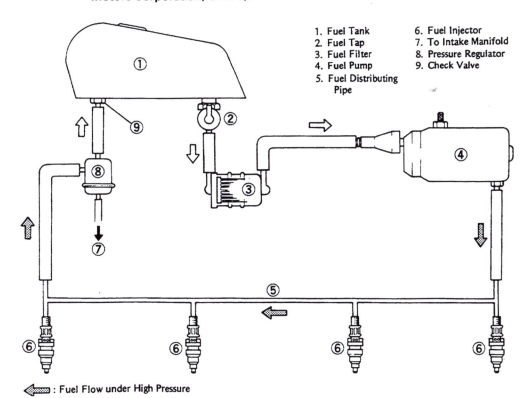

1. Fuel Tank
2. Fuel Tap
3. Fuel Filter
4. Fuel Pump
5. Fuel Distributing Pipe
6. Fuel Injector
7. To Intake Manifold
8. Pressure Regulator
9. Check Valve

⟨▭▭▭ : Fuel Flow under High Pressure

Figure 8-33 Schematic diagram of fuel system (Kawasaki Motors Corporation, U.S.A.).

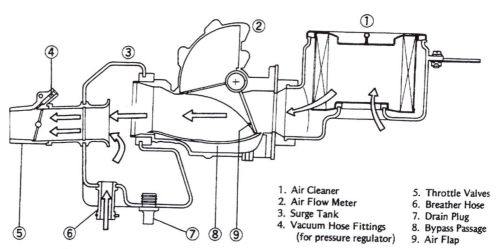

1. Air Cleaner
2. Air Flow Meter
3. Surge Tank
4. Vacuum Hose Fittings
   (for pressure regulator)
5. Throttle Valves
6. Breather Hose
7. Drain Plug
8. Bypass Passage
9. Air Flap

Figure 8-34 Schematic diagram of air system (Kawasaki Motors Corporation, U.S.A.).

to the computer. After passing through the airflow meter, the air enters the surge tank. The large volume of the surge tank is designed to reduce the pulsating movement of the air traveling from the airflow meter and allows an equal distribution of the air to the cylinders. As the air leaves the surge tank and begins traveling down the intake track, the position of the rider-operated throttle butterfly valve determines the amount of air available to the engine. A sensor monitors this throttle position and the volume of air, and transmits this information to the computer. The air continues toward the cylinder, and at some point between the throttle valve and the intake valve, the correct amount of fuel is injected at the proper time.

Because of the sensitive nature of the system, it is essential to make frequent checks for air leaks and to service fuel and air filters at the proper intervals (Fig. 8-35). Leaks and dirty filters create conditions that are misinterpreted by the computer and engine performance suffers. Battery condition is also essential because the battery supplies voltage for the computer, sensors, and ignition system.

TURBOCHARGING Turbocharging is not new to motorcycle design; turbo kits have been available for many years. But manufacturers have only recently produced turbocharged motorcycles for sale to the public. Turbocharging allows an engine to produce a higher horsepower while still meeting EPA noise and emission standards. In otherwise identical engines of equal displacement and equipped with standard carburetors, the turbocharged engine can produce a 60 percent increase in horsepower and may achieve better fuel economy under certain operating conditions.

The turbo unit consists of a turbine wheel and a compressor wheel that spin on a common shaft. The energy that is normally wasted as exhaust gas drives the turbine, which in turn drives the compressor. The compressor forces more air/fuel mixture into the cylinder. When the volume of exhaust increases to spin the compressor fast enough, a boost pressure is produced. Boost pressure is measured in pounds per square inch over atmospheric pressure. Boost pressure continues to build as engine rpm and exhaust volume increase. To prevent excessive pressure that could cause preignition, detonation, and component failure, the turbocharged motorcycle uses a *wastegate* (Fig. 8-36). The wastegate is either located at the turbo side of the unit or on the exhaust pipe before the turbine. The wastegate measures the amount of boost pressure produced. When a specific level of pressure is reached, it opens a gate or valve, which allows some of the exhaust gas to bypass the turbine housing. This prevents a further increase in boost pressure. Maximum boost pressure is determined by the engine design, component strength, and compression ratio.

The turbine wheel is manufactured with several vanes or fins in a special iron housing which can withstand exhaust temperatures up to 1700°F. The compressor wheel is also designed with vanes but because it does not encounter such excessive heat, the housing is constructed of aluminum alloys. The turbine housing is tapered inward to compress and in-

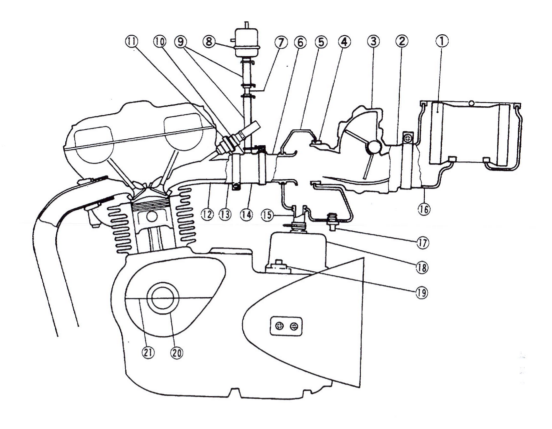

1. Air Cleaner Element	9. Vacuum Hoses	16. Air Cleaner Housing
2. Rubber Fitting	10. Rubber Caps (on	17. Drain Plug
3. Air Flow Meter	hose fittings)	18. Breather Cover
4. Rubber Seal	11. Fuel Injectors	19. Oil Filler Cap
5. Surge Tank	12. Cylinder Head	20. Oil Seal (on crankshaft
6. Air Ducts	13. Throttle Valve Holders	right end)
7. 3-Way Joint	14. Throttle Valves	21. Others (mating surfaces,
8. Pressure Regulator	15. Breather Hose	etc.)

Figure 8-35   Air leak inspection (Kawasaki Motors Corporation, U.S.A.).

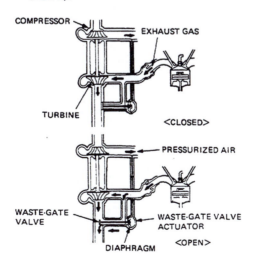

Figure 8-36   Turbocharger with wastegate (American Honda Motor Company).

crease the speed of the exhaust gases. In contrast, the compressor housing flares outward; the increased diameter accommodates the increased volume of air that is pushed toward the cylinder. The shaft uses bearings and thrust washers and is lubricated by oil pressure from the engine. Because the turbine can reach in excess of 180,000 rpm's, floating radial bearings may be used to reduce the bearing rpm by one-half.

Whether the turbo unit is factory-installed or assembled from a kit, several factors must be considered. Two-stroke engines can be turbocharged; however, twin- or multicylinder four-stroke engines operate better with turbocharging because of their smoother exhaust gas output. In any case, because turbocharging increases the load on the engine components, the strength of the engine cases, bearings, pistons, clutch, transmission, final drive, lubrication, and cooling systems should also be increased. Turbo designs also require a lower compression ratio to allow sufficient increase in boost pressure without danger of detonation. Turbocharging can be used in conjunction with standard carburetion or electronic fuel injection (Fig. 8-37). A fuel pump should be used with either system to ensure an adequate amount of fuel.

Most factory-installed turbo units cannot be serviced, but some accessory kits have replacement parts available. Turbo maintenance requires frequent oil changes, the standard fuel system inspection, and a thorough check for air or exhaust leaks. An air leak in the intake could contaminate the fuel and create a lean mixture. An exhaust leak could prevent the engine from reaching the maximum boost pressure.

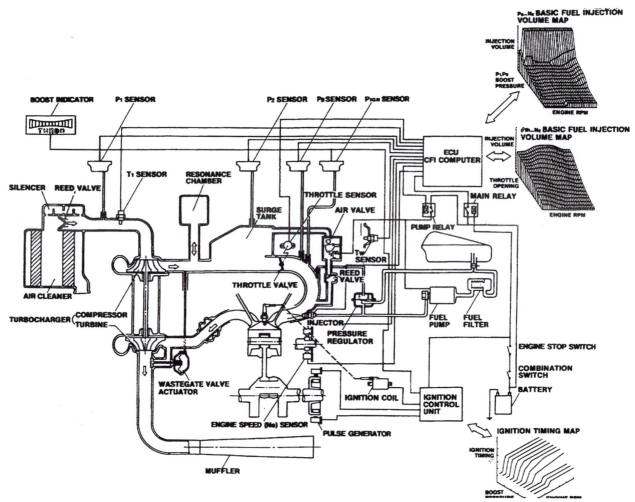

Figure 8-37   Complete turbo system with electronic fuel injection (American Honda Motor Company).

chapter 9

Basic Electrical Theory

A motorcycle's electrical system consists of four major systems and many subsystems. The four major systems are the starting, ignition, lighting, and charging systems. A starting system rotates the engine for starting. An ignition system provides high-voltage sparks to the engine cylinders to fire the compressed air/fuel mixture. A lighting system powers the lights and operates other electrical equipment. A charging system recharges the battery. To produce the electricity these systems require, motorcycles use a direct-current (dc) or alternating-current (ac) generator or battery.

This chapter explains the principles of electricity and magnetism and how they relate to a motorcycle electrical system. The functions of a battery are discussed as well as battery testing and service.

PRINCIPLES OF ELECTRICITY   Understanding certain principles of electricity will clarify how a motorcycle's electrical system operates.

Matter

Matter is anything that has weight and occupies space. Matter exists in three states—solid, liquid, and in a gaseous form—and it can be changed from one state to another. All matter is composed of atoms.

The Atom

An atom is composed of protons, neutrons, and electrons. Protons make up the nucleus of atoms in lighter elements, but in heavier metallic elements we find neutrons which add mass and weight to the atom. Electrons orbit around the nucleus of the atom. Protons and electrons are electrically charged. Protons have a positive charge and electrons have a negative charge. Electrons orbit the nucleus and trace paths called *shells* (Fig. 9-1). Different atoms have different numbers of electrons in the outermost shell, and there may be as many as seven shells. For example, copper has 29 electrons and four shells.

Electron Travel

Electrons, because of their much smaller mass and exterior position in the atom, will travel from one atom to another. Electrons travel from negative to positive. An imbalance be-

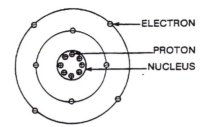

Figure 9-1 Neutral atom (American Suzuki Motor Corporation).

tween negatively charged and positively charged matter creates a force that pushes the negative electrons away from the negatively charged area. This imbalance is called a *potential difference*. Electron travel is *electricity*.

A potential difference can be caused by friction, light, magnetic fields, chemical action, heat, and the bending of crystals. For example, friction occurs when you rub your feet across a carpet. This friction causes electrons to pass from the carpet to your feet. The carpet now has a positive charge because it has lost some electrons, which have traveled to you. You have a negative charge because of the electrons you have picked up. The difference or imbalance of electrons between you and the carpet is the potential difference. This is static electricity. When you touch something with a neutral charge, the extra electrons jump from you to the neutral object and cause a spark.

Conductors, Insulators, and Semiconductors

Some matter conducts electrons, and some matter prevents electron flow. All matter resists electron travel to some extent.

Conductors: A conductor efficiently transmits electrons from one atom to another. Most metallic materials transmit electrons with ease. Silver, copper, gold, aluminum, and lead are excellent conductors.

Insulators: An insulator effectively resists and prevents the flow of electrons. Some insulators that are used on motorcycles are mica, Bakelite, air, plastic, and rubber.

Semiconductors: A semiconductor has the properties of both a conductor and an insulator. Under certain conditions a semiconductor will act as a conductor. It will act as an insulator under other conditions. Silicon and germanium are used as semiconductors.

BASIC TERMINOLOGY   As with any science, electronics has a language of its own. The following terms are necessary for a basic understanding of electrical theory.

Current: Current is the movement of electrons. One ampere of current flow is equal to 1 coulomb in 1 second. Current will be explained in more detail later.

Coulomb: A coulomb is a measurement of electric charge. One coulomb is equal to 6.24 $\times 10^{18}$ electrons.

I: I is the symbol for the amount of electrons flowed in one second, and this current is measured in amperes (amps or A). Therefore, $I = A$.

Electromotive Force: Electromotive force (emf) is the force or pressure that pushes the electrons; it is an imbalance or potential difference.

Volts: A volt is a unit of electric potential and electromotive force.

Resistance: When amperage (current flow) under voltage (the pressure or emf) passes through material, the material resists electron movement. Resistance (R) is measured in ohms (Ω).

Schematics and Symbols: Schematics are wiring diagrams used to plot and trace a circuit on paper. Symbols are used to represent the different devices used in a motorcycle electrical system. A schematic is essential for determining wiring routes (Fig. 9-2). Use the symbol chart provided for reference (Fig. 9-3).

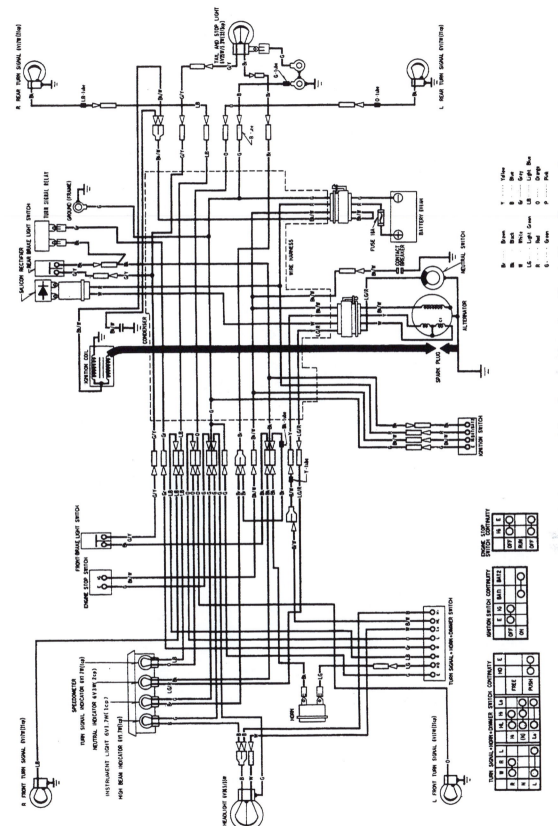

Figure 9-2 Motorcycle electrical system wiring diagram (American Honda Motor Company).

179

CURRENT As stated earlier, current is a continuous flow of electrons. Current may flow at a constant voltage, or the voltage may vary. Current requires a circuit.

Direct-Current Flow

Direct current (dc) that flows at a constant voltage value is known as *pure dc*. A current that varies in voltage value as it flows is known as *pulsating dc*. Both pure dc and pulsating dc never change polarity or direction of flow (Fig. 9-4).

Alternating-Current Flow

Alternating current (ac) changes in voltage value and polarity as it flows. Alternating current flows in one direction until peak voltage is reached and then drops to zero volts. Alternating current then changes direction or polarity until peak voltage is achieved and again drops to zero and again changes polarity. From peak positive voltage to peak negative voltage and back again to peak positive voltage is known as a cycle (Fig. 9-5).

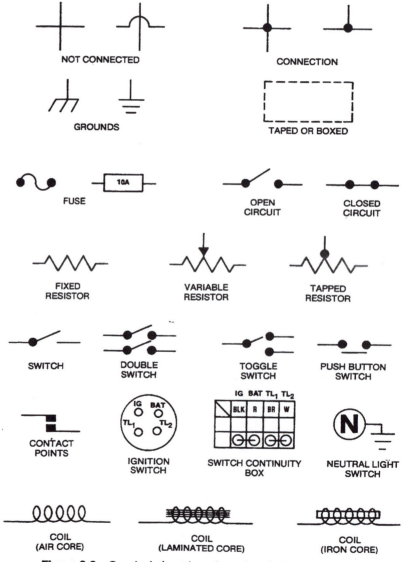

Figure 9-3 Symbol chart (continued on following page).

Circuit

In order to create a continuous flow of electrons, current must have a complete path to follow. A circuit is a closed path that an electrical current can follow. A circuit has a positive and negative side. An ac circuit has alternating negative and positive sides. The following are required to establish a circuit.

A Source of Electromotive Force (Volts):   In a motorcycle electrical system, the source of electromotive force is provided by either the battery or a current generator.

A Set of Conductors: A conductor can take the form of an insulated conductor called *wiring*, or the frame or engine may act as conductors.

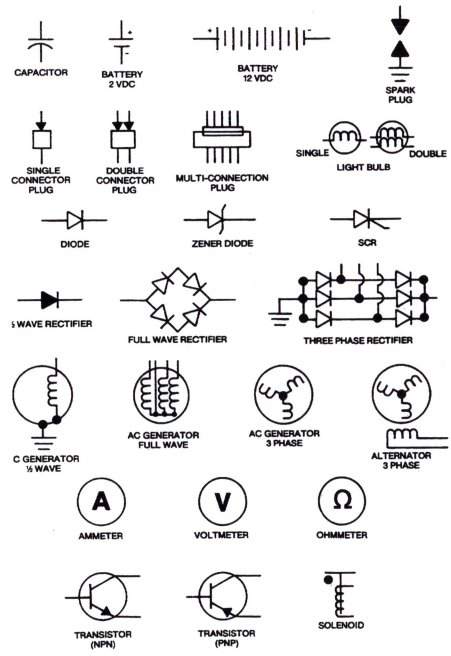

Figure 9-3   Continued.

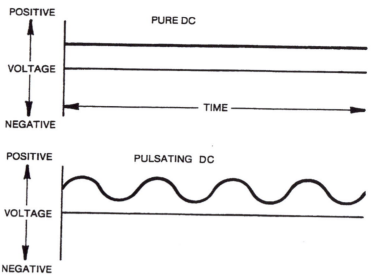

Figure 9-4 Direct current (dc).

A *ground* is the uninsulated side of the circuit and usually has a negative polarity. The frame and engine are used as grounds to eliminate excess wiring. Most motorcycle grounds are connected to the negative side of the battery. This means that not only the negative side of the battery, but also the frame, engine, and anything metallic that is bolted to it, has a negative potential.

A Load to Draw Off Energy: A load is a device that uses electrical energy. Motorcycle lights, coils, resistors, and other devices draw off energy. When the load changes electrical energy into heat or light energy or mechanical movement, the energy is reduced to zero and the current returns to the source of emf.

A Means of Control: A means of control is necessary to turn the current on or off. Some motorcycle electrical systems increase the resistance to current instead of turning the current off. The means of control also includes fuses or circuit breakers to protect the circuit from overheating. Changing the circuit design has a direct effect on circuit resistance. The less resistance a circuit offers, the more current is allowed to flow.

Series Circuit

A series circuit provides one path for current to follow. A motorcycle fuse circuit is a good example of a series circuit (Fig. 9-6). If the fuse breaks, the circuit opens and current stops. If the control switch is open, the circuit is incomplete and current is unable to flow.

In a series circuit, the resistance total is found by adding the value of each resistor. A *resistor* is anything in the circuit that uses electrical energy and reduces the flow of current. If a series circuit has three resistors of a 2-ohm value each, the resistance total equals six: $2 + 2 + 2 = 6$ ohms (Fig. 9-7). If more resistors are added to a series circuit, the resistance total of the circuit is increased and therefore the current is decreased.

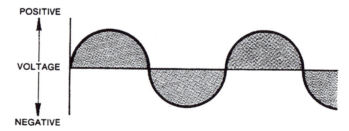

Figure 9-5 Alternating current (ac).

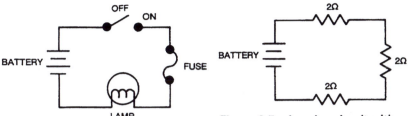

Figure 9-6 A series circuit.

Figure 9-7 A series circuit with three resistors.

Parallel Circuit

A parallel circuit provides more than one path for current to follow. In this system if one device opens the circuits, the current finds a way back to the source because there is another path that it can follow (Fig. 9-8). Finding the resistance total of a parallel circuit is more difficult than finding the resistance total of a series circuit because the resistance total is less than the resistance of any of the resistors. Use the following formula to find the resistance total (R_t):

$$R_t = \frac{1}{\frac{1}{R_1} + \frac{1}{R_2} + \frac{1}{R_3}} \quad \text{or} \quad \frac{1}{\frac{1}{2} + \frac{1}{2} + \frac{1}{2}} = \frac{1}{R_t} = \frac{1}{1.5} \quad \text{or} \quad 0.667 \, \Omega$$

The addition of more resistors in a parallel circuit decreases the resistance total and increases the current.

Combination Circuit

A combination circuit system combines a series and parallel circuit (Fig. 9-9).

To find the resistance total of the circuit in Fig. 9-9, use the following formula:

$$R_t = \frac{1}{\frac{1}{R_2} + \frac{1}{R_3}} + R_1 \quad \text{or} \quad R_t = \left(\frac{1}{\frac{1}{2} + \frac{1}{2}}\right) + 2 \quad \text{or} \quad R_t = 0.5 + 0.5 + 2 = 3$$

MEASURING ELECTRICAL POWER The following laws are useful to calculate the total electrical power used and produced. Ohm's law is the only accurate method for measuring true resistance with current running through a circuit because as heat increases, resistance usually increases.

Ohm's Law

Ohm's law states that current which flows in a circuit is directly proportional to the applied voltage and inversely proportional to the resistance. *Ohm's law* can be stated in three ways:

1. The current in amperes is equal to the pressure in volts divided by the resistance in ohms:

$$I = \frac{E}{R}$$

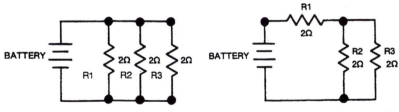

Figure 9-8 A parallel circuit.

Figure 9-9 A combination circuit.

2. The pressure in volts is equal to the current in amperes multiplied by the resistance in ohms:

$$E = I \times R$$

3. The resistance in ohms is equal to the pressure in volts divided by the current in amperes:

$$R = \frac{E}{I}$$

Notice that any one value can be found if the other two values are known (Fig. 9-10).

Let's apply Ohm's law to a motorcycle. A motorcycle ignition coil operates at 12 volts and draws 4 amperes of current. To find the resistance, divide the voltage by the amperes: $12 \div 4 = 3$ ohms of resistance (3 Ω).

Watt's Law

The inventor of the horsepower measurement, James Watt, was also responsible for the volt-ampere measurement, the *watt*. A watt is the measurement for electrical power. It takes 746 watts to equal 1 horsepower. A horsepower measurement is appropriate for large electric motors, but the watt measurement is commonly applied to motorcycle electrical systems. *Watt's law* states:

1. Power in watts is equal to the current in amperes multiplied by the voltage:

$$P = I \times E$$

2. Current in amperes is equal to the power in watts divided by the voltage:

$$I = \frac{P}{E}$$

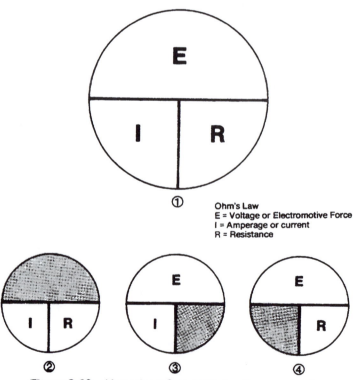

① Ohm's Law
E = Voltage or Electromotive Force
I = Amperage or current
R = Resistance

Figure 9-10 (American Suzuki Motor Corporation).

3. Voltage is equal to the power in watts divided by the current in amperes:

$$E = \frac{P}{I}$$

Notice that any one value can be found if the other two values are known (Fig. 9-11).

Let's apply Watt's law to a motorcycle. A large touring motorcycle can generate 280 watts at 12 volts. It has accessories that use 20 amperes if all of the accessories are turned on at once. The owner installs a 55-watt stereo system. Can all electrical items be run at once? To find the answer:

1. Find the total amperes of generated output:

$$I = \frac{P}{E} \quad \text{or} \quad I = \frac{280}{12} = 23.3 \text{ total amperes output}$$

2. Find the current required for the 55-watt stereo system:

$$I = \frac{P}{E} \quad \text{or} \quad I = \frac{55}{12} = 4.58 \text{ amperes}$$

3. Add the amperes used: 4.58 A + 20 A = 24.5 A

But this system can only generate 23.3 amperes, so with all equipment on, the battery will discharge at a rate of 1.20 amperes per hour. There is not enough current to support all of the accessories for an extended length of time.

PRINCIPLES OF MAGNETISM   All atoms have north and south magnetic poles and a magnetic field that emerges from one pole to the other. Normally, the atoms' poles are not aligned. A magnetic field has the ability to line up many of the poles of atoms in the same direction. Some natural rock called *magnetite* has that ability. Shock or heat disrupts the order of aligned atoms that is produced by a magnet. An iron magnet demagnetizes at approximately 1418°F (770°C).

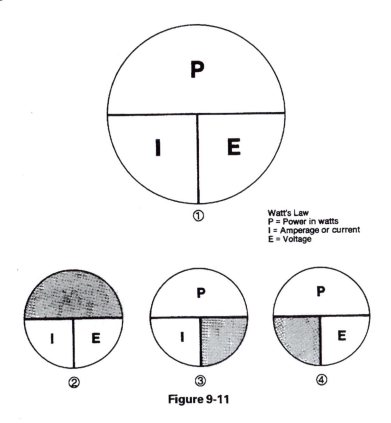

Watt's Law
P = Power in watts
I = Amperage or current
E = Voltage

Figure 9-11

Flux Lines

A magnetic field can be visualized by flux lines. If you put a magnet under a piece of paper and sprinkle some iron filings on the paper, the filings will follow the flux lines. Flux lines travel from the north pole to the south pole in an elliptical path. If two poles of the same polarity are drawn close, the flux lines will repel. But if two poles of opposite polarity are drawn close, the flux lines will connect with each other causing them to attract (Fig. 9-12). There is no known insulator for magnetic flux lines, but some materials pass flux lines more easily than others. Iron, for example, passes flux lines 2000 times more easily than air. The ease with which a material passes flux lines is called *permeability*, and the resistance to flux line flow is called *reluctance*.

PRODUCING ELECTRICITY When a magnet is passed by a coil of wire, electricity is produced. Magnets and coils of wire are used to produce electricity for a motorcycle electrical system. Alnico and Permalloy are two iron alloys that retain their magnetism and are used on motorcycles. These magnets are called permanent magnets. Motorcycles also use soft-iron magnets that weaken quickly after the magnetizing force has been removed. Ignition coils, generators, alternators, and starter motors all use some type of magnetism.

There are two electromagnetic methods by which electric current can be produced for a motorcycle electrical system: electromagnetism and induction. The battery, which produces electricity through electrochemical action, will be explained later in the chapter.

Electromagnetism

Electromagnetism uses electricity to produce magnetism. A magnetic field is produced by passing a current through a conductor which is part of a circuit. The strength of the magnetic field around a conductor when current is passing through it is proportional to the amount of the current flow through that circuit. This means that increasing the current through a conductor increases the magnetic field. This is one way to increase magnetism (Fig. 9-13).

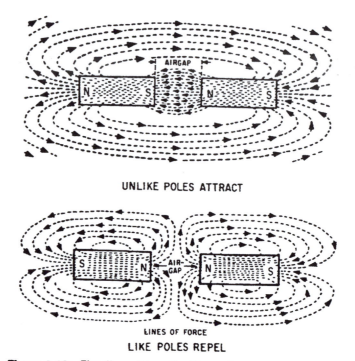

UNLIKE POLES ATTRACT

LINES OF FORCE
LIKE POLES REPEL

Figure 9-12 Flux lines (Yamaha Motor Corporation, U.S.A.).

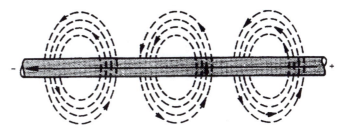

Figure 9-13   Magnetic field surrounding a wire (American Honda Motor Company).

Another method used to increase magnetism is to coil the wire; this causes the fields to combine and increase in strength. To enhance the magnetic field further, the coils are tightly wound to keep the flow directed and strong (Fig. 9-14). An iron core is placed inside many coils to channel the flux lines through the center of the coil (Fig. 9-15). If a movable iron core is placed in the center of a coil but not centered lengthwise, the magnetic flux lines stretch and pull the core to center itself. This device is called a *solenoid*.

Induction

The other method of electromagnetically producing electricity is induction. If a conductor is stationary and a magnetic field is passed across it, emf or voltage is induced and electricity is produced. The conductor is connected to a circuit, and the current flows (Fig. 9-16). The amount of voltage produced depends on the strength of the magnetic field and the speed at which the flux lines are cut by the conductor. Maximum voltage is produced when the magnet's flux lines move at a 90° angle to the conductor. No voltage is produced when the flux lines are parallel with the conductor.

Figure 9-14   Magnetic field of a wire coil (American Honda Motor Company).

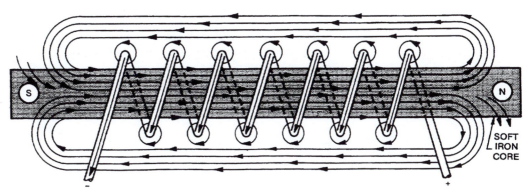

Figure 9-15   Electromagnet (American Honda Motor Company).

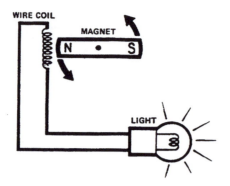

Figure 9-16   Induction (Yamaha Motor Corporation, U.S.A.).

Self-induction

A coil of wire makes a good conductor because the coils form a series circuit. The voltage of each coil is added together, but an increase in coils does not result in a proportional increase of voltage because of self-induction.

A coil of wire producing current flow creates its own magnetic field. Any change in the magnetic field results in self-induction. The coil's magnetic field changes as the magnetic field expands and collapses. The polarity of self-induction is the opposite of the original polarity. The voltage caused by self-induction is opposite to the original voltage. This opposition of current flow, or counter-emf, is a limiting factor in coil output.

THE LEAD-ACID BATTERY   All street motorcycles currently manufactured must have a taillight and brake light that operate when the engine is not running. For that reason a street motorcycle needs a source of energy that can store and discharge energy. A battery is used for this purpose. A battery is an electrochemical device that converts chemical energy into electrical energy. Motorcycles use a lead-acid battery because it can be charged after the stored energy is drained. During charging the current must flow in the opposite direction of discharging.

Lead-Acid Battery Design

A lead-acid battery consists of energy cells that are connected in a series circuit so that the voltage of the battery is increased. There are approximately 2.12 volts of direct current (V dc) per cell. A 6-volt battery has three cells and a 12-volt battery has six cells. Each cell consists of lead plates which are stacked parallel to each other. The plates are made from plain lead and lead peroxide and are arranged alternately: negative, positive, negative. An insulator, usually fiberglass or treated paper, is placed between the opposing plates to prevent direct contact. Current output and capacity increase with an increase in plate surface area (Fig. 9-17).

Electrolyte

Each battery cell contains electrolyte, which is a solution of sulfuric acid and distilled water. The lead plates in the cells are submerged in electrolyte to allow a chemical change to occur. The ratio of acid to water is measured by weight and called *specific gravity*. The specific gravity of most fully charged motorcycle battery cells should be between 1.270 and 1.280. Batteries with a sulfation retardant additive may have an end-of-charge gravity of 1.280 or slightly higher. The specific gravity of batteries in the 12N series may be as low as 1.265 to 1.270.

Battery Operation

A battery produces electricity through electrochemical action. A chemical action between the electrolyte and the cell plates causes an electrical current. The lead peroxide (PbO_2) positive plates and the plain lead (Pb) negative plates react with the electrolyte (H_2SO_4).

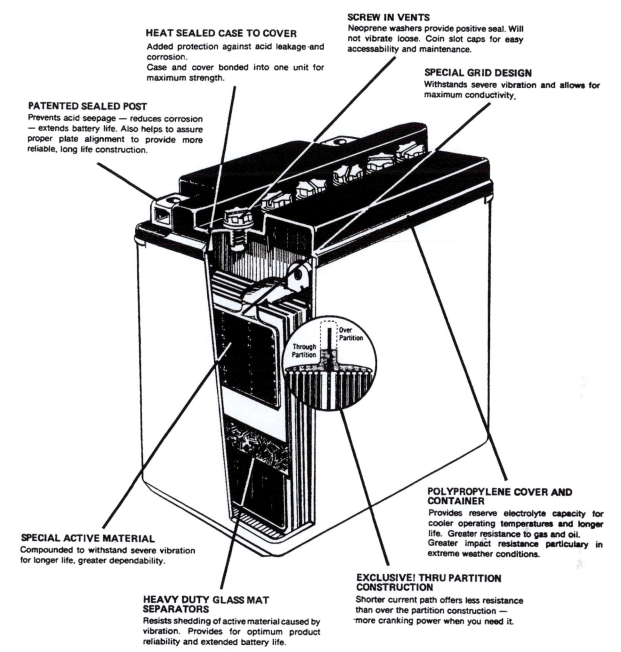

SCREW IN VENTS
Neoprene washers provide positive seal. Will not vibrate loose. Coin slot caps for easy accessability and maintenance.

HEAT SEALED CASE TO COVER
Added protection against acid leakage and corrosion.
Case and cover bonded into one unit for maximum strength.

SPECIAL GRID DESIGN
Withstands severe vibration and allows for maximum conductivity.

PATENTED SEALED POST
Prevents acid seepage — reduces corrosion — extends battery life. Also helps to assure proper plate alignment to provide more reliable, long life construction.

Over Partition

Through Partition

POLYPROPYLENE COVER AND CONTAINER
Provides reserve electrolyte capacity for cooler operating temperatures and longer life. Greater resistance to gas and oil. Greater impact resistance particulary in extreme weather conditions.

SPECIAL ACTIVE MATERIAL
Compounded to withstand severe vibration for longer life, greater dependability.

EXCLUSIVE! THRU PARTITION CONSTRUCTION
Shorter current path offers less resistance than over the partition construction — more cranking power when you need it.

HEAVY DUTY GLASS MAT SEPARATORS
Resists shedding of active material caused by vibration. Provides for optimum product reliability and extended battery life.

Figure 9-17   Cutaway view of battery (Yuasa Exide Corporation).

Discharging: When a motorcycle battery discharges electrical current, the electrolyte separates and becomes H_2 and SO_4. The positive plates separate to form Pb and O_2. In the course of this chemical action, some of the chemicals mix and form different compounds. The hydrogen and oxygen combine to form water, H_2O. This is why a discharged battery can freeze. The SO_4 forms on the positive and negative plates to form lead sulfate, $PbSO_4$, which is known as sulfation.

Charging: When a motorcycle battery is charged, the chemical process is almost reversed. The lead sulfites, $PbSO_4$, split and form lead, Pb, and sulfate, SO_4. The water, H_2O, splits into hydrogen and oxygen. The hydrogen recombines with the sulfate to form sulfuric acid, H_2SO_4. The oxygen recombines with the lead, Pb, to form lead peroxide, PbO_2, the positive plates.

New College Stamford LRC
Drift Road Stamford Lincs.
PE9 1XA
Tel: 01780 484339

Bubbles can be seen in an actively charging battery. These bubbles, called gassing, are hydrogen and oxygen gas, H_2 and O_2, given off by the charging current breaking down the water. The H_2 and O_2 are excess hydrogen and oxygen molecules which cannot combine with the sulfate and lead. The two gases given off not only develop pressure in the battery, but are also very explosive. This is the reason batteries are vented, and no sparks or flame should be exposed to a charging battery.

Ampere-Hour Capacity

The battery's ability to discharge current for an extended period of time is known as the ampere-hour rating. A battery that operates in colder temperatures has a lower ampere-hour rating than a battery operating in a warm climate because cold slows the chemical action. If the battery's internal temperature becomes excessive, plate damage may occur.

Most motorcycle batteries are rated on a scale of 10 hours of discharge at a rate of no higher than the time it takes to drop the cell voltage to 1.75 volts. This means that a 14-ampere-hour battery discharges at a rate of 1.4 ampere-hours for 10 hours. At this point the cell voltage is 1.75 volts, or 10.5 volts for a 12-volt battery, or 5.25 volts for a 6-volt battery. Usually, batteries with a larger plate area have an increased current ampere-hour rating.

Batteries may also have a cold-start rating. To determine this rating, the battery is discharged at a high rate: for example, 150 amperes at 0°F (-17.8°C). A voltage meter is used to measure battery voltage. When each cell is discharged to 1 volt, the test stops. The length of time for the test is also measured.

BATTERY SERVICE AND TESTING

Use the following procedures for setting up a new battery, battery testing, and battery charging.

Setting Up a New Battery

When manufactured, battery plates are dry-charged, installed in the battery housing, and sealed. A new battery is vacuum-sealed and delivered with a vent tube, a charging rate chart, and a card that indicates the month and year the battery was manufactured. A new battery has an indefinite shelf life if it remains sealed and stored at room temperature. Once the battery is unsealed and subjected to atmospheric pressure, it should be prepared, charged, and installed into a motorcycle charging system.

To break the vacuum seal, remove the vent tube plug. To set up a new battery, remove the filler caps and pour electrolyte into each cell until the fluid reaches the upper level line. When each cell is full, the battery will have 80 percent of its charge (Fig. 9-18). Connect the battery to a battery charger that produces 3 amperes or less.

During charging, frequently check the level of the electrolyte and periodically add distilled water to maintain the level. The electrolyte level may rise above the upper level line during charging. After charging, rock the battery to release the trapped gases. The electrolyte level should return to and must be at the upper level line. Install the vent tube. On some models, this tube is routed through the motorcycle frame. Allow the battery to cool for 2 hours; this time can be shortened by partially submerging the battery in water.

Battery Testing

Before making any tests, inspect the battery. Check to see if the battery is clean; a dirty battery discharges across the grime on top of the case. The terminal posts should be clean and free of corrosion. Check the fluid level; it must be between the upper and lower level lines. The casing should not be cracked or leaking. The sediment on the bottom of the cell must not be touching the plates or shorting will occur. Inspect for sulfation and mossing. A white deposit on the plate surfaces may be sulfation. This is caused by a low fluid level or exces-

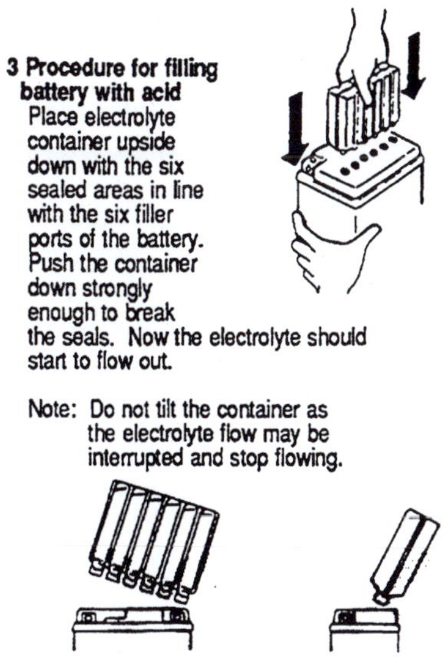

3 Procedure for filling battery with acid Place electrolyte container upside down with the six sealed areas in line with the six filler ports of the battery. Push the container down strongly enough to break the seals. Now the electrolyte should start to flow out.

Note: Do not tilt the container as the electrolyte flow may be interrupted and stop flowing.

Figure 9-18 Filling a battery (Yuasa Exide Corporation).

sive discharging. Mossing looks like little red hairs and is caused by overcharging, overheating, or freezing. Check for proper vent tube routing. The vent tube should exit away from the drive chain and from below the swing arm, and it should not be kinked or pinched. Small cuts in the tube near the battery vent are used to prevent a gas buildup from forming in the event of restricted flow.

Before testing, clean the battery's outer surface with a mild grease-cutting soap and warm water. A soft brush works well for cleaning around the cell caps. A wire brush can be used for cleaning the terminals. Baking soda is not recommended for cleaning batteries because it neutralizes the acid if it enters the cells. However, baking soda works well to clean battery mounting boxes. If the battery fluid is low, fill the battery with distilled water only. Some water contains minerals that will damage batteries. Charge the battery before any test to ensure that the water has mixed well with the electrolyte.

There are basically two types of battery tests: unloaded and loaded. An unloaded test is made on a battery without discharging current. A loaded test is performed with either a low- or high-current load. The unloaded test is the simplest, but it is not as accurate as a loaded test.

Unloaded Test: One of the easiest ways to measure a battery's state of charge is with a hydrometer. The hydrometer measures the specific gravity of each cell, which should be 1.280. This reading indicates a good battery if the cell variation is no greater than 0.050 specific gravity. A hydrometer reading of 1.230 to 1.260 indicates the battery should be charged before testing and/or installation.

The battery's specific gravity changes with temperature. If the battery's electrolyte temperature is above 77°F (25°C), a temperature correction factor should be made by adding 0.001 to the specific gravity reading for each 3°F over 77°F. If the temperature is under 77°F, subtract 0.001 from the specific gravity reading for every 3°F. The cell voltage can be found by adding 0.84 to specific gravity.

Replace the battery if the case or cell partition is cracked, or if one cell is shorted, or if there is a variation in cell gravity after charging. After proper charging, the cell voltage should be at least 2.00 each, or 6.00 V dc for a 6-volt battery, and 12.00 V dc for a 12-volt system.

Load Tests: There are two types of load tests that can be performed on a motorcycle battery. The first is a low-load test. Many motorcycle headlights and taillights come on when the ignition key is turned. This 4- to 10-ampere load is sufficient to remove the surface charge. To load motorcycles with an ac headlight, such as Enduro models, turn on the taillight and stoplight. All voltage tests performed during the load will be made at the battery.

The battery in a 12-volt system should have at least 11.5 V dc with a light load; a 6-volt system should have at least 5.75 V dc. If the battery voltage drops below the given level, the battery must be charged.

A high-rate discharge test is the best test of actual battery conditions under a starting load. Use a load tester device that has an adjustable load. Apply a load of three times the ampere-hour rating or one-half the cold-start rating for 15 seconds. Check the battery's voltage 14 seconds into the test. A good 12-volt battery will have at least 10.5 volts; a good 6-volt battery will have at least 5.25 volts. If the battery voltage falls below these specifications, the battery must be charged.

Battery Charging

When the motorcycle's battery is discharged, a charge is needed to restore it to full capacity. Direct current flowing in the opposite direction of discharge is used. Most motorcycles that use a battery have some type of charging system, but a shop normally uses some type of battery charger that plugs into a wall socket. Leads from the charger to the battery must be hooked positive to positive and negative to negative. There are five types of battery chargers: pulse, high rate, taper, trickle, and constant current.

Pulse Charger: The pulse charger is the newest technology. A pulse charger monitors the battery voltage during the charging and standby charging modes. When the battery voltage reaches a specified low level, the charger delivers a full battery charge. The pulse charger then automatically reduces the charge when the battery reaches a specified high voltage.

High-Rate Charger: A high-rate charger forces a high current into a battery and should not be used for motorcycles, as it may damage the plates and overheat the battery.

Taper Charger: A taper charger charges the battery at a fixed voltage. As the battery voltage increases with the charge, the current drops accordingly. A battery in good condition can be charged in this manner, but a badly sulfated battery may not accept the charge. If the battery is severely discharged, it may take a long time to restore a full charge to the battery. Check the battery temperature frequently. If the battery's temperature becomes excessive, gassing and a loss of electrolyte may occur.

Trickle Charger: A trickle charger charges the battery at a fixed rate. The trickle charge rate should be 1/20 of the ampere-hour rating of the battery.

Different ampere-hour batteries require different charge rates. Most motorcycle batteries should be charged at one-tenth of the rated ampere-hour value. The charging time for a completely discharged battery can be found by multiplying the ampere-hour rating by 1.3.

The battery's voltage increases with the amount of charge. Charging voltage should not exceed 14 to 15 volts for antimony batteries, which are the most common. Charging voltage should not exceed 15 to 16 volts for the more premium low-maintenance batteries and sealed types. Excessive charging shorts the plates by breaking down the plate separators. Full charge is 1.280 specific gravity.

Be cautious while charging a battery. Combined hydrogen and oxygen gases can cause a violent explosion. Never smoke or allow sparks near the battery during charging. Always wear a face shield when working around charging batteries. Be sure that the battery does not become hot to the touch during charging. If this occurs, discontinue charging and allow the battery to cool to room temperature before charging again. To prevent sparks, unplug the charger from the wall socket before removing the charger leads from the battery terminals.

Constant-Current Charger: A constant-current charger maintains a constant supply of current to the battery at all levels of charging. When using this type of charger, you can select the charging current. During charging, as the battery's internal voltage increases, the charger automatically increases the charging voltage to maintain the selected current output.

LOW-MAINTENANCE BATTERIES

Low-maintenance batteries are made of lead calcium plates. The plates absorb the gases generated during charging. Some low-maintenance batteries are not vented to release gases, so the fluid level in the battery remains constant. This provides a couple of advantages: distilled water never needs to be added, and the battery can be used in a tilted position without fear of leaking electrolyte.

The specific gravity of some low-maintenance batteries may differ from conventional batteries. Specific gravity for some low-maintenance batteries is 1.320 at 68°F (20°C). These low-maintenance batteries also use different charging voltage and current.

TEST EQUIPMENT

Most modern test equipment uses a movable pointer and a scale and operates using a magnetic field. A permanent magnet, usually a horseshoe type, is located inside the meter and a movable coil of wire with a pointer attached is placed between the magnet's poles. The coil pivots on jeweled bearings but has stops to prevent rotation. As direct current passes through the coil, a magnetic field is established around it. This electromagnetic field is in opposition to the field of the permanent magnet. The greater the flow of current, the more the pointer will deflect. A change in coil polarity changes the direction of pointer movement (Fig. 9-19).

Voltmeter

A voltmeter is used to test the state of charge of a low-maintenance battery. When fully charged, the open circuit terminal voltage should read 12.8 V dc or higher. Motorcycle testing requires the use of a voltmeter that can measure both ac and dc voltage (Fig. 9-20). A voltmeter is always connected parallel to the circuit being measured. Most voltmeters read from left to right. Proper polarity must be observed during hookup to ensure that the pointer travels in the proper direction. A range of 0.1 to 1000 volts can be obtained by adding resistance to the meter's coil circuit. An ac voltmeter incorporates a rectifier to change ac to dc because ac flowing through the meter coil will read zero. Voltmeters normally have a very high resistance. The more ohms per volt, the greater the accuracy of the meter.

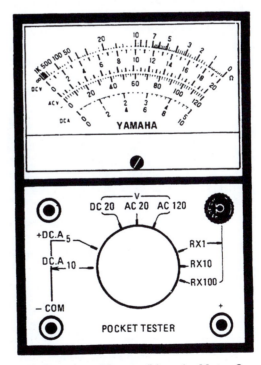

Figure 9-19 Pocket multitester (Yamaha Motor Corporation, U.S.A.).

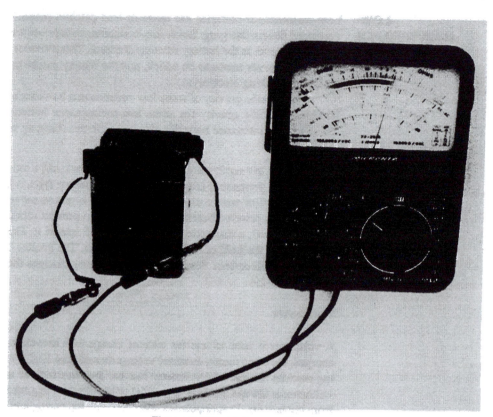

Figure 9-20   Using a voltmeter.

Ammeter

An ammeter is used to measure current flow and is always connected in series with the circuit being tested (Fig. 9-21). An ammeter operates like a voltmeter, but it uses a shunt to bypass excessive current flow around the coil. The coil senses the voltage drop past the shunt and the pointer moves accordingly. Different ranges can be obtained by changing the resistance value of the shunt. An ammeter normally has a very low resistance and does not restrict current flow in the circuit being tested. Observe proper polarity while hooking up the ammeter. An ammeter with a range of 0 to 10 amperes is needed for most testing.

Figure 9-21   Using an ammeter.

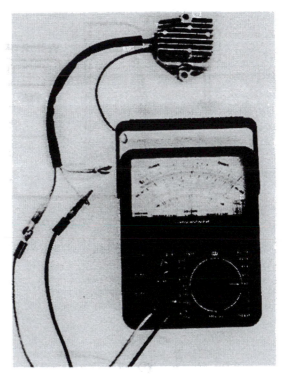

Figure 9-22   Using an ohmmeter.

Ohmmeter

An ohmmeter is used to measure the resistance of a circuit device. An ohmmeter is always connected directly across from the resistor with the power disconnected (Fig. 9-22). The ohmmeter has a power source, usually a battery. A current of predetermined value is passed through a resistor. The ohmmeter senses how much current flows through the meter. Most ohmmeter scales are read from right to left. The far right side of the scale indicates zero or no resistance; the left side indicates a very high or infinite (∞) resistance. By changing the internal resistance of the meter, different sensitivities can be obtained. Each time the meter is changed, readjust the zero knob. Most ohmmeters used to test motorcycles range from 1 to 10,000 ohms.

VOLTAGE DROP   When electrical current flows through resistance, the output voltage is less than the input voltage. The amount of voltage drop across a device should be proportional to the amount of resistance and the amount of current flowing through a device. An increase in resistance or current flowing through a device will increase the voltage drop and decrease the output voltage.

Voltage Drop Testing

Voltage drop testing is performed using a voltmeter to determine the amount of resistance in a switch, connector, or battery cable. Because the amount of resistance is slight, it is not normally detected by an ohmmeter.

   When performing a voltage drop test, the voltmeter selector should be set to a low dc scale and current must be flowing in the circuit. Connect the voltmeter tester leads across the switch, connector, or battery cable you are testing, and read the amount of voltage drop indicated by the voltmeter (Fig. 9-23). Note that a voltmeter may be damaged when testing in reference to ground.

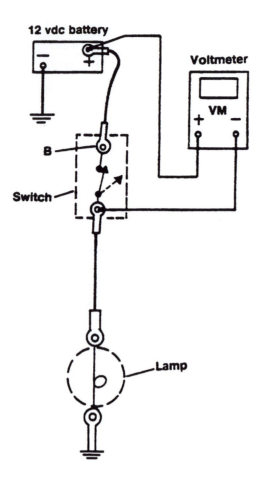

Figure 9-23   Sample voltage drop test connections (Harley-Davidson Motor Company, Inc.).

chapter 10

Ignition Systems

Ignition occurs when a spark from the spark plug ignites the air/fuel mixture in the combustion chamber. The purpose of the ignition system is to furnish high-voltage sparks to the engine cylinders to fire the compressed air/fuel mixture. This chapter explains the components basic to all ignition systems, the operation of specific motorcycle ignition systems, and describes the troubleshooting procedure for each system.

IGNITION SYSTEM COMPONENTS

The basic elements of electrical ignition systems are (Fig. 10-1):

> Voltage source
> Timing device
> Capacitor
> Ignition coil
> Secondary wiring
> Spark plugs

Voltage Source

The voltage source may be either a coil and a rotating magnet, or a battery.

Timing Device

There are different timing device designs. Some timing devices consist of contact breaker points and a cam that is driven off the engine by a shaft. In this type of system the points are timed to open and close in relation to the crankshaft. The timing unit determines when the contact points turn the current on or off. Some systems use a solid-state triggering device, coil and magnetic field, or a light beam instead of contact points.

Most street motorcycles use some form of timing device to advance spark. A motorcycle timing device must begin spark advance at a certain rpm and stop advancing at a cer-

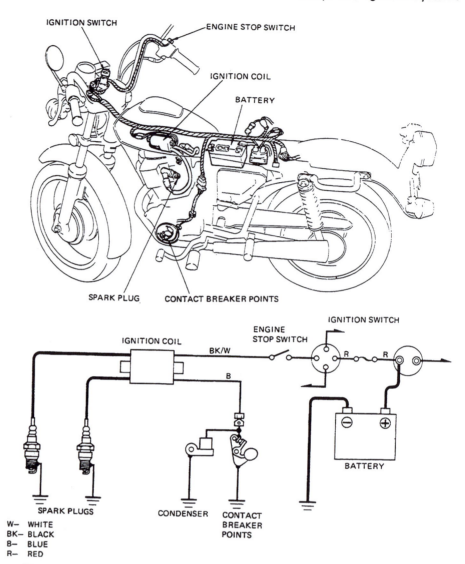

Figure 10-1   Battery-point ignition system (American Honda Motor Company).

tain higher rpm. Spark advance makes the adjustments necessary for changes in load conditions and speed. When the motorcycle is idling, the timing unit is in a retarded position. The spark plug fires a few degrees before the piston reaches top dead center. But when the engine speed increases, combustion must begin earlier. The timing of the spark is advanced to allow for combustion lag. The advance in timing boosts horsepower, but only so much advance is beneficial because of the risk of detonation. Advance curves vary between models (Fig. 10-2).

Mechanical Spark Advance: Motorcycle mechanical advance units consist of a rotating plate to which weights are attached (Fig. 10-3). A rotating shaft spins, and the weights are thrown outward, which causes the timing lobe(s) to advance. Springs are used to keep the weights from being thrown outward at low speed. Weight stops keep the unit from over-advancing. A timing pin or key drives the unit. Some motorcycle advance units are driven off the camshaft, and some are driven off the crankshaft. But all centrifugal advance is controlled only by engine speed or the advance mechanism, not the load on the engine.

Vacuum Advance: Some of the larger motorcycles are equipped with a vacuum advance unit. The main advantage of a vacuum advance unit is increased fuel economy at part throt-

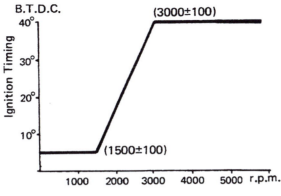

Figure 10-2 Ignition timing/ engine rpm relationship (Kawasaki Motors Corporation, U.S.A.).

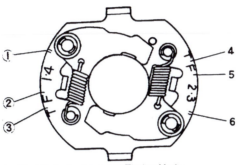

1. #1, 4 Cylinder Advanced Timing Marks
2. #1, 4 Cylinder Timing Mark
3. #1, 4 Cylinder TDC Mark
4. #2, 3 Cylinder TDC Mark
5. #2, 3 Cylinder Timing Mark
6. #2, 3 Cylinder Advanced Timing Marks

Figure 10-3 Centrifugal timing advancer (Kawasaki Motors Corporation, U.S.A.).

tle. At part throttle the volumetric efficiency of most engines is low. This creates a less compressed mixture which must be ignited farther from top dead center. Advancing timing with no engine load at part throttle allows the engine to burn a leaner, cleaner mixture.

The vacuum advance unit operates through intake manifold negative pressure (Fig. 10-4). A vacuum diaphragm is attached to a movable backing plate. When negative pressure is present on the diaphragm, the backing plate rotates to advance ignition timing. This occurs only at part throttle with no-load conditions. During all other conditions, the vacuum advance is set in its retarded position. This prevents the ignition timing from over-advancing when the engine has a high load.

Solid-State Advance: Solid-state advance units are used on some electronically controlled ignition systems. These units advance the timing at a higher rpm. At higher rpm trigger coils generate more voltage, so the voltage rises sooner to the necessary level to fire the ignition (Fig. 10-5). Figure 10-5 shows the trigger coil output at various rpm's and the timing changes that are brought about.

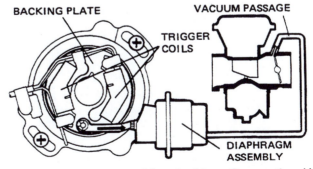

Figure 10-4 Vacuum advance (Yamaha Motor Corporation, U.S.A.).

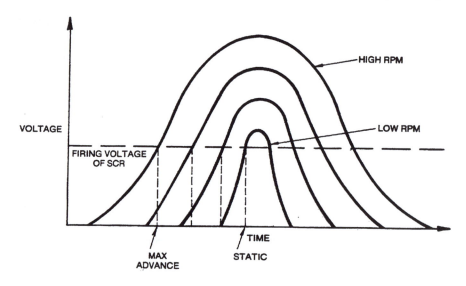

Solid-state advance units are used on some electronically
controlled ignition systems. These units advance the
timing at higher RPM. Generally, they rely upon the fact
that at higher RPM trigger coils generate more voltage.
So the voltage rises sooner to the necessary level to fire
the ignition. The diagram shows the trigger coil output at
various RPM's, and the timing changes brought about.

Figure 10-5   Solid-state advance graph.

A solid-state advance unit is a complex circuit contained in a sealed box. It may use special external coils. The advance curve cannot be adjusted. If the unit does not operate properly, it must be replaced.

Capacitor

A capacitor, also called a *condenser*, stores and discharges electrons (Fig. 10-6). A capacitor is composed of two metal plates with an insulator or dielectric between them. The capacity of the device depends on the size of the conductive areas, the distance between the conductive areas, and the material used for the dielectric. Some common dielectrics are made of paper, wax, mica, and various oxides. The conductive areas can be composed of aluminum, copper, or silver and may take the form of sheets, foil, or plates. Different capacitors have different voltage capacities.

Figure 10-6   Capacitor.

Usually, a capacitor is used to assist the collapse of the primary field and to protect the point gap surface from heavy arcing by providing a place for the current to flow. A capacitor is made of sheets of foil laminated to an insulator or dielectric. The foil and dielectric are rolled and hermetically sealed into a canister. One foil is grounded to the canister, and the other is attached to an insulated wire terminal. The capacitor has a specific capacity that is based on the storage ability of the surface area and the dielectric. The smaller the dielectric's surface area, the larger the capacity of the capacitor. Capacity is measured in microfarads.

Ignition Coil

The ignition coil is used to step up a low voltage to a voltage that is high enough to create a spark at the plug. This voltage surge is carried by a high-tension wire to the spark plugs, where it produces a spark across the spark plug gap. Very high voltage is required at the plug because of the extreme resistance of the plug gap.

There are three phases in the sparking process. The first is the inductive phase. Before the spark occurs, voltage builds up across the spark plug gap. This voltage causes an electric field to develop within the air/fuel mixture in the area. That electric field, when strong enough, causes the mixture to ionize, electrons to flow, and a spark to occur. The instant the spark begins, the voltage at the spark plug drops to a level that is sufficient to sustain the spark.

The length of time between the beginning of the voltage at the plug and the beginning of the spark is called *rise time*. Rise time should be as short as possible to prevent plug fouling. The length of time the spark occurs is called *spark duration*. Spark duration must be long enough to ignite the air/fuel mixture fully.

The second phase of the sparking process is called the *capacitive phase*. It begins when the voltage has dropped so low that the spark stops. In this phase the capacitor and spark plug coil interact to dissipate any electrical energy that was not consumed by the spark.

The last phase is called *point cam dwell angle* or simply *dwell*. During this phase the ignition points are closed, and the magnetic field in the ignition coil is building up for the next spark.

The ignition coil changes electrical energy into magnetic energy and back into electrical energy. An ignition coil consists of two separate windings of insulated wire that are wound around a laminated steel core. Sometimes the windings are connected together. One winding is called the *primary* and the other is the *secondary*. The primary winding consists of a heavy wire wound a few hundred turns. The secondary winding is fine wire wound tens of thousands of turns. The laminated steel core is used to increase the magnetic conductivity or permeability. In a dc ignition coil the secondary winding is wound around the core, and the primary is wound around the two of them. The winding location is reversed for ac coils. Both windings and core are hermetically sealed with a synthetic resin. Terminals are located on the coil's primary and secondary sides.

The difference in the number of coil windings between the primary and secondary windings is the *turns ratio*. If the primary winding has 100 turns of wire and the secondary winding has 1000 turns of wire, the secondary voltage is 10 times greater than that of the primary. The current in the secondary winding is one-tenth the value of the primary winding.

There are basically two types of ignition coils: ac and dc. The coils look the same, but each uses different turns ratios and voltage to the primary coil, and the ac coil may be internally grounded (Figs. 10-7 and 10-8).

An ignition coil operates on the principle of induction. When a magnetic field is passed through a conductor, voltage is induced in the conductor. Current flows either from a battery, an ac source, or a capacitor through the primary winding of the coil and a magnetic field builds up surrounding the coil. The amount of time for buildup depends on the coil's impedance or the total resistance in the circuit.

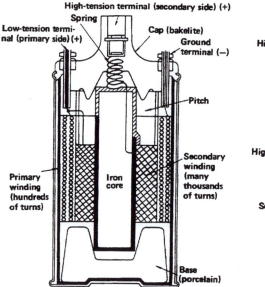

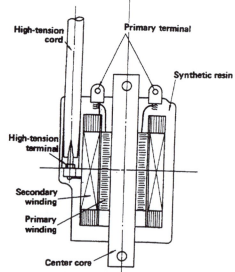

Figure 10-7 Dc primary ignition coil (Yamaha Motor Corporation, U.S.A.).

Figure 10-8 Ac primary ignition coil (Yamaha Motor Corporation, U.S.A.).

Some ignition coils operate on a rapid buildup of the magnetic field; others operate on a rapid collapse of the magnetic field. The current to the primary winding must be interrupted (dc) or varied (ac) for a change in the magnetic field to occur. Since the current in the primary winding is always changing, so is the magnetic field. As current in the primary winding builds, the magnetic field expands outward. When the current stops, the field collapses inward toward the secondary winding. Most coils have the primary and secondary windings wound in opposite directions to ensure that the magnetic field distorts when induction occurs. Some ignition coils use two high-tension terminals to the spark plugs. On this type of ignition coil, one of the leads has a negative polarity, and the other has a positive polarity. The polarity of single lead coils is always negative.

Secondary Wiring

Secondary wiring is the high-tension wire that is connected to the ignition coil and the spark plug caps. The wire is heavily insulated to contain the high voltage it carries. It must resist oil and heat without producing electrical leakage, which is known as *breakdown*. The center core of the wire is constructed either of metallic wire or of carbon-impregnated string.

Spark Plugs

The spark plug carries the high-voltage spark across the gap, converts the potential difference into enough heat to sustain combustion, and controls the engine temperature. A spark plug is an inexpensive, replaceable device that is installed into a combustion chamber. Spark plugs vary in size, heat range, and tip design. Although the design may vary, there are only three main parts of a spark plug: the insulator, shell, and center electrode (Fig. 10-9).

Insulator: The insulator is hollow and usually made of aluminum oxide because of its excellent insulating properties, heat conductivity, and strength. The length of the insulator nose exposed to the hot combustion gases determines the heat range of the plug. The top of the insulator usually has three to five ribs to increase the surface area and to prevent a *flashover*. A flashover occurs when a spark jumps across the surface of the insulator from the terminal to the body of the plug. The insulator nose must withstand hot combustion

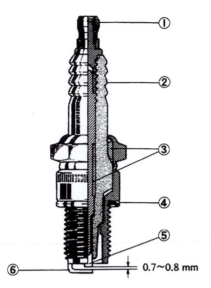

1. Terminal
2. Insulator
3. Cement
4. Gasket
5. Center Electrode
6. Side Electrode

Figure 10-9 Spark plug construction (Kawasaki Motors Corporation, U.S.A.).

gases, engine vibration, high combustion pressures, removal, abrasive cleaning, and installation. The insulator's operating temperature must be at least 650°F or fouling occurs. Preignition will occur if the temperature exceeds 1600°F (Fig. 10-10).

Shell: The shell or body of the plug is made of steel and the threaded portion screws into the cylinder head. A hex head on top of the shell fits a plug wrench. A reusable gasket is

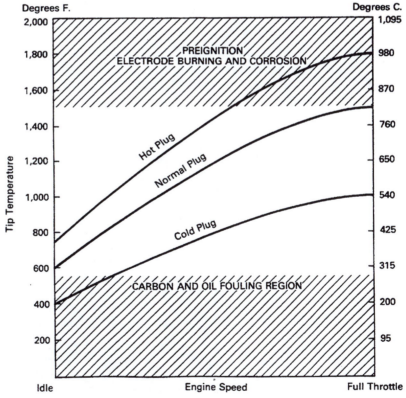

Figure 10-10 Spark plug heat range chart (Champion Spark Plug Company).

attached to the base of the threads to aid in heat transfer and sealing. Different thread diameters, lengths, and hex heads accommodate the many combustion chamber designs. A side electrode is attached to the base of the shell. Most side electrodes are resistance-welded to the shell but can be bent to make gap adjustments. Electrodes are available in many designs.

Center Electrode: A center electrode is contained in the hollow insulator, which is pressed into the shell. The center electrode is composed of different metals, which provide electrical conductivity, thermal dissipation, and resistance to chemical corrosion. The center electrode may include a resistor to reduce radio interference. Some spark plugs have a small gap in the center electrode to reduce voltage bleed-off from the coil. Center electrodes vary in diameter.

The center electrode and the lower portion of the insulator are the hottest parts of the spark plug. This allows the insulator to be burned clean of any deposit that would cause a conductive path for voltage loss. Current flows from the center electrode to the side electrode when a single spark plug lead ignition coil is used. A spark requires less voltage to jump from a hot surface than from a cold surface.

Heat Range: Heat range is the plug's ability to transfer heat from the firing tip to the cylinder head. The rate of heat transfer depends primarily on the distance it must travel. A "cold" plug has a short heat range and a short insulator nose; a "hot" plug has a long heat range and a longer nose (Fig. 10-11).

Tip Design: Tips are coated with gold and platinum to prevent corrosion caused by heat and high voltage. Tip diameters vary. A center electrode with a small tip allows more air/fuel mixture to be exposed to the spark. A projected tip operates well at low speed because the long insulator nose holds heat well, and it operates well at high speeds because the incoming air/fuel mixture cools the tip and prevents preignition. A disadvantage of the projected tip is the clearance it requires. A spark plug with a retracted tip is used where very high temperatures are present and a projected ground electrode would overheat. The side electrode of this type of plug is located inside the shell to keep it cooler. This type of plug is subject to low-speed fouling because of the retracted tip. A surface gap plug is used when preignition is a problem. The insulator of this type of plug is extended to the base of the shell. The side electrode is located at the base of the shell, and the center electrode is flush with it. Surface gap plugs require a very high voltage to fire.

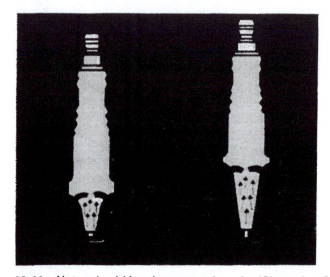

Figure 10-11 Hot and cold insulator nose lengths (Champion Spark Plug Company).

There are specific testing and servicing procedures for each ignition system component.

Battery

When servicing a battery-assisted ignition system, inspect and service the battery as described in Chapter 9. Perform a load test and check the battery's charging rate.

Capacitor

Ignition capacitors usually have a capacity of 0.18 to 0.26 microfarad. Special electrical testing equipment must be used to measure microfarads. The surface condition of the contact points also indicates inefficient capacitor operation. Metal transfer is caused by arcing at the point's surface. If the system is negatively ground, metal transfer will occur from the fixed, negative contact point to the positive side contact point as a result of low capacity. If the metal transfer is from the positive to the negative side, the capacity is too large. Remember this "3M rule" for contact point condition and capacity: if minus (negative) point is minus metal (pitted), the capacitor is minus capacity. Contact point surface must offer low resistance and good heat transfer, and must be flat, smooth, and clean (Fig. 10-12).

Not all point arcing is caused by capacity faults. Check the grounds and primary windings for low resistance. Points may burn because of high resistance at the contact surface.

Point Gap

Contact point gap is critical. If the point gap is too large, the time the points are closed will be too short. This will not allow sufficient buildup of the ignition coil's magnetic field. If the point gap is too narrow, the heavy current flow will cause burning.

A feeler gauge can be used to measure the point gap, but a dwell meter is more accurate. A dwell meter is connected and operated while the engine is running. It indicates the number of degrees of crankshaft rotation the points are closed. Dwell depends on the number and shape of the lobes.

Use an ammeter connected in series with the primary winding to indicate the current flow when the engine is running. Low current weakens the magnetic field produced, and the secondary ignition voltage will be weak. This may be caused by dirty points. Measure the resistance at the point gap with an ohmmeter to ensure peak coil saturation.

Servicing Ignition Points

Water, oil, dirt, or other contaminants can cause contact point fouling. Spray fouled points with electrical contact cleaner. Misaligned points burn quickly and reduce primary voltage. If the contact points are not aligned, bend only the fixed side, which is usually negative. Inspect the thickness of the heel or rubbing block. As the rubbing block wears, the

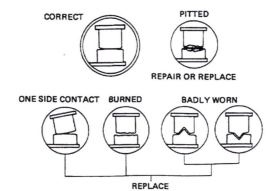

Figure 10-12 Contact breaker point surface conditions (American Honda Motor Company).

point gap decreases, which in turn increases the dwell. Lubricate the rubbing block and pads to reduce wear. Check the service manual for point gap specifications. Replace the points if you have any doubt about their condition (Fig. 10-13).

Ignition Timing

There are two methods used to check ignition timing: static and dynamic. Most engines have timing marks stamped on the flywheel rotor. Usually, the letter "F" identifies the static fire mark. Some two-stroke engines do not have timing marks and a special timing dial gauge must be used to measure the piston travel. Consult the service manual for timing marks and specifications, and use the following procedures for static and dynamic timing.

Static Timing: This method is used only on engines equipped with points. Use a battery-powered test light or a buzz box to time energy transfer ignition systems (Fig. 10-14). Locate the source coil wire, remove the timing cover, and identify the timing marks. Disconnect the source coil wire from the ignition coil and connect the test light or buzz box to the

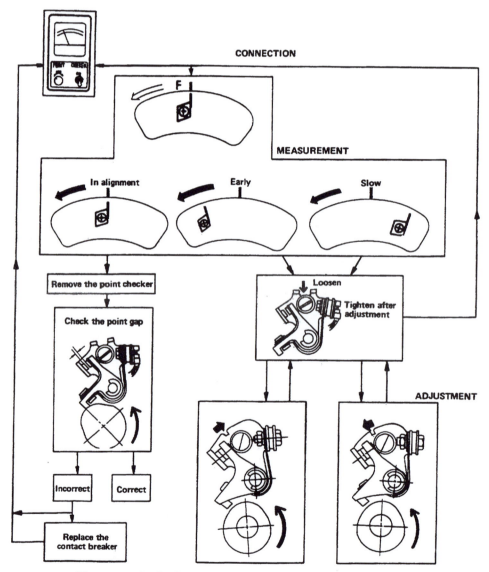

Figure 10-13 Ignition timing adjustments (Yamaha Motor Corporation, U.S.A.).

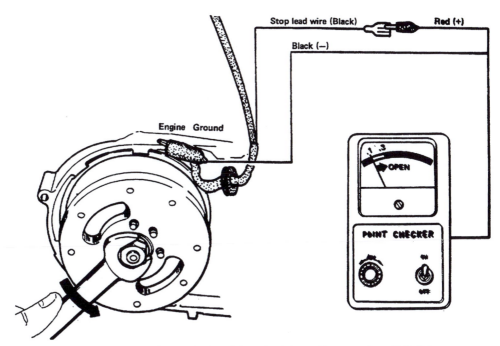

Figure 10-14   Static timing (Yamaha Motor Corporation, U.S.A.).

source coil on the positive side and connect the negative side to a good engine ground. Rotate the flywheel in the direction of normal rotation. The light or buzzer will turn off when the points are open and turn on when the points are closed. An energy transfer system fires the spark plug when the points open. The points should open when the firing mark reaches the stationary pointer and the light or buzzer should come on. If they do not, adjust the point gap so that the points open on the firing mark. On some older models the advance unit must be locked in the full-advance state to static-time the engine.

After setting the timing, check the point gap. If the point gap is smaller than the service specifications recommend, the rubbing block is worn and the points must be replaced. Lubricate the point cam with a small amount of point cam lubrication to lengthen the service life of the rubbing block.

To static-time a dc battery-point ignition system, use a self-powered continuity light and the motorcycle's electrical source. Set the point gap at the widest opening according to the service specifications. Connect the test light with one end to the engine ground and the other to the hot side of the points. Leave all connections connected. Dc battery-point ignition systems fire the spark plugs when the points are open. When the ignition switch and engine stop switch are on and if the battery is fully charged, the test light should come on when the points are open. Set the point gap. Adjust the point breaker plate by rotating the plate in the direction of shaft rotation to retard the ignition timing or by rotating the plate in the opposite direction to advance the timing. The test light should come on as the stationary pointer aligns with the static fire mark.

When timing a twin-cylinder engine with two sets of points, set the left cylinder first and then the right. On four-cylinder engines, set the first and fourth cylinders and then set the second and third cylinders.

Dynamic Timing: Dynamic timing is made with a stroboscopic timing light while the engine is running (Fig. 10-15). Any ignition system that uses timing advance marks and a high-tension spark plug lead can be checked for proper ignition timing with a timing strobe light. The timing light must be powered by an external electrical source. If the motorcycle is not equipped with a battery, use a battery with the proper voltage. Most timing lights are powered by a 12-volt system, but a few can also use 6 V dc. There are three wires on the timing light. Connect the red wire to the positive battery terminal, the black wire to the neg-

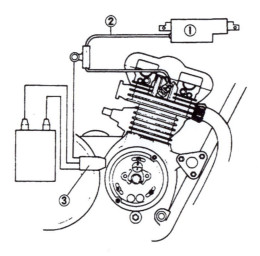

1. Ignition Coil
2. Spark Plug Lead
3. Strobe Light

Figure 10-15   Dynamic timing
(Kawasaki Motors Corporation, U.S.A.).

ative battery terminal, and the trigger lead to the number one cylinder spark plug wire. Most timing lights use an inductive trigger pickup to time the strobe. The inductive pickup is used on each cylinder or cylinder set to check the timing. The timing light will flash when the spark plug fires.

As the engine idles, the timing light should flash at the idle fire mark. As the engine increases in speed, the spark plug should fire sooner to overcome combustion lag. This causes the timing light to flash farther and farther away from the idle timing mark. Advance fire marks should align with the stationary pointer at the proper engine speed. Consult the service manual for the engine advance specifications. If no advance is evident, check for seizure of the advance unit. If the idle fire mark does not remain stationary at idle, check for weak spring tension in the centrifugal advance unit. If the timing exceeds the advance fire marks, check to see if the weight stops are bent on the centrifugal advance unit. The manufacturers usually recommend replacing the centrifugal advance unit if any of these problems are found. Solid-state advance units must be replaced if any advance problems occur.

Test the operation of a vacuum advance unit with a timing light and a vacuum pump, or rotate the unit manually to full advance and block the vent hole on the atmosphere side. When the breaker plate is released, it should not rotate back. If the unit returns, this may indicate a diaphragm leak. Consult the service manual for procedures.

Ignition Coils

There are three tests which can be made on any coil. Consult the service manual for specific testing procedures and specifications.

Performance Test: This is the best test for an ignition coil. The coil should produce a spark that jumps a 7-millimeter gap continuously without breakdown. Do not allow the spark to jump more than 7 millimeters, or the coil's internal insulation may be damaged. Test the coil at operating temperatures to ensure that no breakdown exists.

Resistance Test: A resistance test will not duplicate the high voltage a coil produces, and the resistance value will vary with different types of coils. Test the resistance of the primary and secondary windings (Figs. 10-16 and 10-17). Be sure to remove the spark plug caps before testing the secondary winding, or the caps' resistance will be added to the reading.

Insulation Breakdown Test: With the points open, check the primary winding for continuity and insulation breakdown.

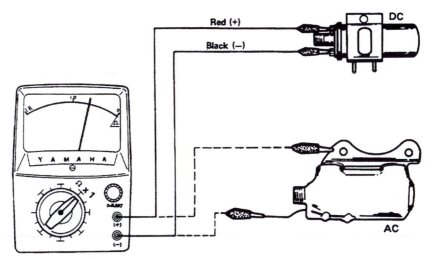

Figure 10-16 Primary winding resistance test (Yamaha Motor Corporation, U.S.A.).

Secondary Wiring

Inspect the high-tension wires. Moisture can cause a wire's metallic core to corrode at the connection. Wire with a carbon-impregnated string core may break if it is pulled too hard and create a spark gap between the wire and connector. The arc will soon erode the string and cause misfiring.

The high-tension wires and plug caps break down with age. Test the wire and plug caps separately with an ohmmeter for specific resistance. Wiggle the wire to check for breakage. Check for corrosion at the cap and high-tension lead. You may have to cut back the wire to get a good connection.

Spark Plugs

The spark plug's appearance indicates the condition of the cylinder (Fig. 10-18). The normal color of the insulator nose should range from light tan to gray. If unleaded fuel is used, the insulator nose will be lighter in color. The electrodes should be flat. These are indica-

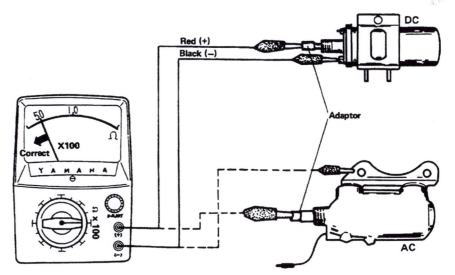

Figure 10-17 Secondary winding resistance test (Yamaha Motor Corporation, U.S.A.).

NORMAL
Correct heat range

SPLASHED DEPOSITS
Containment from combustion environment

WORN
Replace with new spark plugs

HIGH TEMPERATURE GLAZING
Varnish-like deposit from combustion, coating the plug insulator

OIL DEPOSITS
Poor oil control; common in four-cycle engines

OVERHEATED
Improper heat range plug or increased combustion chamber temperature

CARBON DEPOSITS
Incorrect heat range, rich mixture, or weak ignition; common in four-cycle engines

PREIGNITION
Improper heat range plug, incorrect ignition timing, lean fuel/air mixture, or "hot spots" in cylinder

ASH DEPOSITS
Poor oil control, improper oil, or fuel/oil additives

DETONATION
Wrong fuel; increased fuel octane requirement from incorrect timing or air/fuel ratio; overheating

GAP BRIDGE
Deposits bridging gap space

MECHANICAL DAMAGE
Improper plug reach, improper gapping, handling, or foreign object in engine

Figure 10-18   Spark plug firing end conditions (Champion Spark Plug Company).

tions of good heat range for the tested speed and engine load. There may be some variations for two-stroke engines.

Before removing the plug, clean the area around the hole, so that rocks, rust, and sand do not enter the combustion chamber. Apply air pressure around the plug threads before removing it with the last few turns. If multiplugs are used, note which cylinder each plug came from. Make sure that the washer is attached to the spark plug and not left in the head. Inspect the plug for fouling.

Spark Plug Fouling

There are several types of fouling.

Carbon Fouling: A carbon-fouled plug is coated with dry, fluffy carbon. The carbon deposits are caused by a cold heat range, long idling or continued low speed, an over-rich fuel mixture, restricted air passage, or retarded ignition. To cure carbon fouling, use a hotter plug, or set the ignition timing or mixture ratio.

Lead Fouling: Lead fouling is found only when leaded gasoline is used. The compounds in leaded gas are deposited on the insulator. The compounds will not conduct until the plug temperature increases. Plug temperature increases when the throttle opens, but opening the throttle to clean the plug will result in fouling. Engine speed should be increased slowly to prevent lead fouling. The insulator of a lead-fouled plug will vary from white to yellow, or brown to black. To correct lead fouling, use a hotter plug or unleaded fuel if permissible.

Oil Fouling: In a two-stroke engine, oil fouling is caused by an over-rich premix ratio or internal leaks. In a four-stroke engine, it is caused by oil control problems. An oil-fouled plug is black and shiny. To correct the problem, set the mixture and make a leakdown test.

Silica Fouling: Silica fouling is caused by sand that has entered the combustion chamber. Make a compression test and check for top-end damage before replacing the plug.

Wet Fouling: Wet fouling is caused by an excessively rich mixture or by no-spark conditions.

When inspecting the spark plugs, also inspect the insulators and electrodes. An overheated insulator is bleached and spotted, or split. Check to see if the glue has melted around the center electrode. Overheated electrodes are burned and purple. Overheating is caused by incorrect heat range, low-octane fuel, advanced spark timing, a lean mixture, or insufficient cooling. To correct overheating, use a colder plug, higher-octane fuel, set the spark timing or mixture ratio, or increase the cooling.

Preignition will burn away the electrodes and possibly the insulator. Look through the spark plug hole for a gray area on the piston surface. If preignition continues, the piston will melt, resulting in aluminum deposits on the spark plug. If deposits are found, check for engine damage at the top end.

Because the electrodes are corroded by chemicals and electricity, the spark plug gap becomes wider. The sharp edges of the electrode become rounded, causing a larger gap and increased resistance at the gap. The voltage requirement increases to the point of misfire. Replace the plug before the electrode is completely eroded.

Servicing Spark Plugs

A fouled plug can be cleaned and regapped. Use the following procedure:

1. Blast the insulator with cleaning sand to remove all deposits.
2. File the electrodes flat if the tip is not fine wire. Fine wire will bend under the pressure of a file.
3. Spray the plug tip and shell threads with electrical contact cleaner to remove any remaining blast material.

4. Use a spark plug gapping tool to reset the electrode gap to specifications. Measure with a wire feeler gauge. Pits in the electrode surface will give a flat feeler gauge a false reading.

5. Apply a light coating of antiseize lubricant to the center threads.

6. Screw the plug in hand-tight to avoid cross threading.

7. Use a torque wrench to tighten the plug. A loose plug will not dissipate heat quickly. A plug that is too tight may cause the electrode to change the gap clearance, or it may lose its gastight seal. Tighten the plug according to the following general guidelines:

10-mm plug	to 7–10 lb (1.0–1.5 kilograms mass, or kgm)
12-mm plug	to 10–14 lb (1.5–2.0 kgm)
14-mm plug	to 14–18 lb (2.0–2.5 kgm)

Heat Range

Great care should be taken when changing the heat range. If you select a heat range that is too cold, the insulator or tip may foul. When selecting a heat range, try to use the hottest plug possible without creating preignition. At low speed or idle, a hot plug will burn off carbon deposits on the insulator.

FACTORS AFFECTING IGNITION

Spark advance, engine design, and the type of fuel used affect ignition design and operation.

Spark Advance

Spark advance is a major consideration in ignition design. The ignition is timed to deliver the spark from the coil to the spark plug at the proper time for the power stroke. Ignition advance moves the ignition spark forward in time. The faster the piston travels, the less time is available to overcome combustion lag and for active combustion to take place. Advancing spark timing creates efficient combustion at higher speeds.

Engine Design

Differences in engine design and fuel produce different ignition needs.

Less engine load	Combustion is slower, more spark advance is required.
More engine load	Combustion is faster, less spark advance is required.
High engine speed	Combustion has less time to occur, more spark advance is required.
Low engine speed	Combustion has more time to occur, less spark advance is required.
Cold engine temperature	Combustion is slower, more spark advance is required.
Hot engine temperature	Combustion is faster, less spark advance is required.
Large cylinder bore	Combustion is slower, more spark advance is required.
Small cylinder bore	Combustion is faster, less spark advance is required.
Low compression ratio	Combustion is slower, more spark advance is required.
High compression ratio	Combustion is faster, less spark advance is required.

Fuel Characteristics

The type of fuel used affects combustion and ignition timing.

Low-volatility fuel	Combustion is slower, more spark advance is required.
High-volatility fuel	Combustion is faster, less spark advance is required.
Lean air/fuel mixture	Combustion is faster (up to lean misfire zone), less spark advance is required.
Rich air/fuel mixture	Combustion is slower (up to fouling range), more spark advance is required.
High-octane fuel	Combustion is slower, more spark advance is required.
Low-octane fuel	Combustion is faster, less spark advance is required.

Other Factors

The combustion chamber shape, the position of the spark plug in the cylinder head, carbon deposits, and lingering exhaust gases in the combustion chamber also affect ignition.

IGNITION SYSTEMS

There are two types of motorcycle ignition systems: battery-assisted ignition systems and ignition systems without batteries. This section explains how each ignition system functions.

Battery-Assisted Ignition Systems

There are four battery-assisted ignition systems.

Battery-Point Ignition: This system has been used for years in four-stroke motorcycles; it produces a long-lasting spark at the plug gap. The system consists of a battery, ignition coil, contact points, a capacitor, system wiring, and some type of timing advance. When the ignition switch is turned on, current flows into the primary side of the ignition coil from the contact points. A spring is used to close the points. The point springs are made of two metals, so heat will not change spring tensions. When the points are closed, the current flows and the ignition coil's magnetic saturation begins. A cam is used to open the points. The contact points are wired in a series circuit to interrupt the primary coil dc flow. This interruption in direct current causes the magnetic field to collapse. The collapse is timed with a point cam and breaker contact points. The capacitor assists in the collapse of the magnetic field and protects the point gap surface from heavy arcing by providing a place for current to flow (Fig. 10-19).

Transistor-Assisted Contact Ignition (TAC):   The first attempt to eliminate the heavy current flow at the contact points was made with the use of a transistor. A transistor is a solid-state switch which can handle a higher current flow than its mechanical counterpart. An emitter, collector, and base are contained in the sealed transistor box. Current flows from the emitter to the collector as long as a trickle of current flows through the base. The con-

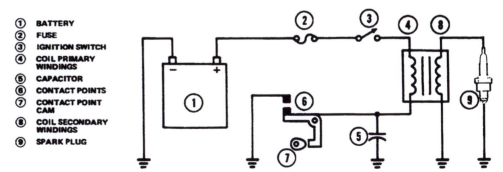

① BATTERY
② FUSE
③ IGNITION SWITCH
④ COIL PRIMARY WINDINGS
⑤ CAPACITOR
⑥ CONTACT POINTS
⑦ CONTACT POINT CAM
⑧ COIL SECONDARY WINDINGS
⑨ SPARK PLUG

Figure 10-19   Battery-point ignition system (American Honda Motor Company).

tact points control the trickle of current. Instead of 3 amperes at the contact points, this system has less than 1 ampere. There is little erosion at the point surfaces because of the reduced current flow. The primary current flow from the emitter to the collector is turned on quicker and shut off faster than conventional systems. Timing is more precise because the switching process is quicker. Higher ignition coil current can be used and this produces a shorter rise time and a higher voltage output. Decreased rise time and higher voltage produce less plug fouling and increased performance.

Transistor Pointless Ignition (TPI): Transistor pointless ignition eliminates the problems associated with TAC and increases timing accuracy (Fig. 10-20).

Instead of using the contact points to trigger the transistor, a magnetic switching device or pulse generator is used. The pulse generator is located on the breaker plate. A timing lobe called a *reluctor* is used in place of the breaker cam. The pulse generator is mounted so that the reluctor spins freely inside of it. An air gap is maintained between the reluctor and the pulse generator. Since no contact is made between them, adjustments are eliminated and timing should not change.

The pulse generator consists of a permanent magnet and a pickup coil. The reluctor is made of steel to enhance the magnetic field. When the reluctor is not moving, a weak magnetic field is established in the pickup coil. As the reluctor begins to rotate, the air gap between the pickup coil and the reluctor decreases. The strength of the magnetic field increases and as it builds and moves around the pickup coil, an electric field is induced in the coil. This electric field is positive at one end of the coil and negative at the other end. The magnetic field continues to build until the reluctor is as close as possible to the pickup coil. When the reluctor passes the closest point and the air gap begins to increase, the pickup coil's magnetic field begins to collapse. This reverses the coil's polarity. The positive end of the coil is now negative, and the voltage pulse is sent to an amplifier. Once the pulse generator's signal has been amplified, it is sent to the base side of the primary circuit transistor, which then shuts off the current flow to the ignition coil and voltage is induced in the secondary winding. When the air gap between the pulse generator and reluctor increases to a certain point, the pickup coil becomes positive again. This action turns on the primary circuit transistor, and current flows again to the ignition coil.

Digitally controlled ignition systems are found on some late-model dc ignitions that use a pulse generator as the timing device. This system uses an integrated circuit (IC) chip

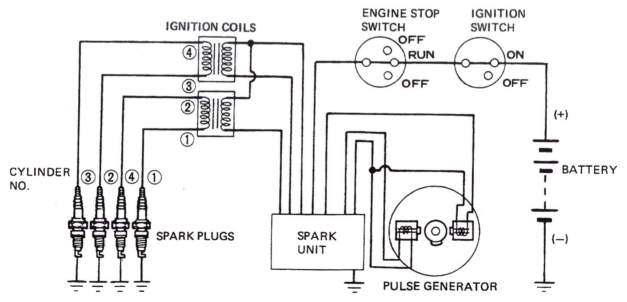

Figure 10-20 Transistor pointless ignition system (American Honda Motor Company).

to control the advance curve. The IC chip is made of semiconductor material and contains multiple circuits. No repairs can be made to an IC chip.

A digitally controlled ignition system provides very accurate timing which creates lower emissions and a more consistent power output. Unlike standard electronic or centrifugal advance units that determine timing advance based on a linear curve, the timing of the advance spark is variable based on the engine's rpm. In some cases the advance curve adjusts for throttle position and gear selection (Fig. 10-21). The motorcycle manufacturer performs extensive engine testing to determine the optimum advance timing curve from idle to the engine's maximum rpm. This information is then programmed into the IC chip's memory.

Hall Effect Transistorized Controlled Ignition: This type of ignition system uses a Hall effect generator as a triggering device for the ignition control unit. This unit is similar to the pulse generator used in a transistorized pointless ignition system (Fig. 10-22).

The Hall effect generator consists of a stationary sensor plate and a rotating timing disk or rotor. The stationary sensor plate contains a Hall integrated circuit and a magnet. The magnet is placed at right angles to the Hall integrated circuit. The solid portion of the timing disk separates the Hall integrated circuit and the magnet. The timing disk also has a window which exposes the Hall integrated circuit to the magnet at times that correspond to the ignition cycles. When battery current flows through the Hall integrated circuit and the circuit is exposed to the magnet's magnetic field, the circuit redirects voltage to the ignition control unit.

Ignitions without Battery

A magneto ignition is a self-contained system that produces high voltage and distributes it to the spark plug at the correct instant. A magneto system does not require assistance from a battery. There are three motorcycle magneto ignition designs: the high tension, energy transfer, and capacitor discharge. The high-tension magneto system does not use any external coils to produce high voltage, but the capacitor discharge and energy transfer systems do.

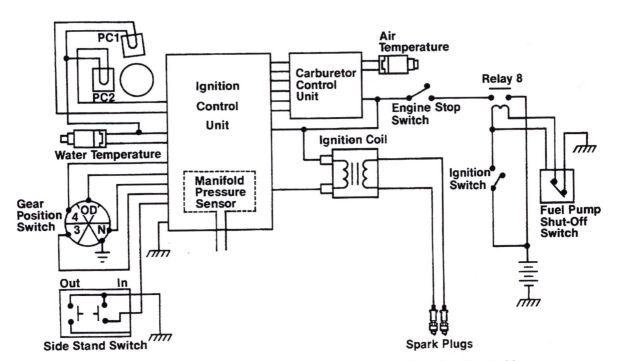

Figure 10-21 Digital ignition system (American Honda Motor Company).

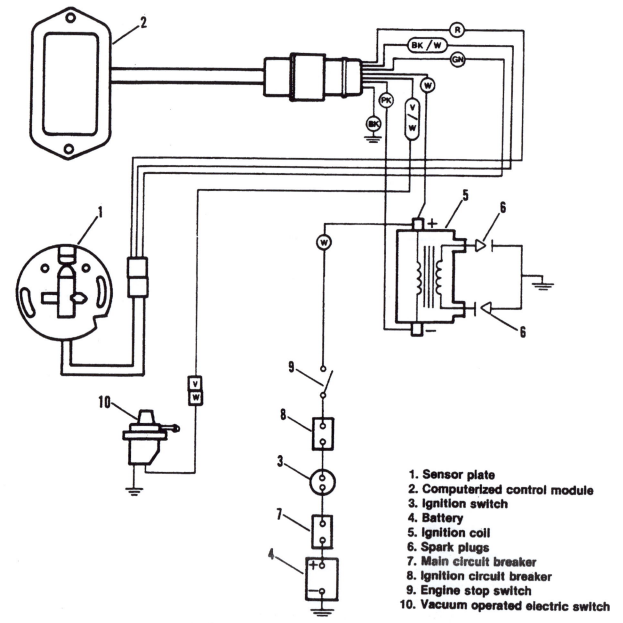

Figure 10-22 Hall effect transistorized controlled ignition (Harley-Davidson Motor Company, Inc.).

1. Sensor plate
2. Computerized control module
3. Ignition switch
4. Battery
5. Ignition coil
6. Spark plugs
7. Main circuit breaker
8. Ignition circuit breaker
9. Engine stop switch
10. Vacuum operated electric switch

   A magneto ignition system has three advantages over the battery-assisted ignition systems: no battery or external source of current is needed to operate a magneto system, a quicker rise time is produced, and the potential voltage output increases with the magneto's speed. However, a magneto system has low voltage at starting speed and little advance capability.

High-Tension Magneto Ignition: The high-tension magneto system found on some early motorcycles consists of a permanent magnet rotor. A laminated iron horseshoe is mounted around the rotor. An induction coil is wound around the core of the laminated horseshoe. The primary winding of the induction coil is wired in series with contact points. As the magnetized rotor revolves inside the horseshoe, a primary current is established. The points are in the closed position. As the rotor continues to rotate, the field builds to a peak. When the primary current is at its peak, the contact points open. The collapse of the peak primary

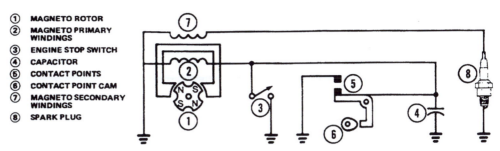

Figure 10-23 High-tension magneto ignition system (American Honda Motor Company).

voltage in the primary coil induces high voltage in the secondary coil, which causes a spark at the plug gap. A capacitor assists in the collapse of the primary field and protects the point gap surface (Fig. 10-23).

Energy Transfer Magneto Ignition: The energy transfer magneto ignition system uses a flywheel with permanent magnets which rotate around a laminated core with coil windings. An external step-up induction coil sparks the plug. Extra coils that power lights or charge a battery may be located under the flywheel. Points are used in parallel along with the capacitor. The induction coil differs from one used in battery-point ignition in that the primary is wired to ground. Normally, the breaker points are closed. The points are opened only for the amount of time it takes for flux reversal in the generating coil. Some energy transfer systems use a centrifugal timing advance, but the design creates very limited advance curves.

The energy transfer system uses a two-legged laminated iron core with coil windings wound over the top. The flywheel's magnets rotate around the poles. When one north pole magnet and one south pole magnet line up with the two poles, a magnetic flux line is established. As the flywheel continues to rotate, the poles change polarity. This change in polarity is timed with the contact point opening, and voltage is induced into the primary side of the ignition coil (Fig. 10-24). The rapid voltage surge that flows into the primary side of the induction coil causes the secondary coil to build up. It is this rapid buildup that makes the coil produce spark at the plug. Because it only takes two magnets to operate the system, and most systems have more than two, the points stay closed for about 320° of crankshaft rotation (Fig. 10-25).

Because of the energy transfer ignition design, peak generated voltage only lasts for approximately 20° of crankshaft movement. This limits the amount of advance that can be used. The maximum spark voltage varies with engine speed, and the manufacturer must compromise on a timing point. The timing point must not vary from the manufacturer's specifications, or optimum performance will not be obtained.

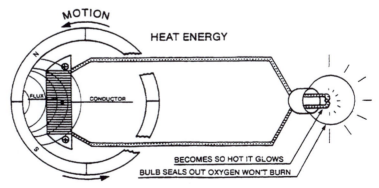

Figure 10-24 Magnet passing a coil wire (American Suzuki Motor Corporation).

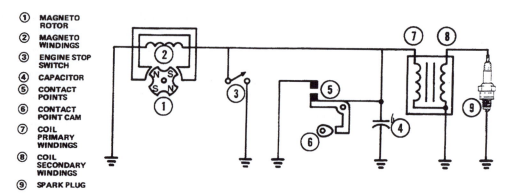

①	MAGNETO ROTOR
②	MAGNETO WINDINGS
③	ENGINE STOP SWITCH
④	CAPACITOR
⑤	CONTACT POINTS
⑥	CONTACT POINT CAM
⑦	COIL PRIMARY WINDINGS
⑧	COIL SECONDARY WINDINGS
⑨	SPARK PLUG

Figure 10-25 Energy transfer ignition system (American Honda Motor Company).

Capacitor Discharge Ignition (CDI): Because of the demand for higher voltage and quicker rise times, the capacitor discharge ignition system is used on many motorcycles today. This completely solid-state ignition has maintenance-free magnetic timing that operates at high speed. Some CDI units have incorporated an electronic timing advance. Capacitor discharge ignition uses a method of rapid buildup of coil field that is similar to the energy transfer system.

The CDI consists of an exciter coil or ac generator which charges the capacitor with up to 500 volts. A diode acts as a one-way valve to prevent the capacitor from discharging before the appropriate moment. The capacitor stores the voltage until the timed discharge. A zener diode protects the capacitor from overcharging by allowing the excess voltage to bleed away. A trigger coil triggers the voltage at the silicon-controlled rectifier (SCR), which discharges the capacitor when trigger voltage is present at the gate. The capacitor discharges through the ac ignition coil and induces high voltage to the spark plug gap. The primary and secondary windings share a common ground (Fig. 10-26).

As the rotating permanent magnets move around the exciter coil, a positive waveform is produced. This positive charge flows through the diode and charges the capacitor. Capacitor discharge is blocked by the diode and zener diode. The zener diode discharges in reverse bias only if the voltage is too high. This allows complete charging at low ac generator speed and prevents overcharging at high speed. After the capacitor has been charged, the rotating permanent magnets move past the exciter coil and on to the trigger coil. A small trigger voltage is induced which turns on the SCR when the voltage value is high enough. When the SCR completes the circuit, the capacitor discharges its voltage through it and into ground. Voltage continues to flow into the pulse transformer's primary windings and onto the back side of the capacitor. It is this rapid discharge of voltage into the primary winding that produces extreme voltage at the secondary winding.

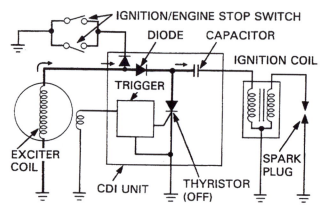

Figure 10-26 Capacitor discharge ignition system (American Honda Motor Company).

There are many advantages to this ignition system. Because the magnetic field builds rapidly, rise times are very short. High voltage appears at the spark plug gap before fouling can discharge voltage across the insulator. Larger spark gaps can be used because of increased voltage. Capacitor discharge ignition systems are maintenance-free, and many have a fixed timing point. High starting voltage is achieved at low speed because of the zener's ability to limit voltage at high ac generator speeds. This means that the exciter coil's output can be high at low speed without damaging components at high speed.

Timing advance is easily incorporated into the CDI system. Since the timing operation is controlled by trigger voltage at the SCR, an earlier voltage increase will advance ignition timing. As the permanent magnets rotate at increased speed, the voltage buildup in the trigger coil occurs sooner. This advances the ignition timing in direct relation to engine speed. Some solid-state advance systems incorporate a limiter to prevent excessive advance. A test of the advance system can be made only by performance testing.

TROUBLE-SHOOTING IGNITION SYSTEMS

A logical system of testing will reveal the problem when an ignition system fails to operate. The following procedure applies specifically to battery-point ignition, but it can be generally applied to each ignition system. Differences and additional procedures will be provided for each ignition system.

Troubleshooting Battery-Point Ignition

Consult the service manual for specifications and use the following procedure:

1. Service and test the battery.
2. If the battery test results are positive, use a voltmeter to check for a voltage drop at the primary side of the ignition coil with the points closed. If the voltmeter fluctuates or fails to register, the contact points may be at fault. If there is no voltage to the coil, consult the service manual for ignition switch testing procedure.
3. Make a point resistance test to determine if there is any loss in the contact surface voltage. Inspect the points. Lubricate the point opening lobe to prevent gap closure caused by wear. If metal transfer at the point surface is excessive, test the capacitor.
4. Test the ignition coil.
5. Inspect the system's wiring.

Troubleshooting TAC

Consult the service manual and follow the procedure given for battery-point ignition. As the rubbing block wears, the point gap decreases, which increases dwell and changes timing. High-speed point bounce, slow-speed sticking, and general sluggish movement may occur because of the extended life of the point surface. If the ignition coil test results are positive, voltage is present at the primary side, the points are in good operating condition, and the system wiring is functional, then the transistor may be at fault. Consult the service manual for testing procedures.

Troubleshooting TPI

Follow the standard troubleshooting procedure. In addition, check to see if the reluctor is spinning while cranking the engine. Check the air gap between the reluctor and the coil. Sometimes the timing pin or key is sheared off when the engine is improperly manually rotated (Fig. 10-27). Test the pulse generator by connecting an ohmmeter to each end of the coil's wiring. This will measure coil resistance. Compare this with the service manual specifications.

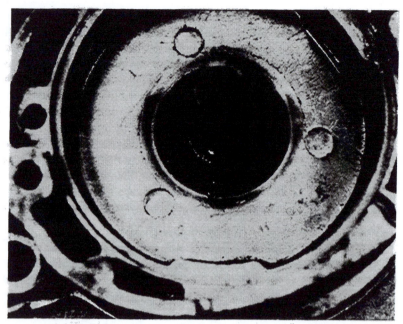

Figure 10-27 Sheared ignition timing pin on camshaft.

Troubleshooting Photo-Optic Ignition

Most of the problems with this system are caused by the lighting device. The output of light-emitting diodes may vary with temperature changes. Dirt and contamination may block the light beam. Consult the service manual and follow the standard troubleshooting procedure.

Troubleshooting High-Tension Magneto

Test the voltage source for voltage. If the voltage does not meet specifications, make a resistance test and an insulation breakdown test. Follow the standard troubleshooting procedures for the ignition coil, ignition switch, contact points, and system wiring.

Troubleshooting Energy Transfer Magneto

Follow the procedure given for high-tension magneto.

Troubleshooting CDI

Troubleshooting capacitor discharge ignition is similar to troubleshooting the transistor pointless ignition. The exciter coil, trigger coil, and pulse transformer can be checked for continuity and insulation breakdown. The spark units or CDI box cannot be successfully tested with an ohmmeter. A voltmeter may be used to performance-test the CDI system if the manufacturer lists the voltage specifications. Check the output of the exciter coil, trigger coil, and CDI black box. A shop service tester or replacing the unit with a functional part are the best tests, but they are not always the most convenient or the least expensive methods. Before drawing any conclusions, make sure that all connections are complete and have continuity. Follow the troubleshooting procedure as described in the TPI section and consult the service manual. Remember, a capacitor discharge ignition operates with extremely high voltage and can hurt you or become damaged if it is improperly handled.

chapter 11

Charging Systems and Starter Motors

Almost every motorcycle that uses a battery has some type of battery charging system. Without a charging system, a motorcycle would require an enormous battery to run for an extended period. The charging system operates while the motorcycle is running. It replaces the current that the battery loses while starting the engine and operating all of the other electrical devices. There are many different systems that may be used to charge a battery and maintain a system's voltage (Fig. 11-1).

This chapter first explains the fundamentals of battery charging systems and how to check the charging rate. Then the design, operation, and testing procedures for each charging system are presented. Chapter 6 explained the design and operation of motorcycle starting systems but did not include the design, operation, and testing procedure for starter motors. This information is presented in this chapter.

PRINCIPLES OF OPERATION

When a battery-equipped motorcycle operates without a charging system, or the system is not functioning, the current is removed from the battery and lost. This is known as *total loss*. In a total-loss system the battery is the only source of electrical energy. But as the battery's state of charge drops, the efficiency of the electrical devices also drops. For example, the ignition spark of a total-loss system would fire only as long as the battery's state of charge would allow. As soon as the battery voltage becomes low enough to weaken induction in the ignition coil sufficiently, the system would fail.

A charging system restores current to the battery when the battery voltage and specific gravity are low. The charging voltage is higher than the battery's voltage in order to force current into the battery. As the battery's specific gravity begins to increase, the charging voltage also increases to maintain a constant high-charge rate. The amount of charging voltage and the charging rate are determined by the battery and the voltage control device. As the battery voltage rises to the level set by the voltage control device, the charging current gradually tapers off.

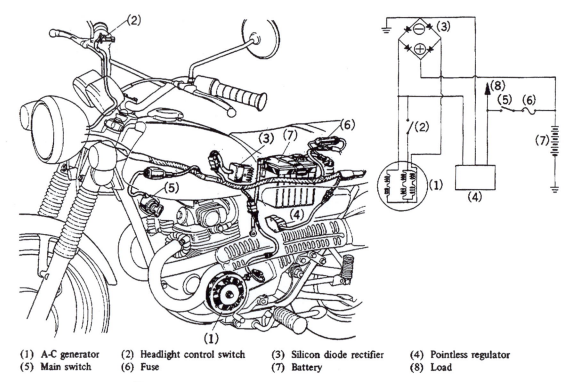

| (1) A-C generator | (2) Headlight control switch | (3) Silicon diode rectifier | (4) Pointless regulator |
| (5) Main switch | (6) Fuse | (7) Battery | (8) Load |

Figure 11-1 Charging system (American Honda Motor Company).

CHECKING CHARGING SYSTEMS

The charging system of any motorcycle can be checked with the following procedures:

1. Battery inspection and service
2. Testing battery load voltage
3. Testing charging voltage
4. Testing charging current
5. Testing ac output voltage

This section describes these five steps, which can also be used to indicate a problem in the charging system. The battery should be fully charged and the motorcycle must be at operating temperature during any charging system test. If a problem is discovered, each component in a charging system can be tested, and this will be described later in the chapter.

Battery Inspection and Service

This procedure was explained in Chapter 9. Remember that excessive charging voltage or charging rate can damage the battery. The effects of overcharging are evident by mossing between the battery plates and plate warping, which occurs as a result of overheating. Heavy gassing can also occur, and this lowers the level of the electrolyte. If the fluid drops below the top of the plates, sulfation forms on the plates.

Testing Battery Load Voltage

This procedure was explained in Chapter 9.

Testing Charging Voltage

Use a voltmeter with a range of 0 to 20 V dc. The motorcycle must be running at operating temperature. You may need jumper cables to provide access to the battery terminals for the voltmeter hookup. Do not allow shorting of the jumper to ground.

Start the engine and run it to 3000 rpm or to the service manual specifications. Hook up the voltmeter in parallel to the battery and read the charging voltage. You must test for at least 2 minutes because the voltage does not rise instantly. Use cooling fans to prevent the engine from overheating.

The voltage reading should be 7 to 8 V dc for a 6-volt system or 14 to 15 V dc for a 12-volt system. The extra voltage forces the charging current into the battery. Consult the service manual for the voltage specifications.

Testing Charging Current

This is a three-part test.

First you must determine the *system draw*, which is how much current the motorcycle uses with the main systems on. Remove the negative battery cable and hook up an ammeter in series with the negative ammeter lead to the negative battery terminal and the positive ammeter lead to a good ground (Fig. 11-2). The ammeter reading to the right of zero will give the total discharge. Turn the main switch on, but do not start the engine. The ammeter reading indicates the total current drawn from the battery to run the system. The charging system must produce at least this much current so that the battery will not discharge. A high system draw could indicate an overload, too many electrical devices, or a short in the system. Zero system draw indicates an open circuit, such as a broken or separated fuse.

The second part of this test determines the engine speed in rpm's at which the charging system begins to charge the battery; this is called *break-even speed*. Connect an ammeter as described previously, and kickstart the motorcycle. Do not use an electric starter with an ammeter in series; the electric starter will exceed the range of most meters. Instead, touch the battery cable to the battery terminal when starting the motorcycle with the electric starter and then hook up the ammeter.

As the engine idles, check the ammeter. If the needle on the meter reads to the left of zero, the charging system is charging below idle speed. For most motorcycles, it is normal for the needle to read to the right of zero but to swing left of zero with a slightly higher rpm. If the ammeter always reads a discharge, go on to the next step, "Testing Ac Voltage Output," which is explained on page 224. Use a tachometer. A break-even speed at or around idle is normal. If the break-even speed is greatly above the idle speed, a low charging output or excessive electrical load is indicated.

The third test of the charging current determines the charging system's output at speed. Connect the ammeter positive tester lead to the negative battery terminal and the negative tester lead to a good ground. The ammeter reading to the right will now give

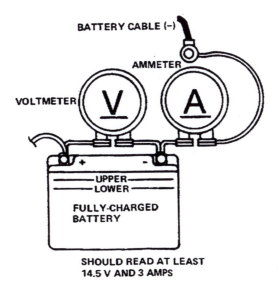

**SHOULD READ AT LEAST
14.5 V AND 3 AMPS**

Figure 11-2 Using an ammeter and voltmeter to test charging current (American Honda Motor Company).

the charging amperage. Speed up the engine to approximately 3000 rpm and measure the amount of current charging the battery. As the battery voltage increases, the current flow decreases. A battery in a low state of charge charges more than one that is fully charged. The charging system output should be at least one-tenth the ampere-hour rating for that battery.

If a separate voltmeter and ammeter are available, the charging voltage and charging current can be tested at the same time.

Testing Ac Output Voltage

This procedure is not necessary if you are testing the charging rate of a motorcycle with a dc generator or if the charging voltage and current have tested within specifications. If the ac charging system is not operating within specifications, testing the ac output voltage will determine if the problem is caused by the ac generator or by the regulation device.

This test determines whether or not the alternating current output is within the correct limits. The test is made by bypassing the voltage regulation system. Because ac output test hookups vary with the different designs, this test will be explained later in the chapter.

AC CHARGING SYSTEM DESIGNS   There are basically two types of ac charging systems: those that use permanent magnets to create induction (Fig. 11-3) and those that use an electromagnet powered by the battery to create induction (Fig. 11-4). For clarity in this text, the permanent magnet charging system is referred to as an ac generator, and the electromagnet charging system is referred to as an alternator. Most manufacturers do not distinguish between these two charging systems and refer to all ac charging systems as "alternators."

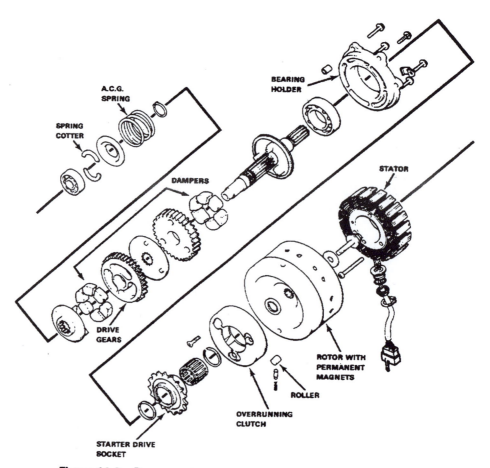

Figure 11-3   Permanent magnet system (American Honda Motor Company).

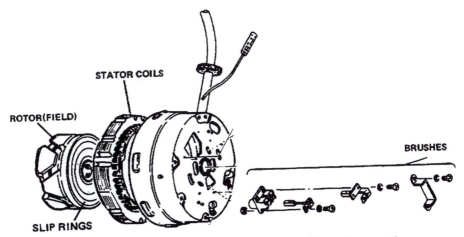

Figure 11-4 Electromagnet system (Yamaha Motor Corporation, U.S.A.).

Most ac charging systems require a voltage control device to prevent overcharging the battery. Most manufacturers refer to this device as a "regulator." In this text, the device used with an ac generator is called a *current limiter*. The device used with an alternator is called a *voltage regulator*. The current limiter and voltage regulator both control charging voltage to the battery, but they function differently as explained later in this chapter.

Diodes are used in all of the ac charging systems to convert alternating current to direct current. A diode is a semiconductor that acts as a conductor in one direction known as forward bias and as an insulator in the opposite direction known as reverse bias. A diode is made of silicon, selenium, or germanium, and impurities are added to create an excess of free electrons or a lack of them. The extra electron side (N) donates electrons to the vacant side (P). The stator coil's polarity is always changing, and the diode blocks the flow in the reverse bias but allows forward-bias charging current to the battery when the ac positive wave is greater than the battery voltage. High resistance in reverse bias prevents the battery from discharging through the diode (Fig. 11-5).

Half-Wave Charging Systems

This charging system is the smallest and simplest of the ac charging systems. It is used on many small dual-purpose motorcycles. This system consists of a flywheel with permanent magnets, a stationary stator coil, one diode, and system wiring (Fig. 11-6). The half-wave system is usually used with a 6-volt battery. Many half-wave charging systems do not use any extra means of voltage control. The maximum charge output is only enough to maintain the load devices and support the battery. This is called a *balanced system*.

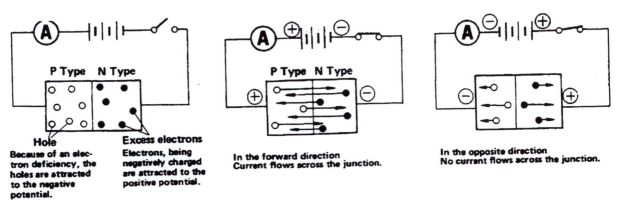

Figure 11-5 Diode operation (Yamaha Motor Corporation, U.S.A.).

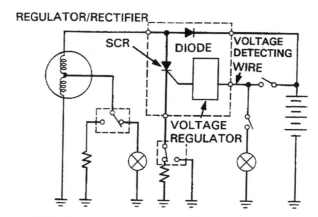

Figure 11-6 Permanent magnet half-wave charging system (American Honda Motor Company).

A rotating flywheel is usually mounted to the crankshaft. This flywheel or rotor has permanent magnets cast or bolted into it, and it functions to vary the magnetic fields at the coil. As the rotor spins, the poles of the magnets move continuously past the stator. The stator coil is placed close to the rotor with a set air gap between the two. As the rotor spins, a magnetic field is induced in the coil. As the rotor continues rotating, the field weakens to zero and then begins to build in the opposite polarity. The voltage induced in the coil starts at zero and builds to a peak just as the magnet is closest to it. The voltage drops back to zero as the pole revolves away. The polarity of the coil then reverses, builds to a peak, and drops to zero again. The alternating current is then rectified to direct current by the single diode.

The single diode is connected in series between the ac source and the battery. Only the positive wave is allowed to flow; the negative does not. The half-wave system is so named because only half of the ac charging coil output is used. The stator coil is grounded on one end at the stationary stator plate to complete the circuit to the negative side of the battery.

Full-Wave Charging Systems

A full-wave charging system uses four diodes instead of one. This allows a full wave to be used for battery charging. The stator windings are not grounded to the frame but are wired to the rectifier. The full-wave system has almost twice the wattage of a half-wave charging system at the same speed. Because of the increased output, a current limiter is required (Fig. 11-7).

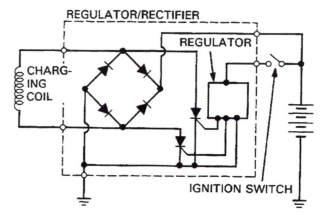

Figure 11-7 Full-wave permanent magnet charging system (American Honda Motor Company).

Current Limiter: A current limiter incorporates a silicon-controlled rectifier (SCR) and a zener diode to provide a path of least resistance for the alternating current. The SCR has three connections: the anode or positive side, the cathode or negative side, and the gate which is the triggering lead. The zener diode passes current in both forward and reverse bias if the voltage in reverse bias is great enough to achieve breakdown. The diode is wired in series with the positive side of the battery and the triggering or switching gate of the SCR. If the battery begins overcharging, the diode breaks down and passes current to the gate. The SCR is wired to ground one-half of the alternating current. The battery voltage trips the diode, which triggers the SCR and grounds one ac coil. This limits the current output from the ac generator. When the diode blocks the flow and the SCR turns on again, the battery begins charging at a greater rate and the process starts all over again.

More than one ac charge coil may be grounded with the use of multiple limiters. When the limiter is operating, it changes a full-wave into a half-wave, a three-phase into a full-wave, and on some multiple units it will shut the charging system completely off. A current limiter is not adjustable and it cannot be repaired, but it can be tested and replaced. Some limiters are incorporated with the rectifier and the whole assembly must be replaced if the limiter does not function properly.

Most of the full-wave systems built before 1978, and some later models, have two sets of charge coils: day coil windings and night coil windings. The night coil windings are connected to the rectifier only when the headlight switch is turned on. This extra charge coil is used only when the headlight removes more current than the daytime charge system can handle (Fig. 11-8).

The headlight switch is a two-part design. One part controls the direct current to the headlight, and the other part controls the alternating current for the night coil windings.

Three-Phase Charging Systems

A three-phase charging system is usually used on motorcycles because of the high charging output that is produced at low speed. A three-phase charging system may be either a permanent magnet or electromagnet type. Both designs consist of stator coils, diodes, system wiring, and a voltage control device to control the high output. A minimum of six diodes is stacked in three rows to create a rectifier. The rectifier is connected to the ac stator by wires.

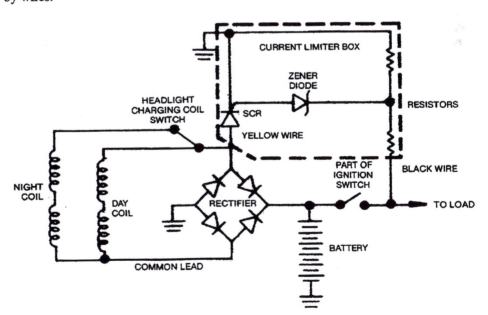

Figure 11-8 Ac generator with current limiter and night coil (American Honda Motor Company).

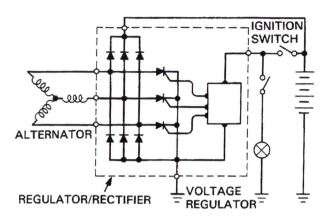

Figure 11-9 Three-phase permanent magnet charging system (American Honda Motor Company).

Three-phase charging system stators consist of three ac coil wires. These coils are connected to form either a "Y" or "delta" configuration. In the Y-wound stator design, the three ac coils are connected in the middle to form a "Y." This type of connection causes the coils to be in series with each other, thereby producing a high voltage and a steady current flow. Delta-wound stator coils are connected at each end to form a triangle. This type of connection causes the coils to be in parallel with each other, which also produces a high voltage and steady current flow.

Ac Generators: A three-phase ac generator uses permanent magnets to produce a strong magnetic field at all speeds. Most three-phase ac generators begin to charge the battery at or slightly below idle. A current limiter is used on all three-phase ac generators to ground the ac coils when the battery voltage is high and to reconnect the ac coils to the rectifier when the battery voltage is low (Fig. 11-9).

Alternators: An alternator consists of a field coil, a rotor, six or more diodes, one stator coil, system wiring, and a voltage regulator (Fig. 11-10).

An alternator uses one of two types of field coils: a brushless type or a brush type. A brushless field coil is stationary, and a rotor is used to cut the flux lines between the field coil and the stator winding. The rotor is constructed so that it passes flux lines but does not become a magnet. A small amount of residual magnetism is left in the rotor to self-induce the stator winding. In a brush-type field coil, the coil and rotor are combined to form one piece. This assembly is mounted to a shaft and spins (Fig. 11-11). Electrical contact brushes and slip rings connect the rotating field coil to the battery.

Some alternators use nine rather than six diodes. The additional three diodes are wired parallel with the standard three diodes on the positive side. These extra diodes pass the positive current to the field coil through the voltage regulator (Fig. 11-12).

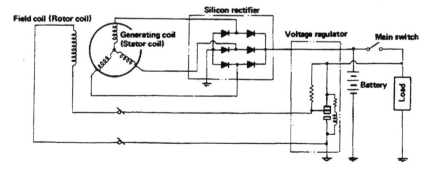

Figure 11-10 Diagram of an alternator with six diodes (Yamaha Motor Corporation, U.S.A.).

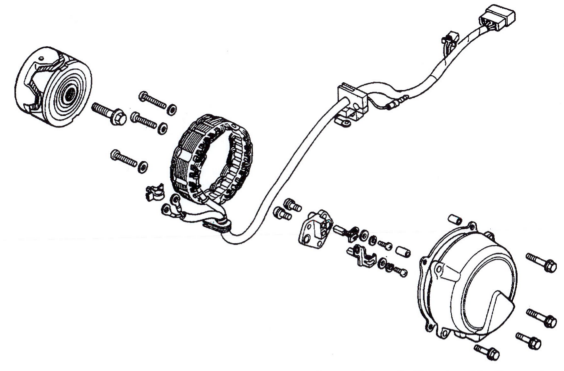

Figure 11-11   Three-phase brush-type alternator (American Honda Motor Company).

Voltage Regulators: A voltage regulator is used to vary the electromagnetism in the field by accurately controlling the field coil's direct current. Voltage regulators may be solid-state or mechanical. Both types control the amount of current flow through the field coil. The more current a regulator allows to flow, the stronger the magnetic field and the greater the ac output from the stator windings. When the regulator blocks the current to the field coil, very little output occurs at the stator windings. A solid-state regulator controls current in an even gradation. A mechanical regulator operates in steps.

Mechanical voltage regulators: A mechanical voltage regulator assembly consists of a voltage coil, points on a movable arm, springs, resistors, and three terminals (Fig. 11-13). Each step or mode of operation changes the amount of current to the field. Mode 1 occurs when the battery voltage rises to 13.5 to 14 V dc, mode 2 occurs at approximately 14 to 14.5 V dc, and mode 3 occurs above 14.5 V dc.

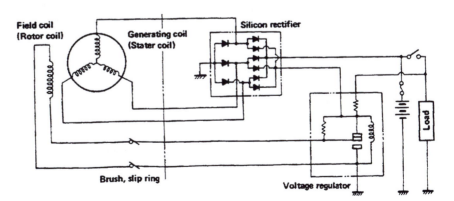

Figure 11-12   Diagram of an alternator with nine diodes (Yamaha Motor Corporation, U.S.A.).

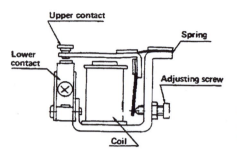

Figure 11-13 Mechanical voltage regulator (Yamaha Motor Corporation, U.S.A.).

During mode 1 the battery voltage is low, and a low-resistance path is provided for direct current to the field. As the battery voltage rises, the voltage coil in the regulator strengthens its magnetic field. When the magnetic field is strong enough to pull down the point arm, which is held by an adjustable spring, the low-resistance current path is broken. Mode 2 is now in operation and the point arm is centered between the two fixed contacts.

During mode 2 the current to the field coil passes through a field resistor of set value. This lowers the current flow and reduces the field's magnetic strength. If the battery voltage continues to rise, the voltage coil inside the regulator pulls the point arm down even farther, to the lower contact point. This is mode 3.

In mode 3 the current follows the path of least resistance, which is to the field resistor and then to ground. The current to the field is zero, so the alternator output is very low.

The operation of a mechanical regulator varies with temperature, so temperature-compensating springs and resistors are often used. A metal cover protects the regulator and contains the magnetic field.

Solid-state voltage regulators: There are many different solid-state voltage regulator designs. Most are not adjustable and must be replaced if a problem develops.

Most solid-state voltage regulators work off of the ground side of the rotating field coil or rotor coil (Fig. 11-14). The solid-state voltage regulator controls the amount of current through the rotor coil to ground. When the battery has less than a full charge, maximum current is allowed to flow through the rotor coil. When the battery is fully charged, the solid-state voltage regulator shuts off the current flow through the rotor coil. This reduces alternator output.

TESTING AC CHARGING SYSTEMS

After using the first four steps for checking the charging rate that are described at the beginning of the chapter, the following tests may be made to determine ac voltage output and to test ac charging system components.

Testing Ac Voltage Output

If the charging rate test measures below specifications, an ac voltage output test must be made. This performance test determines if the problem is in the ac generator or alternator or if there is a voltage control problem. Hook up an ac voltmeter in parallel with the charge coil(s) (Fig. 11-15). On a half-way system, connect between the ac side of the rectifier and to the frame ground. Do not disconnect the ac lead from the system wiring because this is a test of output under load. Start the motorcycle and run it up to 3000 rpm. The ac voltmeter should read slightly above the battery voltage. Consult the service manual for the specifications. A half-wave system may require higher rpm's for this test.

If the system being tested uses a field coil and very low or no output is indicated, make sure that magnetism is present at the field coil. Hold a thin, flat feeler gauge as close to the field coil cover as possible without touching it. If the feeler gauge is attracted to the cover when the charging system is on, go to the next test. If it is not attracted, test the field coil.

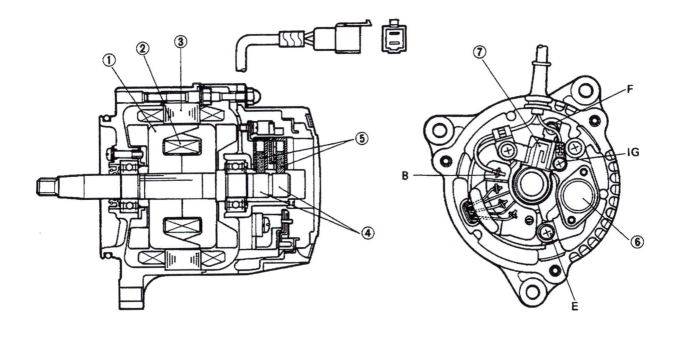

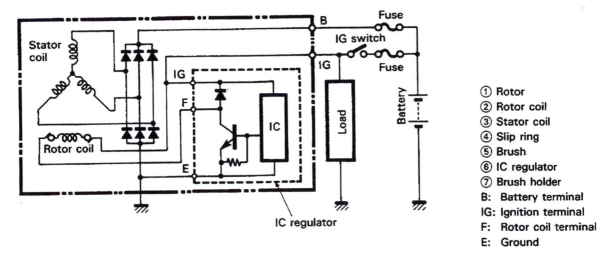

① Rotor
② Rotor coil
③ Stator coil
④ Slip ring
⑤ Brush
⑥ IC regulator
⑦ Brush holder
B: Battery terminal
IG: Ignition terminal
F: Rotor coil terminal
E: Ground

Figure 11-14 Three-phase IC alternator (American Suzuki Motor Corporation).

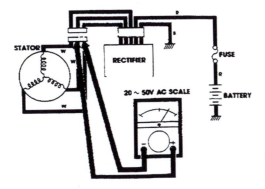

Figure 11-15 Testing ac voltage output (Yamaha Motor Corporation, U.S.A.).

Stator Continuity Test

If the ac voltage output test indicates little or no voltage, a stator continuity test must be made. Shut off the engine. Disconnect the ac coils from the system wiring and hook up an ohmmeter to the ac wires. Consult the service manual for the resistance figures and measure the resistance between all of the ac wires. For half-wave systems with only one ac lead, ground the other tester lead to the motorcycle engine. Check the wiring diagrams before starting this test and do not use an ohmmeter in a live circuit.

Stator Insulation Test

The stator insulation test ensures that the ac coils do not ground to the motorcycle engine. On half-wave systems the ac charge coil is normally grounded at one end, and the grounding terminal must be removed first to insulate it from ground. Test full-wave and both three-phase systems for continuity between the ac wire and the engine ground. No continuity should occur to ground during the test. Replace the stator if the results of the test fall below the service specifications.

Rectifier Tests

Consult the service manual and the wiring diagram before testing the rectifier. If the ac output test measured within specifications, a test of the rectifier is the next step. Each diode can be tested with an ohmmeter. In the forward bias, most diodes test at approximately 5 to 40 ohms. In the reverse, the ohmmeter should read 2000 ohms or more. Both forward and reverse tests must be made on each diode (Fig. 11-16).

Three-phase rectifier testing involves the same diode-testing procedure, but there are two tests per diode. Some rectifier testing may not be possible if a voltage regulator or limiter is integrated with the rectifier. Consult the service manual for the testing procedures.

Current Limiter Tests

Some current limiters that are not part of the rectifier can be tested. The test procedure is actually a process of elimination. If the charging system has sufficient ac output but does not charge, disconnect the limiter. Start the motorcycle and run it at approximately 3000

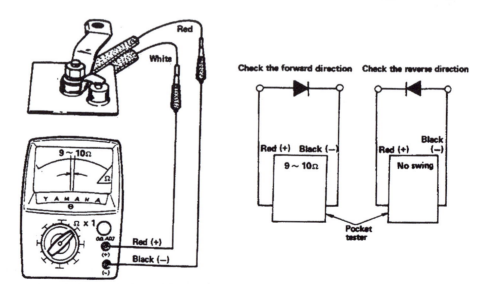

Figure 11-16 Checking forward and reverse bias of a single diode (Yamaha Motor Corporation, U.S.A.).

rpm. Use cooling fans to prevent the engine from overheating. Measure the dc charging voltage at the battery. If the battery voltage rises while the limiter is disconnected, the limiter is grounding out when it is connected. Allow the battery voltage to increase over the limiter's set level. Plug the limiter back in and see if the voltage at the battery drops. Note at what battery voltage the limiter activates and compare this voltage with the service manual specifications.

Most limiters can be bench tested with a variable dc power supply such as a model train transformer, a voltmeter to measure the charging voltage, and a powered test light. You may also need a filter to stabilize the direct current. Hook up the dc power supply with the correct polarity to the limiter. Hook up the positive side of the test light to the ac lead and the negative test light lead to the limiter's ground. Increase the dc voltage supply to the limiter's set level, which should be approximately 14 to 15 V dc. The test light should turn on at that voltage level. If the light does not go on, the limiter is not operating. If the test light stays on, the limiter is shorted. Limiters cannot be repaired and must be replaced.

Regulator Testing and Adjustment

If the alternator output test reading is low, test the voltage regulator. Determine if the field terminal side of the regulator has dc voltage. If the voltage at the field terminal is approximately the same as the battery voltage with the ignition key on and the engine not running, proceed to the field coil test. If there is no voltage at the field terminal, test for voltage at the battery side of the regulator. Again, the voltage at the battery side of the regulator should be approximately the same as the battery voltage. No voltage or low voltage indicates an open or high-resistance circuit. Consult the service manual for the specific test procedures for the model you are testing.

On most motorcycles it is possible to bypass the regulator and hook the field coil directly to the battery and test the alternator voltage. This test is called *full fielding*. If the alternator output is within specifications after performing a full-fielding test, the regulator is at fault (Fig. 11-17).

Solid-State Regulator Test: Solid-state regulator functions can be measured with an ammeter connected in series with the regulator and field. When the battery voltage is low, current should flow into the field at approximately 2 amperes. Start the motorcycle and allow the battery charging voltage to increase. As the battery voltage increases, the current flow to the field should decrease. If there is no current flow to the field or if the current flow does not decrease as the battery voltage increases, replace the regulator.

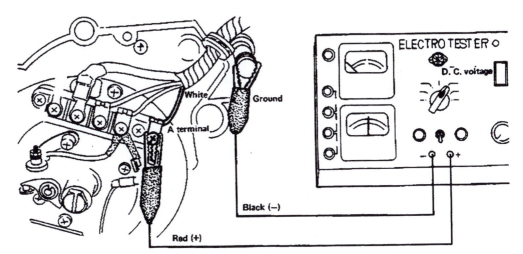

Figure 11-17 Mechanical voltage regulator adjustment (Yamaha Motor Corporation, U.S.A.).

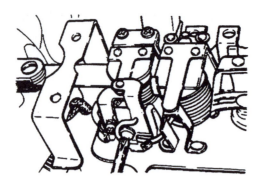

Figure 11-18   Measuring the core gap (Yamaha Motor Corporation, U.S.A.).

Mechanical Regulator Testing and Adjustment: Perform the same test as for a solid-state unit. If the mechanical regulator does not meet specifications in the function test, it can be bench tested and the core gap, point gap, and voltage setting can be adjusted.

Measure the resistance of all resistors, coils, and contact point surfaces. If the resistor or coils do not meet specifications, replace the regulator. If the contact points offer high resistance, clean them with electrical contact cleaner and run a clean piece of paper between the surfaces. Do not file the regulator points. Replace the regulator if the points are burned or pitted. Measure the distance between the voltage coil and the point arm with a flat feeler gauge (Fig. 11-18). This distance is the core gap. Adjust this gap if it does not meet specifications. Measure the point gap with a flat feeler gauge and adjust the gap to specifications (Fig. 11-19). Either reinstall the regulator or use the variable dc voltage supply to test for the voltage setting.

Consult the service manual for the procedure and test the three modes of operation. If the voltage setting does not meet specifications, adjust the spring that holds the point arm in mode 1. More spring tension will increase the charging voltage; less spring tension will reduce the charging voltage.

Field Coil Tests

As with any coil, testing a field coil requires a two-part test. The first test determines the coil's resistance. Hook up an ohmmeter to the disconnected field wires. Measure the total resistance of the field coil and compare the reading with the service specifications. Replace the field coil if it does not meet specifications. On models with brushes and slip rings, check the brush length and clean the slip rings with contact cleaner.

The second test is for insulation breakdown. Test between one field coil wire and ground. No continuity should occur unless the coil is internally grounded. Replace the field coil if it does not meet specifications.

System Wiring Tests

If the charging system components test within specifications and there is still a problem, test the system wiring. Measure the resistance or the voltage drop and make an insulation breakdown test on all charging system wiring. Usually, connectors are the cause of a system malfunction.

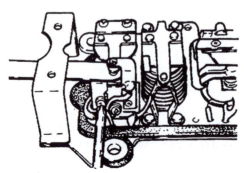

Figure 11-19   Measuring the point gap (Yamaha Motor Corporation, U.S.A.).

DC CHARGING SYSTEM DESIGNS   Some motorcycles use a dc generator, which is a device that converts mechanical energy into electrical energy. Unlike the ac generator, the dc generator mechanically converts alternating current to direct current before the current leaves the generator to charge the battery.

Dc Generators

Basically, a dc generator consists of rotating coils, stationary electromagnets, a commutator, and two brushes. Dc generator design is simple, but the operation is extremely complex. What follows is a basic explanation of dc generator operation (Fig. 11-20).

A dc generator uses rotating coils and stationary electromagnets to induce voltage. The rotating coils are electrically connected to the commutator. The whole assembly is mounted on a shaft and called the *armature*. The armature spins on bearings or bushings that are pressed into the generator housing. The housing, which is sometimes called the *generator frame*, also supports the magnets. The electromagnets have a small amount of residual magnetism to start the induction process. Some generators use a cooling fan that is mounted to the armature shaft. Most generators are gear- or shaft-driven, but a few use a belt.

The commutator is segmented with a series of copper bars, and each armature coil is electrically connected to each copper bar. If the commutator were not segmented, the current would be ac. The leads of each rotating coil are connected to the commutator segments. Usually, a negative brush and a positive brush ride on the commutator. Each segment of the commutator is insulated from the other and the brushes remain the same polarity. Dc generators use many coils in the armature to overlap the neutral points that result when the voltage in one coil peaks and drops to zero. The number of voltage peaks in one 360° revolution is proportional to the number of coils in the armature.

When the dc generator is operating, the magnetic field between the armature windings and the field coils becomes distorted. The distortion of the magnetic field changes the neutral point in the armature. The commutator brushes are therefore shifted toward the direction of rotation instead of centered between the field coils.

Dc generators feature a shunt design. A shunt design generator is one that has the battery, field, and armature all wired in parallel. In a shunt design, the battery provides the least resistance and so receives the most current flow. If any additional load is applied to the battery through the lighting, ignition, or other systems, the total resistance of the parallel circuit decreases. With the decrease in resistance, the field coil receives less current and the system's charging voltage drops. If the loads are light and the battery is fully charged, the field will receive more current and this increases the charging voltage. For this reason a shunt design generator requires a voltage and current control.

Most motorcycles that use a dc generator will use one of two shunt designs: the externally grounded field or the internally grounded field. There is no particular advantage to using one over the other. Both designs require some type of external voltage and current control, and a regulator is used for this purpose (Fig. 11-21).

Externally Grounded Field Generator: The externally grounded field generator is commonly used on American models and a few European models. The field coils are wired in parallel with the battery. Some of the current from the armature passes through the field coils and to the regulator for generator regulation.

Internally Grounded Field Generator: The internally grounded field generator is similar to the externally grounded generator except for the way field current is regulated. The field coils are wound the same as the externally grounded generator. The difference is the current for the field coils is regulated by passing through the regulator before passing through the field coils.

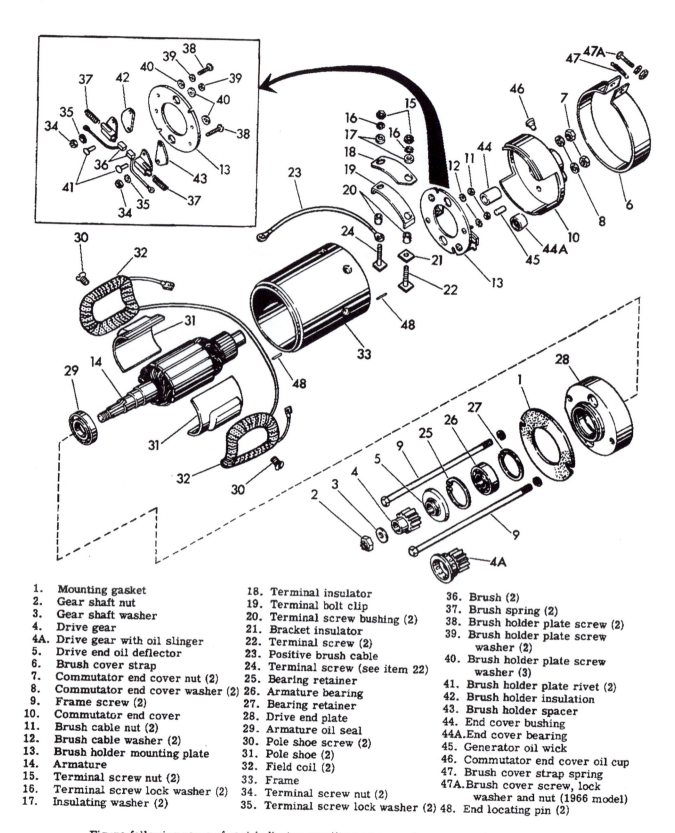

1.	Mounting gasket	
2.	Gear shaft nut	
3.	Gear shaft washer	
4.	Drive gear	
4A.	Drive gear with oil slinger	
5.	Drive end oil deflector	
6.	Brush cover strap	
7.	Commutator end cover nut (2)	
8.	Commutator end cover washer (2)	
9.	Frame screw (2)	
10.	Commutator end cover	
11.	Brush cable nut (2)	
12.	Brush cable washer (2)	
13.	Brush holder mounting plate	
14.	Armature	
15.	Terminal screw nut (2)	
16.	Terminal screw lock washer (2)	
17.	Insulating washer (2)	
18.	Terminal insulator	
19.	Terminal bolt clip	
20.	Terminal screw bushing (2)	
21.	Bracket insulator	
22.	Terminal screw (2)	
23.	Positive brush cable	
24.	Terminal screw (see item 22)	
25.	Bearing retainer	
26.	Armature bearing	
27.	Bearing retainer	
28.	Drive end plate	
29.	Armature oil seal	
30.	Pole shoe screw (2)	
31.	Pole shoe (2)	
32.	Field coil (2)	
33.	Frame	
34.	Terminal screw nut (2)	
35.	Terminal screw lock washer (2)	
36.	Brush (2)	
37.	Brush spring (2)	
38.	Brush holder plate screw (2)	
39.	Brush holder plate screw washer (2)	
40.	Brush holder plate screw washer (3)	
41.	Brush holder plate rivet (2)	
42.	Brush holder insulation	
43.	Brush holder spacer	
44.	End cover bushing	
44A.	End cover bearing	
45.	Generator oil wick	
46.	Commutator end cover oil cup	
47.	Brush cover strap spring	
47A.	Brush cover screw, lock washer and nut (1966 model)	
48.	End locating pin (2)	

Figure following name of part indicates quantity necessary for one complete assembly.

Figure 11-20 Dc generator (Harley-Davidson Motor Company, Inc.).

236

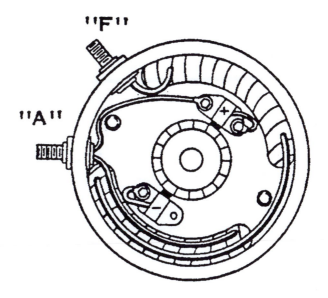

"F"

"A"

MODEL 65A-12V.

Figure 11-21 Externally grounded dc generator (Harley-Davidson Motor Company, Inc.).

Dc Regulators

The purpose of a dc regulator is to control charging voltage and charging current and to disconnect the field coils from the battery when the generator's output voltage is lower than the battery's (Fig. 11-22). A dc regulator consists of a cutout relay, voltage relay, and a current relay. Each relay has a set of contact points on a movable arm, resistors, and a single core with two windings.

The cutout relay operates only when the generator output is less than the battery output. The relay operates to disconnect the generator and reconnect the generator when the

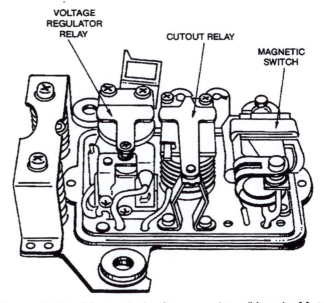

VOLTAGE REGULATOR RELAY

CUTOUT RELAY

MAGNETIC SWITCH

Figure 11-22 Mechanical voltage regulator (Yamaha Motor Corporation, U.S.A.).

generator output is greater than the battery output. The set of contact points is wired in series with the armature output, and the single coil with two windings is located directly under the movable arm. Normally, the arm is held open by an adjustable spring. When the output is low, the current flow in the cutout windings does not produce a sufficient magnetic field on the point arm to pull the arm. The points are open. As the generator's output builds due to residual magnetism, the current flow in the cutout winding increases and the magnetic field becomes strong enough to pull the contact points. This completes the circuit from the generator to the battery.

The voltage relay controls the charging voltage. The voltage regulation coil is made of many windings of fine wire, and it is wired between the armature and ground. The voltage regulation coil senses the output voltage from the armature and produces a magnetic field. When the voltage is great enough, the magnetic field pulls the contact points, which are normally closed, apart.

The voltage control points are wired to ground on externally grounded field generators. The points are wired between the armature and the field on internally grounded field generators. The resistors are wired in parallel with the voltage points. The resistors reduce the field current when the points open the circuit.

The voltage points vibrate and open and close many times in a second. This creates a constant voltage and allows the current to taper off when the voltage reaches the set level. The loads and current output of a generator may vary, but it should maintain a constant voltage.

Dc regulator coils have copper windings, and the current passing through them increases the operating temperature and the resistance. Bimetallic strips prevent the settings from changing.

The current relay controls the total current output from the generator. The current relay winding is wired in series with the cutout relay. A set of contact points is located above the heavy winding of the current relay. The points are wired with the field and vibrate, but they do not vibrate as fast as voltage contact points. The current relay points open to reduce a high current flow. The generator produces high current when the battery is discharged or if high loads are placed on the generator. High current at the brushes creates arcing at the commutator and increases the operating temperature.

TESTING DC CHARGING SYSTEMS

Before testing a generator, determine if it is externally or internally grounded. To identify the generator, disconnect the field wire from the generator. Do not allow the wire to touch ground. Start and idle the engine. Connect a voltmeter to the field terminal at the generator and connect the other lead to ground (Fig. 11-23). If the voltmeter indicates voltage, the generator is externally grounded. If no voltage registers, the generator is internally grounded. The location of the brushes will also reveal the generator design. The field coil is connected to the positive brush on an externally grounded generator and to the negative brush on an internally grounded generator.

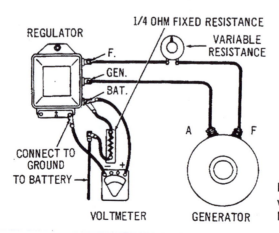

Figure 11-23 Testing a dc generator with a voltmeter (Harley-Davidson Motor Company, Inc.).

Testing Dc Generator Output

The output of both internally and externally grounded generators can be tested with an ammeter with a range of 0 to 30 and a voltmeter. Consult the service manual for specifications and special notes. Use a process of elimination to determine if the generator or the regulator is at fault.

Bench Testing

Bench testing a dc generator will indicate if there is a problem with the system. Use a self-powered continuity light to bench-test both types of generators for a grounded circuit. Install a piece of paper between the negative brush and the commutator. Disconnect the field wire at the negative brush grounding point on an internally grounded model. On both models, connect the test light between the armature terminal and the generator frame. If the light comes on, something is grounded somewhere in the generator. To determine which circuit is grounded, insulate the positive brush and test again. The armature is grounded if the light goes out. The field coils or brush holder is grounded if the light stays on. When a grounded field is found, check the regulator for burned points.

To test an externally grounded generator for open circuits, connect the test light between the armature and the field. Connect the light between the field and ground on internally grounded models. The light should go on if the circuit is not open.

Use the motorcycle's battery and an ammeter to test for short circuits. Connect the ammeter between the battery and the field, and ground the field. Consult the service manual for the current flow specifications. If more current is measured than specified in the manual, the field is shorted. Check for burned regulator points.

Use a testing device called a *growler* to determine if the problem is in the armature. Consult the service manual and make sure the brushes are within the service limits. Inspect the mica that insulates the commutator segments; the mica should be undercut below the segment (Fig. 11-24). Clean the commutator with fine crocus cloth and contact cleaner. Inspect the bushings or bearings and lubricate them if necessary.

Polarizing Generators

If a generator is disconnected, it should be polarized to ensure that the charging current flows in the proper direction. To polarize an externally grounded model, make the connections as usual but jump the battery to the armature. On internally grounded models, disconnect the field wire at the generator and use a jumper cable to touch the positive side of the battery.

Testing Regulators

There are many different regulator designs. Consult the service manual for the appropriate testing procedure for the model you are working on.

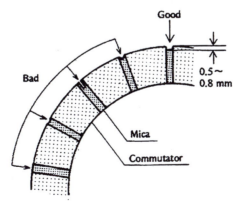

Figure 11-24 Inspecting commutator segments (Kawasaki Motors Corporation, U.S.A.).

Testing System Wiring

Excessive resistance in the charging circuit decreases the current to the battery and increases the generator voltage. To check the voltage drop, connect the positive side of a voltmeter to the armature terminal and the negative side to ground. With the engine running and everything connected, the voltage drop should not exceed 0.75 volt. Check the voltage drop between the armature terminal and the regulator. The terminal voltage should be less than 0.25 volt. Check from the regulator A terminal to the positive side of the battery. The voltage should not drop more than 0.25 volt. Check from the generator frame to the negative battery post; the voltage should not exceed 0.5 volt.

STARTER MOTORS   Basically, the operation and components of starter motors are the same as dc generators. But most motors use four field coils and the field coils are larger than those of dc generators. The brush location in a starter motor is also different (Figs. 11-25 and 11-26).

A motorcycle starter motor changes electrical energy into mechanical energy with sufficient torque and speed to start the engine. When the starter motor armature carries current, a magnetic field is established around the armature. The armature moves from a strong magnetic field to a weak one. A distortion of the magnetic field occurs because the armature carries current. One side of the armature is pushed and the other side is pulled by the magnetic field. Opposite reactions take place on opposite sides of the armature and this creates a twisting movement of the armature. The armature is connected by gears, a chain, or both to the starter drive system (Fig. 11-27).

TESTING STARTER   Test a starter motor as you would an internally grounded field generator. Test for voltage
MOTORS   drop between the positive battery terminal and the starter motor terminal and between the negative battery terminal and the starter frame. The voltage should drop no more than 0.75 volt.

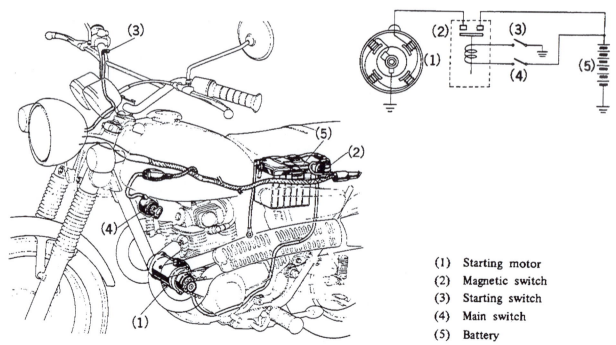

(1)   Starting motor
(2)   Magnetic switch
(3)   Starting switch
(4)   Main switch
(5)   Battery

Figure 11-25   Electric starting system (American Honda Motor Company).

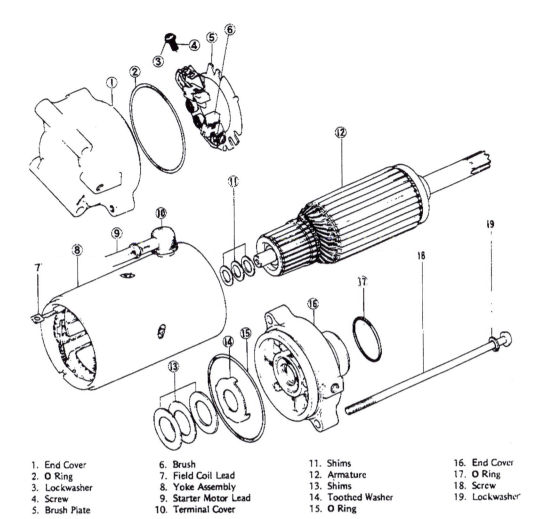

1. End Cover	6. Brush	11. Shims	16. End Cover
2. O Ring	7. Field Coil Lead	12. Armature	17. O Ring
3. Lockwasher	8. Yoke Assembly	13. Shims	18. Screw
4. Screw	9. Starter Motor Lead	14. Toothed Washer	19. Lockwasher
5. Brush Plate	10. Terminal Cover	15. O Ring	

Figure 11-26 Starter motor (Kawasaki Motors Corporation, U.S.A.).

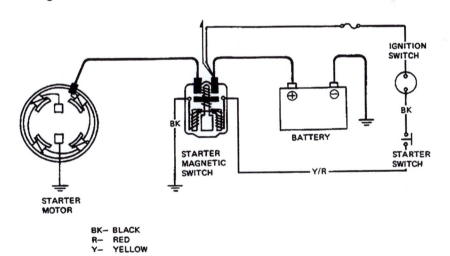

BK— BLACK
R— RED
Y— YELLOW

Figure 11-27 Starter motor circuit (American Honda Motor
Company).

chapter 12

Lighting and Accessory Systems

In the past motorcycles have been equipped with a minimum number of lighting and accessory systems. But today's motorcycles are equipped with many lighting, warning, and safety systems. These systems are designed to inform the rider and protect the motorcycle. While these systems greatly increase the safety and convenience of motorcycling, they also frustrate inexperienced mechanics when a problem develops. This increases the work load in a shop and the demand for qualified technicians.

This chapter explains the basic operation and design of lighting, warning, safety, and accessory systems. Because these system designs vary so much between manufacturers and models, only general information and some service tips can be presented. You must consult the service manual for specific details and servicing procedures.

LIGHTING SYSTEMS A motorcycle lighting system may include a headlight, taillight, stoplight, turn signals, and instrument illumination.

Headlights

Motorcycle headlight systems differ in circuit design and voltage supply depending on when the motorcycle was manufactured and its purpose and size.

Most street motorcycles that can also be used for off-road riding use an ac-powered headlight. A lighting coil located under the rotating flywheel supplies alternating current. A high- and low-beam selector switch is wired in series with the lighting coil and headlight. The headlight bulb has a twin or dual filament, and the bulb and reflector may be combined as a single unit known as a *sealed beam*. Most ac headlights are 6-volt systems and some use the same wattage for high- and low-beam operation (Fig. 12-1).

Most street motorcycles use a dc headlight that is powered by the battery (Fig. 12-2). Unlike the ac headlight system, this system uses a fuse and the high/low-beam selector switch is wired in series between the headlight fuse and the headlight. Some dc headlights require large amounts of current and may use a relay to shorten the length of the wiring.

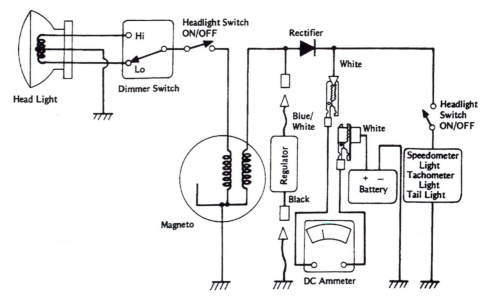

Figure 12-1 Ac lighting and charging systems (Kawasaki Motors Corporation, U.S.A.).

The relay is an electric switch that is wired between the headlight and fuse. The relay is turned on or off by low-amperage wiring that runs to the handlebar switch.

Dc headlights may feature sealed-beam construction or the bulb may be replaceable (Fig. 12-3). There are many types of headlight bulbs. Use caution when handling quartz bulbs; your fingers will create a hot spot on the glass, which shortens the bulb's service life. Handle these bulbs with a clean, lintfree cloth.

The horizontal and vertical positions of both ac and dc headlights can be adjusted and should be adjusted with a load on the motorcycle. The vertical adjustment screw is usually located right next to the headlight. When adjusting, always back the screw out farther than necessary and then screw it in until the adjustment is correct. This ensures correct spring

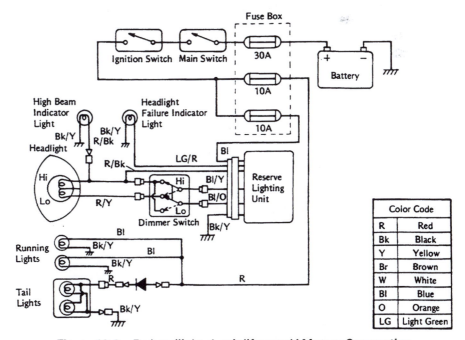

Figure 12-2 Dc headlight circuit (Kawasaki Motors Corporation, U.S.A.).

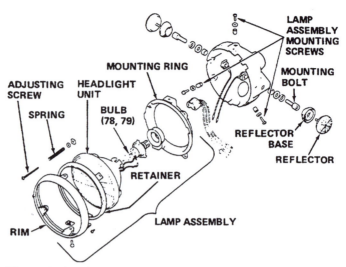

Figure 12-3   Headlight assembly (American Honda Motor Company).

tension. The horizontal adjustment is made at the headlight housing mounting bolts or with an adjusting screw on models with fairings. Loosen the screw, make the adjustment, and retighten. The correct horizontal and vertical headlight positions vary with the local law, but usually the headlight is positioned slightly lower and to the right of center.

Taillights

All street motorcycles are required by law to have a dc battery-powered tail spotlight so that the taillight will remain on if the engine stalls. All street motorcycles also include a red taillight lens and some form of license plate illumination. A gasket should be used between the lens and base to prevent corrosion or shorting caused by water. Be careful not to overtighten the lens screws. The taillight assembly must be free of corrosion or neither the taillight nor stoplight will operate (Fig. 12-4).

Most dc taillights use a twin-filament, replaceable bulb; one filament lights the taillight and the other lights the stoplight. Some motorcycles use two bulbs to increase the brightness of the taillight and stoplight.

Most street motorcycles include a parking light. The parking light is actually the taillight that is activated when the main switch is placed in the "park" position.

Because of federal regulations, ac taillights are used only on off-road motorcycles.

Stoplights

The stoplight filament in the twin-filament bulb used for both taillight and stoplight has less resistance, so the stoplight shines more brightly than the taillight. A stoplight switch controls the light and activates it when the brakes are applied. Stoplight switches vary. Some

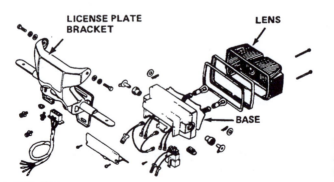

Figure 12-4   Taillight assembly (American Honda Motor Company).

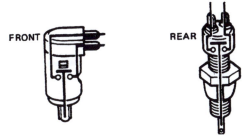

Figure 12-5   Brake light switches (American Honda Motor Company).

have continuity when pushed or pulled; others operate on hydraulic brake line pressure (Fig. 12-5).

Turn Signals

Most street motorcycles include turn signal lights on each side, front, and rear. These lights are wired to operate in a flashing mode when the front and rear lights of the right or left side are activated. A flasher unit is wired in series between the main switch and the turn signal switch on the handlebar. The turn signal switch operates on pulsating dc; the flasher unit interrupts the current flow. The flasher unit is either constructed with points or as a solid-state unit. Some front turn signal lights use a twin-filament bulb, which allows them to also function as running lights. The filament with the least resistance lights the turn signal.

When the turn signals on both sides fail to flash, check for voltage at the flasher unit. If only one side flashes and only one bulb on the opposite side lights up, check for an open circuit or a bad ground. The front and rear bulbs must use the same amount of wattage.

Some motorcycles include a canceling device and a four-way hazard flasher with the turn signals. Turn signal canceling units vary among manufacturers. Some use a lean-angle detector that is activated when the motorcycle turns. The canceling control unit then measures either the distance traveled or the amount of time after the turn and cancels the turn signals accordingly (Fig. 12-6). A four-way hazard system activates each turn signal to flash at the same time. To accomplish this, most street motorcycles have a hazard switch wired in series with the turn signals and a hazard flasher unit.

Instrument Lighting

Most motorcycles that include instruments also include either direct or indirect lighting for the instrument. When the bulb is inside the gauge, it is directly lit. Indirect lighting is external and reflected to the appropriate area. Instrument lighting is wired in parallel.

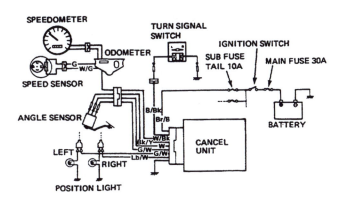

Figure 12-6   Turn signal circuit with cancel unit (American Honda Motor Company).

WARNING Warning systems include sensors and gauges or lights that alert the rider to speed or engine
SYSTEMS temperature, or to low fuel, oil, brake fluid, battery voltage, or electrolyte levels. Factory-
installed or accessory horns allow the rider to warn others on the road.

Speedometers

Some motorcycles have a digital speedometer; others use a speedometer with a mechanical pointer that is operated by a cable driven by the front wheel. In a digital speedometer
system, the cable driven by the front wheel spins a small pulse generator. The voltage output from the pulse generator increases with the speed that the unit is spun. The voltage output is converted to a digital readout; the higher the voltage output, the higher the digital
reading (Fig. 12-7).

Some models use speed sensors in conjunction with mechanical pointer speedome-
ters. But this speed sensor, which is a small pulse generator, is used to assist the operation
of other devices, such as turn signals, cancelers, buzzers, stall preventers, and suspension
warning devices.

Temperature Gauges

Many motorcycles include temperature sensors and gauges that indicate engine temperature. A temperature indicator system includes a gauge, sensor, and voltage regulator. Sometimes the voltage regulator regulates the voltage to more than one gauge. The resistance of
the temperature sensor varies with changes in temperature. More heat creates less resistance. The higher the temperature, the more voltage is at the gauge, which swings the
needle in the gauge more to the right.

Water temperature is monitored on liquid-cooled engines, and some fuel-injected
models include air temperature indicators. Air temperature sensors are usually wired to the
fuel injection control unit. One motorcycle uses two air temperature sensors. One sensor
monitors the temperature of air coming into the air box; the other monitors air temperature
after the turbocharger.

To test a temperature indicator system, first measure the voltage at the regulator, then
at the gauge, and finally at the sensor. To test a water temperature sensor, it must be suspended in a pan of oil so that it does not touch the sides of the pan. It must be suspended in
oil, not water, because water can be heated only to 212°F in an unpressurized container.
Measure the sensor's resistance when it is cold, then heat the oil to 250°F and measure the
resistance again (Fig. 12-8). More resistance should be indicated when the sensor is cold
than when it is hot.

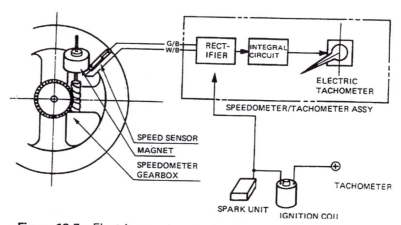

Figure 12-7 Electric speedometer/tachometer (American Honda
Motor Company).

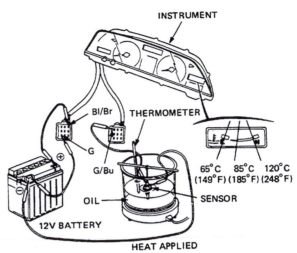

Figure 12-8 Testing temperature gauge sensor (American Honda Motor Company).

Fuel-Level Indication System

Some motorcycles are equipped with this system, which includes a fuel gauge, fuel-level sensor, and a voltage regulator (Fig. 12-9). The fuel gauge operates like a voltmeter. The voltage at the fuel gauge is higher when the gauge reads full. The voltage regulator maintains a constant voltage of approximately 7 volts. The fuel-level sensor varies the volts to the fuel gauge. The fuel sensor or float is a variable resistor that changes resistance as the float arm moves up or down. It has less resistance when the float arm is up and more when the arm is down and the gauge reads empty (Fig. 12-10). The battery's starting voltage may vary between 10 and 15 volts, and this affects the accuracy of the fuel gauge reading.

This system can be tested by first measuring the voltage at the regulator, then at the gauge, and finally at the fuel-level sensor. Do not exceed 7 volts at the gauge. To check the operation of the sensor, connect an ohmmeter and measure the resistance when the fuel tank is full and empty. There should be more resistance at empty.

Oil Indicator Systems

Some motorcycles have sensors and indicator lights for oil pressure and level. Most oil indicator systems operate on battery voltage. The oil pressure sensor is a simple switch that is activated by a pressure loss (Fig. 12-11). When no pressure is applied, the switch has con-

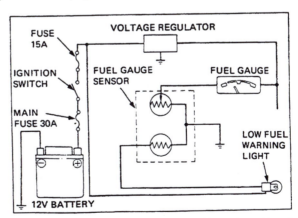

Figure 12-9 Fuel level indication system (American Honda Motor Company).

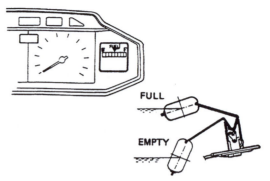

Figure 12-10   Fuel level sensor (American Honda Motor Company).

tinuity between the terminal and ground. This continuity ceases when pressure of approximately 5 pounds per square inch is applied. Oil-level sensors operate in a similar way. With the proper oil level, the sensor does not have continuity and the indicator light is off. When the oil level is low, the sensor has continuity and the light comes on.

Make sure that the light bulb is operational before testing the oil indicator system. Then test oil pressure and level sensors for voltage and continuity. A light that stays off may indicate a system failure or the sensor may be stuck. A light that stays on may indicate a grounded sensor or system wiring.

Brake Fluid Indicators

Some motorcycles have sensors that indicate the level of the hydraulic brake fluid in the reservoir. The fluid-level sensor in the reservoir is usually a simple switch. When the float at the end of the sensor drops below a minimum level, the sensor has continuity and the indicator light in the instrument cluster comes on.

Battery Condition Indicators

Some motorcycles are equipped with a battery condition indicator that may consist of a voltmeter, a fluid-level sensor, or both. The voltmeter gives a good indication of the battery's condition if you know what to look for. Loaded battery voltage should be approximately 11.5 V dc, starting voltage should not be lower than 10 V dc, and charging voltage should not be higher than 15 V dc.

The fluid-level sensor is installed inside a battery cell and usually replaces one of the cell caps. It functions to light an indicator light in the instrument cluster if the electrolyte drops below a minimum level. When the electrolyte level is sufficient, the sensor does not have continuity. When the level is low, the sensor has continuity and lights the indicator.

Horns

Street motorcycles may have one or two factory-installed or accessory horns. Accessory horns are either air or electric and usually require large amounts of current and a relay. Most factory horns do not use large amounts of current and do not use a relay. When the button

Figure 12-11   Oil pressure sensor switch (American Honda Motor Company).

is pushed on a factory horn, the current either flows through the pushbutton from the internally grounded horn or from the ground at the pushbutton to the externally grounded horn. When an accessory horn with a relay is used, two current paths must be completed. When the button is pushed, current runs from ground to the pushbutton and then to the electromagnet in the relay. When the electromagnet is energized, the second current path from the ground through the relay and back to the positive side of the battery is completed.

Most horns have an adjustment screw to clear the tone. Loosen the locknut, turn the screw in either direction until you reach the desired output, and retighten the locknut. Faulty horns are easier to replace than fix.

SAFETY SYSTEMS

Safety devices include starting and ignition override systems, additional sensors, and reserve lighting units.

Starting Override Systems

All motorcycles with an electric starting system use some form of starter override system to prevent the electric starter from engaging while the engine is running or until certain devices are in the start mode. The starting override system may consist of a simple, one-way starter clutch switch or electrical devices that override the starter circuit when the charging system is operational.

The clutch switch is used on many models and is usually located at the clutch lever on the handlebars. When the clutch is disengaged, the clutch switch completes the circuit loop and allows the motorcycle to start in gear. If the operator tries to start the engine in gear while the clutch is engaged, the circuit is incomplete and the motorcycle will not start.

Some motorcycles may be started while the clutch is engaged, but the transmission must be in neutral. On some other motorcycles, whether in neutral or in gear, the clutch must be disengaged for starting (Fig. 12-12). A neutral transmission switch allows the operator to find neutral with the aid of an indicator light. Once in neutral, the clutch switch may be bypassed.

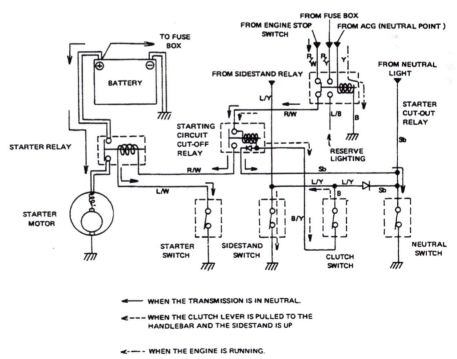

Figure 12-12 Starting override system (Yamaha Motor Corporation, U.S.A.).

Some motorcycles include a sidestand switch that prevents the engine from starting if the sidestand is down and the transmission is in any gear other than neutral.

Most late-model motorcycles interrupt the flow of current to the headlight when the electric start button is pushed. This allows the extra current to the headlight to be used to start the engine. The headlight interrupt device may be either a simple switch wired to the starter button or a complex, solid-state device.

Ignition Override Systems

Ignition override systems of the simple "kill" switch design have been in use for many years. The complexity of the ignition override system has been increased with the addition of safety devices such as lean-angle indicators, sidestand switch cutouts, "knock" sensors, and pressure retard devices.

A *lean-angle indicator* automatically shuts off all ignition systems and stops the engine if the motorcycle falls over while it is running. A *sidestand switch* operates under this condition, but its function is to cut off the ignition while the engine is running when the sidestand is down and while the rider selects a gear other than neutral.

A *"knock" sensor* prevents excessive detonation by retarding ignition timing. This sensor is located near the cylinder head, and at the first sign of detonation it retards the timing as much as necessary to prevent detonation. Turbocharged motorcycles use a *pressure sensor* to slow ignition timing. As the boost pressure rises, the risk of detonation increases. The pressure sensor is located on the intake manifold side and wired to a control unit. When activated by the sensor, the control unit retards the ignition timing with respect to intake manifold pressure.

Additional Sensors

Some additional devices that may be found on motorcycles include pressure, vacuum, throttle, and airflow sensors. These sensors are wired into the ignition control unit to help the motorcycle run smoother, cleaner, and safer.

Reserve Lighting Units

Some street motorcycles include a reserve lighting unit. This solid-state device automatically switches to the other functional headlight beam if one of the headlight filaments burns out. This device also lights an indicator light located in the instrument panel if a headlight failure occurs.

ACCESSORY SYSTEMS Some of today's touring motorcycles include a complete audio system and cruise control. The audio system components can include an AM/FM stereo radio, a cassette tape deck or CD player, a 40-channel CB radio, front and rear speakers, headphones for both rider and passenger, and an intercom system between the rider and passenger. Some models also include an automatic volume control that operates to increase the audio volume to the speakers as the motorcycle's speed or outside noise increases.

Audio system service and maintenance involves three areas: reception, electrical wiring, and components.

Reception: AM and FM radio reception is limited. AM radio has a longer range than does FM radio. During normal AM radio broadcasting, AM radio waves curve around the horizon and bounce off the stratosphere. FM radio waves travel straight along the line of sight. Reception "dead spots" are caused when the AM or FM waves reflect off buildings or mountains. AM waves will mix, causing two stations to come in at once. FM radios will cancel out the weakest wave and pull in the strongest. CB radio transmission is limited on a motorcycle because of the small amount of antenna reflective surface.

If the AM reception is strong, but the FM reception is weak, the antenna may be the cause for the poor reception. If the FM reception is strong, but the AM reception is weak, the problem may be caused by electrical interference from the motorcycle's ignition or charging system or by outside interference such as power lines.

If cassette deck sound is poor, the heads may be dirty. Heads should be cleaned regularly.

Electrical Wiring: Each audio component normally has a separate wiring harness that is isolated from the rest of the motorcycle's wiring to reduce electrical interference. When an audio component fails to function, first check the fuse and then check the connectors. Follow the troubleshooting guidelines in the appropriate service manual.

Components: If an audio system component fails and cannot be restored by following the manufacturer's troubleshooting guidelines provided in the service manual, then the component must be removed and sent to an authorized repair facility.

Cruise Control

Some motorcycles are equipped with electronic cruise control that automatically maintains the vehicle's speed. To set the speed to be maintained, the rider accelerates to the desired speed and then presses a set button located on the handlebars. This button activates an electric servo motor that holds the throttle in the set position. A microprocessor monitors the speedometer or tachometer, gear shift indicator, brake switches, clutch switch, and throttle position sensor and relays this information to the servo motor to ensure that the correct throttle opening is maintained.

Before the rider activates the cruise control system by pressing the set button on the handlebars, the motorcycle must be moving at a minimum speed of approximately 30 miles per hour. Some models limit maximum cruise control speed to 80 miles per hour.

The cruise control automatically shuts off when the brakes are applied, the throttle is returned to the idle position, or the clutch is disengaged. If the resume button is pushed, the cruise control will open the throttle to increase the speed of the motorcycle to the original presetting. If the cruise control switch or motorcycle is shut off, a new speed setting must be programmed.

These are only some of the lighting, warning, and safety systems you may encounter during your training and work as a motorcycle technician. Read the service manual carefully before servicing any lighting or accessory system.

chapter 13

Wheels and Tires

Early motorcycles had wooden wheels and did not provide a comfortable or safe ride on roads that were rough with mudholes and ruts. Wire-spoke wheels were pioneered by motorized bicycles in the 1880s and are still popular today. As tires have become more complex in construction, new wheel designs have appeared to accommodate them.

This chapter explains the basic wheel components, designs, and servicing. The service information will include preventative maintenance, minor repairs, lacing and truing of spoke wheels, and wheel balancing. Later in the chapter, tires and tire service are discussed.

BASIC WHEEL COMPONENTS

The basic wheel parts are the hub, axle, rim, spokes, and bearings (Fig. 13-1). At the center of the wheel is the hub. The hub is an aluminum casting that carries the load. Sometimes there is a steel or iron drum pressed in for brake linings. Except for disk brake systems, the braking device is located inside the hub, and a flange is cast on the hub's outer diameter. The flange has holes in it for the spokes that support the wheel. The hub assembly consists of wheel bearings, a spacer, and when the bearings are not sealed, the hub will have its own seals. The wheel rotates on wheel bearings and is attached to the motorcycle by the axle. The axle is mounted at the lower end of the front fork or the rear swing arm. The purpose of the rim is to support the tire. The rim is designed to permit tire removal and installation. The rim is made of either steel or aluminum. It is ring-shaped with a recess along the center (Fig. 13-2). Spoke holes and a tire valve hole are located along the center of the rim. There are three types of valve stems: side, center, and L-shaped. A rim lock is included on some tube-type rims to prevent the tire from slipping on the rim during operation. The rim flanges are machined to provide greater rigidity, as is the drop center in the rim. The drop center has three basic functions: to provide rigidity, to position the spoke nipples out of the way of the tire and tube, and to aid tire changing.

WHEEL DESIGNS

There are four basic types of motorcycle wheels on today's market. They are the aluminum or magnesium cast wheel, the assembled wheel, the split rim wheel, and the spoke wheel. Each type of wheel is designed to support the weight of the motorcycle and rider and to assist in providing the driving, braking, and steering forces. To ensure a comfortable and safe ride, wheels are designed to be light yet strong.

Figure 13-1   Basic wheel components.

Aluminum and Magnesium Cast Wheels

Aluminum cast wheels are designed to use either tube or tubeless tires (Fig. 13-3). Check the rim to determine which type of tire to use. Magnesium cast wheels can be used only with tube tires. Select a cast wheel carefully. Check the standards for cast wheel manufacturing which are published and obtainable. There are tolerances for radial and lateral deflection and precise standards for the rim contours. The rim should never be less than half the width of the tire. Measure the rim width at the inside of the flange.

Assembled Wheels

The hub and rim of the modern assembled wheel are made of aluminum (Fig. 13-4). The spokes, which may be aluminum or steel, are permanently riveted to the rim and bolted to

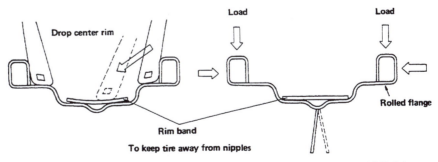

Figure 13-2   Rim construction (Yamaha Motor Corporation, U.S.A.).

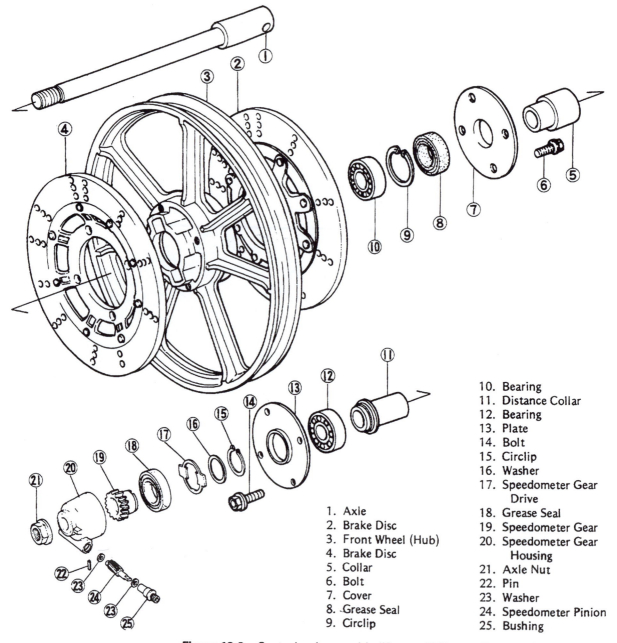

1. Axle
2. Brake Disc
3. Front Wheel (Hub)
4. Brake Disc
5. Collar
6. Bolt
7. Cover
8. Grease Seal
9. Circlip

10. Bearing
11. Distance Collar
12. Bearing
13. Plate
14. Bolt
15. Circlip
16. Washer
17. Speedometer Gear Drive
18. Grease Seal
19. Speedometer Gear
20. Speedometer Gear Housing
21. Axle Nut
22. Pin
23. Washer
24. Speedometer Pinion
25. Bushing

Figure 13-3   Cast wheel assembly (Kawasaki Motors Corporation, U.S.A.).

the hub. This wheel should not be disassembled. Cast alloy wheels require very little maintenance. Keep them balanced and check them periodically for cracks and trueness.

Split Rim Wheels

Split rim wheels have two-piece rims and are used on some three wheelers, four wheelers, and small trail bikes (Fig. 13-5). A tire can be fitted to a split rim wheel without any levering of the beads down into the well and up over the opposite rim flange. Once a split rim assembly is complete, the tire cannot roll off the rim. Two-piece steel rims require tube tires except when a rubber sealing band and tubeless cover are fitted to the rim to prevent air from leaking.

Figure 13-4
Assembled wheel.

Spoke Wheels

A properly constructed spoke wheel is strong, lightweight, and resilient (Fig. 13-6). The spokes are made of a strong wire that transfers the force to the hub to help keep the wheel true (Fig. 13-7). Almost all spoked wheels are laced with a cross pattern. The cross pattern is determined by the number of times one spoke crosses other spokes that are in the opposite direction from the same side of the hub and rim. Usually, spoke wheels have one to four cross patterns. The higher the cross-pattern number, the more radial and vertical strength the wheel has. The constant pull of alternate spokes during starting and stopping eventually stretches and loosens the spokes so that servicing becomes necessary.

Figure 13-5
Split rim.

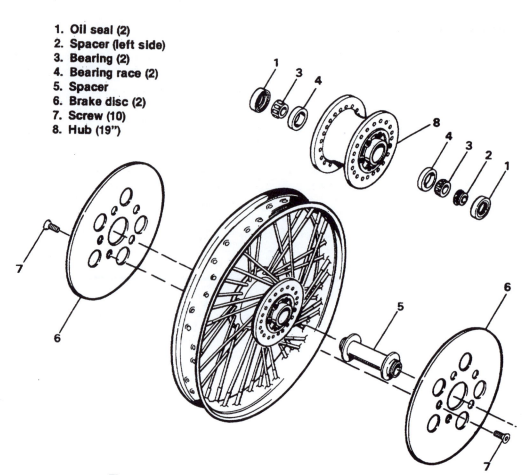

1. Oil seal (2)
2. Spacer (left side)
3. Bearing (2)
4. Bearing race (2)
5. Spacer
6. Brake disc (2)
7. Screw (10)
8. Hub (19")

Figure 13-6 Spoke wheel assembly (Harley-Davidson Motor Company, Inc.).

WHEEL MAINTENANCE The first step of wheel maintenance is an inspection of the spokes, wheel bearings, and axle nuts.

Spokes

Spokes should be checked frequently, especially if the motorcycle is used under high load conditions, over rough terrain, or for racing. One day's riding may loosen the spokes. All spokes must have equal tension for optimum wheel performance. To check the spokes, use one of the following methods:

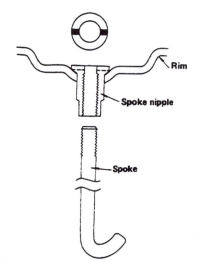

Figure 13-7 Spoke assembly (Yamaha Motor Corporation, U.S.A.).

1. Rotate the wheel and lightly tap all spokes with a screwdriver. Listen for a ringing "ping" as each spoke is contacted. A dead "plunk" from any spoke indicates that the spoke is loose and in need of tightening.

2. Grasp each pair of spokes around the wheel. Squeeze them together to find any that "give" more easily than the others. If the spokes "give," they are loose and need to be tightened.

If your inspection indicates any loose spokes, they may be tightened up to $1\frac{1}{2}$ turns without concern that the spoke ends will come through the nipple and later cause a flat tire. Avoid overtightening in any area, as this will throw the wheel out of true.

Inspect the rim strip over the top of the spoke nipple heads to make sure it is in good condition. If necessary, replace it with an appropriate rim strip to protect the tube from the sharp edges of the spoke nipples.

Make sure the spoke nipples and threads are serviceable.

Wheel Bearings

There are two common types of wheel bearings used on motorcycle wheels: caged ball bearings and tapered roller bearings. The manufacturers usually pack caged ball bearings with grease and seal at least one side of the bearing. Caged ball bearings cannot be serviced and should be replaced when there are any signs of damage, when there is excessive movement of the balls inside the bearing cage, and whenever the caged ball bearing is removed from the hub of the wheel. Bearings that have been removed from the hub should never be reused.

Caged wheel bearings are removed using the bearing remover recommended by the motorcycle manufacturer. Right and left bearings must be installed in a specific order. Consult the appropriate service manual to determine which bearing is to be installed first. If one side of the bearing is sealed, it should be installed in the hub so that the sealed side faces the outside of the hub. If both sides of the bearing are sealed, the bearing should be installed so that the stamped mark indicating the bearing's size faces the outside of the hub. A new caged bearing is installed by using the appropriate tools to drive it into the hub. Never strike the inner race of the caged bearing as this will damage it. The distance collar must be installed in the correct direction before installing the other bearing. Right and left bearings should be replaced in pairs.

Tapered roller wheel bearings require regular servicing. Consult the motorcycle service manual for the maintenance schedule. During servicing, all parts of the bearing, except the oil seals, should be cleaned in a low-flash-point solvent. After cleaning, inspect the bearing and bearing cups or races for damage or wear.

Tapered roller wheel bearings must be replaced in sets. Replace old oil seals with new ones. If the bearing races are removed for replacement, lubricate the new races with bearing grease or oil. Press one race into each side of the wheel hub using the wheel bearing race installer recommended by the manufacturer. Place the wheel hub center spacer into the hub. Coat the bearings with bearing grease, and install one into each side of the wheel hub. Replace the remaining spacer(s). Press an oil seal into each side of the hub so that it is flush with the outer surface of the hub.

Wheel bearing end play is set by the manufacturers and should not be altered. Consult the appropriate service manual for the proper wheel disassembly and assembly order and all torque specifications.

Axle Nuts

All good-quality cycle wheels are made with an internal bushing that is located between the two wheel bearings. This internal bushing allows the axle nuts to be drawn up tightly without damaging the bearings. Make sure that axle nuts are tight by checking them often. Use a lock-type axle nut or castle nut.

MINOR WHEEL Minor repairs are indicated if you find a dented rim, a broken spoke, if more than 1½ turns
REPAIRS are necessary to tighten any spoke, or if the wheel wobbles from side to side. You must
remove the wheel, dismount the tire and tube, and repair, true, and balance the wheel as
described in the next section.

Rim Repair

Hammering out a dented rim is not recommended, but if the rim is only slightly bent,
resulting in a flat spot, sometimes turning the wheel will compensate for the flat spot.
Otherwise, replace the rim.

Wheel Bearings

After removing the wheel, inspect the wheel bearings. If bearing problems are indicated,
replace both bearings before continuing the wheel repair. Consult the service manual if
taper bearings are present and require servicing.

Bearing Removal

To remove the bearings from the hub, lay the wheel on a barrel or workbench. Be sure to
support the hub just outside the bearing area. If there is a seal, remove it with a seal remover. Be careful not to score the hub. If the spacer has a side hole, remove the bearings
by inserting an L-shaped steel rod in the spacer hole and tapping the bearing out with a
hammer (Fig. 13-8). To remove bearings with a straight spacer, tap the spacer bushing to
one side with a 10-mm- or ¼-inch-diameter drift and then tap out the bearing. Reverse the
wheel and remove the second bearing. If retaining clips are present, remove them first.

Bearing Installation

To install new bearings, press or tap them in one at a time. Always replace bearings in pairs
and be careful to keep them straight. Bearings should be packed with wheel-bearing grease.
Be sure to replace the internal spacer bushing or the bearings will be damaged when the
axle nuts are tightened. If the bearings are sealed, install a new seal and grease the seal lips
thoroughly. If the hub is distorted or cracked, or if the bearings fit loosely, replace the complete hub assembly.

Wheel Lacing

Lacing is an important element of wheel repair, and not all wheels are laced the same way.
Before lacing a wheel, refer to the service manual for the model you are working on. What
follows is a basic procedure for wheel lacing.

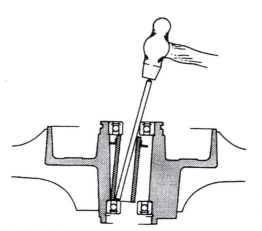

Figure 13-8 Bearing removal
(Kawasaki Motors Corporation,
U.S.A.).

Identify the hub, wheel, and cross-number pattern of the spokes. Check the spokes to see if all of the heads are bent at the same angle and to determine the length of the spokes. If there is a difference, sort the spokes into each head type and/or length. If half of the spoke heads are less angled than the other half, these spokes are the inside spokes. Check the spoke angle by placing a spoke in the hub. The positioning of the spokes can also be determined by their head length. You may find that the head-to-bend distance varies. The longer head-to-bend spokes should be used as outside spokes (Fig. 13-9). If all the spokes are identical, they can be used as either inside or outside spokes. If the hub is a conical type with one flange much smaller than the other, the spoke lengths will be very different. The longer spokes are used on the small flange side of the hub. There may also be a higher number in the cross pattern on the small flange side. It is common to have a four-cross pattern on the small flange side and only a two-cross or single-cross pattern on the large flange or brake side.

The wheels and spokes in all Japanese designs can be identified by the lacing pattern. A common rule of these patterns is that an equal-flange, 36-spoke wheel will have a 3–6 pattern. This means there will be three holes between like spokes and six holes between key spokes. A 36-spoke wheel has 18 inside spokes and 18 outside spokes.

To begin lacing, start with the inside spokes. Take a spoke and place it in a hole in the flange closest to you. Now take an inside spoke and insert it in the hole just to the right of the first spoke on the bottom flange. These two spokes are called the *key spokes* (Fig. 13-10). Put a piece of tape on these spokes for easy identification later. Now take each inside spoke and place it in the flange, skipping every other hole. Place the top flange inside spokes counterclockwise, and place the bottom flange spokes in the opposite direction. Place the rim over the hub and spokes. Start with the first top inside key spoke, which is one hole left of the valve stem hole. Place a nipple on the spoke with just a couple of turns. Too much tightening now will make it more difficult to finish lacing the wheel later. Now take the next top inside spoke to the left of the top key spoke and, skipping three rim holes, place it into the fourth hole. Start a nipple and continue in the same manner until all the top inside spokes are in the rim holes. Now take the second inside key spoke on the bottom flange and, skipping six holes, place it in the seventh hole. You have now established the 3–6 pattern. Continue with the bottom inside spokes, but skip only three holes between each spoke. You are now half finished. Take an outside spoke and place it in any hole so that it comes up and over the flange. Place it in the opposite direction of the inside spoke and line it up with a hole on the rim (Fig. 13-11). Start a nipple. Continue this procedure until all outside spokes are in place.

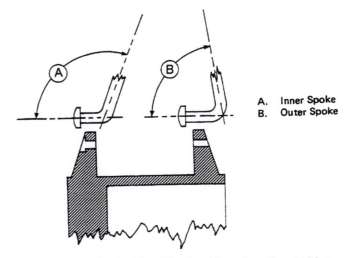

A. Inner Spoke
B. Outer Spoke

Figure 13-9   Spoke identification (American Suzuki Motor Corporation).

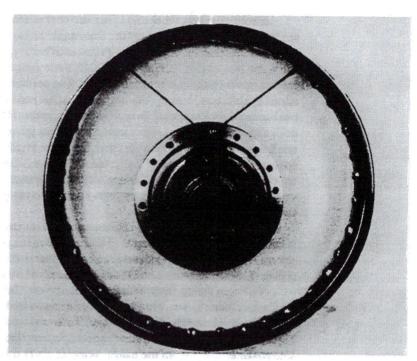

Figure 13-10 Key spokes.

The procedure is the same for a 40-spoke wheel except for the placement of the key spokes. A 40-spoke wheel usually has a 3–10 pattern with three holes between like spokes and 10 holes between key spokes (Fig. 13-12). The bottom inside key spoke is placed by skipping 10 holes between key spokes.

Truing

After lacing, a wheel must be made true. Truing a wheel requires equal tensioning of all spokes. Start by using a screwdriver to tighten four sets of four spokes 90° apart until there is equal tension. A truing stand with dial indicators for checking wheel runout is ideal for easy truing (Figs. 13-13 and 13-14). However, any fork jig or vise that holds the axle can

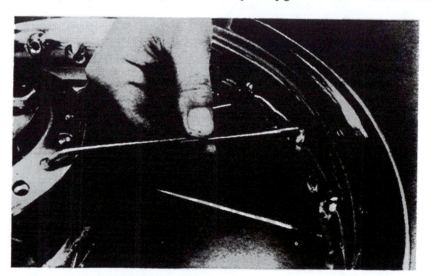

Figure 13-11 Position the outer spoke in the opposite direction of the inside spokes. The spoke will point at a rim hole (*Motorcyclist Magazine*, Peterson Publications).

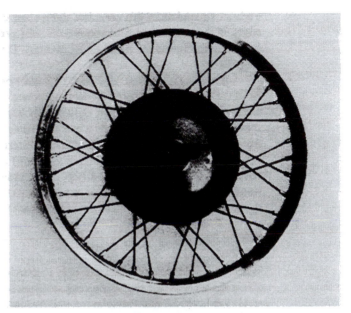

Figure 13-12   40-spoke wheel.

be used in place of a truing stand. Some cycle rims are deliberately laced off-center to the hub to accommodate rear chain alignment or front brake clearance. This is called *rim off-set*. To determine if a wheel is laced off center, put a straightedge across the hub and measure from the straightedge on the hub to the edge of the rim. Measure both sides and compare the measurements. If the measurements are within 1/16 inch (1.6 mm) of each other, the wheel is center-laced. If there is more than a 1/16 inch (1.6 mm) difference, the wheel was probably intended to be off-center. Note this off-center measurement so that this distance is maintained as you proceed. After tightening each spoke until all appear to have the same tension, rotate the wheel. The wheel might wobble from side to side or have an out-of-round "hop."

Correct the out-of-round hop first. Rotate the wheel and mark the highest point of the wheel with chalk. In most cases, a fairly wide area of four or more spokes will be high.

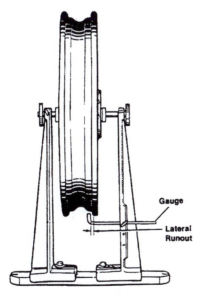

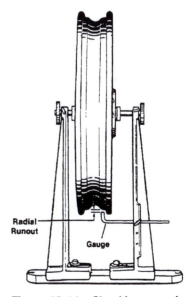

Figure 13-13   Checking cast rim lateral runout (Harley-Davidson Motor Company, Inc.).

Figure 13-14   Checking cast rim radial runout (Harley-Davidson Motor Company, Inc.).

Tighten all spokes in this area, but tighten the center spokes more than the spokes at the edge. If the spokes seem to require a lot of pressure when tightening them, loosen the spokes in the low areas by an equal amount. This permits the rim to become round again (Fig. 13-15).

If a wheel is within 1/32 inch (0.8 mm) or less out of round, eliminate the wobble. Hold the chalk at the side of the rim and rotate the wheel. Again tighten the spokes in the chalk-marked area, but tighten only the spokes on the side away from the marks. If the spokes require a lot of pressure when tightening them, loosen equal amounts of spokes on the marked side of the wheel. Continue to alternately loosen and tighten spokes until the side wobble is reduced to 1/32 inch (0.8 mm) or less. After the wobbling is eliminated, check again for an out-of-round hop. To complete the wheel repair, check all spoke tensions and see that no spoke ends are sticking out of the nipples. Grind or file protruding spoke ends flush and smooth to the nipple head. Check the off-center lacing measurements.

Wheel Balancing

Wheel balancing is important not only to provide handling and a smooth ride; it can also affect the wear of the tire. Balancing is achieved by determining where the wheel/tire assembly is heaviest, and then placing small weights opposite the heavy portion of the wheel. The weights are placed either on the spokes or on the rim. Different types of weights are used for spoke and cast wheels (Fig. 13-16). There are several ways to balance a wheel. Two of the most common methods are static and spin balancing.

Static Balancing: If a wheel balancing machine is not available, a wheel can be balanced on the motorcycle. First remove the wheel assembly and set the backing plate assembly aside. Mount the wheel on the motorcycle without the backing plate assembly. Rotate the wheel; it will stop with the heaviest point down. Mark this area with chalk. Assuming that the mark is at 0°, mark the wheel at 120° and 240° from the first mark. Add weight at 120° and 240°. When the wheel does not come to rest in the same spot each time it is rotated, the balancing is completed.

Figure 13-15   Tightening spokes (*Motorcyclist Magazine*, Peterson Publications).

Figure 13-16 Balancing weight on a cast wheel.

Static balancing can also be achieved using a bubble balancing machine. Remove and clean the wheel and place it in the machine. The air bubble in the machine will indicate where the wheel weights should be installed. The bubble will be in the center of the circle when the wheel is balanced.

Spin Balancing: Spin or dynamic balancing is also done with a machine. The wheel is spun at different rates of speed. The heavy portion of the wheel is determined through the use of lights.

It is important to balance wheels frequently no matter what technique is used. Balancing wheel/tire assemblies should be accomplished by adding weights to the wheel as previously described. Liquid balancers and liquid balance/sealers are not recommended as alternatives to wheel weights. Properly balanced wheels and tires last longer and provide a smooth ride.

TIRES Because tires are the link between the motorcycle and the road, they are critical components. Tires help to provide stability as well as the required steering and braking response. They also cushion road irregularities and assist in acceleration.

There are two types of tires: tube and tubeless (Fig. 13-17). The primary difference between these two types of tires is the way they are designed to hold air.

Tubeless Tires

These tires share most of the design features of tube tires, but tubeless tires use an inner liner and chafer instead of a tube to hold air. The inner liner is a layer of soft rubber which covers the inside of the tire carcass. This rubber is similar to the rubber of most innertubes. It provides a barrier to minimize normal air loss from inside the tire and to prevent rapid deflation when a puncture occurs. The air pressure forces the inner liner tightly around any small penetrating object to slow the rate of air loss.

A chafer is an additional layer of airtight rubber located at the bead area of a tubeless tire. The chafer helps to seal the bead of the tire where it makes contact with the rim. The chafer also provides protection from damage that may be caused by the rim or by tire mounting and dismounting.

Tires marked "Tubeless" on the sidewall should be used only on tubeless wheels and should never be used with a tube. Using a tube in a tire marked "Tubeless" will create ex-

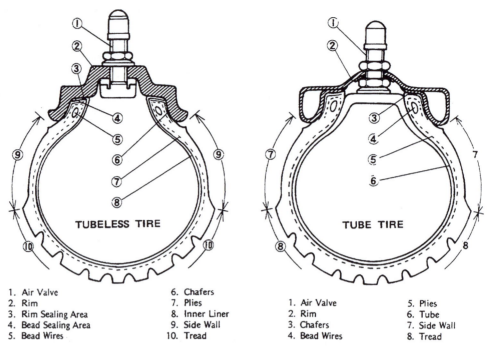

1. Air Valve   6. Chafers
2. Rim   7. Plies
3. Rim Sealing Area   8. Inner Liner   1. Air Valve   5. Plies
4. Bead Sealing Area   9. Side Wall   2. Rim   6. Tube
5. Bead Wires   10. Tread   3. Chafers   7. Side Wall
                                                    4. Bead Wires   8. Tread

Figure 13-17 Tube and tubeless tire construction (Kawasaki Motors Corporation, U.S.A.).

cess friction and heat. Heat eventually causes chemical and physical deterioration which weakens the tire structure.

Tires with sidewalls labeled "Tubeless: On tube-type rim fit tube" can be used without tubes when fitted on an appropriate tubeless wheel. They may also be used with a tube when fitted on a tube-type wheel.

Tube Tires

Tube tires do not have an inner liner and chafer and therefore must be used with an inner-tube. When changing to a new tire, a new tube should be fitted. Previously used tubes become thin through stretching and can crease and crack. When fitting a new tube to a tire, be sure that the tube size and tire size markings are exactly the same to ensure that the tube is the right size for the tire.

TIRE SELECTION Because tires are so critical to motorcycle performance and safety, appropriate tire selection is essential. If you decide to replace a tire with one of a different manufacturer or marking, be sure the tire is approved for the motorcycle model by either the motorcycle or tire manufacturer. Check the technical data published by the manufacturers, and consider the tire size, motorcycle use, tire construction, load and speed ratings, and tread pattern. Use the following guidelines for correct tire selection.

Tire Size

When replacing a tire, it is best to select one that is the same size as the tire originally provided by the manufacturer. Changing to a different size can cause problems. When considering larger tires, you must determine whether there is sufficient clearance. A larger front tire must have proper clearance between the tire and front forks, as well as between the tire and fender. A larger rear tire must have sufficient clearance between the tire and swing arm, as well as between the tire and fender. All tires expand a bit after being initially installed and inflated. Although this expansion is not excessive, it is a factor that must be considered when determining tire clearance.

When considering wider tires, make sure that the relationship between the size of the front and rear tires is correct. Vehicle geometry is a critical aspect of motorcycle design, and changes in the geometry as a result of improper tire sizes can dangerously affect handling and stability. You must also be sure that the wheel rim is wide enough for the tire.

Do not replace the original tire with a tire that is smaller.

Motorcycle Use

Although tires designed for all-round operation are still available, many are designed specifically for sport, high-performance, high-mileage touring and sport touring. Make sure that the tire you select meets the specific needs of the rider and motorcycle. Check the technical data available from the tire manufacturer.

Tire Construction

Until the early 1970s motorcycle tires were constructed using a standard bias design. Improvements in motorcycle design and performance resulted in the development of various tire constructions. Bias, bias belted, and radial tires are now available to maximize motorcycle performance.

Some bias belted and radial tires include a letter next to the speed rating on the sidewall to identify the type of construction. "B" indicates bias belted; "R" indicates radial construction. Consult the tire manufacturer's technical data to determine the best tire construction based on the motorcycle model and use.

Load and Speed Ratings

Load information and the tire pressure specification are located on the sidewall of street-legal tires. The load rating indicates the maximum load the tire should carry. The tire pressure specification is the amount of inflation pressure appropriate for that load. The tire pressure specification is not the recommended inflation pressure for all load conditions. Refer to the owner's manual or the tire manufacturer's technical data to determine the appropriate inflation pressure when operating at less than maximum load.

On some tires, the load rating is expressed as a ply rating, a load range, or a number that appears after the size marking. These are industry codes that should be observed, but use the load indicated on the sidewall when determining the appropriate tire. Never replace the original tire with one that has a lower load rating.

The speed ratings are included with the tire size or load rating number. Speed ratings are indicated by the letters S, H, V, or Z. An S-rated tire has performed during laboratory tests at maximum load and pressure and is qualified for sustained road speeds of up to 112 miles per hour. An H-rated tire is qualified for speeds up to 130 miles per hour, a V-rated tire for speeds up to 150 miles per hour, and a Z-rated tire for speeds above 150 miles per hour. A Z rating is awarded to only qualified radial tires.

Tread Patterns

Tread patterns vary depending on whether the tire is designed for street or off-road use. Street tire tread pattern is designed to displace water when the road is wet and to provide the best balance of wet and dry road grip. Street tire tread patterns vary depending on the type of use. Tires for high-mileage touring at highway speeds usually have wider and deeper grooves than those designed for high-performance use. High-performance motorcycles used in dry conditions require tires with greater areas of rubber and less grooves. A tire that is heavily grooved with a deep tread pattern could cause instability under high-power/high-speed operation.

Because no single tread pattern can provide optimum performance over a range of ground conditions, off-road tires are available in three basic tread designs. Soft-terrain (S/T) tires have widely spaced knobs to clear mud, loose dirt, and sand. Hard-terrain (H/T) tires have closely spaced knobs that provide traction and resist wear on hard surfaces. Intermediate-terrain (I/T) tires attempt to provide a compromise between S/T and H/T tires.

Tread compound also varies according to the type of tread pattern. The compound of an S/T tire is harder than that of an H/T tire. This allows the smaller knobs of an S/T tire to penetrate the soft ground. The softer compound of the H/T tire allows the large knobs to provide traction on slippery hard ground.

Trials universal tires are primarily designed for off-road use but must also provide acceptable road performance. A trials universal tire has closely spaced knobs and a flexible carcass. This combination, when used with appropriate tire pressure, provides ideal performance for trials competition and secondary use.

TIRE MAINTENANCE AND REPAIR

There are many tire care and maintenance procedures that should be observed. Most tire manufacturers publish a list of tire maintenance and repair procedures. This section provides an explanation of some of the most important procedures.

Checking Air Pressure

Checking tire inflation pressure is perhaps the single most important maintenance procedure because all tires lose air over time (Fig. 13-18). Incorrect inflation pressure will affect tire tread wear, so it is essential to check air pressure on a regular basis to ensure efficient tire operation. When a tire is underinflated, the center tread does not contact the road, and the tire buckles inward putting additional load on the tire ribs and shoulder. Therefore, the center tread of an underinflated tire will show little wear, but the adjoining ribs and shoulder area will be heavily worn and scuffed. An overinflated tire does not properly deflect the road surface. The center tread will show most of the wear and little or no wear will occur on the tread pattern ribs or shoulder.

Determine the appropriate tire inflation pressure and check the air pressure regularly. Checking air pressure regularly will indicate when normal air leakage is sufficient to require adding air to the tire. It will also provide a warning if the air loss that has occurred since the last check is greater than expected. If significant air loss has occurred, check the tire for cuts or punctures. Air pressure loss may also be caused by a worn or badly sealed valve core. Inspect the valve core and replace it if it is worn or tighten it for correct seating.

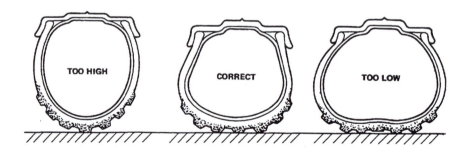

High tire pressure:
High tire pressure will result in inferior riding comfort. It will also cause the tire to skid and the tread to wear at its center.

Low tire pressure:
Low tire pressure fails to support a specified load, or causes heat due to bending of the side wall. It also causes the cord layers to separate and wears the sides of the tread.

Figure 13-18   Tire air pressure (Yamaha Motor Corporation, U.S.A.).

Tire Inspection

When checking the air pressure, also inspect the outside of the tire. Examine the sidewalls and tread for damage that may have been caused by objects run over on the road. Discovering minor damage will allow you to prevent tire failure and accidents or injuries.

Tire Repair

A tire can be repaired only if it has been punctured in the center of the tread. A puncture in the tread shoulder cannot be effectively repaired because the puncture may have damaged the belt endings. Repairing punctured sidewalls is also not effective because of the high degree of flexing in those areas. Repaired tires are not recommended for continuous use.

A tire can be repaired using either a machine or tire tools. Tire tools are more commonly used. Do not use screwdrivers or any other sharp tool. Many tires with tubes also have rim locks to help secure the tire bead to the rim, which keeps the tire from slipping on the rim. Most off-road motorcycles have rim locks, and you must loosen the nut on the rim lock and remove the tire valve core (Fig. 13-19). Break the tire bead from the rim. Insert the tire tool near the valve stem and pry the bead up over the rim flange while pushing the tire bead into the low portion or center of the rim opposite the valve stem. Be careful not to insert the tire tool deeply, or the tube will be damaged. Coat the tire bead with tire-mounting lubricant to make tire removal easier. Pull out the tube and replace the valve core. Check the tire at the point where the tube is damaged to determine whether or not there is also tire damage. Rub a cloth, not your hand, inside the tire to locate any sharp objects. Bend the sidewall and check for cracks which could cause the tire to burst under stress.

To reinstall the tire, put one tire bead on the rim. If there is an arrow indicating rotation, place the tire so that the arrow points in the direction of travel. Install the rim lock and tighten the nut a couple of turns. Insert the valve stem through the rim and install the nut loosely with a couple of turns. Make sure that the valve stem is straight. If there is a dot on the tire, align it with the valve stem. Push the remaining bead opposite the valve stem onto the rim. Carefully insert the tire irons and work them alternately from side to side. When nearing the wheel lock, push the lock into the tire so that the bead will go under it. Use this same procedure for the valve stem. Tire-mounting lubricant can aid in mounting. Fill the tire with air until the bead is in the proper place, and then obtain the correct air pressure.

Tubeless Tire Repair

To repair a tubeless tire, use an inside combination plug/patch (Fig. 13-20). Remove the tire and find the puncture by rubbing a cloth inside the tire. Clean and smooth the puncture with contact cleaner and a file. If necessary, ream the puncture to enlarge the hole for the plug.

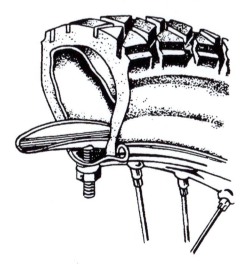

Figure 13-19 Rim lock (Kawasaki Motors Corporation, U.S.A.).

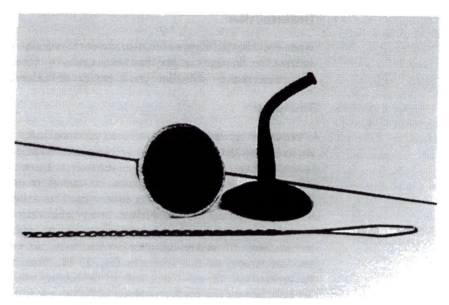

Figure 13-20   Tubeless tire combination plug/patch.

Apply glue and install the patch on the inside. Pull the plug up through the hole until the patch is flush with the tire. Roll the patch with a round object and allow the glue to dry. Install the tire and check for leaks.

Tire Storage

How a tire is stored when not in service can affect its mileage and performance later. Stored tires should not be subjected to extreme temperatures or sunlight. Sunlight ages tires quickly and causes them to harden and crack. Do not store tires where electric motors are present; the high concentration of ozone also ages tires quickly. Do not store tires where oil and gasoline could contaminate the rubber.

Wheels and tires are essential elements in the driving, braking, and steering forces. Frequent inspection of wheel and tire components and proper servicing and repairs are necessary for a safe ride.

chapter 14

Frame and Suspension

The frame is the "skeleton" of the motorcycle; it is designed to support the rider and the engine and to provide attachment points for the frame's components. The suspension system supports the motorcycle on its wheels and axles. The suspension system, frame, and frame components provide the handling characteristics of the motorcycle.

The first section of this chapter describes frame construction, geometry, and components. Service, maintenance, and frame repair are also presented. The second section of the chapter describes the principles of suspension, the front and rear suspension system components, and how to service these systems.

FRAME CONSTRUCTION A frame may be made of steel or aluminum. Some frames are constructed of a combination of tubes and pressed steel. The construction of the frame determines the frame's stability and rigidity.

FRAME DESIGN The motorcycle's handling ability is based in part on the shape of the frame. There are several basic frame designs:

Diamond Frame

The diamond frame's tubular construction is lightweight yet strong, and it provides stability at high speeds. This design is open between the front down-tube and the engine-mounting bracket. The engine is bolted into this area and becomes part of the frame's structure, which is why this type of frame is also called an *engine-stressed frame*. This design provides rigidity and effective load distribution (Fig. 14-1).

Cradle Frame

This frame is composed of a combination of triangles and similar shapes and features either a single or double down-tube. The double down-tube design places the two ends of the down-tube widely apart to form a triangle. This results in improved lateral rigidity. Engine

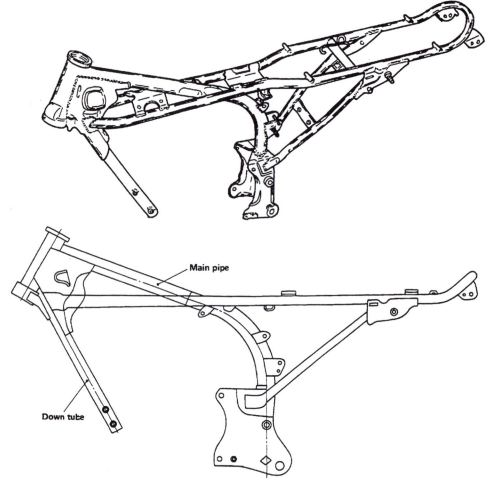

Figure 14-1   Diamond frame (Yamaha Motor Corporation, U.S.A.).

vibration is a major consideration in the design of the cradle frame. Because of the frame's ability to absorb vibration from a high-rpm engine, it is often used for road models with medium- to large-displacement engines (Fig. 14-2).

Backbone Frame

The backbone frame, also called a *monocoque*, is a one-piece assembly that is formed by welding together pressed steel plates or tubes. The backbone frame is used primarily with small- to medium-displacement engines (Fig. 14-3).

Underbone Frame

This is a variation of the backbone frame. The frame slopes down to the engine from the head pipe and up to the seat to provide comfortable riding and easy mounting and dismounting. The engine is supported by the engine bracket, which extends downward from the frame. The underbone frame is used primarily for mopeds and small-displacement engines (Fig. 14-4).

Perimeter Frame

This frame design is suited for the demands of super sport motorcycles. The frame is made of lightweight aluminum or steel. The dual box sections wrap around the engine from the steering head to the swing arm to provide superior performance rigidity (Fig. 14-5).

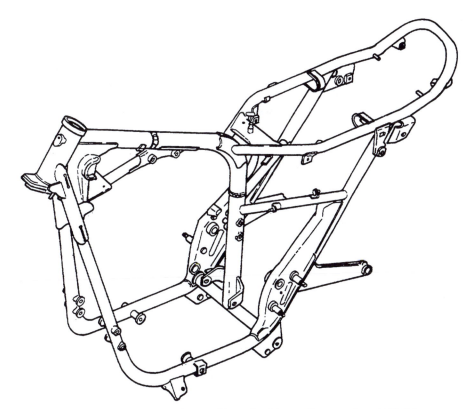

Figure 14-2   Cradle frame (Yamaha Motor Corporation, U.S.A.).

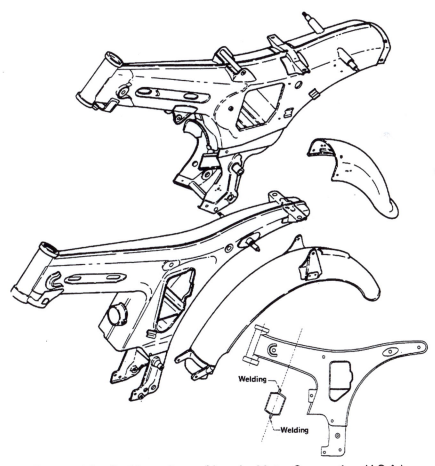

Welding

Welding

Figure 14-3   Backbone frame (Yamaha Motor Corporation, U.S.A.).

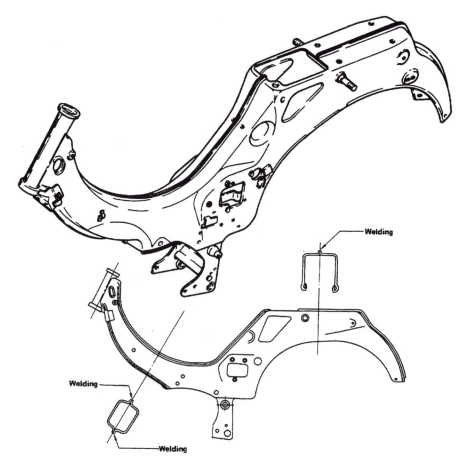

Figure 14-4 Underbone frame (Yamaha Motor Corporation, U.S.A.).

Twin-Spar Frame

The twin-spar frame consists of a very strong aluminum or steel triangle between the steering head and swing arm pivot. This design, referred to as a deltabox frame and used on some Yamaha models, provides very distinctive and responsive handling characteristics (Fig. 14-6).

Rubber-Mounted Frames

Several manufacturers utilize some form of rubber mount system to isolate power train vibration from the frame and rider. Harley-Davidson systems suspend the power train on two or three rubber mounts. One mount is located in the front, near the engine, and one or two mounts are located in the rear, behind the transmission. A system of adjustable stabilizers provides adjustment for the horizontal and vertical alignment of the power train (Fig. 14-7).

FRAME COMPONENTS   The major frame components that are attached to the frame include:

> Front-end steering head
> Triple clamp assembly and handlebars
> Steering stem
> Engine mounts
> Rear-wheel swing arm
> Footpegs and other mounting areas

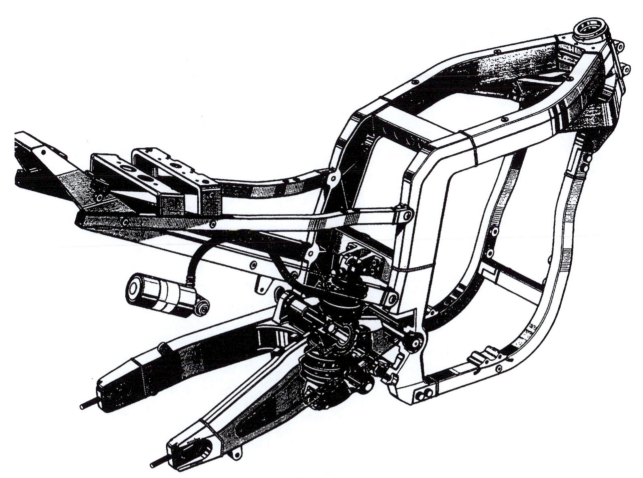

Figure 14-5 Perimeter frame (American Suzuki Motor Corporation).

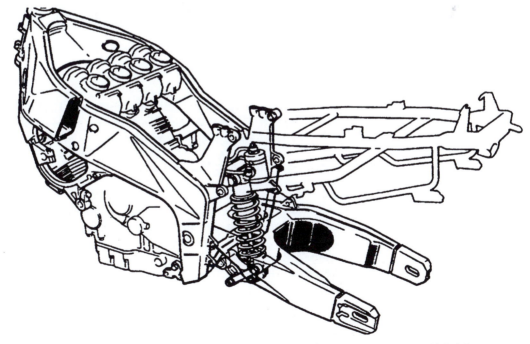

Figure 14-6 Deltabox frame (Yamaha Motor Corporation, U.S.A.).

Figure 14-7   Frame with rubber-mounted engine.

Front-End Steering Head

The steering head is the tube at the top and front of the frame. The steering head is supported by the steering stem and is welded at a given angle to provide the proper fork angle. Included in the steering head are two bearing races on which ball or tapered roller bearings rotate.

Triple Clamp Assembly and Handlebars

The purpose of this assembly is to hold the front forks in position. A triple clamp assembly consists of the steering stem and two brackets that position the fork tubes. The upper portion of the triple clamp can be used for the handlebar mounts, lights, and instrumentation. The bottom portion of the triple clamp can incorporate steering stops, a steering lock, and part of a steering damping device.

When the handlebars are turned, the front fork turns with them and changes the position of the front wheel. Handlebars can be solid or rubber-mounted to help decrease vibration. Rubber bushings are usually placed between the handlebar clamps and the top of the triple clamp. The handlebars are secured to the mounts by bolts and alloy caps. A mark on the cap indicates the correct cap position. Early motorcycles used sheet-metal clamps or U-bolts.

Steering Stem

The steering stem is an axle that enables the front end to turn. The steering stem is either bolted or welded to the bottom of the triple clamp, or a bearing race or tapered bearing is installed over the stem to rest on the bottom clamp. This assembly goes up through the steering head and another race or tapered roller bearing is installed on top. The top of the steering stem is threaded on the outside, and in some cases it is also threaded on the inside. The outside threads and preloading nut allow the bottom clamp to be fastened to the steering head separately from the top clamp (Fig. 14-8). Most front-end designs include dust covers that are placed before the nut to protect the bearings from dust and dirt. The top clamp is secured with a bolt, and sometimes a pinch bolt is used to provide more holding strength.

Engine Mounts

There are various methods of engine mounting. Each frame design uses a different engine-mounting technique and different engine-mounting areas. Metal or aluminum tabs or mounts are used to secure the engine to the frame. Metal tabs are either welded or bolted to the frame; aluminum tabs must be bolted. Some engines are rubber-mounted.

Rear-Wheel Swing Arm

The rear wheel is linked to the frame by the swing arm (Fig. 14-9). The swing arm allows the wheel to move up and down, but prevents it from moving laterally and flexing at the pivot point. The swing arm is made of steel or aluminum. Included in the swing arm assembly are: a sleeve, bearing or bushing, O-ring, cap, pivot shaft or locating pins, chain adjuster and guide, adjuster bolt, and brake stay. Some swing arm designs use needle bearings in place of bronze, iron, or nylon bushings.

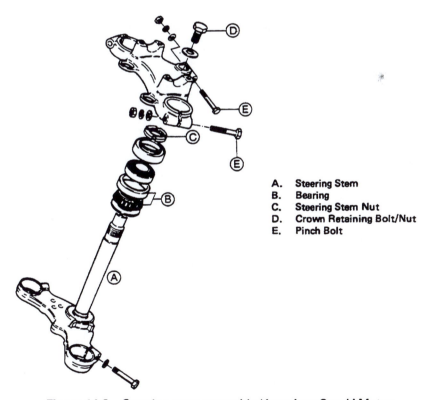

A. Steering Stem
B. Bearing
C. Steering Stem Nut
D. Crown Retaining Bolt/Nut
E. Pinch Bolt

Figure 14-8 Steering stem assembly (American Suzuki Motor Corporation).

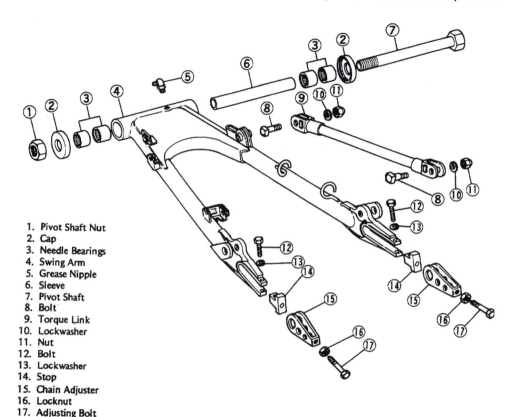

1. Pivot Shaft Nut
2. Cap
3. Needle Bearings
4. Swing Arm
5. Grease Nipple
6. Sleeve
7. Pivot Shaft
8. Bolt
9. Torque Link
10. Lockwasher
11. Nut
12. Bolt
13. Lockwasher
14. Stop
15. Chain Adjuster
16. Locknut
17. Adjusting Bolt

Figure 14-9   Swing arm assembly (Kawasaki Motors Corporation, U.S.A.).

Footpegs and Other Mounting Areas

Most footpegs are bolted to the frame. Gussets, which are flat pieces of metal used for support, are added to ensure strength. On some motorcycles the footpegs are mounted to the engine. Other important mounting areas are the rear brake, rear shocks, gas tank, seat, fenders, air box, and side plates. Most of these items are rubber-mounted to absorb shock.

FRAME MAINTENANCE   Minor repairs can be made on a frame, but it is best to avoid the need for repairs and practice preventative maintenance. Keep the motorcycle clean and inspect the frame frequently.

Frame Inspection

There are portions of the frame that are particularly susceptible to stress and wear. Frame wear is expected and usually obvious on off-road motorcycles, but it should not be overlooked on any motorcycle. The following areas are the frame's main stress points. Inspect these areas carefully and be alert for cracks, flaking or chipping paint, and any other signs of bending or flexing.

Front-End Steering Head: Constant movement of the front forks during stopping and bouncing over changes in terrain cause stress on the steering head. This area is usually reinforced with extra gussets, but it is still subject to cracking.

Engine-Mounting Areas: Engine vibrations and improper tightening of the engine mount bolts can create stress here.

Swing Arm Pivot Area: Wear is caused here by the movement of the swing arm and by the forces put on the rear end during turning and acceleration.

Rear Shock Mounting Area: This is a critical area of stress, especially if the rear shocks are worn or if the motorcycle is used for off-road or other hard riding.

Other Stress Points: Check the footpeg-mounting area, rear brake-mounting area, the kickstand, centerstand, and steering stops.

Servicing Frame Components

Use the following procedures to service the front-end assembly, the engine-mounting area, and the swing arm.

Front-End Assembly Service: To maintain the front-end assembly, check the bearings and races for pitting and excess dirt and grit. Worn or damaged bearings must be replaced. Bearings must be cleaned and repacked with wheel-bearing grease. Consult the service manual for the front-end assembly tightening specifications.

Engine-Mounting Area Service: Engine-mounting areas must be checked and tightened periodically because engine vibrations and road shocks can loosen the engine mount bolts or enlarge the holes.

Swing Arm Service: Swing arm bushings or bearings should be lubricated periodically and checked for looseness. Try to move the swing arm sideways. Any sideways movement could indicate one or more problems: a worn swing arm axle, a loose swing arm axle nut, improper tightening of the swing arm axle nut, or worn bushings or bearings. It is important not to overtighten the swing arm axle, as this could cause excess friction and wear of the bearings and bushings. Consult the service manual if replacing a part is necessary.

SUSPENSION A motorcycle suspension system consists of front forks, shock absorber springs, and a swing arm. These components support the motorcycle on its axles and wheels and affect the handling of the motorcycle (Fig. 14-10). The development of lighter, faster motorcycles has led to significant changes in frame geometry, shock absorbers, and swing arm arrangements. Frame and suspension technology advances each year, especially for off-

Figure 14-10 Front and rear suspension systems within a frame (American Honda Motor Company).

road and road-racing motorcycles, which in turn affects the technological development of all other types of motorcycles. To comprehend these rapid changes, it is first necessary to have a clear understanding of suspension theory and terminology.

FACTORS AFFECTING SUSPENSION

There are many factors and components at work to provide suspension and the handling characteristics of a motorcycle. Much of the engineering of a suspension system is based on the motorcycle's sprung and unsprung weight. These two factors affect the choice of springs that are required for efficient suspension system operation. The springs and the factors involved in their operation determine the amount of damping the shock absorber must provide.

Sprung and Unsprung Weight

Sprung weight includes the parts of the motorcycle that are supported on springs (Fig. 14-11). The masses involved in sprung weight are the fork tube, engine, triple clamp, frame, and any other components that are supported on springs.

Unsprung weight is not supported on springs and includes the wheel assembly, fork sliders, rear shocks, a portion of the swing arm, the chain or shaft drive, one-half of the spring, and on some models, the front fender.

When the masses of the wheels and tires are put in motion, a gyroscopic effect is created which helps to stabilize the wheels. This gyro action is affected by the wheel diameter, wheel weight, and rpm.

The more unsprung mass a motorcycle has, the more momentum is built up during the up-and-down travel of the suspension system at increased speed. A heavier spring is required to slow and return the suspension system to its normal position after encountering a bump.

Compression and Rebound

Springs are major suspension system components. A spring cushions the road shocks by flexing and twisting. The spring changes shape under stress or pressure, and this is called

□ SPRUNG MASS
■ UNSPRUNG MASS

FRONT UNSPRUNG MASS   REAR UNSPRUNG MASS

(TIRE, WHEEL, BRAKES,   TIRE, WHEEL, BRAKES, SPROCKET
FORK, DAMPER, AND ONE   REAR HALF OF SWING ARM
HALF OF SPRING)   ONE HALF OF CHAIN
SOMETIMES FENDER   ONE HALF OF SHOCK
                                                 ONE HALF OF SPRING

Figure 14-11   Sprung and unsprung weight (S & W Engineered Products).

the *compression stroke*. The spring returns to its original shape when the stress or pressure is removed, and this is called the *rebound* (Fig. 14-12).

Operation of a Spring

There are several factors that affect the operation of a spring.

Free Length: A spring's free length is determined by measuring the spring's length without a load.

Mechanical Preload: Mechanical preload is determined by measuring the spring while it is installed in the front fork or on the rear shock in an extended position.

Static Preload: Static preload is the amount of spring compression when the motorcycle is resting on its suspension with its own weight.

Coil Bind: Coil bind occurs when the coils of a spring are compressed and there is no clearance between each coil.

Spring Rate: The spring rate indicates the stiffness or softness of a given spring. The spring rate is the amount of force or weight that is necessary to compress a spring a given distance, and it is measured in pounds per inch or in kilograms per centimeter (kg/cm). A 100-pound single-rate spring depresses 1 inch with a 100-pound load, 2 inches with a 200-pound load, and so on (Fig. 14-13).

Three factors determine spring rate: the number of active coils, the diameter of spring wire, and the mean diameter of the spring. Active coils are the coils that are free to move. The more active coils a spring has, the lower its spring rate. Spring rate decreases with an increase in length and diameter of the spring wire.

Progressive Spring Rates: To accommodate a variety of road conditions, springs must provide a progression of spring rates (Fig. 14-14). The spring must be soft enough to compress on small bumps, and yet be strong enough to withstand larger road shocks. There are several methods used to achieve progressive spring rates. The coils can be wound tighter at one end of the spring, or the coil wire can be partially dipped in acid to decrease its diameter. An air spring, which can also be used in the front suspension, provides a natural progressive spring rate. This spring operates according to *Boyle's law*, which states that a volume of gas that is compressed by one-half will double its original pressure. Compressed by one-half again, the existing pressure will double again (Fig. 14-15). If an air spring leaks, the suspension system fails.

Dual-rate springs are stacked. An example of stacked springs would be a primary spring with a 65-pound rate stacked on top of a secondary spring with a 100-pound rate.

Damping: Springs require assistance from the shock absorber because when a spring is compressed, it tends to come back or rebound with the same force that compressed it. The shock absorber acts as an opposing force to slow the rebound movement. All shock ab-

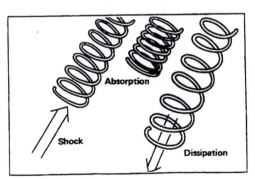

Theory of Operation

Function of Coil Springs
The coil spring absorbs shocks; but immediately dissipates the stored energy and oscillates or vibrates for a considerable time. To damp out these vibrations rapidly, oil damping is employed.

Figure 14-12 Compression and rebound (Yamaha Motor Corporation, U.S.A.).

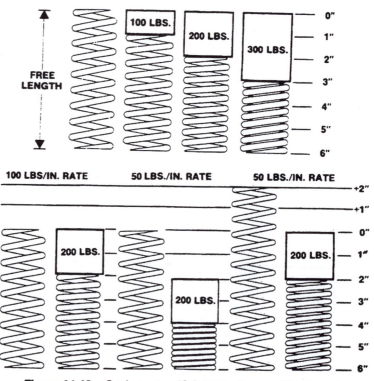

100 LBS/IN. RATE   50 LBS./IN. RATE   50 LBS./IN. RATE

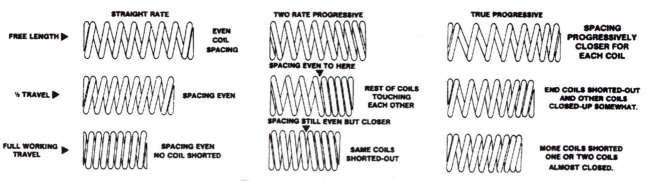

Figure 14-13 Spring rates (S & W Engineered Products).

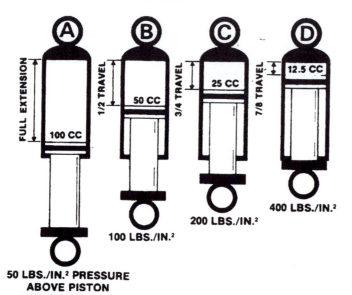

Figure 14-14 Progressive spring rates (S & W Engineered Products).

Figure 14-15 Boyle's law as it relates to an air shock (S & W Engineered Products).

sorbers use some form of damping to turn oil resistance into heat energy (Fig. 14-16). Shock absorbers use oil moving through holes in a piston to provide proportional damping over a wide range of speeds. Damping is directly affected by the size of the orifice in the piston, the oil viscosity, and the type of damping control. Damping operates on the following principles:

Oil does not compress.

Oil flows through the path of least resistance.

Oil flows from chamber to chamber to equalize pressure.

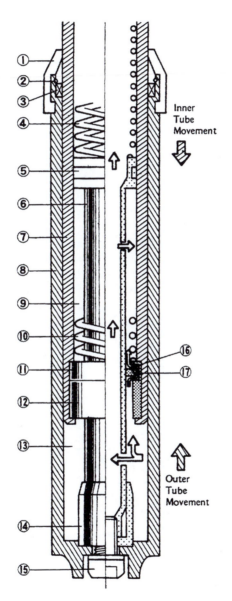

Inner
Tube
Movement

Outer
Tube
Movement

1. Dust Seal	9. Upper Chamber
2. Retainer	10. Spring
3. Oil Seal	11. Spring Seat
4. Spring	12. Collar
5. Piston Ring	13. Lower Chamber
6. Cylinder and	14. Cylinder Base
Piston Unit	15. Allen Bolt
7. Inner Tube	16. Spring
8. Outer Tube	17. Non-return Valve

Figure 14-16 Damping of a front suspension unit (Kawasaki Motors Corporation, U.S.A.).

REAR SUSPENSION COMPONENTS   The basic rear-end suspension components include the swing arm, rear shock absorber(s) and spring(s), and linkage if a single shock absorber is used.

Swing Arm

The swing arm has a single pivot point that connects it to the frame near the rear of the engine and allows the rear-wheel assembly to move up and down. This up-and-down movement is controlled by one or two springs and shock absorbers. Usually, a pair of coil springs are placed one on each side of the swing arm, and each spring is combined with a shock absorber. A single-shock system uses one spring and one shock absorber, and they are mounted on the forward middle portion of the swing arm by linkages or levers (Fig. 14-17).

Springs

The springs are attached to the shock absorbers, which are attached to the frame on pivots and to the two legs of the swing arm near the rear-wheel axle. The springs extend and compress to cushion the road shocks as the swing arm moves up and down. Springs are single rate, dual rate, or progressive rate.

Shock Absorbers

Shock absorbers are designed to prevent excessive wheel movement and to cushion secondary wheel movement caused by road irregularities. Most shock absorbers are placed inside the coil springs.

All rear shock absorbers use some form of hydraulic damping. Hydraulic damping was first used over 100 years ago to dissipate the recoil energy produced by field artillery. A piston pushes through an oil-filled cylinder and forces oil through small orifices, where friction converts the motion into heat. The damping force so produced is proportional to the velocity squared. This damper provides almost no resistance at low speeds, an appropriate level of resistance at an intermediate speed, and quickly becomes almost rigid in response to high speeds.

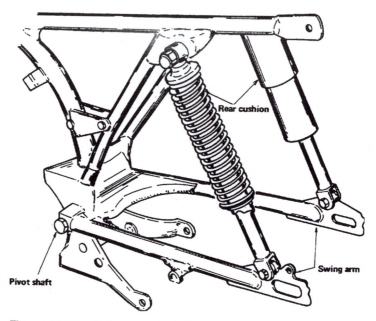

Figure 14-17   Swing arm and shock absorber (Yamaha Motor Corporation, U.S.A.).

Damping Unit Controls: Motorcycle suspension must provide proportional damping over a wide range of speeds, so the orifice area must increase with fluid pressure proportional to the speed of the shock. If a shock absorber had the same damping effect on the compression stroke as it did on rebound, the motorcycle would be thrown upward by the force of the bump as well as by the spring force. A shock absorber uses one of several types of damping unit controls.

Spring Washer: This unit uses a piston with a ring. The piston is fastened to the shaft of the shock and has many orifices for compression and rebound damping. A number of different-sized spring washers are stacked over the holes on both sides of the piston to cover the holes. When the shock moves up or down, the oil must move the washer and go through the orifices because oil cannot be compressed. The spring rate, size of the spring, oil viscosity, and the size of the orifices determine how much damping the unit provides.

Spring-Loaded Balls: In this design the piston has from five to eight damping holes of varying sizes depending on the motorcycle and its intended use. Some of the compression damping holes contain small steel balls that serve as check valves. Usually, one of these balls is free-floating within the piston. This free-floating ball pops the damping hole open and allows oil to pass through at the slightest bump. The remaining check valve balls are spring-loaded with springs in a variety of tensions and preloading lengths. These check valves open progressively based on the severity of the bump.

One-Way Valve: Another method used to adjust damping is to equip the damper piston with a one-way valve that opens by compression to let the oil flow without resistance. On the rebound this one-way valve quickly closes under the pressure of a return spring. Now the oil must flow through smaller orifices, which stiffens the rebound. Some damper assemblies can be externally adjusted for both compression and rebound.

Shock Absorber Designs

Because oil cannot be compressed, the sliding piston rod that drives the damper piston cannot move into the oil-filled cylinder without displacing oil. The pressure would either blow out the rod seal or cause the damper cylinder to bulge. Shock absorbers either mix the oil with air or segregate the oil from the air. Manufacturers recommend the use of nitrogen instead of air because nitrogen is not contaminated and responds more consistently to temperature changes.

Nonsegregated Atmospheric Damper: Early hydraulic shock absorbers use a reservoir connected to the bottom of the damper cylinder. The damper cylinder is filled with oil, but the reservoir is only half filled. As the piston rod enters the damper cylinder on the compression stroke, the oil runs into the reservoir through a small hole and compresses the clearance air there slightly. When the damper reverses its motion on the rebound, the displaced oil rushes back in from the reservoir to the damper.

Dual-Wall Shock Absorber: This design places the damper cylinder inside the reservoir cylinder and is easier to assemble on the motorcycle. The clearance gas is at atmospheric pressure and is not segregated from the oil. This damper must be mounted upright or the nitrogen gas in the reservoir is drawn into the damper. The mixing of oil and nitrogen gas, known as *aeration*, creates foam which makes the damping action erratic. In motocross applications even a carefully designed nonsegregated damper gets clearance gas into the oil (Fig. 14-18).

Atmospheric dampers are also subject to erratic action at high wheel velocities because the movement of the damper piston creates pressure in front of the piston and a vacuum behind it. Only 14.7 pounds per square inch of air pressure is available at sea level to force the oil into the damper. When the piston moves fast enough, oil cannot meet the demand and does not rush in quickly enough to fill the vacuum completely. This causes the

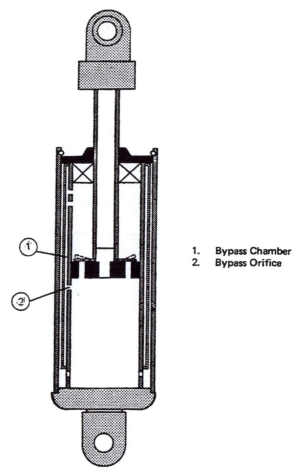

1.   Bypass Chamber
2.   Bypass Orifice

Figure 14-18   Dual-wall shock absorber (American Suzuki Motor Corporation).

sudden formation and collapse of low-pressure bubbles, which is known as *cavitation*. When the piston reverses its motion, the chamber that has cavitated cannot produce damping. Using lightweight oil in shocks allows the oil to flow better under the available pressure.

Emulsion Damper: This design was developed in an attempt to eliminate cavitation. In an emulsion damper the clearance gas and oil are deliberately mixed and there is no reservoir. Mixing the oil with air makes this shock absorber suitable for the large wheel movements that are common in off-road use (Fig. 14-19).

Pressurized Segregated Damper: Cavitation and aeration problems led to the development of the pressurized segregated shock absorber, in which high-pressure gas is held apart from the shock oil in a rubber or plastic bladder or floating piston (Fig. 14-20).

Construction of the Shock Absorber Unit

The shock is linked to the frame and swing arm at the eyes with a bolt, steel bushing, and rubber cushion. Some eyes have swivel bushings that are used when the shock is mounted to the side of the swing arm at an outward slant. The eyes may be linked to a linkage, or to a lever and bell crank.

The shaft or damping rod is usually threaded at both ends to incorporate the eye on one end and the piston and damping arrangements on the other. A seal is placed between the eye and the piston. The seal is held in place in the shock body by a seal holder cap or

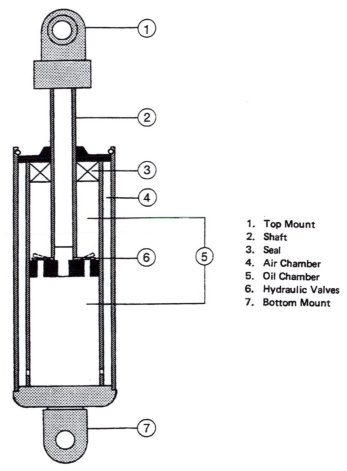

1. Top Mount
2. Shaft
3. Seal
4. Air Chamber
5. Oil Chamber
6. Hydraulic Valves
7. Bottom Mount

Figure 14-19   Emulsion damper (American Suzuki Motor Corporation).

by snap rings in the body. The shock also incorporates an external rubber bumper to slow the shock movement when the motorcycle bottoms out and the shock is completely compressed and no longer free to move.

The outside of the shock body may have notches and a clip to allow different spring preload positions. Other shock bodies may be threaded or use a preload ring for the same purpose. The shock body may have a reservoir attached. Segregated shocks use either a floating piston or a bladder with an attached or remote reservoir. Shocks can be mounted to the motorcycle at different angles.

Single-Shock Systems

Single-shock systems use a bell crank that pivots with the movement of the swing arm and a linkage to connect the shock absorber to the swing arm. As the wheel moves up over a bump, the linkage articulates and the ratio of shock-piston speed to rear-wheel movement changes. The force required to compress the suspension progressively rises with additional travel, and the result is a rising rate of rear shock damping (Figs. 14-21 and 14-22).

Troubleshooting and Repairing Shock Absorbers

Three common damping problems are pumping down, topping out, and heat. Pumping down is caused by too much damping, which overrides the return force of the springs and does not allow for a complete return of the wheel after a bump. Topping out is caused by

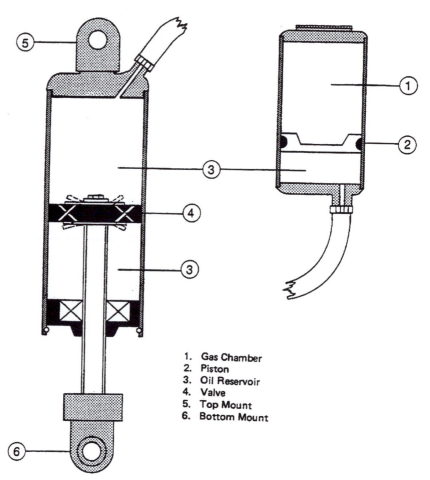

1. Gas Chamber
2. Piston
3. Oil Reservoir
4. Valve
5. Top Mount
6. Bottom Mount

Figure 14-20 Pressurized segregated damper with floating piston (American Suzuki Motor Corporation).

too little damping; the springs overcome the damping force. Friction and heat can break down the oil viscosity. When this occurs, the shock has very little damping. Bottoming and topping out can cause the shaft to break or bend, the frame to crack, and leaks at the seal.

To determine if the shock is damaged, remove it from the motorcycle and remove the spring. Push and pull on the shaft of the shock. It should move smoothly with some resistance. If the movement is not smooth, the shaft may be bent or there may be a loss of oil. Usually, if a loss of oil has taken place, oil will appear at the top of the shock body where the shaft enters the seal. This indicates that the seal is damaged and must be replaced. Consult the service manual for the procedure. Many shock absorbers can be rebuilt. Consult the service manual for the shock in question to determine if rebuilding is possible.

FRONT SUSPENSION AND STEERING

The front fork assembly supports the front wheel and allows it to pivot from side to side for steering by means of the triple clamp, steering head, and stem. One or two springs are placed inside the fork tube, which is held in place with a fork cap and fork slider damping rod. The triple clamp holds the steering damper if one is included.

Early motorcycles used heavy, external leaf springs without damping to create some flex at the front end (Fig. 14-23). The springer fork assembly was an obsolete fork design of the leading link fork family until revived by Harley-Davidson. Once again in production, this assembly consists of a rigid fork, which is attached to and pivots in the frame's steering head bearing. A spring fork slides through the rigid fork bushings and is attached to the rigid fork by two rockers. The rockers pivot on self-lubricating Teflon bushings. Suspension is provided by six compression springs and two rebound springs with a single hy-

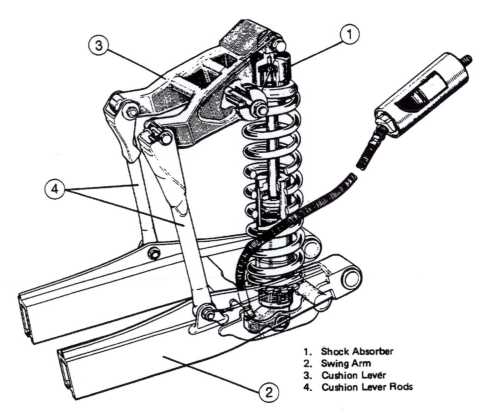

1. Shock Absorber
2. Swing Arm
3. Cushion Lever
4. Cushion Lever Rods

Figure 14-21 Single shock system (American Suzuki Motor Corporation).

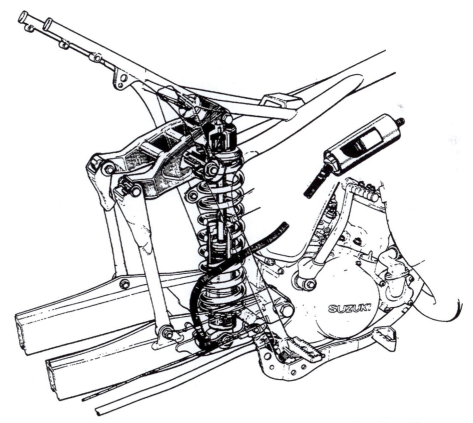

Figure 14-22 Full-floating single shock system (American Suzuki Motor Corporation).

Figure 14-23   Springer-type front end.

Figure 14-24   Trailing link suspension system.

draulic shock for dampening. This fork design provides a natural antidive effect. When the front brake is applied, the front brake caliper pivots on the front axle and induces a downward pressure on the rockers. This counteracts the natural tendency of the front end to compress the springs as the weight shifts forward.

The trailing link suspension system uses a link to mount the wheel to the rear of the front tubes, but it does not cushion braking loads efficiently. The leading link suspension system uses a link to mount the wheel to the front of the tubes and provides antidive braking (Fig. 14-24). This system works well, but it is expensive to manufacture and involves a lot of unsprung mass. The telescopic front end is the most commonly used suspension system.

Telescopic Front End

This system keeps the wheel-axle assembly evenly aligned between each fork. Because of its construction, it allows for varying spring rates and damping control to provide a smooth ride over varying road conditions (Fig. 14-25). The telescopic assembly consists of:

> Fork tube
> Fork cap
> Fork suspension spring
> Topping-out spring
> Oil and dust seals
> Fork slider
> Damper rod
> Damper piston
> Bottoming sleeve and stop
> Bypass valve
> Rebound and compression orifices

Basic Telescopic Damper

Like the rear shocks, the front forks have compression and rebound strokes. Suspension movement pumps oil through small passages and produces friction that controls unwanted wheel movement. The compression and rebound strokes are affected by:

> Oil viscosity
> Amount of oil
> Size of the damping holes in the damping rod
> Whether or not the forks have air caps and are pressurized
> Amount of air pressure

Front Fork Designs

There are two basic front fork designs: an oil fork and an air-oil fork. There are many variations of each design.

Oil Forks: These nonpressurized telescopic forks use an internal spring and oil in the fork slider to cushion the wheel movement on the compression stroke. Earlier models used external springs for the same purpose. The bottom of the damping rod is connected to the slider by an Allen bolt or Phillips screws. The top of the rod is a piston. In most cases the slider and damping rod are held to the fork tube by a snap ring, or they may be held together by a snap ring above an oil seal, or by a screw on the front fork slider seal holder. As the wheel moves up, the wheel's axle moves the fork slider up, and oil is forced through orifices in the damping rod.

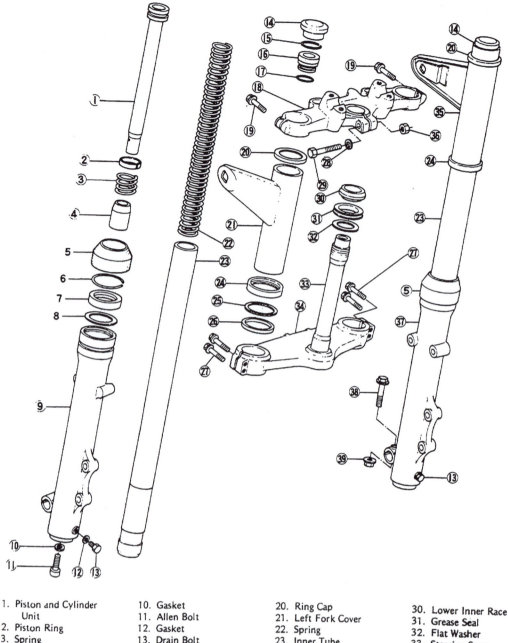

1. Piston and Cylinder Unit	10. Gasket	20. Ring Cap	30. Lower Inner Race
2. Piston Ring	11. Allen Bolt	21. Left Fork Cover	31. Grease Seal
3. Spring	12. Gasket	22. Spring	32. Flat Washer
4. Piston Base	13. Drain Bolt	23. Inner Tube	33. Steering Stem
5. Dust Seal	14. Rubber Cap	24. Base Cover	34. Stem Base
6. Retainer	15. Retainer	25. Damper Ring	35. Right Fork Cover
7. Oil Seal	16. Top Plug	26. Rubber Damper	36. Nut
8. Flat Washer	17. O Ring	27. Lower Clamp Bolt	37. Right Outer Tube
9. Left Outer Tube	18. Stem Head	28. Lockwasher	38. Clamp Bolt
	19. Upper Clamp Bolt	29. Clamp Bolt	39. Nut

Figure 14-25 Telescopic front fork assembly (Kawasaki Motors Corporation, U.S.A.).

Air-Oil Forks: This is basically the same design as the oil fork, but an air cap is provided to insert air and create pressure. This pressure assists the spring on the compression stroke.

Early air forks were designed to operate without a wire spring and required higher pressure. Friction heated the air and caused air and oil leaks. When the fork lost pressure, the suspension system failed.

With the addition of a spring, air pressure could be decreased. A softer spring rate is used in pressurized air forks, and the use of air and different oil levels allows a wider range of spring rates.

Cartridge dampener forks include a hollow piston/rod that fits into the existing dampening rod to form a cartridge. Most of the fork oil stays within the cartridge, which maximizes the dampening efficiency. An adjuster located at the bottom of the fork slider allows the rider to change the oil flow, thereby providing more accurate compression dampening.

Inverted cartridge forks have a cartridge within the inverted fork that operates very similarly to the cartridge dampener forks. The upper tubes in the inverted cartridge fork design have a greater diameter than those of cartridge dampener forks. This larger upper tube design gives the system more damping surface area, which increases the front fork's resistance to unwanted flexing.

Troubleshooting and Repairing Front Forks

Changing the fork oil and seals is the most common maintenance procedure. If the fork tubes are damaged, they may need to be replaced. Consult the service manual and use the following procedure to service the front fork:

1. If the fork caps are under air pressure, release the pressure.
2. Remove the front wheel, brake assembly, and fender.
3. Loosen the top pinch bolts on the top triple clamp and then loosen the fork caps.
4. Loosen the bottom triple clamp bolts and pull the fork assembly down and out while turning the fork tube. Sometimes the fork caps must be removed.
5. Remove the fork caps. Remember that the caps could be under spring preload pressure, and use care when removing them.
6. Remove the spring from inside the fork tube and drain the oil.
7. To remove the fork tube from the slider, remove the bolt at the end of the slider and pull the tube from the slider.
8. Remove the damping rod from the fork tube.
9. Inspect the fork tube, slider, bushing, and piston for scoring, scratches, and excessive or abnormal wear. Replace the parts that cannot be reused.
10. Check the fork tubes for runout by setting the fork tube in V-blocks with a dial indicator (Fig. 14-26). Consult the service manual for the appropriate service limits.
11. If the tubes do not meet specifications, replace them.
12. Clean all parts and assemble the forks with proper fork fluid. Consult the service manual for the fluid-level specifications.

STEERING GEOMETRY Several factors are involved in providing steering. The two factors that most affect steering are rake and trail. Rake and trail work together to provide motorcycle handling. Rake is the angle of the steering head measured in degrees. Trail is the distance between the actual contact patch and the imaginary point where the steering head axis strikes the ground (Fig. 14-27). Early motorcycles did not allow for sufficient rake and trail and did not have high-speed stability for that reason.

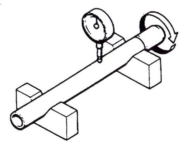

Figure 14-26 Checking fork tube with a dial indicator (American Honda Motor Company).

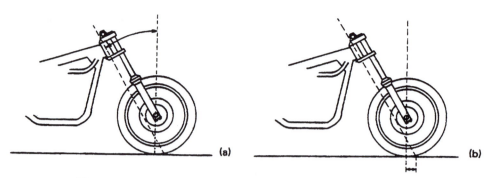

Figure 14-27   (a) Rake and (b) trail (American Suzuki Motor Corporation).

Different types of motorcycles use different degrees of head angle, so they handle a little differently. The steeper the head angle, the more quickly the motorcycle will turn, but the less high-speed stability it will have. More rake and trail creates slower turning but increases the high-speed stability.

The fork crown offset and the position of the front axle also affect the steering geometry. Fork crown offset is measured in inches from the center of the steering head crown to the center of the fork tube, where it is held by the triple clamps (Fig. 14-28). These components must be considered when troubleshooting a steering problem. If the frame or suspension system components are bent, they must be repaired to the original specifications.

TROUBLE-SHOOTING HANDLING PROBLEMS

If the motorcycle is hard to steer, the problem could be caused by one or more of the following:

A faulty steering head bearing

Excessively tight bearing adjustment nut

Insufficient tire pressure

Faulty tire

If the motorcycle steers to one side, the problem could be caused by one or more of the following:

Unevenly adjusted right and left shock absorbers

Bent fork tube, front axle, and/or frame

Incorrect wheel installation

Faulty steering head bearings

Worn wheel bearings

Figure 14-28   Fork crown offset (American Suzuki Motor Corporation).

If the front wheel wobbles, the problem could be caused by one or more of the following:

Bent front rim
Worn wheel bearings
Faulty tire

If the front suspension is too "soft," the problem could be caused by one or more of the following:

Weak front telescopic fork springs
Insufficient fork fluid
Incorrect fork fluid weight

If the rear suspension is too "soft," the problem could be caused by one or more of the following:

Weak shock springs
Incorrect damper adjustment
Leaking oil, air, or gas from the damper unit

If the front suspension is too "hard," the problem could be caused by one or more of the following:

Bent forks
Incorrect fork fluid weight
Clogged fork fluid passages
Excessive fork fluid

If the rear suspension is too "hard," the problem could be caused by one or more of the following:

Incorrectly mounted suspension components
Incorrect damper adjustment
Bent swing arm pivot shaft
Damaged swing arm bearings or bushings
Faulty suspension linkage

Avoid creating problems by keeping the motorcycle clean and making frequent inspections. Loose, worn, or damaged suspension parts may impair vehicle stability and control. Check the suspension system for excess oil leaks. Check the frame at the stress points. Keep all metal-to-metal parts clean and lubricated and ride responsibly.

Brake Systems

A brake is an energy-conversion device that converts the energy of motion into heat energy. Basically, a brake system consists of one or more brake assemblies and operating and control mechanisms. Friction is created within the brake assembly to increase the friction at the tire and road surface to slow and stop the motorcycle.

This chapter briefly presents the development of motorcycle brake systems and focuses on the four systems that are most commonly used today. Troubleshooting and maintenance procedures for each modern braking system are explained. Many modern motorcycles also include a floating backing plate, an antidive system, or a unified brake system. The basic design and operation of these systems are also presented.

A BRIEF HISTORY

Because the first motorcycles were no more than bicycles with small engines, they required only a lightweight braking system. Some models used coaster or back-pedaling brakes, and others used bicycle saddle brakes. Saddle brake pads were activated by the brake lever to clamp against each side of the rim of the rear wheel.

Later models used a band brake. This system consisted of a drum attached to the rear wheel. A band connected to the activating lever and encircled the drum. The inside of the band was coated with asbestos. When the lever was pulled, the band contracted around the drum to slow and stop the motorcycle. This system was used for about 20 years.

V-pulley brakes were popular until 1925. This system used a friction material that was attached to a pulley belt for braking. This was the first system that used a friction material. This system and all of the previous braking systems were exposed to the elements and moisture reduced the friction at the brake assembly.

BRAKE SYSTEMS

When motorcycles were designed to be larger and more powerful, drum brakes and later disk brakes were developed. These systems, and the cable-disk brake system, which is a combination of the two, are now standard on most motorcycles. Some new models are equipped with an antilock braking system.

Drum Brakes

Until the early 1980s, drum brakes were common on most motorcycles (Fig. 15-1). This system consists of:

Brake lever or pedal
Rod or cable
Cam and cam lever
Brake shoes and linings
Brake drum
Pivot pins
Springs
Backing plate

The operation of drum brakes is based on leverage, pressure, and friction. Most motorcycles use front and rear brake assemblies (Fig. 15-2). Pressure at the brake lever on the handlebars is transferred by a cable to pull the cam lever to operate the front brake. Pressure at the brake foot pedal is transferred by a rod or cable to the cam lever to operate the rear brake. The cam lever is designed and manufactured to a specific length to exert the proper amount of force on the cam. Manufacturers determine the cam lever length based on the length of the brake pedal. The brake lever and pedal allow the rider to exert a little force at the lever or pedal to create a larger force at the brake cam and linings to slow the motorcycle and bring it to a stop.

The brake drum is part of the hub and rotates with the wheel. The brake shoes, which are lined, the cam lever, pivot pins, and springs are secured to the backing plate (Fig. 15-3). The backing plate holds these components inside the brake drum. The plate is attached to the frame or swing arm and does not rotate with the wheel.

The cam is rectangular and positioned between the ends of the brake shoes. The other ends of the brake shoes are secured to the backing plate by the pivot pins and springs. When pressure is exerted on the lever or pedal, the force pulls the cam lever to turn the cam. When the cam turns, it pushes the brake shoes apart and forces them against the inside of the brake drum. The pressure creates friction against the rotating drum and the friction is transferred to the wheel and tire to slow the motorcycle. There are springs attached to the inside of the brake shoes; these springs pull the shoes back into place once the pressure at the lever or pedal is released.

A single leading shoe drum brake system is activated when force is applied against the brake lever or pedal cable or rod that is attached to the brake mechanism. A threaded

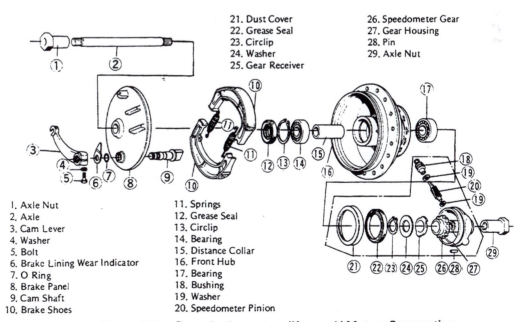

21. Dust Cover
22. Grease Seal
23. Circlip
24. Washer
25. Gear Receiver

26. Speedometer Gear
27. Gear Housing
28. Pin
29. Axle Nut

1. Axle Nut
2. Axle
3. Cam Lever
4. Washer
5. Bolt
6. Brake Lining Wear Indicator
7. O Ring
8. Brake Panel
9. Cam Shaft
10. Brake Shoes

11. Springs
12. Grease Seal
13. Circlip
14. Bearing
15. Distance Collar
16. Front Hub
17. Bearing
18. Bushing
19. Washer
20. Speedometer Pinion

Figure 15-1   Drum brake system (Kawasaki Motors Corporation, U.S.A.).

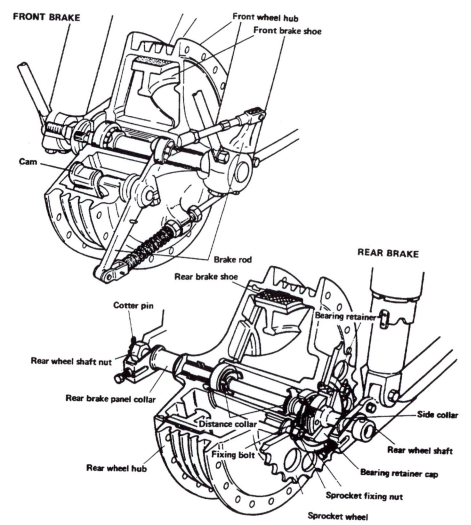

Figure 15-2 Front and rear drum brake systems (Yamaha Motor Corporation, U.S.A.).

adjuster on the end of the brake-activating cable or rod controls the precise brake activation point. The adjuster moves against a pivot on the end of the brake arm. The brake arm is clamped to and turns a brake-activating cam. This cam transfers the rotating force from the outside of the drum through the protective brake panel to the inside of the drum. The cam then spreads one end of the two crescent-shaped shoes. The other end of the shoes pivots against a common pin that is set into the brake panel. The rotation of the wheel slows as both shoes press against the inside surface of the drum. The friction created by the shoe-to-drum contact slows the wheel.

The front shoe pressed against the drum is called the leading shoe. The back shoe pressed against the drum from the common pivot pin is called the trailing shoe (Fig. 15-4).

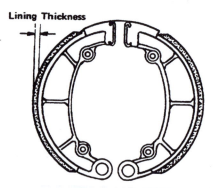

Figure 15-3 Brake shoes (Kawasaki Motors Corporation, U.S.A.).

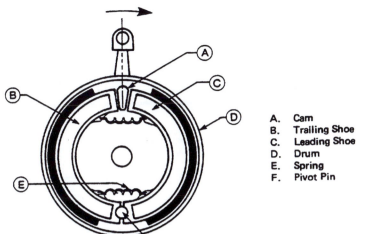

A. Cam
B. Trailing Shoe
C. Leading Shoe
D. Drum
E. Spring
F. Pivot Pin

Figure 15-4 Single-cam mechanical drum brake system (American Suzuki Motor Corporation).

Because of its position within the assembly, the leading shoe creates more force against the drum than the force that is applied to it. This increased force capability is called a *self-energizing effect*. The trailing shoe creates less force against the drum than the force that is applied to it.

Cams are used to activate the shoes in a dual leading shoe drum brake system (Fig. 15-5). Two cams, located on either end of the brake panel, simultaneously press the shoes against the drum. This creates two leading shoes and produces a braking force that is noticeably greater than a single leading shoe system of similar size when the same amount of force is applied to the brake lever or pedal.

The brake drum is made of either a hard iron or a soft metal coated with hard chrome so that it can withstand the heat created by friction without warping or wearing. The outside of the hub is usually made of aluminum or magnesium to dissipate the heat efficiently. Some drum brakes have air vents that allow fresh air to cool the linings and hub. Other hubs are manufactured with fins that aid in cooling.

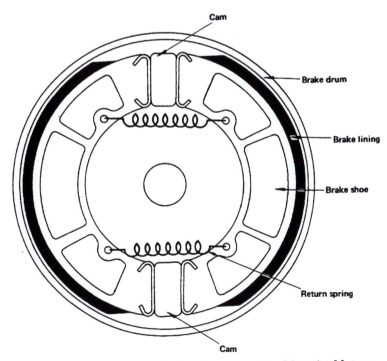

Figure 15-5 Dual-cam brake shoe assembly (Yamaha Motor Corporation, U.S.A.).

Hydraulic Disk Brakes

The introduction of heavier, faster motorcycles created the need for added stopping power and stronger brakes. Hydraulic disk brakes fill this need (Fig. 15-6). The hydraulic disk brake system consists of:

> Brake lever
> Master cylinder assembly
> Hydraulic lines
> Brake fluid
> Caliper assembly
> Disk
> Brake pads

This brake system operates using hydraulic pressure and friction. A small force exerted at the brake lever is transformed into hydraulic pressure at the master cylin-

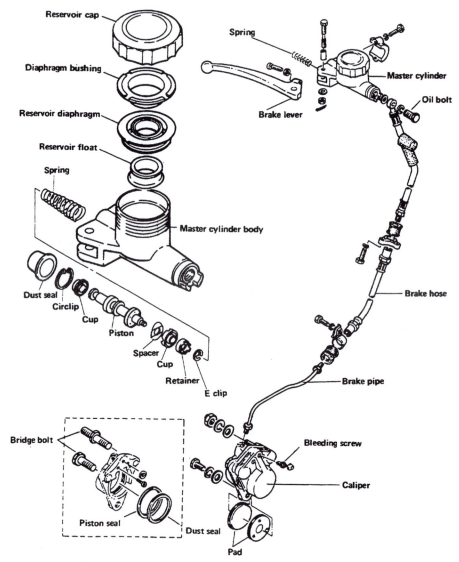

Figure 15-6 Hydraulic disk brake system (Yamaha Motor Corporation, U.S.A.).

der assembly. This hydraulic pressure is transferred by hydraulic lines to the caliper assembly, where the leverage increases to create friction at the brake pads to slow or stop the motorcycle.

A master cylinder consists of the master cylinder body, a check valve, a return spring and seat, a piston, and primary and secondary cups. The cylinder body contains a reservoir for brake fluid and a piston chamber. When the brake system is at rest, the brake fluid from the reservoir fills the piston chamber and most of the fluid in the chamber is pushed into the hydraulic lines. The primary rubber cup fits over the end of the piston and expands when the piston pushes into the chamber to prevent fluid from leaking past the piston. The secondary cup acts as a return seal for the spring that returns the piston when the pressure at the brake lever is released. The movement of the piston into the chamber pressurizes the brake fluid throughout the system.

There are two common types of caliper brake assemblies: fixed and floating. A fixed caliper, which is also known as a double-action caliper, is rigidly mounted to the front fork leg. The caliper contains movable pistons, and a crossover passageway inside the caliper connects both halves of the caliper (Fig. 15-7). When the brakes are applied, equal amounts of hydraulic pressure are applied to the pistons on each side of the brake caliper. The movable pistons and pads then simultaneously pinch the disk as the brake is applied.

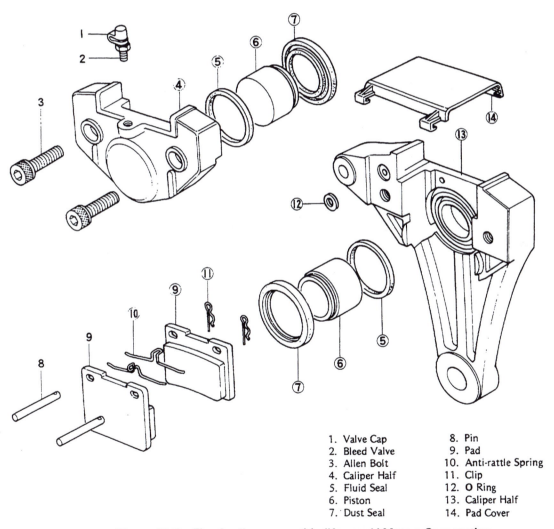

1. Valve Cap	8. Pin
2. Bleed Valve	9. Pad
3. Allen Bolt	10. Anti-rattle Spring
4. Caliper Half	11. Clip
5. Fluid Seal	12. O Ring
6. Piston	13. Caliper Half
7. Dust Seal	14. Pad Cover

Figure 15-7 Fixed caliper assembly (Kawasaki Motors Corporation, U.S.A.).

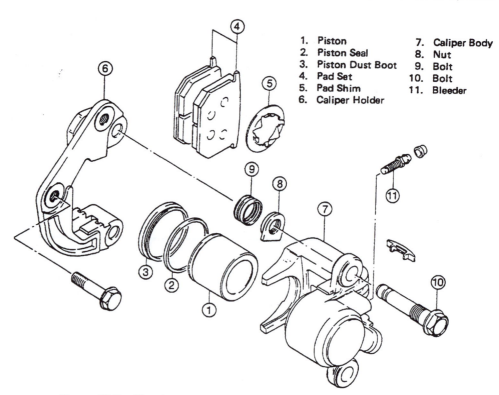

1.	Piston	7.	Caliper Body
2.	Piston Seal	8.	Nut
3.	Piston Dust Boot	9.	Bolt
4.	Pad Set	10.	Bolt
5.	Pad Shim	11.	Bleeder
6.	Caliper Holder		

Figure 15-8   Floating caliper assembly (American Suzuki Motor Corporation).

The single-action floating caliper has movable piston(s) and pad(s) and one stationary pad. The movable pad is positioned next to the piston, and the fixed pad is located on the opposite side. The caliper body is mounted on a bracket with pivot or sliding pins, which allow limited sideways movement (Fig. 15-8). When the brake is activated, the brake piston moves. The piston movement causes the caliper to "float" or move on the mount to pinch the disk between the pads. As the pressure continues, the caliper body slides over until the fixed pad is pressed against the opposite side of the disk (Fig. 15-9).

Brake Pads: There are different types of disk brake pads (Fig. 15-10). When disk brakes were originally implemented, asbestos-based pads were used. Asbestos pads were later re-

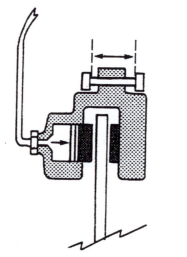

Figure 15-9   Floating caliper operation (American Suzuki Motor Corporation).

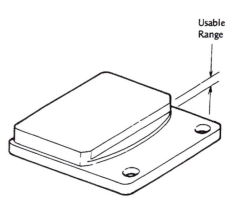

Figure 15-10   Rear brake pad (Kawasaki Motors Corporation, U.S.A.).

placed with pads of organic materials that were impregnated with small metal particles to increase the service life of the pad and improve wet braking performance. Most motorcycle manufacturers now design their brake systems to be used with sintered brake pads, which are impregnated with fine particles of copper and other metals. Sintered metal brake pads provide wet braking performance that is equal to their dry braking performance. Insulation is used on the back of the brake pad to shield the hydraulic brake fluid from heat and reduce braking noise.

Brake pad manufacturers must comply with ratings published by the U.S. Department of Transportation which rate brake pad materials according to the effective heat range in which they operate.

Brake pads should always be replaced in sets; never replace just one pad.

Brake Fluid: There are three main types of brake fluid that are rated by the U.S. Department of Transportation (DOT) and used in hydraulic brake systems: DOT 3, DOT 4, and DOT 5. DOT 3 and DOT 4 are both glycol-based brake fluids. DOT 5 is a silicon-based brake fluid. DOT 4 can be mixed with and used in place of DOT 3. However, DOT 3 should not be used in place of DOT 4. DOT 4 has a higher boiling point than DOT 3 and is normally found on motorcycles that use semimetallic or metallic brake pads, which generate higher braking temperatures. Loss of braking could occur if the fluid were to boil. Both DOT 3 and DOT 4 brake fluids are hygroscopic, which means they absorb moisture from the atmosphere. This contaminates the fluid, which lowers its boiling point and leads to corrosion in the brake system. DOT 3 and DOT 4 are harmful to plastics and painted surfaces, so use care when draining or adding these brake fluids.

Water or moisture does not mix with DOT 5 brake fluid, nor can DOT 5 be mixed with DOT 3 or DOT 4. DOT 5 is not harmful to painted or plastic surfaces. DOT 5 emulsifies easily; do not shake the container.

DOT 3 and DOT 4 have additives that counteract the fluids' natural tendency to cause seals to shrink. DOT 5 has additives that counteract the fluid's tendency to make seals swell. These additives impregnate the seals. If you change from one type of fluid to the other, the seals and all rubber parts should be replaced to prevent brake system failure.

Water, air, and dirt that contaminate the fluid affect the efficiency of the hydraulic disk brake system. If water contaminates the brake fluid, the water can get hot and boil. The steam creates bubbles in the system. The piston must compress the bubbles before it can move the fluid to the pads. This condition is apparent when there is a lack of resistance at the pedal or lever and reduced stopping power. Water can be removed only by changing the fluid. Air that contaminates the system can be bled from the system through the air bleed screw.

Any dust or dirt in the fluid causes the rubber seals, pistons, and other moving parts to wear quickly and results in fluid and air leaks. Any discoloration of the fluid indicates contamination and the fluid must be replaced. Brake fluid should be replaced at least once a year to maintain efficient brake operation.

Cable-Disk Brakes

This system, which is used on smaller motorcycles, is a combination of drum and disk brake designs but does not use hydraulic pressure. The caliper assembly is operated by a cable and cam instead of hydraulic fluid. When pressure is applied to the brake lever, it pulls the cable which is attached to the cam. The cam pushes against a piston to push the brake pad against the disk.

Antilock Brakes

Antilock brakes are based on the concept that braking torque should be controlled while the rider is operating the motorcycle. Controlling braking torque during operation ensures optimum tire-to-road surface traction during braking. The antilock brake system also provides an extra margin of safety by helping to prevent wheel lock during hard braking or when braking on low-traction surfaces.

The antilock brake system is only activated when the rider applies the front or rear brakes hard enough to lock the wheel. The system operates by modulating brake fluid pressure, which then varies the braking torque to allow the wheels a limited amount of controlled slipping.

FLOATING BRAKE MOUNTS

Some motorcycle braking systems are allowed to pivot on the axle as the wheels move up and down. This design eliminates the effects of the wheel and suspension movement on the braking operation and prevents the braking force from being transmitted to the motorcycle's suspension system. The floating brake mount has a rod that is attached to one end of the mount and to the motorcycle frame or fork. The axle goes through the mount so that the mount can float or pivot on the axle as the suspension compresses and rebounds. Suspension movement has less effect on braking, and the braking forces are transferred to the frame or fork rather than the suspension system.

Drum brakes use a floating backing plate (Fig. 15-11). Disk brakes use a floating caliper mount.

ANTIDIVE SYSTEMS

Some motorcycles use an antidive system to reduce front fork compression during braking (Fig. 15-12). Before antidive systems were developed, very stiff springs were used in the front forks to reduce the compression, but this also reduced the front-end response. When a motorcycle travels over a rough surface, the front forks must respond to the bumps and holes and maintain stability during braking. Most antidive systems use increased compression damping in the front forks and the front brake assembly to prevent excessive fork compression and to improve handling when the brakes are applied by keeping the weight evenly distributed.

There are many different antidive systems; generally, antidive systems operate in conjunction with the brake and brake fluid and with the front fork damping unit. An antidive system consists of a brake-activated valve and piston assembly, a piston and valve seat assembly, and some type of adjusting mechanism. These components are held in the antidive housing, which is attached near the bottom of one or both fork legs. The valve is placed in the hydraulic damping circuit, through which the fork oil flows when the fork is compressed. When pressure is applied at the brake lever, some of the brake fluid from the

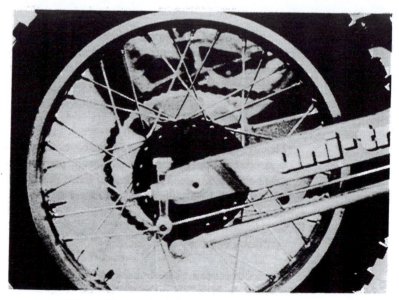

Figure 15-11   Floating brake mount assembly.

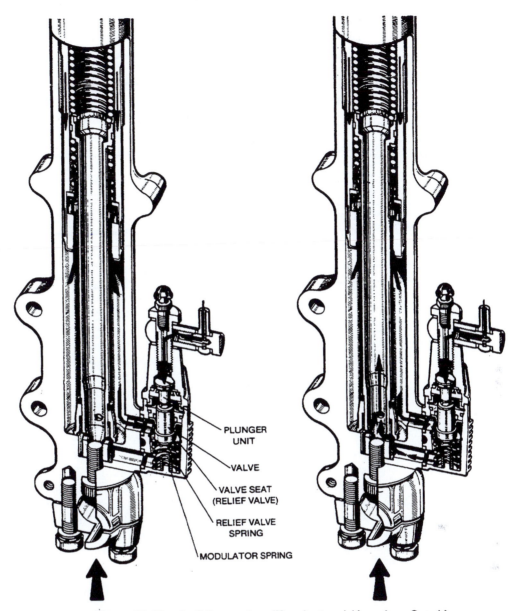

Figure 15-12   Antidive system (Kayaba type) (American Suzuki Motor Corporation).

caliper is diverted into the antidive housing to create pressure at the piston to close the compression damping valve. This gradually restricts the fork oil flow so that the compression damping is increased during braking.

If a bump is encountered during braking, the pressure in the fork compression circuit increases rapidly. The increased pressure overrides the antidive system through the use of a spring-activated valve. The spring-loaded valve and valve seat, which are separate from the brake-activated valve, allow the fork oil to flow through its normal path. If the brake is still applied when the road becomes smooth again, the compression damping circuit returns to normal and the spring-activated valve returns to the valve seat. This allows the brake-activated valve piston to resume its stabilizing effect.

Most antidive systems use a soft spring and an adjusting mechanism to allow different riding and load conditions.

One simple type of antidive system used exclusively on Harley-Davidson models utilizes the principles of Boyle's law to increase compression force when braking. The system consists of a conventional air-assist front end, an air manifold, an air reservoir in the handlebar, and an electric air valve.

The system operates in two modes: brakes off and brakes on. The handlebar reservoir has a valve in which a small amount of pressure can be applied. This air pressure compresses when the front end compresses. When the brakes are off, the brake light switch circuit is off, and the air compresses in the forks, manifold, and reservoir. Increasing pressure builds slowly as the air compresses into a large volume.

When the brakes are on, the brake light circuit is also on, and it sends current to the electric air valve. The valve closes, so the air that is being compressed in the forks cannot reach the reservoir. As the front end compresses, the air pressure rises quickly, which stiffens the front suspension.

UNIFIED BRAKE SYSTEMS

Most motorcycles incorporate front and rear brake systems, and most experienced riders know how to coordinate front and rear braking. But many riders are uncertain as to how much front brake pressure to apply and usually apply too much rear brake pressure.

The optimum braking effect is created by static friction. Static friction occurs when the friction at the braking assembly is gradually applied to allow the motorcycle to slow to a stop without skidding. Kinetic friction occurs when sudden friction created at the braking assembly causes the wheel to lock and the motorcycle skids. When a motorcycle skids, the tire does not hold to the road and there is less braking effect and an increase in heat buildup at the tire. Over 60 percent of the weight of the motorcycle and rider is transferred to the front tire when the brake is applied. If pressure to the front and rear brakes is not applied correctly, the rear tire loses much of its static friction and the rear wheel may lock and skid.

To aid in coordinating front and rear brake operation, some manufacturers have developed a braking system that automatically operates the front and rear systems when the rider applies pressure to the rear brake pedal (Fig. 15-13). A unified braking system automatically applies more braking power to the front end to prevent the rear wheel from locking. Usually, a unified brake system consists of three disk brakes, two in the front and one at the rear. When pressure is applied at the brake pedal, the system provides simultaneous and proportioned activation of the rear and left front calipers. When the pressure is applied to the brake lever only, the right front caliper is activated. Most unified brake systems use a proportioning valve installed in a hydraulic disk brake system that links with the left front and rear brake calipers. Most of these valves are no larger than a master cylinder, and in some cases they are located under the seat.

SERVICING BRAKE SYSTEMS

Because the brake system is so important to the rider's safety, it must be carefully maintained and serviced.

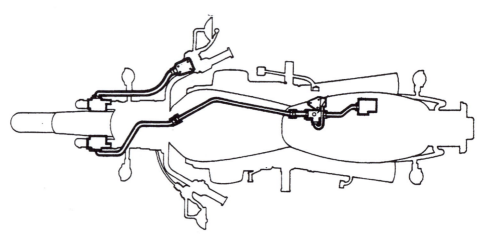

Figure 15-13 Unified brake system (Yamaha Motor Corporation, U.S.A.).

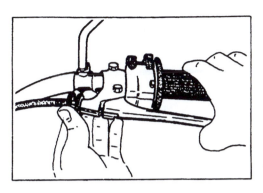

Figure 15-14   Adjusting the play of the brake lever (Yamaha Motor Corporation, U.S.A.).

Servicing Drum Brakes

Make sure that all metal-to-metal parts are clean and lubricated. The brake linings must be clean. If they are glazed, they will not create sufficient friction at the drum. Use a fine-grit sandpaper and brake cleaner to remove the glaze. When removing the glaze with sandpaper, do not create a low spot and reduce the amount of lining contacting the drum. Check for internal wear of the brake shoes.

Inspect the cables for fraying and make sure that they are clean and lubricated. Replace frayed cables. Correct cable routing is essential. On front brake systems, make sure that the cable does not catch between the triple clamp and the stop that is mounted on the steering crown as this could pinch the cable. Turn the handlebars from side to side and make sure that the cable does not pull tight and lock the brakes.

Inspect the position of the cam lever. It should be approximately 90° from the brake rod or cable. If it is much more than 90°, the effectiveness of the leverage is reduced. You can correct the angle on some models by removing the cam lever and repositioning it.

Drum Brake Adjustments: To adjust single-cam front brakes, loosen the bracket on the adjuster at the handlebar (Fig. 15-14). Loosen the adjusting screw until depressing the lever one-fourth of its travel activates the brake. If the brake shoes are rubbing the drum, use the adjuster at the wheel. Loosen the nut until the wheel rolls freely.

Rear brake systems use one adjuster nut on the end of the brake rod or cable. Adjust this nut until there is approximately 1/2 inch of travel at the brake pedal (Fig. 15-15).

When adjusting dual leading shoe drum brakes, it is critical that each shoe engages the drum at the same time and at the same rate. Poor adjustment of the shoes can result in erratic braking action. Adjust the brake balance bar or connector link between the two cam levers so both brake shoes contact the drum simultaneously and with the same amount of force. To make this adjustment, shorten or lengthen the ends of the bar as required. Consult the appropriate service manual for the proper adjustment procedure.

When servicing mechanical drum brakes, be sure to use a method designed to minimize the hazard created by airborne asbestos fibers. Asbestos fibers have been found to cause respiratory disease and cancer. Never use an air hose or dry brush to clean mechanical drum brake assemblies. Consult the service manual for the appropriate cleaning method.

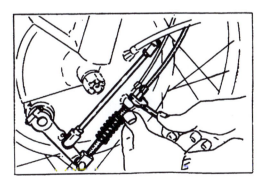

Figure 15-15   Adjusting the brake cable (Yamaha Motor Corporation, U.S.A.).

Troubleshooting Drum Brakes: Consult the service manual and use the following procedures when troubleshooting drum brakes.

Brakes squeal	Clean the linings or pads.
	Replace worn linings or pads.
Brakes stick	Clean the cables.
	Check the return springs.
	Clean or replace the brake lever.
	Remove and clean the cams.
	Check the linings for wear, and replace them if the tapered ends are worn down.
Brakes fade	Check for glazed or worn linings.
	Check for scored linings or drum.
	If brake shoes are scored, replace them.
	Turn or replace the drum depending on how badly it is scored.
Brakes grab	Check for foreign material between the linings and drum.
	Check the linings and make sure the tapered ends are not worn off.

Servicing Hydraulic Disk Brakes

If a fluid leak develops, a great deal of fluid can escape when under pressure. Check the fluid reservoir frequently for the correct amount of fluid. If you need to add fluid often, check for leaks. Replace the brake fluid at least once a year or whenever it is contaminated.

The brake pads usually do not glaze because they are out in the open and air circulates around them to keep them cool. The disk wipes the pads clean of dirt and must be kept clean; excessive dirt will score it. Brakes that squeal under light pressure are annoying, but the noise does not affect braking efficiency. Cleaning or replacing the pads should cure the problem. Do not drill holes in the brake pads. This weakens them and causes them to hold dirt. Do not oil the pads, as this affects the stopping power (Fig. 15-16).

Consult the service manual for the simple bleeding procedure if air gets into the lines.

Troubleshooting Hydraulic Disk Brakes: Consult the service manual and use the following procedures to troubleshoot hydraulic disk brakes.

Brakes squeal	Clean the linings or pads.
	Replace worn linings or pads.
Brakes stick	Inspect and clean the brake lever.
	Check brake lever free play.
	Check the brake pads for wear and dirt between the pad and the piston.
	Inspect the master cylinder for dirt around the piston and rubber seals.
	Check for air in the system.
Brakes fade	Check for air in the system.
	Check for worn or glazed pads.
	Check for low fluid level.
Brakes grab	Inspect the pads for wear.
	Inspect for dirt between the pad and the disk.

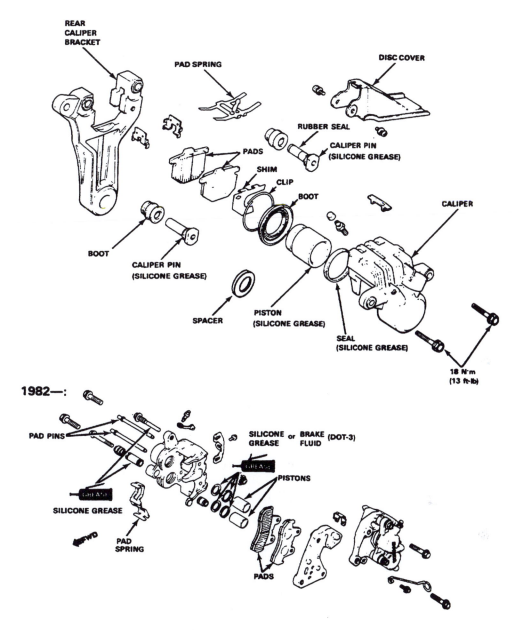

Figure 15-16   Hydraulic disk brake lubrication areas (American Honda Motor Company).

SERVICING ANTIDIVE SYSTEMS   The brake fluid and fork oil must be changed at the manufacturer's specified intervals. Consult the service manual for the procedures, and use the fluid and oil that are recommended by the manufacturer. With the exception of O-rings, the entire unit must be replaced if a problem develops with an antidive system.

chapter 16

Shop Safety and Tools

Shop safety and the correct selection, use, and maintenance of tools are essential elements of motorcycle service and repair. This chapter first presents the basic shop safety rules and the reasoning behind them. The majority of the chapter focuses on the most commonly used hand tools and explains how to select and maintain these tools. The need for thread repair is common when working on motorcycles, and this procedure is also explained.

SHOP SAFETY Certain safety rules should always be followed in a shop environment and any time you are working with power tools or internal combustion engines.

Shop Safety Rules

As you will see, shop safety rules are designed for your protection.

1. *Be careful when working with or around gasoline.* Of all the dangers related to working with internal combustion engines, gasoline is probably the main cause of injuries. Drain or remove the gas tank before working on a motorcycle. If fuel is needed during the course of maintenance, use an auxiliary tank that contains a small amount of fuel.

   If you spill gasoline, take the time to clean it up properly before continuing your work. Of course, there should be no smoking when working around any combustible material.

2. *Properly ventilate your work area.* Sometimes, when servicing or repairing a motorcycle, it is necessary to run the engine for lengthy periods. When you do this, be aware that exhaust gases contain dangerous carbon monoxide. Make sure that your work area is adequately ventilated to fresh air to allow these gases to escape.

   Hydrogen gas, which is highly explosive, is emitted from a battery when a battery charger is used. The area around the batteries and charger should be properly ventilated, and again, no smoking.

3. *Keep your work area neat.* Always keep your work area as neat as possible, and keep the floor free of tools, oil, and other lubricants. If oil is spilled, use an "oil dry" to absorb the spill and then clean the floor thoroughly. Never wax the floors where you are planning to work.

4. *Be careful when using solvents and other cleaners.* Protect your eyes when you are using solvents and other cleaners. Read the labels and take the necessary precautions if the cleaner is an irritant to the skin. If your eyes become contaminated, flush them thoroughly with an eye-cleaning solution or water.

5. *Never ride a motorcycle inside the shop area.* Even when it appears to be clean, there will always be enough contamination on the floor to make it slippery. Riding a motorcycle in the shop can easily result in a fall.

6. *Wear eye protection when working with metal against metal.* Always wear goggles or a face shield when grinding, drilling, cutting, or hammering on metal, or using a press.

7. *Keep a fire extinguisher and first-aid kit near your work area.* Always have a fire extinguisher located near your work area. Know how to use it, and mark it clearly so that it can be easily found by people who may not be familiar with your work area (Fig. 16-1).

Even if you follow all of these rules and are extremely careful, an accident could happen. In case of an accident, there is no substitute for an adequate first-aid kit. It is also a good idea to post the local ambulance, fire department, and emergency center numbers beside the first-aid kit.

SPECIAL TOOLS Tools that are used to repair and service motorcycles can be divided into two categories: special tools and common hand tools. Special tools are designed by motorcycle manufacturers to make certain tasks easier. A list of special tools for all motorcycle designs would include thousands of different tools. Consult the service manual for the model you are working on to determine what special tools are required. Special tools can be purchased through local motorcycle dealerships.

HAND TOOLS This section describes the most commonly used hand tools and explains how to select and take care of them. Whether or not a job is done smoothly is based in part on how well you have chosen your tools and how you maintain and use them.

Bench Vises

Vises take a lot of punishment, and you would be wise to purchase a model that will last. The size of a vise is based on the width of the jaws; standard sizes run from 3 to 6 inches. Be sure that the vise has a maximum jaw opening to suit your purpose.

The jaw facings are the surfaces that grip the material, and they should be removable so that they can be changed from soft to hard and replaced when worn. The jaws should be made of high-carbon tool steel, and the hand extension should be heavy enough to provide the necessary strength and support. Select a vise with a long-lasting finish. Inspect the thread screw; this provides the clamping force, and it must be strong and well tempered. For your convenience, select a model with a built-in anvil at the rear of the vise.

If you have selected the vise properly, maintenance should be minimal. Remove the thread screw and clean and lubricate it periodically. Replace the jaws when they are worn. Do not use an extension on the vise handle; the screw was designed for the pressure of the handle alone. The anvil area is the only place where a hammer should be used. Never hammer material that is clamped in the jaws.

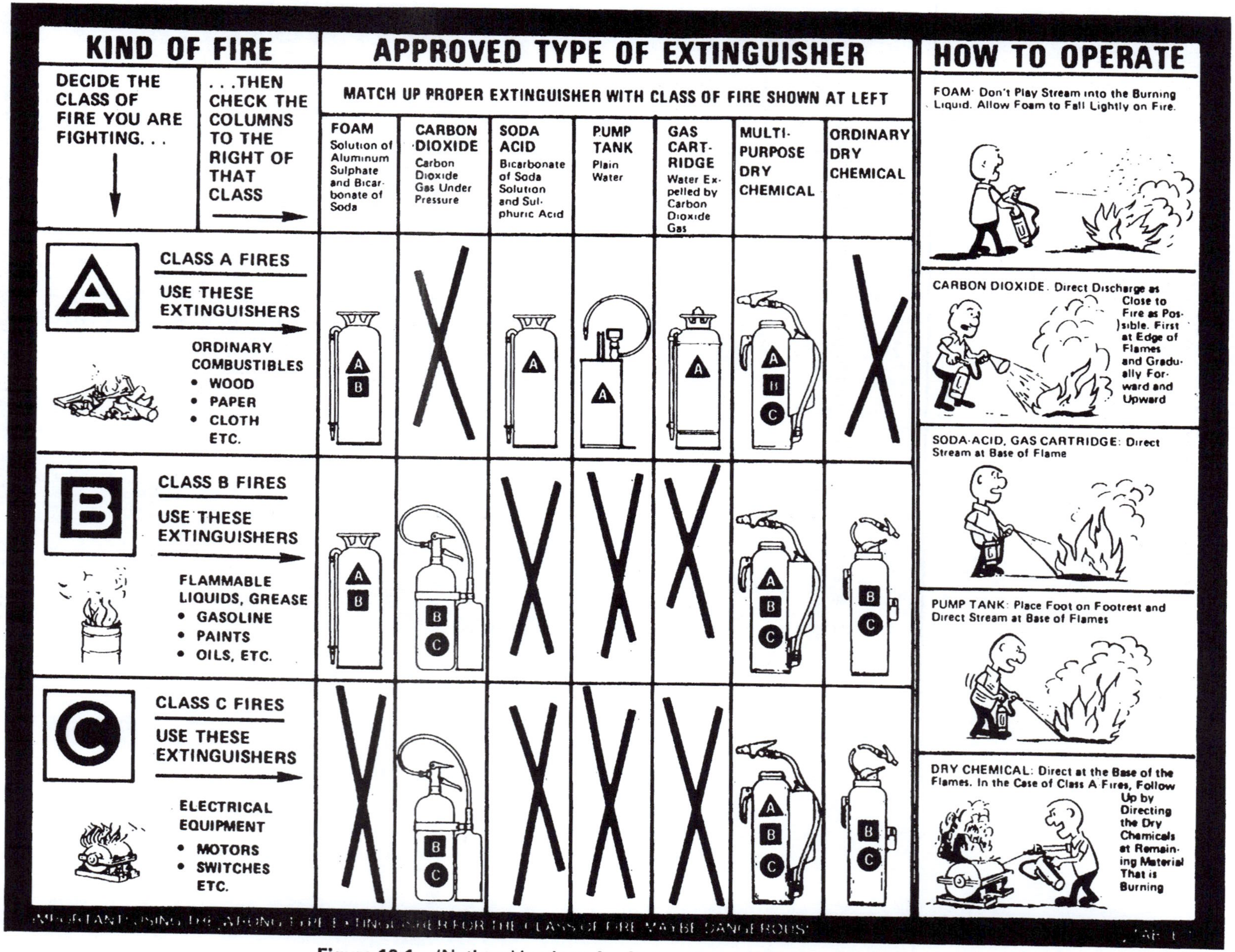

KIND OF FIRE

DECIDE THE CLASS OF FIRE YOU ARE FIGHTING. . . . → . . .THEN CHECK THE COLUMNS TO THE RIGHT OF THAT CLASS →

CLASS A FIRES

USE THESE EXTINGUISHERS

ORDINARY COMBUSTIBLES
- WOOD
- PAPER
- CLOTH
  ETC.

A

CLASS B FIRES

USE THESE EXTINGUISHERS

FLAMMABLE LIQUIDS, GREASE
- GASOLINE
- PAINTS
- OILS, ETC.

B

CLASS C FIRES

USE THESE EXTINGUISHERS

ELECTRICAL EQUIPMENT
- MOTORS
- SWITCHES
  ETC.

C

APPROVED TYPE OF EXTINGUISHER

MATCH UP PROPER EXTINGUISHER WITH CLASS OF FIRE SHOWN AT LEFT

	FOAM Solution of Aluminum Sulphate and Bicarbonate of Soda	CARBON DIOXIDE Carbon Dioxide Gas Under Pressure	SODA ACID Bicarbonate of Soda Solution and Sulphuric Acid	PUMP TANK Plain Water	GAS CARTRIDGE Water Expelled by Carbon Dioxide Gas	MULTI-PURPOSE DRY CHEMICAL	ORDINARY DRY CHEMICAL
Class A	A B	X	A	A	A	A B C	X
Class B	A B	B C	X	X	X	A B C	B C
Class C	X	B C	X	X	X	A B C	B C

HOW TO OPERATE

FOAM: Don't Play Stream into the Burning Liquid. Allow Foam to Fall Lightly on Fire.

CARBON DIOXIDE: Direct Discharge as Close to Fire as Possible. First at Edge of Flames and Gradually Forward and Upward

SODA-ACID, GAS CARTRIDGE: Direct Stream at Base of Flame

PUMP TANK: Place Foot on Footrest and Direct Stream at Base of Flames

DRY CHEMICAL: Direct at the Base of the Flames. In the Case of Class A Fires, Follow Up by Directing the Dry Chemicals at Remaining Material That is Burning

Figure 16-1   (National Institute for Occupational Safety and Health).

Torque Wrenches

There are three common types of torque wrenches: audible-click, deflecting-beam, and the dial indicator type. These torque wrenches are accurate in the middle of their range and are not as accurate in the first 18 percent and last 10 percent of their range. Torque wrenches are available in a variety of torque ranges and should be selected so that when they are most commonly used, they will read in the middle 80 percent of their range. A torque wrench with a range of 0 to 75 foot-pounds is sufficient for most motorcycle servicing. Using an extension will alter the torque wrench reading.

Audible-Click Torque Wrench: Most technicians prefer the audible-click torque wrench (Fig. 16-2). The torque is set by turning the handle to the setting on the calibrated scale on the wrench shaft. When this preset torque is reached, you will hear a click.

This wrench is dependable if certain maintenance rules are followed. The torque wrench should be set at zero when it is stored. This is a precision instrument and should be treated accordingly. Never surpass the maximum torque setting, and never use it as a breaker bar or ratchet. Calibrate the torque wrench semiannually.

Deflecting-Beam Torque Wrench: The deflecting-beam torque wrench is the most difficult of the three torque wrenches to use, but it is also the least expensive (Fig. 16-3). This torque wrench is designed with a beam running from the head that deflects when torque is applied to the handle. Torque is read on a scale. Maintenance of this torque wrench is the same as for the audible-click torque wrench.

Dial Indicator Torque Wrench: The dial indicator torque wrench uses a dial to indicate the torque that is applied. Some of these wrenches have a light that goes on when the torque is reached and guards that protect the dial. The dial needle should move in both directions for left and right threads.

Figure 16-2 Audible-click torque wrench (S-K Hand Tool Div./Dresser Ind.).

Figure 16-3 Deflecting-beam torque wrench (S-K Hand Tool Div./Dresser Ind.).

Screwdrivers

You will need two types of screwdrivers: the flat-tip and the Phillips.

Flat-Tip Screwdrivers: Select a variety of flat-tip screwdrivers to meet your needs. A flat-tip screwdriver should be selected so that the tip fits snugly into the groove of the fastener and is exactly the width of the fastener. Flat-tip screwdrivers can be ground when the end becomes damaged, but be sure not to overheat or oversharpen the end.

Phillips Screwdrivers: Phillips screws come in four common sizes, and the Phillips drivers are numbered according to size. The number one indicates the smallest and most pointed of the tips; number four is the largest and bluntest of the tips. Select your Phillips screwdriver accordingly, and it should fit snugly into the head of the screw. Clean the screw slot when it is dirty or rounding out of the head will result.

Screwdrivers should be used only for tightening and loosening fasteners. To maintain your screwdrivers, do not abuse them. Do not use them as pry bars, chisels, center punches, or gasket scrapers.

Hand Impacts

Hand impacts are commonly found in two sizes, 3/8 and 1/2 inch, but the 3/8 inch is sufficient for most jobs. The bits that are included with the impact come in various sizes. Make sure that you use the proper bit for the job. Keep the impact clean of dirt and grease to ensure a firm hold.

Drill Motors

Most shops use drill motors of two chuck sizes. The maximum sizes are 1/2 and 3/8 inch with variable speeds, forward and reverse. The larger 1/2-inch drill motor is usually used for honing a cylinder and is occasionally used when a larger hole must be drilled in a frame or mounting bracket. The 3/8-inch drill is used extensively for easy-outs, taps, screw thread coils, small aftermarket accessories, and small grinding jobs.

When using a drill motor, make sure that there are no cuts or tears in the cord. Be sure that the chuck or drill head is not worn to the point that you are unable to get a firm grip on the drill or stand. Make sure that the key is working well and that you can get a firm grip on the chuck when tightening it. Use plenty of lubrication while drilling metal. This assists in the drilling and helps to prevent the drill from losing its edge.

Die Grinders

There are basically two different types of die grinders: electrical and air-powered. Air-powered grinders are recommended for industrial use because they are dependable and easy to use. Die grinders that exceed 10,000 rpm are used to chamfer ports and for two-stroke engine performance modifications. They are also used for small grinding and cutting jobs.

Always put lubrication in the air-powered die grinder before using it. If it is being used for a long period of time, occasionally unhook the hose and apply more oil, especially if the compressor has heavy condensation in it. After you have finished grinding or cutting an object, keep in mind that the item is hot. If you must pick it up, use a pair of gloves or pliers.

Files

The file is the most commonly used of all metalworking tools. There are more than 3000 types of files. The files that are commonly used in motorcycle repair are the single-cut, double-cut, and vixen files.

Single- and Double-Cut Files: The two basic files are single-cut and double-cut files. A single-cut file has one unbroken row of teeth across the face of the file. These files are available in six different grades: rough cut, coarse cut, bastard cut, second cut, smooth cut, and dead-smooth cut. Single-cut files are used when a smooth finish is desired.

Double-cut files have two broken rows of teeth crossing each other. This file can remove metal more quickly, but it does not give as smooth a cut as a single-cut file. Double-cut files are also available in the six different grades listed previously.

Vixen Files: In motorcycle repair, it is necessary to file soft metals such as lead and aluminum. A special file known as a vixen or circular cut file should be used for this purpose. It removes soft metal quickly and produces a smooth surface after each stroke.

When filing, position the material so that your forearm is parallel to the floor. The file cuts only on the forward stroke. The file may be coated with chalk, wax, or turpentine to prevent the teeth from becoming clogged.

After using a file, clean it with a file card. Store it in a dry place and keep the files separated or the abrasive action of two or more files striking each other will ruin the cutting surface.

Hacksaws

Hacksaws are usually adjustable from 8 to 16 inches. A 10–32 blade indicates that there are 10 teeth per inch and the blade is a grade 32. The larger the last two numbers are, the harder the metal you can cut. If you are cutting a thin piece of metal, always use a higher-numbered blade because it will have less give. Use the proper blade for the job.

Select a hacksaw with a hand guard. Before using the tool, make sure that the teeth are not excessively worn, and lubricate the blade. Be careful after cutting the metal; it will be hot.

Sockets

There are a number of different sockets manufactured. Standard, fluted, Phillips, and Allen-head sockets are used in the motorcycle industry. When selecting sockets, examine them carefully. Make sure that they are designed for maximum clearance and have a good grip. It is best if they are made of a high-grade steel and plated for easy cleaning.

Standard Sockets: Standard sockets are usually six-point or twelve-point. Four-point and eight-point sockets are manufactured, but they are uncommon. A six-point socket is the best all-purpose socket. It has strong sides and a good grip on the fastener. Twelve-point sockets should be used when clearance is limited, but they are not as strong as a six-point socket because of their thinner walls, and they have a tendency to break under high torque (Fig. 16-4).

Fluted Sockets: The fluted socket is a variation of the standard socket. It is designed to put pressure on the flat side of the fastener rather than on the point, which lessens the chances of rounding the head of the fastener. This socket is excellent for use with air-powered impacts and at other times when high torque is used.

Phillips Sockets: The Phillips and standard screwdriver sockets are available in a variety of sizes and are designed for use with a hand impact or ratchet handle. They are available in different lengths and a variety may be needed.

Allen-Head Sockets: Hex-head sockets or Allen-head sockets are available in a range of sizes in both metric and SAE. Many motorcycle manufacturers are changing from the Phillips head to this design because the Allen heads have a longer service life and are easier to maintain.

Socket Handles

Usually, a 3/8-inch drive ratchet with a 6- to 7-inch handle is all that is needed in motorcycle repair. The larger 1/2-inch drive socket handle or a socket handle with a longer length is likely to damage threads or break bolts because of the low torques used on motorcycles.

Although you will normally use a ratchet handle, at times such variations as a speed-handle, T-handle, or breaker bar are needed. Speed-handles and T-handles are used for quick extraction of bolts after they are initially loosened. The breaker bar should be used in areas where high-torque valves are used and for axle bolts and swing arm pivot nuts.

The ratchet handle should be disassembled, cleaned, and lubricated periodically. Rebuild kits are available for good-quality ratchets in case of damage to the ratcheting unit.

Wrenches

The most common wrench designs are the open- and box-end.

Open-End Wrenches: The open-end wrench is open on two sides and is best for reaching in tight areas, but it tends to flex open when high torque is applied (Fig. 16-5).

The double-angle open-end wrench has the same size head on both ends, but each head has different angles. The angles are commonly set at 30° on one end and at 60° on the other; this provides a 180° range for use in tight places.

Figure 16-4   Standard 12- and 6-point sockets (S-K Hand Tool Div./Dresser Ind.).

Figure 16-5   Open-end wrench (S-K Hand Tool Div./Dresser Ind.).

Box-End Wrenches: The box-end wrench is closed on all six sides and does not spread under high torques, but it has limited maneuverability. Some wrenches are available with an open-end design on one end and a box-end design on the other (Fig. 16-6). Whenever possible, use box-end wrenches and sockets instead of open-end wrenches. Box-end wrenches are less likely to damage nuts and bolts.

Adjustable Open-End Wrenches: Adjustable open-end wrenches should never be used in place of a box- or open-end wrench. Adjustable open-end wrenches are adjusted by turning the knurled nut to open the jaws to a designated size. Although these wrenches can be pulled in either direction for light loads, they have the greatest strength when pressure is applied to the fixed jaw.

   Wrench jaws should be kept clean to prevent rounding a fastener head or slipping on a nut. Whenever possible, pull on a wrench to prevent injury. If you must push, use the palm of your hand so that if the wrench slips, you are less susceptible to injury. Never use a hammer or extension on your wrenches. They were not designed for the higher torque and will be damaged.

Punches

Motorcycle technicians commonly use taper, drift, and center punches.

Taper Punch: Taper punches vary in size, but they all have a long tapered shank and a flat point. A taper punch is used for inserting shims and washers. It is also used for aligning the wheels and axles, swing arms, and aftermarket accessories.

Drift Punch: A drift punch, which is also called a *pin punch*, is similar to the taper punch, but it is not tapered. It is used for driving out pins or fasteners. Select the correct size so that you remove the pin without enlarging or distorting the hole.

Center Punch: The center punch has a tapered bit and a sharp point. The center punch is used for making an indentation in a piece of metal as a guide for a drill.

   To maintain these punches, always keep the head of the punch dressed and the point sharp.

Figure 16-6   Box-end wrench (S-K Hand Tool Div./Dresser Ind.).

Chisels

The cape chisel and the flat chisel are usually used in motorcycle repair.

Cape Chisel: The cape chisel is used for cutting narrow grooves in metal and is handy for grooving Phillips heads if they become damaged. Keep a narrow cutting point on the chisel, and do not let it get too hot when sharpening it. Cool it with water regularly as the heat will destroy the temper of the metal.

Flat Chisel: A flat chisel has a 60° to 70° bevel on both sides, and it is used for cutting and chipping metal. Do not allow the chisel to get too hot when sharpening it. If possible, determine what the chisel will be used on before putting an angle on it. Soft metal requires less of an angle than hard metal.

Pliers

Pliers are one of the most versatile tools in the mechanic's tool box. Choose good-quality pliers that are forged from hardened steel and machined to close tolerances. Pliers come in a variety of designs.

Slip-Joint Pliers: The slip-joint pliers are the most common, all-purpose pliers. Choose one with insulated handles (Fig. 16-7).

Interlocking Slip-Joint Pliers: Interlocking slip-joint pliers are sometimes referred to as *channel locks.* They are a variation of the slip-joint pliers, but they have an angled jaw and longer handles for better leverage (Fig. 16-8).

Lockjaw Pliers: Lockjaw pliers can be adjusted by tightening the handles to lock onto objects. Use these pliers carefully or you may damage the object clamped between the jaws (Fig. 16-9).

Figure 16-7   Slip-joint pliers (S-K Hand Tool Div./Dresser Ind.).

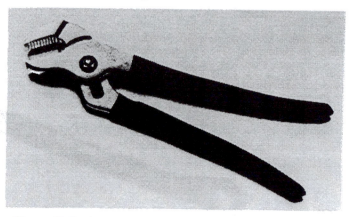

Figure 16-8   Interlocking slip-joint pliers (S-K Hand Tool Div./Dresser Ind.).

Figure 16-9 Lockjaw pliers (S-K Hand Tool Div./Dresser Ind.).

Needlenose Pliers: Needlenose pliers have thin, tapered jaws and are handy for reaching tight spaces. Select one with insulated handles because these pliers are commonly used in electrical repair (Fig. 16-10).

Cutting Pliers: Cutting pliers are sometimes known as *dykes* and are used for cutting wire or removing cotter pins. The jaws of these pliers can be sharpened with a small file if they become dull or pitted (Fig. 16-11).

Lock Ring Pliers: Lock ring pliers may also be called *snap ring pliers*, and they are used for removing retaining rings. These pliers are commonly used when repairing transmissions. Choose a variety of shapes and sizes to meet your needs (Fig. 16-12).

As with all tools, it is important to keep pliers in good working condition. Keep the joints well oiled and clean and check the gripping surfaces regularly for wear. Use pliers for holding, not turning.

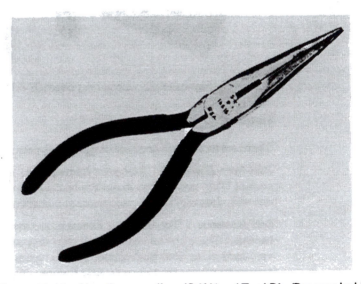

Figure 16-10 Needlenose pliers (S-K Hand Tool Div./Dresser Ind.).

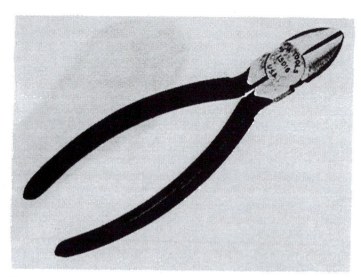

Figure 16-11 Cutting pliers (S-K Hand Tool Div./Dresser Ind.).

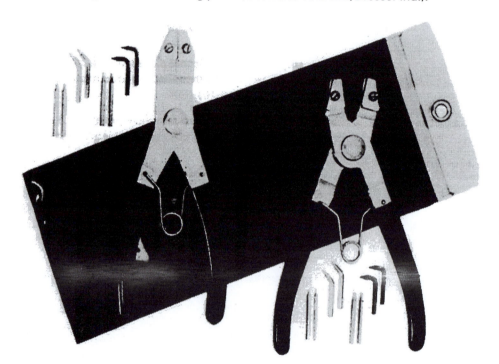

Figure 16-12 Lock ring pliers (S-K Hand Tool Div./Dresser Ind.).

Hammers

There are three basic hammer designs: ball-peen, soft hammers, and brass hammers.

Ball-Peen Hammers: Ball-peen hammers are available in weights from 2 ounces to 3 pounds. They are used to round the heads of rivets and to pound round surfaces. Choose one with a hickory handle, and make sure that the wedges are tight (Fig. 16-13).

Soft Hammers: The best soft hammers are available with replaceable tips that vary in hardness. These tips can be replaced after they are worn. Neutral-colored tips are made of very hard nylon. Red tips indicate the next hardness, blue tips are medium, green tips are soft, and gray tips are very soft. Soft hammers do not mar the surface and are used for separating cases and removing crankshafts (Fig. 16-14).

Figure 16-13 Ball-peen hammer (S-K Hand Tool Div./Dresser Ind.).

Figure 16-14 Soft hammer (S-K Hand Tool Div./Dresser Ind.).

Brass Hammers: Brass hammers are used for striking heavy blows without damaging parts, and they will not produce sparks. They are used for crankshaft rebuilding. Always keep a brass hammer dressed so that the brass does not splinter when striking a blow.

Keep all of these hammers clean of dirt and grease.

FASTENERS This section provides information about threaded and nonthreaded fasteners. Threaded fasteners include capscrews, bolts, machine screws, nuts, internal and external threads, washers, and specialty threaded fasteners. Nonthreaded fasteners include cotter pins, dowel pins, slotted spring pins, and retaining rings.

Descriptions of each type of fastener are provided in this section, as well as information about threaded fastener stress forces, standards, and grading.

Threaded Fasteners

The main purpose of a threaded fastener is to join two or more materials together. The inclined plane or wedging action provides a *clamping force* by stretching the screw like a spring. The clamping force, which is also known as *preload*, is created by tightening a threaded fastener that holds two or more pieces together. Clamping force is usually expressed in pounds.

Stress Forces

Threaded fasteners must be able to withstand many types of stresses including:

Shear force—forces that pull the joined materials away from each other in a direction that is perpendicular to the centerline of the threaded fastener.

Tension—forces that pull the joined materials away from each other in a direction that is parallel with the centerline of the threaded fastener.

Bending—forces that pull on an angle to the centerline of the threaded fastener.

Vibration—the oscillating or shaking motion that results when running most machinery.

The *elastic limit* is the maximum amount a bolt or capscrew can be stretched and still return to its original length after the tension is released. When the elastic limit is exceeded, the fastener is weakened. The elastic limit varies with fastener size and grade.

Threaded Fastener Standards and Grading

In recent years laws have been enacted in the United States to ensure the quality and safety of threaded fasteners. Fasteners manufactured in the United States must be marked with a logo to indicate the manufacturer. Fasteners must also be marked to indicate the grade and must meet the standards assigned to the specified grade. Fasteners manufactured outside of the United States are not required to comply with these laws.

Standards for rating and maintaining uniform threaded fasteners have been established by the Society of Automotive Engineers (SAE), the American Society for Testing Materials (ASTM), the International Standards Organization (ISO), and the Industrial Fastener Institute (IFI). Grading is based on the fastener's hardness, alloy properties, heat treatment, and tensile strength. Tensile strength is the load required to cause tension or stretch failure. Tensile strength is usually expressed in pounds per square inch (psi) or megapascals (MPa). One MPa equals 145 psi. The grade assigned to a bolt or screw can usually be identified by special markings on the head. The grade assigned to a nut can be identified by special markings located on the top, bottom, or around the circumference.

Types of Threaded Fasteners

There are many types of threaded fasteners available and commonly used in the motorcycle industry. This section provides descriptions and information about the following types of threaded fasteners: capscrews, machine screws, tapered pipe threads, internal and external threads, nuts, bolts, washers, and specialty threaded fasteners.

American threaded fasteners can easily be identified by their shank size and thread pitch. Shank size is usually expressed in fractions of an inch that range from 1/4 inch and up. Thread pitch is usually expressed as the number of threads per inch. For example, 3/8–16 indicates the following:

3/8 = the diameter of the shank is 3/8 inch

16 = 16 threads per inch

American threaded fasteners may also include the letters "UNC" (unified national coarse) or "NF" (national fine) after the size and thread pitch. These letters indicate a standardized thread pitch for the specified diameter.

Metric threaded fasteners are also identified by shank size and thread pitch. The shank size is normally expressed in millimeters. The thread pitch is expressed as the number of millimeters from the peak of one thread to the next. For example, the marking M 10 × 1.5 provides the following information:

M = metric

10 = the diameter of the threaded shank is 10 millimeters

1.5 = there is a distance of 1.5 millimeters from the peak
      of one thread to the peak of the next

Figure 16-15 Hex-head capscrews (Bowman Distribution, Barnes Group, Inc.).

Capscrews: Capscrews are externally threaded fasteners that are manufactured to a closer tolerance than a conventional bolt and therefore provide a more precise fit. Capscrews are available in a wide variety of head styles such as hexagon, hexagon with flange, 12-point, spline, Torx, socket-head, Phillips, Reed and Prince, and Posidrive (Fig. 16-15). A capscrew is *semifinished*, which means it has a bearing surface or washer face on the underside of the head. Capscrews are available in a wide variety of materials including steel, brass, aluminum, stainless steel, and titanium. A variety of coatings such as zinc, chromium, cadmium, and parkerizing are used on capscrews.

Capscrews are also available in a variety of grades. American thread hex-head capscrews of grade 1 and grade 2 have a smooth hex head. Grade 5 hex-head capscrews have three short straight raised lines on the head. Grade 8 hex-head capscrews have six short straight lines on the head. American thread hex nuts are usually similarly marked.

The property class assigned to metric thread hex-head capscrews can be identified by the raised decimal or whole numbers on the top of the head. The decimal numbers used to indicate property classes include 5.8, 8.8, 9.8, 10.9, and 12.9. Metric hex-head capscrews that are marked with whole numbers correspond to property classes as follows: 0 and 8 denote property class 8.8, 10 denotes property class 10.9, and 12 denotes property class 12.9. Metric thread hex nuts are also marked with numbers that correspond to their assigned property class.

Socket-head capscrews, also commonly called Allen screws, do not always have grading marks. American thread socket-head capscrews are not usually marked for grade and can be grade 8 or higher. However, the heads of most metric socket-head capscrews are marked with raised decimal numbers that indicate the assigned property class. Many of the socket-head capscrews used on 1992 and newer Harley-Davidson motorcycles are marked with the symbol "GRD 8" on the side of the head to indicate grade 8.

Machine Screws: Machine screws come in most of the same head styles, materials, and coatings as capscrews (Fig. 16-16).

American thread machine screws are available in shank sizes ranging from 0.021 inch to 3/4 inch. Sizes that range from 0.021 to 0.216 inch are indicated by whole numbers: "0000" indicates 0.021 inch; "12" indicates 0.216 inch. Sizes that range from 1/4 to 3/4 inch are indicated by fractions. The thread pitch is indicated as the number of threads per inch.

Figure 16-16 Machine screws: Hex washer head, slotted truss head, and slotted oval head (Bowman Distribution, Barnes Group, Inc.).

Metric thread machine screws are marked in the same way as metric thread cap-screws. For example, the marking "M 3.5–0.7" specifies the following information:

M = metric

3.5 = the diameter of the threaded shank is 3.5 millimeters

0.7 = the distance from the peak of one thread to the next is 0.7 millimeters

Tapered Pipe Threads: Tapered pipe threads are marked to indicate the inside diameter of the pipe and the number of threads per inch. The inside pipe diameter is expressed in fractions of an inch. The thread pitch is provided in threads per inch. For example, "1/8–27 NPT" indicates the following:

1/8 = the inside diameter of the pipe is 1/8 inch

27 = there are 27 threads per inch

NPT = national pipe thread; indicates this thread is tapered to a specific degree,
and the thread pitch is standard for the specified pipe diameter

Internal Threads: Internal threads are usually cut with a tap. A regular hand tap, which is used to start and finish the threading procedure, is available with three types of chamfers. Taper taps have the first seven to ten threads chamfered and are used to start the threading process. Plug taps have the first three to five threads chamfered and are used to continue the threading process. Bottoming taps have the first or second threads chamfered to cut threads to the bottom of a hole. Damaged internal threads can sometimes be repaired by using a rethreading tap. A rethreading tap restores the original thread by reforming it.

Two procedures are commonly used to replace damaged internal threads. Damaged threads can be removed by drilling the hole to a larger size. Then a special tap is used to cut new threads into the freshly drilled hole. The tap used to cut the new threads has a larger diameter but the same thread pitch as the original thread. A diamond-shaped wire thread coil is then compressed and threaded into the hole. The other method of thread repair requires drilling out the damaged threads, tapping the hole with a standard tap, and then threading a solid insert into the newly threaded hole. Some inserts require a locking agent, whereas others have locking keys that are driven down after installation.

External Threads: External threads can be cut with a die or a lathe. If they are not severely damaged, external threads can be repaired using a rethreading die or thread file. A rethreading die restores the original thread by reforming it. Thread files have teeth that are cut and spaced to repair specific thread pitches. Thread files are available in most common thread sizes. Typically, the shank of the thread file has a different thread pitch on each of the four sides on each end, thereby providing a total of eight different pitches.

Nuts: Nuts are available in a variety of finishes. A *regular* nut has no washer face, a *semifinished* nut has a washer face, and a *heavy semifinished* nut has a washer face and a thicker body for extra strength. Nuts are produced in a variety of styles to fit specific needs. Some common nuts include: jam, castellated, slotted, self-locking, self-locking with a nylon insert, wing, acorn, spline, 12-point, hexagon, hexagon with a flange, and square (Fig. 16-17). The size of a nut is based on the maximum internal thread diameter and the thread pitch. Nuts are available in the same materials, surface coatings, and grades as capscrews. To provide maximum clamp strength, a nut should be the same grade as the bolt or screw with which it is to be used.

Figure 16-17   Hex high nuts (Bowman Distribution, Barnes Group, Inc.).

Bolts: Bolt sizes are determined by the diameter of the threaded portion of the bolt, not the size of the head. Bolt threads should always be cleaned before using a bolt. Consult the manufacturer's recommendations to determine whether the bolt threads should be dry or lubricated before torquing the bolt. For maximum strength, a bolt should be threaded into a component to a depth of at least one and a half times its diameter.

Washers: Flat washers and lock washers are commonly used in the motorcycle industry. Both are made in many different grades and coatings.

The purpose of a flat washer is to spread the load more evenly to the pieces that are clamped together by the fastener and to prevent damage to those pieces. Flat washers are manufactured so that one side is flat and has sharp edges. The other side of the washer is rounded. The rounded side should always be placed against the nut or head of the bolt. This prevents stress from being induced into the bolt radius between the shank and head.

Three types of flat washers are used on motorcycles: fender washers, USS washers, and SAE washers. Fender washers are most easily identified because the outside diameter is much greater than the inside diameter. SAE washers have a much smaller outside diameter in relation to the inside diameter. The inside diameter of an SAE washer is usually a very close fit to the fastener with which it is used. The outside-to-inside diameter ratio of a USS washer is somewhat larger than an SAE washer. The fit to the fastener is looser, and often USS washers are thicker than SAE washers. The following comparison illustrates the differences between these three types of flat washers:

Type of washer	Diameter	Inside diameter	Outside diameter	Thickness
Fender	5/16 inch	11/32 inch	1-1/4 to 1-1/2 inch	0.051 to 0.080 inch
USS	5/16 inch	3/8 inch	7/8 inch	0.064 to 0.104 inch
SAE	5/16 inch	11/32 inch	11/16 inch	0.051 to 0.080 inch

Lock washers are used to prevent threaded fasteners from loosening under stress and vibration. The following types of lock washers are commonly used: helical spring lock washers or split lock washers, cone spring lock washers, external tooth lock washers, internal tooth lock washers, and internal/external tooth lock washers (Fig. 16-18).

For maximum clamp strength, select a flat washer or lock washer that is the same grade or a grade higher than the fastener with which it will be used. Do not reuse washers if they are distorted or collapsed. When both flat washers and lock washers are used in an assembly, place the lock washer between the flat washer and nut. If a nut is not used in the assembly, place the lock washer between the flat washer and the head of the bolt.

Specialty Fasteners: A wide variety of specialty fasteners are used in the motorcycle industry for different specific applications. For example, Harley-Davidson Motor Company uses a grade 9 material stud to hold the cylinders and heads on the V-twin engine. These studs cannot be reused because the stress of removing and reinstalling them exceeds the elastic limit. Once removed, new studs must be installed. To ensure an even stretch of the cylinder studs, the torque turn method must be used when tightening the head bolts on these studs. First torque the bolts 7 to 9 foot-pounds in the manufacturer's specified pattern. Then torque the bolts 12 to 14 foot-pounds in the same pattern. Finally, turn the bolts a quarter turn in the same pattern.

The uniform bearing stress (UBS) bolt is another commonly used specialty fastener. UBS bolts are used in high-tension areas such as cylinder head bolts, motor mounts, and

Figure 16-18 Lock washers (Bowman Distribution, Barnes Group, Inc.).

Figure 16-19   Hammer-lock-type cotter pin (Bowman Distribution, Barnes Group, Inc.).

other critical chassis applications. UBS bolts are manufactured with a flange head and an undercut where the shank meets the head. The bottom side of the flange is sloped to help prevent loosening.

The Spiralock thread form incorporates a 30° wedge ramp at the root of the female thread. This ramp does not affect the free-spinning relationship of the male/female threads until the clamp load is applied. At that point, the crests of the male threads on the standard screw are drawn tightly against the wedge ramp. This creates continuous spiral contact along the entire length of the thread engagement, spreading the clamp force more evenly over all the threads.

Nonthreaded Fasteners

Nonthreaded fasteners include cotter pins, dowel pins, slotted spring pins, and retaining rings.

Cotter Pins: Cotter pins are designed to fit a hole in a shaft or bolt to prevent components from sliding off or loosening. Cotter pins are made in different styles and many sizes (Fig. 16-19).

Dowel Pins: Dowel pins are used to hold parts in a fixed position or to maintain alignment when parts are disassembled and reassembled. Dowel pins can be tapered or straight, and the ends may be rounded, chamfered, or square. Dowel pins are hardened and ground to size.

Slotted Spring Pins: Slotted spring pins and coiled spring pins are often used in the same way as dowel pins, but they may also be used to hold a component on a shaft or to hold an assembly together (Fig. 16-20). Spring pins come in many sizes. The diameters range from 1/32 to 3/4 inch, and the lengths range from 3/16 to 6 inches. Slotted spring pins and coiled spring pins are made of carbon steel, steel alloys, or beryllium copper alloy.

Retaining Rings: Most retaining rings are manufactured with one flat side, and the other side is beveled, tapered, or rounded. Beveled and tapered retaining rings are installed with the flat side against the load or thrust. Round or wire-type retaining rings are unidirectional and can be installed either way. All other retaining rings are installed with the flat side facing the direction of thrust.

There are two types of retaining rings: external and internal (Figs. 16-21 and 16-22). External retaining rings are available in a number of styles including basic, E-ring, inverted, bowed, beveled, locking prong, bowed E, crescent, reinforced E, interlocking, and circular self-locking. External self-locking rings slide onto a shaft in only one direction, and the prongs grip the shaft to prevent movement. All other external retaining rings fit into the groove of a shaft to provide a shoulder to locate parts. Many external retaining rings are installed with special pliers that expand the ring enough to slide down the shaft. This is called an *axial assembly*. Other external retaining rings are installed by expanding them and sliding them onto the groove of a shaft. This is called *radial assembly*.

Figure 16-20   Rolled spring pins (Bowman Distribution, Barnes Group, Inc.).

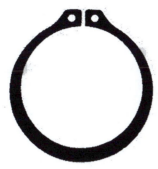

Figure 16-21   External retaining ring (Bowman Distribution, Barnes Group, Inc.).

Figure 16-22   Internal retaining ring (Bowman Distribution, Barnes Group, Inc.).

Internal retaining rings are available in basic, inverted, bowed, and beveled styles. Internal retaining rings fit into a groove in the recess or bore of a component to either locate or retain parts.

THREAD REPAIR   Thread repair is a common motorcycle repair procedure because of the use of aluminum and magnesium, which are softer metals. The most common causes of thread failure are overtightening of fasteners, wear, corrosion, and vibration. Wear is common when the threaded assembly is repeatedly taken apart, as is the case with spark plugs and timing cover inspection plates. Corrosion is common at the intake manifold, where gasoline can work its way into the threads and eat them away. Corrosion is also common if the battery leaks electrolyte (Fig. 16-23).

There are two commonly used procedures for repairing damaged or worn threads. One procedure requires the installation of a spring-loaded screw thread coil. The other involves the installation of a threaded insert. This section briefly explains the steps of each procedure.

Screw Thread Coil: Screw thread coils are designed to repair a damaged screw thread (Fig. 16-24). Threaded inserts are designed to be retained in the hole with a springlike action. In the free state they are greater in diameter than the tapped hole into which they are installed. When the torque is applied, the diameter of the leading coil decreases and the insert can enter the tapped threads. At the end of the procedure, when torque is released, the coil expands with a springlike action to anchor it in place. Because the insert is made of wire, it automatically adjusts whenever the parent material expands or contracts.

Read the instructions accompanying the thread repair kit. The installation of the threaded insert consists of three steps:

Figure 16-23   Stripped hole (Heli-Coil Products, Division of Mite Corporation).

Figure 16-24   Repaired hole (Heli-Coil Products, Division of Mite Corporation).

1. Drill the hole to remove the damaged threads. Drill to the designated size for the insert. Remember to lubricate the drill bit and clean the drilled hole before tapping. The hole must be drilled straight or the insert will cause the fastener to cross-thread or the mating surfaces will not align.
2. Tap the hole to the size of the insert with the tap provided in the insert kit.
3. Use the installer designed for that type of insert and install the threaded insert (Fig. 16-25).

Threaded Insert: Threaded insert repair kits, which are available in most American and metric thread sizes, contain a drill bit, cutting tap, insert driver, and parkerized steel inserts. Thread repair using one of these kits is performed as follows:

1. Lubricate the drill bit and drill out the old threads. Keep the drill square to the surface of the hole during drilling.
2. Lubricate the cutting tap. Tap into the full depth of the drilled hole. Be sure to hold the cutting tap square to the surface of the hole.
3. Clean the hole and be sure to remove all metal chips.
4. Manually start the steel insert in the hole.
5. Lubricate the insert driver. Use a tap wrench to screw the driver into the insert. Then screw the insert into the threaded hole. When the insert is seated, the driver will begin to tighten up in the hole. Apply more pressure and continue to rotate the insert driver until it loosens, indicating that the insert is locked in place.

Regardless of the thread repair method you select, if you follow the procedure carefully, you should have a repaired thread that is equal to or better than the original thread.

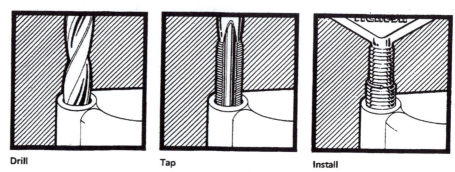

Drill   Tap   Install

Figure 16-25   Repair procedure (Heli-Coil Products, Division of Mite Corporation).

Four-Stroke Engine Tune-Up and Service

A basic tune-up consists of inspecting, testing, and adjusting the engine. Some engines may require replacing the ignition points and condenser. The purpose of a tune-up is to restore engine performance. Service is the term used to indicate the maintenance of all other motorcycle components.

Restoring engine performance increases gas mileage, and a carefully serviced motorcycle is also more reliable, which is especially important for long-distance riding. For example, a rear drive chain that has not been checked and properly adjusted could jump off the sprockets and lock the rear wheel, which could cause serious damage to the motorcycle and the rider. Conscientiously following the entire tune-up and service procedure will help produce safe and efficient motorcycle operation.

The basic tune-up and service procedure includes:

1. Compression check
2. Battery inspection
3. Oil and filter change
4. Spark plug inspection
5. Ignition system service
6. Ignition timing
7. Cam chain adjustment
8. Valve adjustment
9. Air filter service
10. Carburetor synchronization
11. Clutch adjustment
12. Brake adjustment
13. Cable inspection
14. Tire inspection

15. Rear chain and sprocket inspection
16. Drive shaft service
17. Safety inspection
18. Test ride

Tuning and servicing a four-stroke motorcycle requires the use of the motorcycle manufacturer's service manual. The service manual will describe the specific tune-up and service procedures. What follows is a brief description of each procedure and some servicing tips.

BASIC TUNE-UP AND SERVICE PROCEDURES

Compression Check

A compression check determines the condition of the engine's valves, pistons, rings, and head gaskets. Install the compression gauge into the spark plug hole (Fig. 17-1). Open the throttle by hand and open the carburetor choke. Using the electric starter or manual kick-start lever, turn the engine over until the compression gauge reading stops increasing. When the gauge needle stops, record the reading and compare it to the manufacturer's specifications. If there is a compression problem, do not continue the tune-up process. Check the valve clearance. Insufficient clearance may be the cause of low compression. Set the valves to specification and recheck the compression. If the compression reading is within specifications, continue the tune-up process. If compression remains low, consult the service manual to determine the exact nature of the problem.

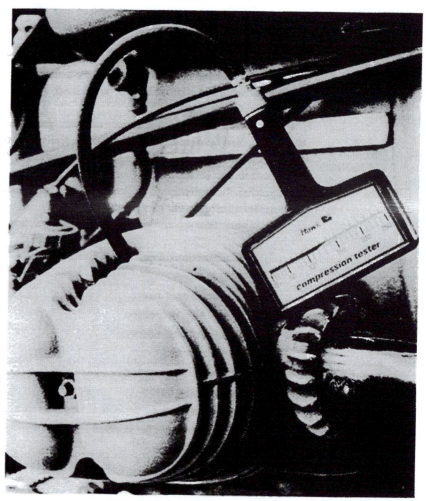

Figure 17-1 Compression check.

Battery Inspection

Use the volt-ohmmeter to check the loaded voltage by turning on the ignition and headlight. For a 12-volt system, the loaded voltage should be no less than 10.5 volts. A 6-volt system should register no less than 5.25 volts. Also make a hydrometer test; the reading should be 1.265 or higher. If indicated, charge the battery. Check the manufacturer's specifications for the charging rate. Remove the battery and check it for cracks and dirty or corroded terminals. If sulfation or excessive sediment deposits are present, replace the battery.

Oil and Filter Change

Before changing the engine oil and filter, run the engine to warm the oil. Remove either the oil level gauge or the filler cap to allow rapid draining. Consult your service manual to determine the location of the drain bolts, and drain the engine oil using all of the drainage areas. After the oil has drained, reinstall the drain bolts.

If the motorcycle uses a paper filter element, remove the oil filter cover and replace the filter element with a new one. Be sure to reinstall the metal washer between the spring and filter element. Reinstall the cover with a new O-ring or gasket.

After removing the filter, clean the filter area with a clean cloth. Before installing a new cartridge filter, spread a thin film of engine oil over the filter O-ring. Consult the appropriate service manual, and follow the manufacturer's oil filter installation procedure. Do not overtighten the filter.

Consult your service manual for the correct quantity and type of oil, and be sure that all drain bolts are installed before adding new oil. After adding oil to the proper level, start the engine and confirm there are no oil leaks.

Spark Plug Inspection

Remove and inspect spark plugs for electrode wear and color. Replace a plug if there is any doubt about its condition. Check plug caps and coil leads for insulation cracks. Consult the manufacturer's specifications for the recommended spark plug electrode gap and spark plug type. Always remove spark plugs before making engine adjustments.

Ignition System Service

Inspect the ignition points for wear. Clean the points with contact cleaner and a point file or flex stone. If points are pitted or worn, they must be replaced. The capacitor must also be replaced if the points are pitted. After the points have been serviced, set the point gap (Fig. 17-2).

Figure 17-2 Ignition advance adjustment (American Honda Motor Company).

If the motorcycle is equipped with an electronic ignition system, very little service can be performed. Verify the timing using a dynamic inductive lead timing light. Normally, an ignition timing adjustment is not required. Consult your service manual for additional information.

Ignition Timing

Time the ignition system statically with a self-powered continuity light or, for battery-assisted ignition systems, with a simple continuity light. With the engine running, check the ignition timing and dwell angle using a timing light and a dwell meter (Fig. 17-3).

Cam Chain Adjustment

Consult the service manual for the location of the cam chain adjuster and follow the man-ufacturer's adjustment procedure. Some cam chain adjusters are self-adjusting (Fig. 17-4).

Valve Adjustment

A valve adjustment should be made when the engine is at room temperature. Set the clear-ance between the valve stem and the valve-activating device (Fig. 17-5). There are differ-

① **STROBOSCOPIC TIMING LIGHT**

② **DWELL METER**

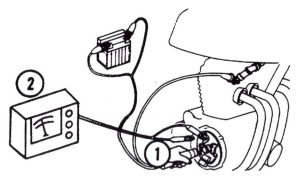

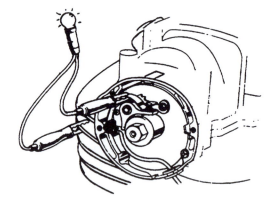

Checking Ignition Timing and Dwell Angle, Using a Stroboscopic Timing Light and Dwell Meter with Engine Running

Checking Static Ignition Timing with a Simple Continuity Light (for battery ignition systems only)

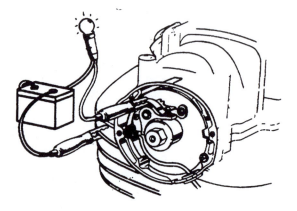

Checking Static Ignition Timing with a Self-Powered Continuity Light

Figure 17-3   Ignition timing (American Honda Motor Company).

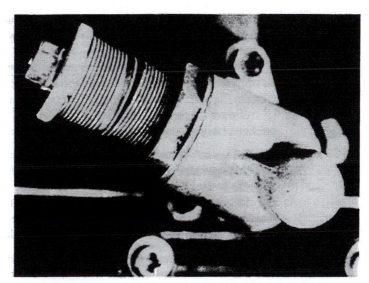

Figure 17-4 Semiautomatic cam chain adjuster.

ent types of valve adjusters and different adjusting procedures for each type. Check the service manual for the specific type of adjustment.

Air Filter Service

Because a dirty air filter can cause an improper air/fuel mixture, manufacturers recommend periodic cleaning or replacement of the air filter. Motorcycles operated in dusty areas require more frequent air filter inspections and service.

The appropriate service procedure depends on whether the air filter has an oiled urethane foam, paper, or gauze element. When replacing air filters, be sure that both the filter and air box or holder are clean and properly secured. If the air filter joint has rubber seals, lightly grease them to increase the sealing ability and prevent water and/or dirt particles from reaching the engine's internal components.

Oiled Urethane Foam Element: Remove the air filter from the air box or holder. Wash away the accumulated dirt by gently squeezing the element in a nonflammable solvent or

(1) Remove the tappet hole caps and generator cover.

VALVE CLEARANCE (IN, EX)

0.05 ±0.02 mm (0.002 ±0.0008 in.)

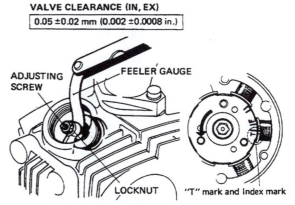

(2) Rotate the A.C. generator rotor in the counterclockwise direction and align the "T" mark on the rotor with the index mark on the stator.

Figure 17-5 Measuring clearance between the valve stem and valve activating device (American Honda Motor Company).

warm soapy water. Allow the element to dry thoroughly before applying air filter oil. Oil applied to a wet or damp element will be diluted by the solvent or water, thereby decreasing the filter's effectiveness.

Use the manufacturer's recommended air filter oil. Apply the oil to the entire surface, and rub the element with both hands to saturate it with oil. Squeeze excess oil from the element. Apply a thin coat of white lithium grease to the sealing surface.

Be sure to correctly oil this type of element. Failure to use air filter oil could result in premature engine wear if the motorcycle is run in extremely dusty conditions.

Paper Element: After removing the air filter, gently tap it to loosen accumulated dirt. Apply low-pressure compressed air to the inside of the filter to remove any remaining dirt from the surface. Reinstall the filter.

If the motorcycle is equipped with a viscous paper element, the filter cannot be cleaned because the element contains a dust adhesive. This type of paper filter must be replaced. Consult your service manual to identify the motorcycle's air filter.

Gauze Element: Remove the filter. Wash the element in a nonflammable solvent to remove dirt and old filter oil. Then wash the element in warm soapy water. Let the element air dry. Before reinstalling the element, apply the manufacturer's recommended filter oil to the entire surface area of the filter.

Carburetor Synchronization

Before starting the carburetor synchronization process, be sure that the valves and cam chain are adjusted and that the ignition timing is set. Allow the engine to warm up but not become excessively hot. Use an electric fan to control the engine temperature. Consult the manufacturer's specifications and adjust the idle to the proper speed. Synchronize the carburetors using mercury sticks or vacuum gauges. Check the idle speed. If a pilot screw adjustment is necessary, adjust it while the gauges are still attached. This enables you to monitor and correct any change in synchronization (Fig. 17-6). Some models have a base carburetor; check the service manual for the base synchronization carburetor.

Carburetor synchronization is important. Out-of-sync carburetors could cause a rough and erratic idle, engine overheating, and poor fuel mileage. Engine noise will also be excessive; the primary and cam chain will make a slapping noise if the carburetors are not synchronized.

Improper carburetor synchronization can increase the carbon monoxide and hydrocarbon readings and result in a violation of EPA laws. If possible, use an exhaust gas analyzer to confirm that the emissions do not exceed the legal limit.

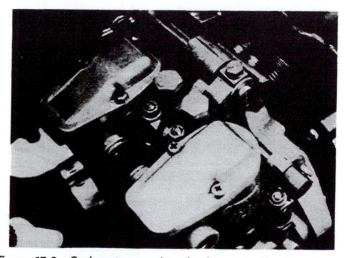

Figure 17-6 Carburetor synchronization and adjusting screws.

Clutch Adjustment

Adjusting the clutch can be accomplished by adjusting the cable, or by adjusting the release mechanism, or both (Fig. 17-7). Lubricate the cable and release mechanism and check them for damage or fraying. If the clutch slips or has a disengaging problem, consult the service manual for the service procedure.

Brake Adjustment

If the motorcycle is equipped with disk brakes, begin the brake adjustment by first checking the master cylinder fluid. If it is low, refill it to the proper level. If the fluid appears to be contaminated with moisture, drain and bleed the system according to the directions in the service manual. The brake adjustment is the same for both front and rear hydraulic disk brake systems. Inspect the brake pads for excessive wear and dirt. Adjust the free play of the hand and foot brake levers according to service manual specifications. If the brake system is cable-operated, inspect the cable for damage. The cable must be lubricated periodically to ensure proper operation. Do not adjust the rear brakes until the rear chain has been adjusted. The chain adjustment will change the cable or rod length on some models.

Cable Inspection

Inspect all cables for fraying or damage. Make sure that cables are routed properly and are not loose or sticking out (Fig. 17-8). Lubricate the throttle, brake, and clutch cables. Lubricate all motorcycle zerk fittings and any metal-to-metal moving parts.

Tire Inspection

Tires should be inspected for their general condition, and you should look for unusual wear, cracks, or cuts. To ensure a safe ride, replace tires whenever necessary. Proper tire pressure is important for good gas mileage and safety. Consult the manufacturer's specifications for the proper tire pressure readings.

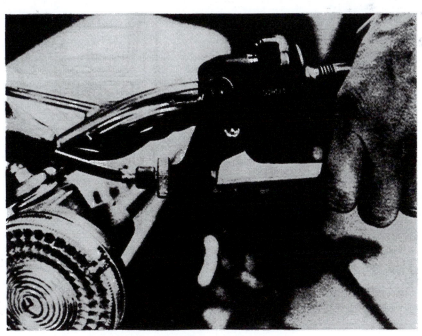

Figure 17-7   Checking clutch lever free play.

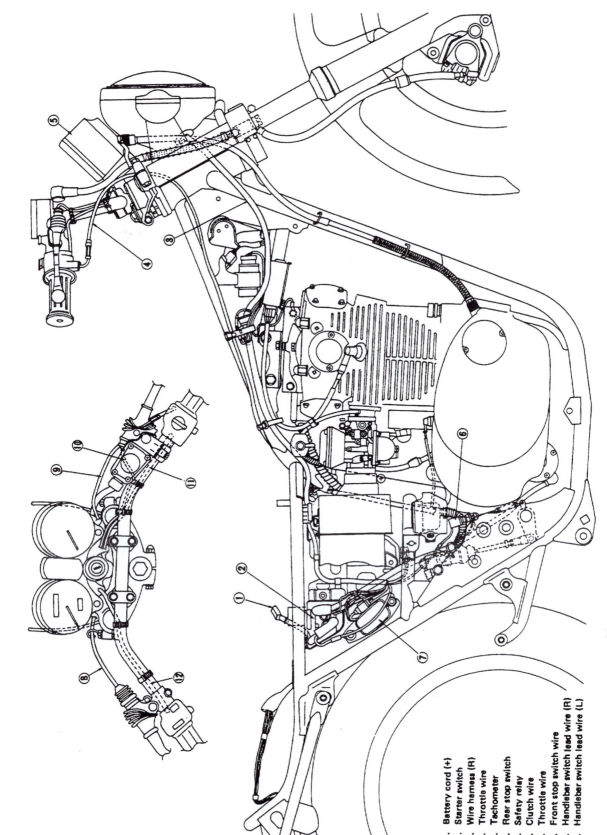

1. Battery cord (+)
2. Starter switch
3. Wire harness (R)
4. Throttle wire
5. Tachometer
6. Rear stop switch
7. Safety relay
8. Clutch wire
9. Throttle wire
10. Front stop switch wire
11. Handlebar switch lead wire (R)
12. Handlebar switch lead wire (L)

Figure 17-8   Cable routing diagram (Yamaha Motor Corporation, U.S.A.).

Rear Chain and Sprocket Inspection

Check the rear drive chain for buckling or excessive pin wear. Check for sprocket wear and proper rear wheel alignment. Replace the chain when necessary. Be sure that the master link clip is installed correctly. A properly lubricated and adjusted chain helps to provide a safe and dependable ride (Fig. 17-9).

Drive Shaft Service

When servicing the drive shaft, check the oil levels and replace contaminated oil. Consult the manufacturer's specifications for the type and quantity of oil to use.

Safety Inspection

After all adjustments and fluid changes have been completed, make a thorough inspection of the motorcycle. Check for any safety related and other potential problems. Evaluate the overall condition of the motorcycle and make a note of any repairs and/or maintenance that may be required in the future. Be sure to make the motorcycle owner aware of these items.

During your safety inspection, check the following areas for leaks, excessive wear, permanent damage, and proper operation:

1. Brakes
2. Cables
3. Control levers
4. Steering
5. Tire/wheel assemblies
6. Chain and sprockets
7. Front and rear suspension
8. Headlight and taillight
9. Brake light
10. Turn signals

Figure 17-9 Checking final drive chain for correct free play.

11. Horn
12. Instrumentation
13. Exhaust system
14. Fuel system

Test Ride

Complete a four-stroke engine tune-up and service with a test ride. Before the test ride, check the overall condition of the motorcycle for safety. Check the brake operation and front wheel alignment. Check for oil leaks and the engine oil level. Check the throttle response and the idle for smoothness and rpm. Be sure to wear an approved safety helmet while riding. During the test ride, the motorcycle should accelerate without hesitation or misfire. After returning from the test ride, make final carburetor adjustments for the idle mixture and rpm.

You have completed a successful four-stroke motorcycle engine tune-up and service.

chapter 18

Two-Stroke Engine Tune-Up and Service

The definitions for tune-up and service as presented in Chapter 17 do not change when applied to a two-stroke motorcycle engine. The reasons for tuning and servicing a two-stroke engine are the same as for a four-stroke engine: to restore engine performance, to improve gas mileage, and to maintain safe operating conditions. However, a two-stroke is more sensitive to state-of-tune than a four-stroke motorcycle engine. A two-stroke engine in need of tuning is susceptible to spark plug fouling. To avoid carbon fouling, it is necessary to remove the carbon buildup from the combustion chambers periodically. Two-stroke ignition timing is critical. Timing that is either too advanced or too retarded can cause damage to engine components. Carefully follow the entire tune-up and service procedure to produce safe and efficient motorcycle operation.

The basic tune-up and service procedure includes:

1. Compression check
2. Main bearing inspection
3. Battery inspection
4. Transmission service
5. Oil injection service
6. Air filter service
7. Spark plug inspection
8. Ignition system service
9. Ignition timing
10. Exhaust system service
11. Clutch adjustment
12. Rear drive chain and sprocket service
13. Brake adjustment
14. Cable inspection
15. Tire inspection

16.   Drive shaft service

17.   Safety inspection

18.   Test ride

Tuning and servicing a two-stroke motorcycle requires the use of the motorcycle manufacturer's service manual. The service manual will describe the specific tune-up and service procedures. What follows is a brief description of each procedure and some service tips.

BASIC TUNE-UP AND SERVICE PROCEDURES

Compression Check

Make a compression check to determine the condition of the engine's pistons and rings. An engine with a low compression reading will be difficult to start. Install the compression gauge into the spark plug hole. Hold the carburetor throttle completely open and make sure that the choke is fully open. Using the manual kickstart lever or electric starter, turn the engine over until the compression gauge reading stops increasing. If the motorcycle has an electric starter, ground the spark plug wire. When the gauge needle stops, record the reading and compare it to the manufacturer's specifications. If there is a compression problem, do not continue the tune-up process. Consult the service manual to determine the exact nature of the problem. Make a crankcase pressure test to determine if there is any crankcase leakage.

Main Bearing Inspection

Two-stroke main crankshaft bearings must be in good working condition or there will be a problem with the ignition system. Check the ignition side crankshaft bearing to determine

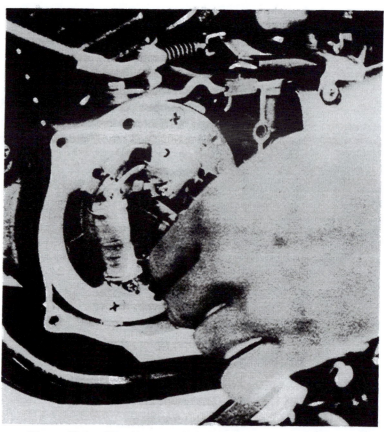

Figure 18-1   Checking crankshaft for loose main bearing.

that there is no up-and-down movement of the bearing. If there is any movement, the bearing should be replaced (Fig. 18-1).

Battery Inspection

Use the volt-ohmmeter to check the loaded charge by turning on the ignition and headlight. For a 12-volt system, the loaded voltage should be no less than 10.5 volts. A 6-volt system should register no less than 5.25 volts. Also make a hydrometer test; the reading should be 1.265 or higher. If a low reading is indicated, charge the battery. Check the manufacturer's specifications for the charging rate. Remove the battery and check it for cracks and dirty or corroded terminals. If sulfation or excessive sediment deposits are present, replace the battery.

Transmission Service

Drain the transmission oil, taking care to use all of the drainage areas. Consult the service manual for tips. Be sure to clean the drain bolt. This is especially important when the drain bolt is magnetic. Always use the transmission oil recommended by the manufacturer. Do not overfill the transmission with oil. Install the drain bolt and oil dip stick before operating the engine.

Oil Injection Service

Check the oil level in the injection tank. If the oil tank has run dry, the oil pump and lines must be bled. Consult the service manual for oil pump bleeding and adjustment procedures (Figs. 18-2, 18-3, and 18-4).

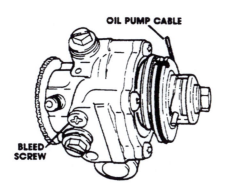

Figure 18-2 Two-stroke oil pump with bleed screw (Yamaha Motor Corporation, U.S.A.).

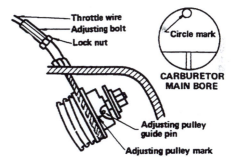

Figure 18-3 Adjusting at the oil pump (Yamaha Motor Corporation, U.S.A.).

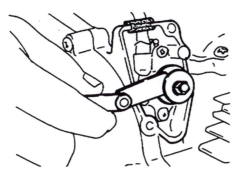

Figure 18-4 Checking minimum pump stroke (Yamaha Motor Corporation, U.S.A.).

Air Filter Service

Because a dirty air filter can cause an improper air/fuel mixture, manufacturers recommend periodic cleaning or replacement of the air filter. Motorcycles operated in dusty areas require more frequent air filter inspections and service.

The appropriate service procedure depends on whether the air filter has an oiled urethane foam, paper, or gauze element. When replacing air filters, be sure that both the filter and air box or holder are clean and properly secured. If the air filter joint has rubber seals, lightly grease them to increase the sealing ability and prevent water and/or dirt particles from reaching the engine's internal components.

Oiled Urethane Foam Element: Remove the air filter from the air box or holder. Wash away the accumulated dirt by gently squeezing the element in a nonflammable, high-flash-point solvent or warm soapy water. Allow the element to dry thoroughly before applying air filter oil. Oil applied to a wet or damp element will be diluted by the solvent or water, thereby decreasing the filter's effectiveness.

Use the manufacturer's recommended air filter oil. Apply the oil to the entire surface, and rub the element with both hands to saturate it with oil. Squeeze the element to remove excess oil. Apply a thin coat of white lithium grease to the sealing surface.

Be sure to oil this type of element. Failure to use air filter oil could result in premature engine wear if the motorcycle is run in extremely dusty conditions. In these conditions, excessive dirt could be drawn into the engine.

Paper Element: After removing the air filter, gently tap it to loosen accumulated dirt. Apply low-pressure compressed air to the inside of the filter to remove any remaining dirt from the surface. Reinstall the filter.

If the motorcycle is equipped with a viscous paper element, the filter cannot be cleaned because the element contains a dust adhesive. This type of paper filter must be replaced. Consult your service manual to identify the motorcycle's air filter.

Gauze Element: Remove the filter. Wash the element in a nonflammable, high-flash-point solvent to remove dirt and old filter oil. Then wash the element in warm soapy water. Let the element air dry. Before reinstalling the element, apply the manufacturer's recommended filter oil to the entire surface of the filter element.

Spark Plug Inspection

Remove and inspect spark plugs for electrode wear and color. Replace a plug if there is any doubt about its condition. Check plug caps and coil leads for insulation cracks. Consult the manufacturer's specifications for the recommended spark plug electrode gap and spark plug type. Always remove spark plugs before making engine adjustments.

Ignition System Service

Inspect the ignition points for wear. Clean the points with contact cleaner and a point file or flex stone. If the points are pitted or worn, they must be replaced. The capacitor must also be replaced if the points are pitted. After the points have been serviced, set the ignition timing (Figs. 18-5 and 18-6). Make sure that the CDI, magneto, or energy transfer system is clean and free of dirt or corrosion (Fig. 18-7).

Ignition Timing

If the motorcycle has more than one set of points, each cylinder must be individually checked, adjusted, and timed. Use a static timing light, buzz box, or some type of resistance reading meter to indicate the point opening. Use a dial indicator to determine the exact

Figure 18-5 Measuring the point gap (Yamaha Motor Corporation, U.S.A.).

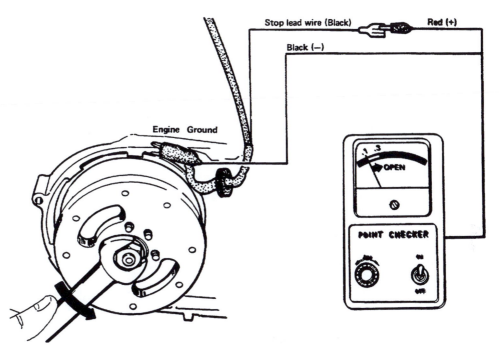

Figure 18-6 Checking the ignition timing (Yamaha Motor Corporation, U.S.A.).

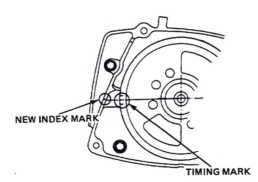

Figure 18-7 Aligning CDI timing marks (American Honda Motor Company).

position of the piston. Consult the service manual for the correct ignition timing setting (Figs. 18-8 and 18-9). If the motorcycle has an electronic ignition system, use a dial indicator or timing light to line up the marks on the rotor and backing plate of the ignition system.

Exhaust System Service

Inspect the exhaust pipe and repair any dents or cracks. Remove the exhaust pipe baffles and clean them to remove all carbon and oil deposits. Exhaust pipes should be burned out periodically to ensure proper engine performance. Follow the service manual recommendations. Do not burn out an exhaust pipe if the outside of the pipe is chrome.

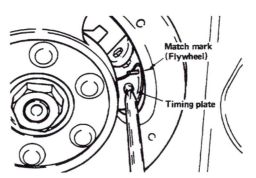

Figure 18-8   Adjusting the timing (Yamaha Motor Corporation, U.S.A.).

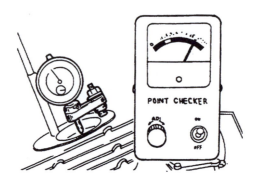

Figure 18-9   Checking the timing with a dial indicator (Yamaha Motor Corporation, U.S.A.).

Clutch Adjustment

Adjusting the clutch can be accomplished by adjusting the cable, or by adjusting the release mechanism, or by adjusting both. Inspect for fraying, lubricate the release mechanism, and check for damage. If the clutch slips or has a disengaging problem, check the service manual for the adjustment procedure (Fig. 18-10).

Rear Drive Chain and Sprocket Service

Inspect the chain for buckling or excessive pin wear. Check for sprocket wear and proper rear wheel alignment. Replace the chain when necessary. If the chain includes a master link clip, make sure that the clip is properly installed with the closed end toward rotation. Always use chain lube, not motor oil, to lubricate the rear chain (Figs. 18-11, 18-12, and 18-13).

Brake Adjustment

If the motorcycle is equipped with disk brakes, begin the brake adjustment by checking the master cylinder fluid. If the fluid is low, refill the cylinder to the proper level. If the fluid appears to be contaminated with moisture, drain and bleed the system according to the

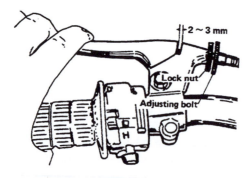

Figure 18-10   Adjusting the clutch hand lever free play (Yamaha Motor Corporation, U.S.A.).

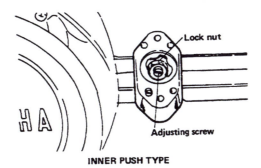

Figure 18-11 Adjusting the release mechanism (Yamaha Motor Corporation, U.S.A.).

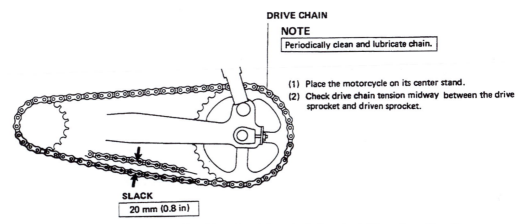

Figure 18-12 Checking the drive chain for slack (American Honda Motor Company).

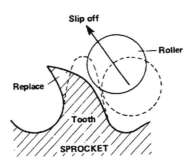

Figure 18-13 Sprocket wear (Yamaha Motor Corporation, U.S.A.).

directions in the service manual. The brake adjustment is the same for both front and rear hydraulic disk brake systems. Inspect the brake pads for excessive wear and dirt. Adjust the free play of the hand and foot brake levers according to the service manual specifications. If the brake system is cable-operated, inspect the cable for damage. The cable must be periodically lubricated to ensure proper operation. Do not adjust the rear brakes until the rear chain has been adjusted. The chain adjustment will change the cable or rod length on some models.

Cable Inspection

Inspect all cables for fraying or damage. Make sure that the cables are routed properly and are not loose or sticking out. Lubricate the throttle, brake, and clutch cables. Lubricate all motorcycle zerk fittings and any metal-to-metal moving parts.

Tire Inspection

Inspect the tires for their general condition and for unusual wear, cracks, or cuts. To ensure a safe ride, replace tires whenever necessary. Proper tire pressure is important for good gas mileage and safety. Consult the manufacturer's specifications for the proper tire pressure readings. Inspect and adjust spokes.

Drive Shaft Service

Check the oil levels and replace oil that is contaminated by gear wear. Check the manufacturer's specifications for the type and quantity of oil to use.

Safety Inspection

After completing all adjustments, maintenance, and repairs, make a detailed inspection of the motorcycle. Check the operation of all components that affect the rider's safety. Evaluate the overall condition of the motorcycle and make a note of any repairs and/or maintenance that may be required in the future. Be sure to make the motorcycle owner aware of these items.

Test Ride

Complete a two-stroke engine tune-up and service with a test ride. Before the test ride, check the overall condition of the motorcycle for safety. Check the brake operation and front wheel alignment. Check for oil leaks and the level of the transmission oil. Check the throttle response and the idle for smoothness and rpm. Be sure to wear an approved safety helmet while riding. During the test ride, the motorcycle should accelerate without hesitation or misfire. After returning from the test ride, make final carburetor adjustments for both the idle mixture and rpm.

You have now completed a successful two-stroke motorcycle engine tune-up and service.

chapter 19

Riding Safety

Motorcycle riding is no longer just a sport; it has become a practical form of transportation for many people. There are over 10 million motorcycles in the United States that are commonly used for commuting as well as for various racing competitions at amateur and professional levels.

Motorcycle manufacturers, dealers, technicians, and the individual rider all play an important role in riding safety. Five major motorcycle manufacturers—Harley-Davidson, Honda, Kawasaki, Suzuki, and Yamaha—have combined their financial support to create the Motorcycle Safety Foundation. The goal of this private, nonprofit organization is to reduce motorcycle accidents and injuries. The Motorcycle Safety Foundation conducts programs dealing with rider education, licensing improvement, public information, and research.

In addition to supporting the Motorcycle Safety Foundation, each motorcycle manufacturer promotes riding safety by delivering a product of high quality. The customer can be assured that the motorcycle has been designed with safety in mind, and that the design and central components work well. It is the responsibility of the motorcycle dealer and technicians to set up the motorcycle properly to ensure safe operating conditions.

ELEMENTS OF RIDING SAFETY Ultimately, riding safety is the responsibility of the individual rider. The most important elements of riding safety are learning how to ride and practicing safe riding habits. However, riding safety also requires preventative maintenance, proper riding apparel, and maintaining the proper attitude while riding.

Preventative Maintenance

Once the motorcycle has been purchased, the owner is responsible for maintaining the motorcycle's mechanical safety. Improvements in overall design, ignition systems, and carburetion have increased the reliability of motorcycles such that they can usually be ridden many miles beyond the recommended service intervals. Consequently, it is easy for the owner to neglect proper maintenance for long periods of time. This can create not only the need for costly repairs in the future, but also unsafe riding conditions. It is important for the owner to read the manufacturer's service recommendations and either personally perform maintenance checks or have a qualified technician provide the necessary inspections and servicing. Inspection and maintenance areas include spokes, wheel bearings, steering head and swing arm bearings, battery, brakes, control cables, rear chain and sprockets, air cleaner, and nuts and bolts.

Proper Riding Apparel

The clothing worn while riding a motorcycle should provide comfort, visibility, and protection. The initial cost of proper riding apparel is minimal when compared to the expense of patching injured skin and bones caused by a fall. Shop carefully and consider quality when investing in a jacket, pants, footwear, gloves, helmet, and some type of eye protection.

Leather jackets provide the best protection, but excellent jackets are also being made of dense nylon cord and Cordura. Most jackets are manufactured with removable liners which make the jackets compatible with a variety of riding temperatures. Denim jackets are acceptable, but they do not provide as much protection as the others. Pants should be at least denim, but leather offers the best protection. It is wise to wear sturdy footwear and gloves.

A helmet and proper eye protection are the most important elements of riding apparel. There are open-faced and full-faced helmet designs made of either molded plastic or fiberglass resin. No matter which type of helmet you choose, it should fit securely and fasten snugly at the chin strap. The helmet should be certified approved by the Department of Transportation, the National Standards Institute, or the Snell Memorial Foundation. The approval certification will be found on the inside label (Fig. 19-1). A helmet that passes the Snell 80 standards is superior to all others in impact absorption and in resisting penetration and chemical damage.

Helmets can be worn with either a face shield or goggles for eye protection. Being able to see clearly is essential for the safe operation of any vehicle, but especially a motorcycle. Wind that blasts into bare eyes while riding is very dangerous; tearing and blurred vision can impair your vision enough to cause an accident. Most states require that some form of eye protection be worn while riding a motorcycle. Shields and goggles are available in a variety of colors. Darkly tinted eye protection can be very helpful in eliminating eyestrain in bright sunlight. But some colors, such as the yellow or smoke tints, can strain the eyes when used in certain lighting conditions or at night.

No matter what level of riding skill you possess, an accident may be unavoidable. Proper riding apparel does not guarantee you will be accident-free, but it will decrease your chances of serious or fatal injuries.

Figure 19-1   Helmet safety approval sticker.

Safe Riding Habits

Learning how to ride and practicing safe riding habits are essential. Safe riding begins before the motorcycle is started.

Preride Check: Begin each ride with a preride check to ensure that the motorcycle will perform safely. Inspect for leakage from the fuel tank, engine cases, and oil tank, and check the engine oil level. Make sure that the tires have the correct air pressure. Check the drive chain for proper adjustment and lubrication. If the motorcycle has a shaft drive, look for leaks at the fill and drain plugs, gasket surfaces, and shaft boot.

Roll the motorcycle and make sure that both brakes positively engage. Start the engine and check for smooth operation of the brake, clutch, and throttle cable. Check the operation of the headlight, taillight, brake light, and turn signals. Check the warning lights for battery charging, fuel level, sidestand position, and brake wear. As you ride away, check to see that the centerstand and sidestand are retracted. During the first few minutes of each ride, continue safety awareness by noting any unusual engine sounds or handling characteristics of the motorcycle.

Riding Skills

Motorcycle operational skills are quite different from those required to drive an automobile. The riding skills that are critical to safe motorcycling include braking, cornering, lane positioning, and evasive maneuvers. Mastery of these skills is not the result of trial and error or experimentation; you must practice the correct response until it becomes almost automatic. One of the best ways to learn the correct approach to handling various riding situations is by completing a thorough motorcycle training program such as the Motorcycle Safety Foundation Rider Course.

Most motorcycle accidents involve excessive speed for the traffic conditions coupled with improper use of brakes. Motorcycles receive 70 percent or more of their stopping power through the front brake that is operated by a lever on the right handlebar. However, to execute a stop, both brakes must be applied smoothly and simultaneously.

Most motorcycle accidents occur on good, dry roads and within the normal field of vision. Be aware of the motorcycle collision contact areas (Fig. 19-2). Keep a 2-second distance behind the vehicle you are following and look well down the road (Fig. 19-3). Never

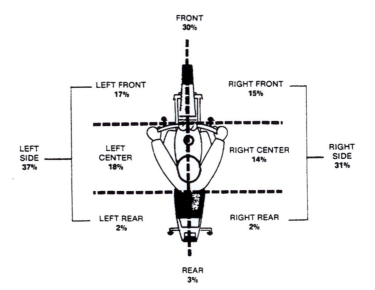

Figure 19-2   Motorcycle collision contact areas (Motorcycle Safety Foundation).

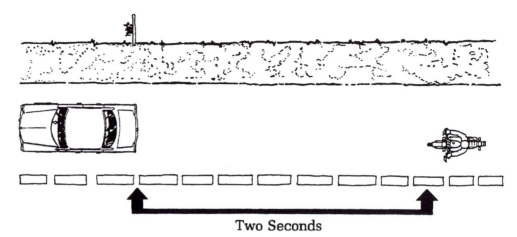

Figure 19-3   Two-second following distance (Motorcycle Safety Foundation).

fix your eyes on one place; survey the entire area in front of you, and glance frequently in the rear view mirror. Be aware of all vehicle and pedestrian activity within your field of vision. You should scan 12 seconds down the road and identify any activity that may become a hazard. Adjust your speed and/or position accordingly (Fig. 19-4).

Ride in the left third of the lane (Fig. 19-5). In this position you are visible to on-coming traffic and can avoid any oil or debris that may be present in the middle of the lane. Make sure that you are visible to the car in front of you by staying out of the driver's blind spot (Fig. 19-6). Keep in mind that a motorcyclist's visibility is even further reduced when following a large vehicle such as a van or truck.

Two-thirds of all motorcycle accidents are caused by another driver who violates the motorcyclist's right-of-way, usually by turning in front of the motorcycle. Knowledge and proper use of evasive maneuvers will prevent many accidents. Evasive maneuvers include swerving to the right or left and emergency braking.

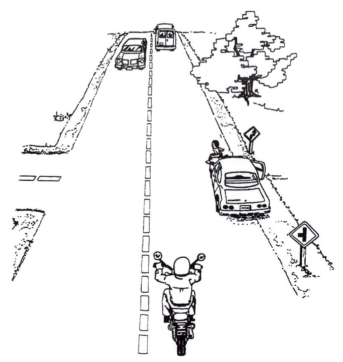

Figure 19-4   Where to look (Motorcycle Safety Foundation).

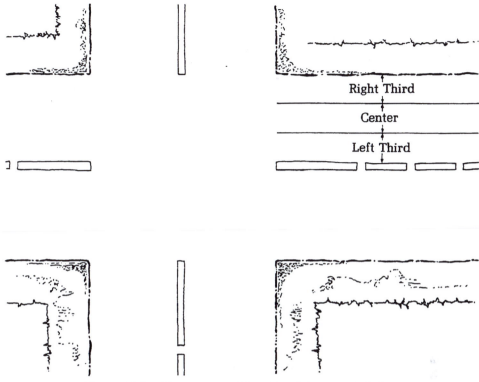

Figure 19-5   Placement within a lane (Motorcycle Safety Foundation).

Figure 19-6   Be visible (Motorcycle Safety Foundation).

Proper cornering involves adjusting speed, leaning the motorcycle, and looking in the direction of the turn. It takes practice to achieve the necessary balance and judgment to complete cornering smoothly. Safe low-speed cornering depends on steering with very little leaning; safe cornering at higher speeds relies on leaning properly. Normally, it is best to keep your body aligned with the motorcycle as you begin to lean into a curve. Enter the corner at the proper speed; excess speed makes it difficult to exit the corner in the proper lane. A sudden decrease in speed while cornering will cause the motorcycle to straighten up and will alter your lane position (Fig. 19-7).

Riding Conditions

Many potentially hazardous road conditions may be encountered while riding. You can choose when and where to ride, but no doubt you will eventually encounter some hazardous conditions and usually more than one at the same time.

Wet pavement offers less traction than dry pavement, so riding speed, braking, and cornering must be adjusted. The most dangerous time to ride in the rain is just as the rain begins and before it has washed the oil from the road. The road, especially painted lines and manhole covers, are extremely slippery at this time.

When riding in cold weather, take care to avoid the effects of hypothermia. As your body becomes colder, you will react more slowly, compromising normally safe habits. Take frequent breaks and dress properly in several layers of clothing that hold in body heat.

When approaching a loose or slippery surface such as gravel, sand, oil, or ice, slow down before reaching the area. Avoid sudden changes in course and hard braking and accelerating. Proceed slowly and smoothly. If you stop, be aware that should you put your foot down, it could slip out from under you and cause a fall.

Railroad tracks, ruts, boards, or tree limbs can be crossed safely at a 45° to 90° angle. Sometimes it is necessary to cross these types of objects squarely so that the motorcycle does not get caught on the object or is deflected from it. Relax and reduce speed (Fig. 19-8).

Caution should always be exercised while riding, but under difficult conditions it is essential. Be alert; it may be necessary to slow down and to lengthen your following dis-

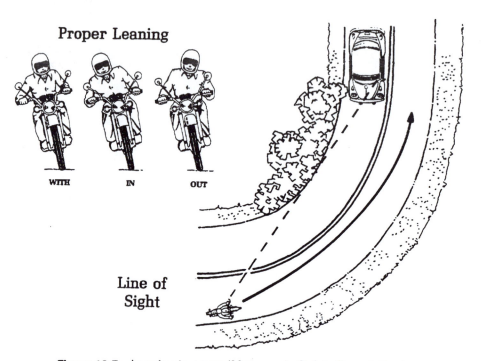

Figure 19-7 Leaning in a turn (Motorcycle Safety Foundation).

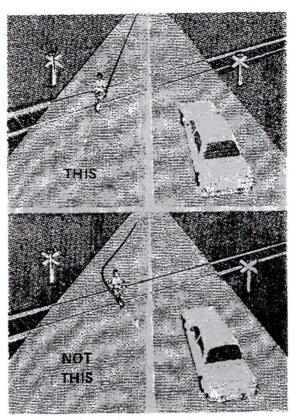

Figure 19-8   Crossing railroad tracks at a 90° angle is acceptable as long as it does not compromise your safety (Motorcycle Safety Foundation).

tance. It may take more effort to control the motorcycle and to maintain the proper lane position. Approach each situation sensibly and with care.

Riding with a passenger is a specialized skill. Balance, handling, and braking are affected by the additional weight. A passenger should never be carried by an inexperienced rider. The motorcycle must be equipped to carry a passenger, and the passenger should be properly dressed and informed of the responsibilities and actions involved.

Proper Attitude

The Motorcycle Safety Foundation states that safe riding is 90 percent mental attitude and 10 percent physical execution of riding skills. A good riding attitude is based on the realization that a motorcycle is more vulnerable on the road than a car. Since the motorcycle is a low-visibility vehicle and weighs less than nearly every other vehicle, the motorcyclist must yield in all situations. This vulnerability also requires that the motorcyclist develop a sharp awareness of potential hazards. A motorcyclist must be alert for a possible conflict, quickly decide how to avoid the conflict, and carry out the safest actions to do so.

Many more motorcycle riding techniques and skills are involved in safe, enjoyable motorcycling than have been mentioned in this chapter. Contact the Motorcycle Safety Foundation, local motorcycle dealers or clubs, or the state Motor Vehicle Department or Department of Transportation for further help in learning how to ride safely. Keep the odds on your side through preventative maintenance, safe riding habits, and defensive riding.

Appendix

English-to-Metric Conversion Table

Multiply:	By:	To obtain:
Length		
inches (in)	25.4	millimeters
inches (in)	2.54	centimeters
feet (ft)	30.48	centimeters
inches (in)	0.0254	meters
feet (ft)	0.3048	meters
miles (mi)	1.609	kilometers
Area and volume		
square inches (sq in)	6.452	square centimeters
square feet (sq ft)	0.0929	square meters
cubic inches (cu in)	16.39	cubic centimeters
cubic inches (cu in)	0.01639	liters
quarts (qt)	0.9463	liters
gallons (gal)	3.785	liters
Weight		
ounces (oz)	28.35	grams
pounds (lb)	0.4536	kilograms
Torque		
foot-pounds (ft-lb)	0.1383	kilogram-meters
inch-pounds (in-lb)	0.0115	kilogram-meters
Pressure		
pounds per square inch (psi)	0.0703	kilograms per square centimeter
Mileage		
miles per gallon (mpg)	0.4252	kilometers per liter
Power		
brake horsepower (bhp)	0.9862	metric horsepower
Temperature		
degrees Fahrenheit (°F)		degrees Celsius (°C)

Formula: $C° = 5/9 (F° - 32)$

Procedure:
1. Take the number of degrees Fahrenheit that you wish to convert.
2. Subtract 32 from that number.
3. Multiply that number by 0.5556, and the answer is the degrees in Celsius.

Metric-to-English Conversion Table

Multiply:	By:	To obtain:
Length		
millimeters (mm)	0.03937	inches
centimeters (cm)	0.3937	inches
centimeters (cm)	0.0328	feet
meters (m)	39.37	inches
meters (m)	3.28	feet
kilometers (km)	0.6214	miles
Area and volume		
square centimeters (cm²)	0.155	square inches
square meters (m²)	10.76	square feet
cubic centimeters (cm³)	0.06102	cubic inches
liters (l)	61.02	cubic inches
liters (l)	1.057	quarts
liters (l)	0.2643	gallons
Weight		
grams (gm)	0.03527	ounces
kilograms (kg)	2.205	pounds
Torque		
kilogram-meters (kg-m)	7.233	foot-pounds
kilogram-meters (kg-m)	86.796	inch-pounds
Pressure		
kilograms per square centimeter (kg/cm²)	14.224	pounds per square inch (psi)
Mileage		
kilometers per liter (km/l)	2.353	miles per gallon
Power		
metric horsepower	1.014	brake horsepower
Temperature		
degrees Celsius (°C)		degrees Fahrenheit (°F)

Formula: $F° = 1.8C° + 32$

Procedure:

1. Take the number of degrees Celsius that you wish to convert.
2. Multiply that number by 1.8.
3. Add 32 to the number, and the answer is the degrees in Fahrenheit.

Glossary

Ac: abbreviation for alternating current, current that changes in polarity as it flows.

Ac generator: an ac charging system device that uses a rotating permanent magnet and a stationary coil of wire to create induction.

Active coils: the working coils in a spring that are free to move.

Additives: chemicals added to oil or fuel to increase its effectiveness.

Advance curve: the ignition timing advance relative to rpm.

Aeration: the process of mixing air or gas with oil.

Air bleed circuit: the passageways in the carburetor body that intersect with various jet outlet passageways to supply additional air to help the atomization process.

Air filter: a filter made of paper, foam, or gauze that prevents contamination in the air from entering the carburetor, usually located inside an air box that is sealed to the carburetor air intake.

Air screw: a screw located at the air filter side of the carburetor that projects into the air bleed circuit and allows adjustments of the air to the slow jet.

Alternator: an ac charging system device that uses an electromagnet powered by the battery to create induction.

Ammeter: a gauge used to measure current flow.

Ampere-hour rating: the length of time a battery discharges current.

Antidive system: a system installed with some brakes that uses front fork damping and the front brake assembly to prevent excessive fork compression and to improve handling when brakes are applied.

Antioxidants: chemicals added to oil to slow the reaction rate of oil with oxygen.

Armature: an assembly consisting of rotating coils electrically connected to a commutator and a shaft that spins on bearings or bushings pressed into the generator housing.

Atom: the basis of all matter consisting of the nucleus, which is made up of protons and neutrons, and orbiting electrons.

Austenitic: a nonmagnetic corrosion resistant steel.

Axle: a shaft used to support a part or parts across the frame or forks.

Backing plate: a mounting plate that holds the brake shoes, cam lever, pivot pins, and springs inside the brake drum.

Ball bearing: a multiple-piece assembly and spherical balls found in crankshafts, camshafts, transmissions, and steering stems, and as wheel bearings.

Battery: a storage device that converts chemical and electrical energy.

Battery-point ignition system: an ignition system consisting of a battery, ignition coil, contact points, a capacitor, system wiring, and some type of timing device.

Bead: the inner reinforced edge of a tire that holds it to the rim.

Bearing: an assembly that carries radial, axial, or thrust loads to cushion movement and reduce friction.

Beveled gear: a gear that is positioned to make an angle change.

Blow-by: combustion gases moving past the piston rings.

Booster port: in a two-stroke engine, the port that allows an extra amount of fuel mixture from the intake port into the combustion chamber.

Bore: the diameter of a cylinder.

Bottom dead center (BDC):   the piston position when the piston is at the bottom of its stroke.

Boundary conditions: metal-to-metal contact caused by extreme pressures or by the absence of a suitable supply of oil.

Brake: an energy-conversion device that converts the energy of motion into heat energy to slow or stop the motorcycle.

Brake drum: the metal outer shell of a drum brake assembly that is part of the hub and that the brake shoes press against to create friction.

Brake fluid: a special oil used in hydraulic brake systems to transmit pressure.

Brake lever: the front brake-activating lever located on the handlebar.

Brake mean effective pressure (BMEP):   the calculated pressure on the pistons measured in pounds per square inch, which takes into account frictional losses caused by rings, pistons, and bearings.

Brake pedal: the rear-brake-activating device.

Brake shoes: in a drum brake assembly, metal pieces lined with friction material that are secured to the backing plate by pivot pins and springs and that press against the inside of the brake drum to create friction.

Brake system: one or more brake assemblies and operating and control mechanisms.

Breakeven speed: the engine speed in rpm's at which a charging system begins to charge the battery.

Bushing: a tubular type of bearing made in one or two pieces.

Cable-disk brakes: a brake system that combines features of drum and disk brake systems and uses a cable and cam to operate a caliper assembly.

Cam chain: a chain running between the crankshaft and camshaft.

Camshaft: a shaft with a least one lobe that turns at one-half the engine speed and initiates and controls valve action in relation to crankshaft rotation, located in the crankcase or over the combustion chamber.

Capacitor: a device used by all motorcycles, usually in the ignition system, to store and discharge electrons; also called a condenser.

Capacitor discharge ignition (CDI):   an electronic ignition system designed to produce very high voltage, consisting of an exciter coil, a capacitor, diode, trigger coil, silicon-controlled rectifier, and ac ignition coil.

Carbon dioxide: a completely burned product of combustion.

Carbon monoxide: a poisonous, colorless, odorless gas produced during combustion by incomplete burning of the air/fuel mixture.

Carburetor: the fuel system component that meters the fuel and air and supplies the proper amounts to the engine.

Cavitation: the sudden formation of low-pressure gas pockets in a liquid that occurs by means of mechanical forces.

Celsius (C):   a metric unit of temperature; a temperature scale on which water boils at 100°C and freezes at 0°C.

Centimeter (cm):   a metric unit of linear measure equal to approximately 0.3937 inch.

Charging system: an electrical system that operates while the motorcycle is running to replace the current that the battery loses while starting the engine and operating all of the electrical devices.

Circuit: a complete, closed path that an electrical current can follow.

Circuit breaker: a device used to protect an electrical circuit from excessive current flow.

Clearance: the space between two parts.

Clutch: the part of the primary drive system that engages and interrupts the power flow from the engine to the transmission and permits gradual engagement.

Coil bind: a condition that occurs when a spring is compressed and there is no clearance between each coil.

Cold starting device: the system included in carburetors to provide and control the richer mixture that is necessary to start the engine.

Combustion: the rapid oxidation or burning of the air/fuel mixture in the combustion chamber.

Combustion chamber: the small space in the cylinder head where combustion takes place.

Combustion lagtime: a period of slow burning that occurs before the burning of the air/fuel mixture spreads throughout the combustion chamber.

Commutator: a series of copper bars insulated from each other and connected to rotating coils; a negative and positive brush ride on the commutator; used in dc generators.

Compression check: a test with a tool that indicates the sealing effectiveness of the cylinder, piston, rings, valves, and gaskets.

Compression ratio: the numerical relationship between the volume in a cylinder at the beginning of the compression stroke and the volume in the combustion chamber at TDC; used to indicate how much the mixture is compressed.

Compression ring: a ring installed on a piston to seal the compression and combustion pressure in the combustion chamber.

Compression stroke: the piston movement from BDC to TDC that compresses the air/fuel mixture in the cylinder while the intake and exhaust valves are closed.

Concentric: having one continuous centerline.

Condenser: a device usually used to assist the collapse of the primary field and to protect the point gap surface from heavy arcing by providing a place for current to flow.

Conduction: the transfer of heat from a high-temperature region through either solid material or stagnant liquid to a low-temperature region.

Conductivity: a measured value of a material's ability to flow current.

Conductor: a material that efficiently transmits electrons from one atom to another; on a motorcycle a conductor may take the form of wiring, the frame, or the engine.

Connecting rod: a one- or two-piece rod that links the piston to the crankshaft and transforms the linear motion created by the descending piston into rotational motion of the crankshaft.

Continuity: a material's ability to flow current that cannot be measured.

Convection: the transfer of heat resulting from air or liquid moving over a hot surface.

Conversion: a rule, usually written as a mathematical formula, for changing a measurement from one measurement system to another.

Coolant: a 50–50 mixture of distilled water and ethylene glycol circulated through a liquid cooling system.

Coulomb: a measurement of electric charge; 1 coulomb equals 6.24×10^{18} electrons past a given point in 1 second.

Counter-rotating balancer: an internal or external gear- or chain-driven device, timed to a specific crankshaft revolution and used to balance the vibration of the throw, rod, and piston.

Crankcase: an engine case that holds the crankshaft and transmission shafts in place and supplies the main engine-mounting points; opened horizontally or vertically.

Crankshaft: a single- or multiple-piece unit that transforms the reciprocating piston motion into useful rotating motion to allow the turning of gears to produce work.

Cubic centimeter (cc):   a metric unit used to measure volume; equal to approximately 0.061 cubic inch.

Current: a flow of electrons, measured in amperes.

Current limiter: a charging system device that limits the charging voltage to the battery from the ac generator.

Cycle: the series of five engine operations that are completed in two or four piston strokes to produce power.

Cylinder: a round, tubelike opening in the cylinder block.

Cylinder head: the part that seals the cylinder bore, provides an adequate combustion chamber and a location for the spark plug, and positions the valves and valve-activating devices on four-stroke engines.

Dc: abbreviation for direct current, current that does not change polarity or direction of flow.

Dc generator: a charging system device that mechanically converts alternating current to direct current before the current leaves the generator to charge the battery; consists of rotating coils, stationary electromagnets, a commutator, and two brushes.

Dc regulator: a dc charging system device that consists of a cutout relay, voltage relay, and current relay to control charging voltage and current.

Desmodromic: a four-stroke valve train that mechanically opens and closes the valves using rocker arms and camshaft(s).

Detonation: a violent explosion of the final portion of the burning combustion gases caused by an excessive rise of pressure and temperature; also called autoignition.

Dial indicator: a measuring tool used to determine small movements.

Diode: a semiconductor that allows the passage of electric current in only one direction, used in all ac charging systems to convert alternating current to direct current.

Direct drive transmission: a transmission system in which the power is transmitted to the input shaft and exits through a shaft inside or outside the input shaft.

Dog: a knob on the side of a gear that aligns or interlocks with a matching dog or hole in an adjacent gear.

Drive train: the drive systems that transfer the power produced by the engine to the rear wheel; includes primary drive, clutch, transmission, and final drive systems.

Dual-range transmission: an auxiliary transmission, also called a subtransmission, that is placed into the power flow between the transmission and the final drive system.

Dwell angle: a phase of ignition that occurs when the ignition contact points are closed, current flows, and the ignition coil's magnetic saturation begins; also called dwell.

Dynamic timing: a test of ignition timing made with a strobe light.

Eccentric: a wheel, disk, or shaft with an offset center.

Electrolyte: a solution of sulfuric acid and distilled water contained in a battery cell.

Electromagnetism: the production of a magnetic field that results when an electrical current is passed through a conductor.

Electromotive force (emf):   the force that causes electrons to travel; an imbalance or potential difference.

Electron: a negatively charged particle that orbits the nucleus of an atom.

Electronic fuel injection: a system that injects fuel into the engine's intake manifold and uses a computer to time and meter the fuel.

Emulsion: the result of adding air or gas to oil.

Energy transfer magneto: a self-powered ignition system that consists of a flywheel with permanent magnets that rotate around a laminated core with coil windings, an induction coil, contact points, and capacitor.

Engine load: the internal losses that the engine must overcome to perform work.

Exhaust gas analyzer (EGA):   a device used to determine the exact amounts of hydrocarbons and carbon monoxide in the exhaust.

Exhaust port: in a two-stroke engine, the passageway located on the upper portion of the cylinder opposite the intake port that channels spent combustion gases to the exhaust system.

Exhaust stroke: the movement of the piston from BDC to TDC that pushes the exhaust gases from the cylinder while the exhaust valve is open.

Exhaust system: the system consisting of the exhaust port, exhaust valve, exhaust pipe, and muffler that delivers burned combustion gases to the atmosphere.

Expansion chamber: a two-stroke engine exhaust system that consists of a header pipe, the first cone, chamber, rear cone, stinger, and silencer.

Feeler gauge: a flexible metal blade used to measure the space between two parts.

Final drive ratio: the number of times the transmission output shaft turns to produce one revolution of the rear wheel.

Final drive system: the part of the drive train that uses a chain, belt, or shaft to direct the power flow from the transmission to the rear wheel.

Fins: metal projections on motorcycle components that provide heat transfer through air cooling and radiation.

Firing order: the staggered sequence of operation in each cylinder of an engine.

Fixed caliper: in a hydraulic disk brake system, the assembly that is mounted stationary to the front fork and holds a piston and brake pad on either side of the brake disk.

Flash-over: a condition that occurs when a spark jumps across the surface of a spark plug insulator from the terminal.

Float bowl: in a carburetor assembly, the reservoir connected to the bottom or side of the carburetor body below the venturi that contains fuel, one or more floats, and usually an overflow tube.

Floating caliper: in a hydraulic disk brake system, the assembly that is connected to a movable arm and holds one piston and both inside and outside brake pads to press against a brake disk.

Float system: in the carburetor assembly, the float arm and pin, float needle and seat, and floats that control the fuel entry and level in the float bowl.

Flux lines: invisible lines that travel in an elliptical path from the north pole to the south pole of a magnet.

Fractional distillation: the heating of liquid to the boiling or separation point.

Frame: the "skeleton" of the motorcycle, made of tubes, steel plates, or pressed steel, that supports the rider and engine and provides attachment points for the frame's components.

Friction: the resistance of motion between two contacting moving parts.

Front fork: the spring and damping device that holds the front wheel in place.

Fuel: the combustible substance made of combinations of hydrogen and carbon atoms known as hydrocarbons.

Fuel filter: a screen used to prevent contamination in the fuel from entering the carburetor or fuel pump.

Fuel pump: a mechanically or electrically driven pump used in the fuel system of engines with fuel injection or turbocharging systems or with motorcycles that position the fuel tank lower than the carburetor.

Fuel screw: a fine-point screw that projects into the slow jet outlet passage, used to adjust the fuel mixture at slow speeds, located at the engine side of the carburetor.

Fuel system: the system that stores fuel, mixes fuel with air, vaporizes the mixture, and delivers it to the engine cylinders.

Full advance: the point at which the advance unit will no longer continue advancing ignition timing.

Full-wave charging system: an ac charging system that utilizes the whole wave for charging and consists of a flywheel with permanent magnets, a stator coil, four diodes, system wiring, and a current limiter.

Fuse: a device used to protect an electrical circuit from excessive current.

Gasket: a treated fiber, aluminum, or copper ring used to seal some cylinder heads, cylinder bases, and side covers.

Gear ratio: the numerical relationship that compares the number of times a drive gear must turn to turn a driven gear one revolution.

Gram (g): a metric unit of mass and weight.

Ground: the uninsulated side of a circuit, usually with a negative polarity.

Gusset: a piece of metal added for support.

Half-wave charging system: a small, simple ac charging system that utilizes one-half of the charging output; consists of a flywheel with permanent magnets, a stator coil, one diode, and system wiring.

Helical gear: a gear with teeth that are cut at an angle to the axis of the gear.

High-tension magneto: a self-contained ignition system that consists of a permanent magnet rotor with a laminated iron horseshoe mounted around the rotor, an induction coil, contact points, and capacitor.

Horsepower (hp): a measure of mechanical power determined by work and its relation to time, a direct result of torque and engine speed.

Hub: the center part of a wheel.

Hydraulic damping: a conversion of oil resistance to heat energy to create a force that opposes input motion.

Hydraulic disk brake: a brake system that exerts pressure through brake fluid to press brake pads against a disk to slow or stop the motorcycle.

Hydrocarbon: a compound that contains only hydrogen and carbon molecules.

Hydrodynamic lubrication: a condition that occurs when a film of oil is constantly maintained between moving parts.

Hydrometer: a device used to measure the specific gravity of electrolyte in each battery cell.

Hygroscopic: a fluid's ability to absorb water.

I: the symbol for amperage, the number of electrons flowed in 1 second.

Ignition: the act of firing the compressed air/fuel mixture in the combustion chamber by a spark from the spark plug.

Ignition coil: a device used to increase a low voltage to a high voltage; changes electrical energy into magnetic energy and back into electrical energy.

Ignition system: the part of the electrical system that provides high-voltage sparks to the engine cylinder to fire the compressed air/fuel mixture, consisting of a voltage source, timing device, capacitor, ignition coil, secondary wiring, and spark plugs.

Impedance: a measure of the total opposition to current flow in an ac circuit.

Indicated mean effective pressure (IMEP): the pressure at the top of the piston.

Indirect drive transmission: a transmission system that receives power from the primary drive into the input shaft or main shaft and then directs the power to the countershaft; the countershaft sprocket transmits the power to the final drive.

Induction: a method of producing electricity by moving a magnetic field through a conductor.

Induction system: a method of filling a two-stroke engine crankcase with an air/fuel mixture.

Innerliner: a layer of soft rubber that covers the inside of a tubeless tire.

Inner race: in a bearing assembly, the part that connects a rotating shaft to the bearing.

Insulation breakdown: electrical leakage.

Insulator: material that effectively resists and prevents the flow of electrons.

Intake manifold: a passageway made of rubber, aluminum, or steel that holds the carburetor to the cylinder head and helps vaporize the atomized air/fuel mixture as it travels from the carburetor to the cylinder head port.

Intake port: in a two-stroke engine, the passageway that allows the air/fuel/oil mixture to travel from the carburetor into the crankcase, located on the lower half of the cylinder opposite the exhaust port on all but rotary valve engines.

Intake stroke: the piston movement from TDC to BDC that occurs as the intake valve opens.

Internal cooling: engine cooling provided by oil, fuel mixtures, and valve overlap.

Jet needle: in a carburetor assembly, the thin, tapered needle that controls the amount of fuel during midrange operation.

Journal: on a shaft, the hardened, polished area that is used with a bearing.

Keystone ring: a wedge-shaped piston ring that allows burning gases to press on the tapered surface.

Kilogram (kg): a metric unit of mass and weight, equal to approximately 2.2 pounds.

Kilometer (km): a metric unit of linear measure equal to 0.621 mile.

Lacing: the positioning of spokes in the hub and rim.

Lighting system: the part of the electrical system that includes the lights and other electrical equipment.

Liter (l): a metric unit of volume, also used as a metric measure of engine-cylinder displacement.

Load: any device that uses electrical energy.

Load motion: rolling or sliding motion found at the bearing surfaces.

Locating pin: a pin that secures a component in place.

Magnetic field: the area around the north and south magnetic poles.

Magneto ignition: a self-powered ignition system that uses points and a condenser.

Main jet: in a carburetor assembly, the circuit that controls fuel at three-quarters to full throttle.

Master cylinder: in a hydraulic assembly, the cylinder that contains brake fluid and where hydraulic pressure is developed when the rider activates the lever or pedal.

Matter: anything that has weight and occupies space; may exist in solid, liquid, or gaseous form.

Mean diameter: the measurement of a coil spring that is computed by adding the inside diameter of the spring to the thickness of the wire.

Meter (m):   a metric unit of linear measure equal to 39.37 inches.

Micrometer: a measuring tool used to determine small distances or the width of a part.

Millimeter (mm):   a metric unit of linear measure equal to approximately 0.03937 inch.

Multigrade oil: an oil that retains its viscosity under varying temperature conditions better than a single-weight oil.

Needle bearing: a type of bearing with long, thin rollers.

Needle jet: in a carburetor assembly, the long jet that provides fuel to the venturi during midrange throttle openings, located in the passageway of the lower portion of the carburetor body directly under the center of the slide.

Ohmmeter: a device used to measure the resistance of a circuit device.

Ohm's law: a physical law that states that current which flows in a circuit is directly proportional to the applied voltage and inversely proportional to the resistance.

Oil filter: paper, wire screen, or rotor designed to keep oil clean and to prevent oil passages from becoming clogged.

Outer race: in a roller bearing assembly, the stationary part that supports the rotating load on the bearing.

Parallel circuit: a circuit that provides more than one path for current to follow.

Permeability: the ease with which a material will pass magnetic flux.

Petcock: the fuel supply valve that is connected to the fuel tank and vacuum-operated or manually operated by a lever.

Photo-optic ignition: a battery-assisted ignition system consisting of a light device, usually a light-emitting diode, rotating disk with slots, phototransistor, control box, and capacitor.

Piston: the part that travels up and down through a cylinder bore.

Piston-port system: a two-stroke intake system that uses the piston to open and close the intake port.

Piston ring: a ring installed on the piston to seal the cylinder bore when it is pushed out against the cylinder by spring tension and the pressure of expanding gases.

Plain bearing: a one- or two-piece assembly consisting of a hard metal backing piece with a softer metal material mated to it.

Polarity: the direction of current flow.

Poppet valve: in a four-stroke engine, the device in the cylinder head that opens and closes to provide and stop the flow of air/fuel and burned combustion gases.

Ports: the passageways cut into a two-stroke engine cylinder that channel gases into and out of the engine.

Postcombustion activity: the last phase of combustion, during which the piston descends, the volume inside the cylinder increases, and the cylinder eliminates spent gases.

Potential difference: a difference in the density of electrons between two places in a circuit.

Power stroke: the piston movement from TDC to BDC, during which the combustion gases act on the piston crown.

Preignition: abnormal combustion that occurs when the air/fuel mixture ignites before the spark plug fires.

Primary drive system: a system of gears, chains, or belts that transmits power from the crankshaft to the transmission; includes the clutch.

Primary winding: part of an ignition coil; a separate winding of heavy wire wound a few hundred turns around a laminated steel core.

psi: abbreviation for pounds per square inch.

Pulsating dc: direct current that varies in voltage value.

Pure dc: direct current at a constant voltage value.

Pushrod: a device used to activate rocker arms to open valves in engines that position the camshaft in the crankcase; also used with some clutches.

Rake: the angle of the steering head measured in degrees.

Rear suspension: the suspension system that consists of the swing arm, rear shock absorber, springs, and linkage if a single shock absorber is used.

Reed valve system: a two-stroke intake system that uses thin flapper valves that are opened by vacuum and closed by pressure.

Reluctance: a material's resistance to magnetic flux flow.

Resistance: the amount a material resists electron movement when current is passed through it, measured in ohms (Ω).

Retaining cage: in a bearing assembly, the part that keeps ball or roller bearings apart.

Rim band: a strip of soft rubber that protects the innertube from the spoke nipples.

Rim offset: the deliberate lacing of spokes off-center to the hub to achieve rear chain or front brake clearance.

Ring end gap: the distance between the ends of the piston rings that is measured when the rings are placed in the cylinder.

Rise time: the length of time between the beginning of the voltage at the plug and the beginning of the spark.

Rocker arm: a part used with a camshaft to activate valves.

Roller bearing: an assembled unit with rollers two to three times as wide as their diameter.

Rotary valve: a two-stroke intake system that uses a partially cut away rotating disk to open and close the intake passage into the crankcase.

Schematic: a diagram used to represent a circuit.

Scraper ring: a piston ring that assists in compression and wipes oil off the cylinder walls.

Secondary winding: part of an ignition coil; a winding of fine wire wound many thousands of turns around a laminated steel core.

Self-induction: the production of voltage resulting from the expansion and collapse of a magnetic field.

Semiconductor: material with the properties of either a conductor or an insulator, depending on circuit conditions.

Series circuit: a circuit that provides one path for current to follow.

Shaft rpm: the number of revolutions a shaft turns in a minute.

Shim: a metal disk or washer manufactured in various thicknesses, used to achieve proper clearances.

Shock absorber: an assembly that uses some form of hydraulic damping to control excessive wheel movement.

Sinter: to fuse metal parts or particles into a material by the application of pressure or heat.

Slide: the component mounted inside some carburetors at the center of the venturi that operates to vary the amount of engine vacuum available to the venturi.

Slow jet: in a carburetor assembly, the small, brass jet located in the passageway at the lower portion of the carburetor body to provide the proper amount of fuel to the venturi at idle and just above idle; also known as the pilot or idle jet.

Spark advance: the adjustments in timing made by the timing device for changes in load, speed, or other conditions.

Spark duration: the length of time spark occurs at a spark plug.

Spark plug: a device installed into a combustion chamber to carry a high-voltage spark across the gap and produce enough heat to sustain combustion; consists of an insulator, shell, and center electrode.

Specific gravity: the weight of a liquid compared to the weight of pure water.

Spin balancing: a method that spins a component to determine its imbalance; also called dynamic balancing.

Spoke: a metal part, often a wire, that runs between the rim and hub of a spoke wheel to transfer force to the hub.

Spring: a coiled wire that varies its length by flexing and twisting.

Spring free length: the length of a spring when measured without load.

Spring mechanical preload: the length or pressure of a spring, measured while it is installed.

Spring rate: the amount of force necessary to compress a spring a specific distance, measured in pounds per inch or kilograms per centimeter, to indicate the stiffness or softness of a spring.

Spring static preload: the amount of spring compression when the motorcycle is resting on the suspension with its own weight.

Sprung weight: the weight of motorcycle components that are supported on springs; includes the fork tube, engine, triple clamp, and frame.

Squish band: the area of the cylinder head that squirts the air/fuel charge toward the center of the combustion chamber and induces turbulence.

Starter motor: a device connected by gears, a chain, or both to the starter drive system that changes electrical energy into mechanical energy with enough torque and speed to start the engine.

Static balancing: a method used to check a wheel assembly for balance while it is stationary.

Static timing: a test of ignition timing made with a buzz box or a continuity light while the engine is at rest.

Steering head: the tube at the top and front of the frame that supports the steering stem and is welded at a specific angle to provide the proper fork angle.

Steering stem: a shaft positioned through the steering head that enables the front end to turn.

Stellite: a material used to coat and produce a hard surface.

Stoichiometric: the theoretically ideal air/fuel ratio at which complete combustion occurs.

Straight-cut gear: a gear with teeth that are cut parallel to the gear's axis; also called a spur gear.

Stroke: how far the piston travels from top dead center to bottom dead center.

Sump: a system for storing oil, either in the crankcase (wet sump) or in a separate tank (dry sump).

Suspension system: a system that consists of front forks, shock absorbers, springs, and the swing arm, used to support the motorcycle on its axles and wheels.

Swing arm: the assembly that links the rear wheel to the frame, allows the rear wheel to move up and down, and prevents the wheel from moving laterally and flexing at the pivot point.

System draw: the amount of current the motorcycle uses when the main electrical systems are operating.

Tapered roller bearing: a bearing specifically designed to handle thrust loads; found in some steering heads, crankshafts, and wheels.

Thermal efficiency: the measurement of how well heat is converted to work.

Thermodynamics: the science of heat, the laws of which predict the effects of heat transfer.

Three-phase charging system: an ac charging system that uses three separate charging waves; consists of either an ac generator or alternator, stator coils, diodes, system wiring, and a voltage control device.

Throttle butterfly: the component mounted inside some carburetors at a point past the venturi and close to engine vacuum that operates to vary the amount of engine vacuum available to the venturi.

Thrust bearing: a bearing specifically designed to handle thrust loads, found on the sides of the big end of a two-stroke connecting rod and on some transmissions and clutches.

Timing unit: a device that determines when the ignition system fires the spark plugs.

Top dead center (TDC):   the position of the piston when the piston has reached the limit of its upward travel in the cylinder.

Top end: all the engine components above the crankcase.

Torque: the twisting force at the end of a rotating shaft, measured in foot-pounds, kilogram-meters, or newton-meters.

Trail: the distance between the center of the tire contact patch and the imaginary point where the steering head axis strikes the ground.

Transfer port: in a two-stroke engine, the passageway located at the bottom of the cylinder that allows the compressed air/fuel/oil mixture in the crankcase to travel to the cylinder.

Transistor-assisted contact ignition (TAC):   an ignition system similar to battery-point ignition but which uses a transistor to eliminate heavy current flow at the contact points.

Transistor pointless ignition (TPI):   a battery-assisted ignition system using a pulse generator to trigger a transistor to fire the spark plug.

Transmission: the part of the drive train that uses a series of gears and shafts to increase the torque and provides gear shifting to allow increases in speed without overworking the engine.

Triple clamp: an assembly that consists of the steering stem and two brackets that position the fork tubes.

Trochoid pump: an oil pump consisting primarily of a pair of rotors.

True: to straighten a shaft, wheel, crankshaft, and so on, so that it rotates without wobble.

Turbocharging: a system that uses the normally wasted exhaust gas to drive a turbine which drives a compressor to force more air/fuel into the cylinders and increase engine power.

Turbulence: the rapid motion of the air/fuel mixture in the combustion chamber.

Turns ratio: the ratio of the number of coils in the primary and secondary windings of an ignition coil.

Unified brake system: a system that automatically coordinates the front and rear brake systems when the rider applies pressure to the brake pedal.

Unsprung weight: the weight of motorcycle components that are not supported on springs; includes the wheel assembly, fork sliders, rear shocks, a portion of the swing arm, the chain or shaft drive, one-half of the spring, and on some models, the front fender.

Valve float: a condition that occurs at high engine rpm when valves do not completely close or fail to close at the proper time.

Valve guide: a device located in the cylinder head that provides a path for the valve stem.

Valve lifter: a cylindrical part that rests on the camshaft lobe and is lifted by cam action so that movement is transferred to the valve and the valve opens.

Valve overlap: a condition that occurs when intake and exhaust valves are partially open at the same time at the end of the exhaust stroke and at the beginning of the intake stroke.

Valve spring: a spring that closes a valve against the valve seat to seal the combustion chamber.

Velocity: the speed of a moving object.

Venturi principle: the physical law that states that air moved through a constriction increases in speed and decreases in pressure at the point of constriction.

Vernier caliper: a measuring tool used to determine the thickness or diameter of a part, or the width or depth of a hole.

Viscosity: the thickness of an oil determined by its rate of flow; a thick oil has a greater viscosity than a thin oil.

Viscosity rating: an oil classification based on the time it takes for an amount of oil to flow through a tube; the higher the rating, the thicker the oil.

Voltage regulator: a mechanical or solid-state device used with an alternator to control the amount of current flow through the field coil.

Voltage source: some type of coil and rotating magnet, or a battery.

Voltmeter: a gauge used to measure voltage.

Volts: a term used to indicate the pressure of electromotive force.

Volumetric efficiency: the measure of how much air is actually inhaled by an engine compared to how much it could hold based on the size of the cylinder.

Watt: the measurement for electrical power; 746 watts equal 1 horsepower.

Wheel balancing: an equal distribution of weight achieved by determining where the wheel is heaviest and then placing weights opposite the heavy portion.

Wrist pin: a pin that attaches the piston to the connecting rod.

Zener diode: a diode that does not allow current to flow until it reaches breakdown voltage.

Zerk fitting: a metal nozzle that injects grease.

Index